ATTITUDES TOWARD PERSONS WITH DISABILITIES

Harold E. Yuker is a Mervyn L. Schloss Distinguished Professor of Psychology and director of the Center for the Study of Attitudes toward Persons with Disabilities at Hofstra University. He has been teaching psychology at Hofstra since 1948, and from 1976 through 1981 served as Provost and Dean of Faculties. He is the author of monographs on elementary statistics and on faculty workload. Dr. Yuker has published extensively in the area of attitudes toward disabled persons, and with his colleagues developed the Attitudes Toward Disabled Persons scales.

Attitudes Toward Persons with Disabilities

Harold E. Yuker, Ph.D.

Editor

SPRINGER PUBLISHING COMPANY

New York

Springer Publishing Company, Inc.
536 Broadway
New York, NY 1001

88 89 90 91 92 / 5 4 3 2 1

Library of Congress Cataloging-in-Publication Data

Attitudes toward persons with disabilities.

  Bibliography: p.
  Includes index.
    1. Handicapped—United States—Public opinion.
  2. Public opinion—United States. I. Yuker, Harold E.
  HV1553.A87   1987   305'.90816   87-23471
  ISBN 0-8261-6190-1

Printed in the United States of America

Contents

Contributors

Barbara Aiello is the founder and director of The Kids on the Block, a troupe of disabled and nondisabled puppets.

Richard F. Antonak is associate professor of developmental disabilities at the University of New Hampshire.

Joan Bailey is studying social and personality psychology at the Graduate Center of the City University of New York.

E. Keith Byrd is associate professor of counselor education and coordinator of the Rehabilitation Counseling Program at Auburn University.

Benzion Chanowitz is assistant professor of psychology at Brooklyn College, City University of New York.

Mark A. Chesler is professor of psychology and co-director of the Program on Conflict Management Alternatives at the University of Michigan.

Barbara K. Chesney is a graduate research assistant in sociology at the University of Michigan.

Timothy R. Elliott is a doctoral candidate in counseling psychology at the University of Missouri.

Catherine S. Fichten is professor of psychology at Dawson College and senior clinical associate at the Sir Mortimer B. Davis Jewish General Hospital Sexual Dysfunction Service in Montreal.

Mary Anne Geskie is school psychologist in the Commack, N.Y., school district.

R. Glen Hass is professor of psychology at Brooklyn College and the Graduate School of the City University of New York.

Mary Elizabeth Hannah is associate professor of psychology and director of the School Psychology Program at the University of Detroit.

Marcia D. Horne is associate professor and chair of the special education area at the University of Oklahoma.

Irwin Katz is professor of psychology at the Graduate Center of the City University of New York.

Ellen Langer is professor of psychology at Harvard University.

Hanoch Livneh is associate professor and director of the Rehabilitation Counseling Program at Rhode Island College.

Henry McCarthy is associate professor in the department of rehabilitation counseling at Louisiana State University.

James Salasek is staff psychologist at Pilgrim Psychiatric Center, West Brentwood, N.Y.

Leora Pedhazur Schmelkin is associate professor of counseling, psychology, and research in education at Hofstra University.

Jerome Siller is professor of educational psychology at New York University.

Joseph Stubbins is professor emeritus at California State University, Los Angeles, and editor of *Social and Psychological Aspects of Disability: A Handbook for Practitioners*.

Nancy Weinberg is associate professor at the University of Ilinois at Urbana–Champaign.

Beatrice A. Wright is professor of psychology at the University of Kansas and the author of the much cited book, *Physical Disability: A Psychosocial Approach*.

Esther Zernitsky-Shurka is on the faculty at the University of Haifa, Israel.

Preface: Attitudes Toward Persons with Disabilities: Progress and Prospects

This volume is designed to provide a perspective on people's attitudes toward persons with disabilities. The attitudes of others are recognized as a major influence on the behavior of disabled persons, and so we have tried to include all aspects of the topic, with coverage by the important people in the field. The attitudes of disabled people themselves are also touched upon.

ORGANIZATION OF THIS VOLUME

The chapters are grouped into five sections. Part I contains two theoretical papers. Beatrice A. Wright documents the frequent negative bias toward disabled individuals and makes recommendations for minimizing this bias. Joseph Stubbins discusses the deleterious and divisive effects of beliefs prevalent among persons who work in rehabilitation and critically examines the effects of such factors as the clinical model, professional interests, the culture of rugged individualism, and the organization of disability groups by medical typologies.

Part II contains six papers dealing with the origins of attitudes. Hanoch Livneh cites empirical evidence pertaining to six perspectives that can be used for examining the origins of negative attitudes. Irwin Katz, R. Glen Hass, and Joan Bailey discuss the theory that attitudes toward members of disadvantaged groups, including disabled persons, tend to be ambivalent and can result in unstable and extreme behavior by nondisabled persons. Jerome Siller states that most studies of attitudes toward disabled persons neglect such intrapsychic constructs as castration anxiety, defensive style, and level of object relationships. He discusses experiments conducted to clarify these relationships. Ellen Langer and Benzion Chanowitz make a distinction between mindless and mindful perception and cite experiments indicating that fostering a mindful approach to the perception of persons with disabilities can have positive effects on attitudes. E. Keith Byrd and Timothy Elliott discuss how disabilities are treated in television, film, and literature, concluding that some media presentations can be effective in producing attitude changes. Esther Zernitsky-Shurka discusses the impact of such societal-cultural variables as nationality, ethnicity, and religion on attitudes toward persons with physical disabilities, with an emphasis on the attitudes of Israeli Arabs and Jews.

Part III deals with attitude measurement. Richard F. Antonak discusses many types of measures that can be used: direct methods, such as opinion surveys, interviews, rankings, Q-methodology, sociometrics, adjective checklists, paired comparison scales, semantic differential scales, probabilistic rating scales, and deterministic rating scales; and indirect methods, such as projective techniques, disguised measures, behavioral observations, and physiological methods. Liora Pedhazur Schmelkin emphasizes the need for multidimensional approaches to replace the unidimensional instruments and designs that have been used to study the images of persons with disabilities.

Part IV deals with the attitudes of members of several specific groups. Nancy Weinberg discusses data indicating that the attitudes of disabled persons toward their disability are extremely variable, ranging from those who are extremely bitter to those who enjoy being disabled and embrace their disability. Mary Elizabeth Hannah discusses the attitudes of teachers toward disabled children and the effects of positive and negative attitudes on teacher–child interaction and the quality of performance of the children. Catherine S. Fichten discusses data pertaining to attitudes of college students with a physical disability and the attitudes of other students, professors, and administrators toward them. Mary Anne Geskie and James Salasek discuss the attitudes of persons engaged in the treatment of disabled persons, including occupational differences and the effects of age, sex, educational level, years of experience, setting, occupational role, and type of training.

Part V deals with attitude change. Marcia D. Horne reviews the effectiveness of procedures designed to modify peer attitudes toward disabled children and concludes that positive attitudes can be facilitated by personal contact, information and discussion, the combination of contact and information, small group experiences, cooperative classroom instruction, or improving the social skills of disabled students. Barbara Aiello discusses the origins and operation of the Kids on the Block, an innovative technique that uses puppets with disabilities to present information about disabilities and ways to interact with disabled persons. Mark A. Chesler and Barbara K. Chesney discuss empowerment attitudes and behaviors, how they can be enhanced by participation in self-help groups, and how they create positive attitudes. Henry McCarthy suggests that employer attitudes represent only one type of barrier to the employment of persons with disabilities and examines the role of persons involved in other aspects of the employment process, such as career education, occupational preparation, and job placement. Finally, Harold E. Yuker discusses types of variables that influence whether the effects of the contact are positive or negative, including characteristics of the person with the disability, the nondisabled person, the interaction, and the environment.

We attempted to use appropriate language throughout, e.g., referring to persons as "disabled" rather than "handicapped," and avoiding such phrases as "the disabled" or "the mentally retarded." We also tried to avoid "victim," "afflicted by," and "confined to a wheelchair," because of their negative connotations. We did use "disabled person," since this is common usage; but we recognize that this refers to "a person who happens to be disabled some of the time." No implication that the person as a whole is disabled is intended.

The references used by each author have been combined in a single listing to increase their utility.

COMMENTS AND SUGGESTIONS

Taken together, these chapters indicate that attitudes toward disabled persons are complex and multifaceted. Many perspectives are possible. Data indicate it is not easy to understand attitudes toward disabled persons, to measure them, or to change them. But we must be able to do all of these if we are to improve the status of persons with disabilities.

These papers summarize our present knowledge, discuss implications, and make suggestions for future research. While we have come a long way, there is still a long way to go. The things to be done include:

1. Recognizing the multifaceted nature of attitudes and their development and ceasing to use univariate approaches and approaches that emphasize only one set of variables, such as subject variables, at the expense of others, such as environmental, perceptual, interactional, and measurement variables.

2. Investigating and discussing the theoretical bases of both positive and negative attitudes, including the fundamental negative bias, the mindfulness/mindlessness distinction, and value ambivalence.

3. Conducting research into the sources of attitudes, seeking to specify the relative influence of (percent of variance explained by) several classes of variables, such as culture, personal experiences, the teachings of significant others, and intrapsychic personality variables.

4. Developing new and better measures of attitudes.

5. Obtaining data pertaining to the attitudes of classes of persons who interact with persons with disabilities, such as parents, rehabilitation and treatment personnel, teachers, and classmates. This research should focus on factors related to within-group differences as well between-group differences.

6. Planning, conducting, and evaluating programs designed to change attitudes toward persons with disabilities. The programs should be multidimensional, using a combination of techniques, should last more than a few hours or a few days, and should include follow up data.

7. Conducting research dealing with the relationship between attitudes and behavior; paying more attention to theory and recognizing that attitudes predict behavior only when appropriate measures are used and when there is correspondence in terms of the target and context (Ajzen & Fischbein, 1977).

8. Finally, recognizing that disability is only one aspect, and often a very minor aspect, of a *person*. We should always attend primarily to the person.

These are exciting possibilities for both theory and research, and we hope to see significant progress in the next ten years.

HAROLD E. YUKER

Acknowledgments

A book of this scope results from the efforts of many people. The contributors were very cooperative in getting their manuscripts in on time and editing them down to size. Dr. Alexej Ugrinsky and the staff of the Hofstra University Cultural Center did an excellent job of running the June 1986 conference, on which this book is based, so that everything happened according to plan. The typing help of Evelyn Parker and Ruth Mangels was invaluable.

My greatest debt, however, is to Hofstra University, its president, James M. Shuart, and the late Dr. Joseph Astman, director of the Hofstra University Cultural Center. In early 1985 I casually mentioned the idea of a conference on attitudes to Dr. Astman. When pressed for a date I suggested mid-1986, and forgot about it. But Joe did not let me forget, and the June 1986 conference was the result. The conference was another illustration of Hofstra's support for persons with disabilities. In 1961 the university made a commitment to making the campus completely accessible. In 1982 Dr. Shuart raised funds to establish the Hofstra University Center for the Study of Attitudes toward Persons with Disabilities. In 1986 the university funded the conference that led to this book. We hope it will make them proud.

PART I
Basic Issues

CHAPTER 1

Attitudes and the Fundamental Negative Bias: Conditions and Corrections

Beatrice A. Wright

The fundamental negative bias is important because it steers perception, thought, and feeling along negative lines to such a degree that positives remain hidden. It is a powerful source of prejudice that ill serves those who are already disadvantaged.

The chapter begins with examples of the fundamental negative bias, selected from the work world of professionals. These examples were chosen partly to show that as professionals we need to become sensitized to contributing inadvertently to disabling myths about particular groups, and partly to show that no one is immune to the fundamental negative bias. To be sure, countless examples from everyday life could also have shown the pervasiveness of the problem.

The basic proposition underlying the fundamental negative bias is then formulated, after which research bearing on the proposed conditions of the bias is presented. Then the implications of the bias for a variety of topics are discussed in terms of their significance regarding attitudes: implications with respect to relationships between strangers, the measurement of attitudes as stereotypes, comparison groups, statistical significance, problem-centered clinical settings, and unsightly and bizarre encounters. Throughout, the understanding of the fundamental negative bias is used to propose counterchecks to its power in promoting prejudice.

PROFESSIONALS AND THE FUNDAMENTAL NEGATIVE BIAS

A Clinical Example

A counselor, seeking consultation concerning the rehabilitation of a delin-quent youth, presented the case of 14-year-old John. The following 10 symptoms were listed: assault, temper tantrums, stealing (car theft), fire setting, self-destructive behavior (jumped out of a moving car), threats of harm to others, insatiable demand for attention, vandalism, wide mood swings, and underachievement in school. The DSM-III diagnosis noted on Axis I was conduct disorder, undersocialized, aggressive, with the possibil-ity of a dysthymic disorder; on Axis II, passive aggressive personality. No physical disorders were listed on Axis III. The psychosocial stressors, rated as extreme on Axis IV, noted the death of his mother when John was a baby and successive placement with various relatives and homes. On Axis V John's highest yearly level of adaptive functioning was rated as poor.

Following perusal of this dismal picture, I asked the counselor whether John had anything going for him. The counselor then mentioned that John keeps his own room in order, takes care of his personal hygiene, likes to do things for others (although on his own terms), likes school, and has an IQ of 140. Notice how quickly the impression of John changes, once positives in the situation are brought out to share the stage with the problems. Before that, the fundamental negative bias reigned supreme. Whereas the fact of John's delinquency had led to the detection of all sorts of negatives about John's conduct and situation, the positives had re-mained sorely neglected.

Although the importance of uncovering the positives seems obvious once it is pointed out, the fundamental negative bias is a powerful decoy that all too frequently directs attention elsewhere.

A Research Example

The fundamental negative bias can be so strong as to lead the evaluator to interpret as negative matters that ostensibly are positive. A case in point is a study that compared reactions of able-bodied persons to confederate-interviewers with and without a disability. (Because there is no need to indict a particular author, this study is not identified here.) Although the major finding was that subjects *consistently* rated the interviewer with the disability more favorably on a variety of personality characteristics, the results were interpreted as supporting "research indicating the operation of a 'sympathy effect' to avoid the appearance of rejection or prejudice"!

The negative interpretation was further elaborated:

> We do not regard the "sympathy effect" as a factor promoting positive inter-
> personal relations between able-bodied and handicapped persons. For exam-
> ple, most people react negatively to the incorrigible flatterer. We refer to such
> an individual as "syrupy," "manipulative," or "phony". . . . Perhaps the physi-
> cally handicapped person perceives behaviors associated with the "sympathy
> effect" in a similar vein, as ingenuine. If we perceive *many* persons around us
> as ingenuine, it may well interfere with the development of effective social
> interactions that help promote personal adjustment.

Is it not curious that the more positive evaluations of the "handicapped
interviewer" (e.g., more likeable, better attitude) should have been gratu-
itously interpreted as reflecting a negative "sympathy effect," that is,
"syrupy, manipulative, or phony"? Why wasn't an alternative explanation
considered, namely, that subjects, in recognizing the orthopedic disability,
appreciated the interviewer's apparent success in meeting challenges and
therefore perceived the interviewer as having special positive qualities as a
cause and, or consequence of such success? Would such a reaction be
"ingenuine" or "phony"? Could the explanation lie in the fundamental
negative bias?

THE FUNDAMENTAL NEGATIVE BIAS: BASIC PROPOSITION

Saliency, value, and context are proposed as three conditions for the free
functioning of the fundamental negative bias: (1) if something that is
observed stands out sufficiently (saliency), and (2) if, for whatever reason,
it is regarded as negative (value), and (3) if its context is vague or sparse
(context), then the negative value assigned to the object of observation will
be a major factor in guiding perception, thinking, and feeling to fit its
negative character.

To place the above proposition in a wider framework, a number of
points should be made explicit. First, it suggests that just as there is a
fundamental negative bias, so, too, there is a fundamental positive bias
that should operate under parallel conditions; namely, that where something is salient, positive, and in a sparse context, the train of thought
should proceed in a positive direction. In fact, a "fundamental affective
bias" could be formulated to refer to the value of an object of observation
as being either positive or negative and so provide the basic set of three
general conditions that would apply to both cases.

Because of our concern with disadvantagement and prejudice, this chapter focuses on the insidiousness of the fundamental negative bias. It is this bias that specifies the conditions underlying what has been called "negative spread effects" in earlier work (Dembo, Leviton, &Wright, 1956/1975).

That the affective value of something, in the absence of counteracting factors provided by the context, can become a powerful force in influencing what a person thinks about and feels can be understood in terms of the concept of similarity as a unit-forming factor (Heider, 1958; Wertheimer, 1923). That is, the similarity between entities, whether they be external objects or intrapsychic events, is a powerful factor in a person's perceiving them as a unit, as belonging together. An especially salient type of similarity between entities is their affective quality. Things that are positive are alike in engendering a force *toward* them; negative things, a force *away from* them. Combining positive and negative qualities subjects the person to forces opposite in direction.

EXPERIMENTS ON CONTEXT

External Contest

A context is the set of interrelated conditions within which something exists and which influences that thing's meaning. The context can refer to conditions present externally to the perceiver or to intrapsychic predispositions of various sorts. A few experiments bearing on the significance of external context in regard to the fundamental negative bias are presented below.

In an important yet simple experiment, people's reactions to the concept of "blindness" as compared to "blind people," and "physical handicap" as compared to "physically handicapped people," were examined (Whiteman & Lukoff, 1965). That the condition itself was evaluated far more negatively than were *people* with the condition is not surprising. Still, the question remains as to how to account for the difference. The fundamental negative bias serves as explanation. Thus, when the condition was being rated, there was no surrounding context to alter its meaning. This allowed its negativity to dominate perception and guide the reaction accordingly. However, the positive concept of "person" provided a context that moderated the preeminent position of the negative condition. In effect, the context determined that different concepts were to be rated. One is reminded of the work of Asch (1952), which clearly showed the importance of context in perception of persons.

The context can be positive or negative. In the above example, the concept of "person" provided a positive context and therefore constrained the negative spread. Research has also shown that, as the positive character of the context becomes even more salient, attitudes become more favorable. This was demonstrated, for example, in an experiment in which attitudes toward a person who was labeled with a particular problem (e.g., former mental patient, amputee) became more positive when that person was described as functioning adequately than when the negative label stood alone (Jaffe, 1966).

If a positive context can constrain negative spread, we might surmise that a negative context could increase the negativity of the object of observation, thereby adding to the grip of the fundamental negative bias in controlling attitudes. Thus, in one experiment, attitudes toward a person described as being physically disabled and as having *undesirable* personality traits were more negative than toward a comparably described able-bodied person (Leek, 1966). Such intensified reactions have also been demonstrated with respect to race (Dienstbier, 1970) and mental disorders (Gergen & Jones, 1963).

The meaning of "external context" or "external conditions" is not limited to a network of prescribed personality or behavior traits of the evaluated person, but includes *the broader situation* that influences how traits will be interpreted. Thus Cook (1969) has shown that interracial contact in *cooperatively* oriented work settings favorably affects the attitudes of extremely prejudiced white adults. Moreover, a cooperative group context reversed the usual decrement in liking for a peer who provides help on a task that involves the recipient's self-respect but cannot be reciprocated (Cook & Pelfrey, 1985).

Intrapsychic Context

In addition to conditions externally imposed, as in the above experiments, intrapsychic factors can also provide the main context for influencing perception. A variety of personal dispositions, such as personality traits and values, are potentially important in this regard. With respect to the fundamental negative bias, we know that people who are ethnocentric are more likely to view outgroup members negatively than persons who are less ethnocentric (English, 1971). This personality trait could provide the kind of internal context that would maximize the saliency of any negative attributes presented by the external stimulus conditions of an outgroup; it could even have the power to lead the perceiver to ignore positive attributes. A similar line of reasoning holds for values. It seems plausible, for example, that a strong value placed on human dignity would have the potential to exert a significant influence in organizing perception in a way that forestalls the fundamental negative bias.

Motivation should be mentioned as still another potentially important internal factor that can affect the potency of the fundamental negative bias. For example, the evaluator might benefit in some way by devaluating another, as when there is a need to feel superior. Such a motive can easily reinforce the fundamental negative bias, even to the extent of discrediting what would ordinarily be regarded as positive aspects of the other person. The converse is also true. For example, humanistic or religious concerns can be a motivating force that creates a positive context of beliefs and principles in which to view people. These are a few examples of personal dispositions that either support or compete with the power of the fundamental negative bias. The reader will be able to think of others.

Of particular importance to clinical and research activities are studies that deal with the contrasting viewpoints of the *insider* and *outsider*, each of which corrals a different set of context conditions in terms of which judgments are made. The insider (also referred to as "actor") is the person himself or herself, the person experiencing or evaluating his or her own behavior, feelings, or problems. The outsider is the person observing or evaluating someone else's behavior, feelings, or problems. Both clinicians and researchers are outsiders with respect to the views of the clients and subjects they are studying. Tamara Dembo (1964, 1970), the distinguished pioneer in rehabilitation psychology, has repeatedly stressed the importance of the different perspectives of the insider and outsider in understanding attitudes. Four groups of investigations involving insider–outsider perspectives are described below.

The "Fortune Phenomenon." First explored by Dembo, Leviton, and Wright (1956/1975), the fortune phenomenon reveals the ease with which devalued groups are regarded as unfortunate, despite the fact that the members of those groups do not view themselves as unfortunate. In one study (Wright & Howe, 1969), women from a variety of groups rated themselves, their own groups, and the other groups in the study on 11-point scales ranging from very fortunate to very unfortunate. Women from the socially devalued groups were mental hospital patients and welfare clients; the groups of higher status were middle-class housewives and college students. An important finding was that virtually all the women from the two socially devalued groups rated themselves, as individuals, average or above average in how fortunate they were. Yet when these groups were identified solely by their label (mental hospital patients, welfare clients), the two groups were rated by all groups of subjects as below average in how fortunate they were. Persons with physical disabilities at a rehabilitation center also rated themselves as individuals at least average in terms of how fortunate they were, whereas, as a labeled group, they were rated below average by others (Wright & Muth, 1965).

The difference in results can be understood in terms of the kind of information being processed. Whereas the label attached to a group defines the salient aspect to be observed and little else (sparse context), when one rates oneself a host of personal and situational aspects enter the field for consideration, and it is this complex that provides the context for one's self-rating. That is, the rating is not based only on one dominant, negative aspect whose meaning derives, not from itself, but from the larger context.

The "Mine–Thine Problem." The "mine-thine problem" also highlights perspective differences between the insider and outsider (Wright, 1983). A simple way to conduct the experiment is to ask subjects to list the initials of five people they know well in one column and beside each initial to indicate that person's worst handicap (i.e., limitation, shortcoming, disability, or problem). Then, next to each of the five handicaps, they are asked to write what they regard as their own worst handicap. They are then asked to consider each of the five pairs of handicaps separately and to circle the one they would choose for themselves if they had a choice. Next, the subjects write two numbers on a slip of paper to indicate the number of times their own and the others' worst handicaps were chosen, the sum of the two normally being five. These slips are then collected so that the number frequencies can be displayed and discussed.

The results are dramatic and consistent. The number of times one's own handicap is reclaimed clearly exceeds choosing the others'. Among the five choices, it is common for subjects to choose their own handicap five, four, or three times, rarely less frequently.

The difference between what is taken into account by the insider and outsider becomes appreciated in a personally direct way in the group's attempt to explain the results. Explanations include: they are used to their own handicap (familiarity factor); they have learned how to deal with it (coping factor); and it is part of the self and the person's history (self-identity factor). Keep in mind that one is an insider when considering one's own handicap, and an outsider when regarding the other person's. Consequently, the other person's handicap more or less stands for a labeled condition and is therefore perceptually more insulated from possible positive contextual features.

Troubling Experiences and the Insider vs. Outsider Perspective. In this experiment, subjects were asked to write an account of two troubling experiences they had had, one highly troubling and the other mildly troubling (Fletcher, 1984). Randomly paired subjects then rated typed versions of their four accounts on several dimensions. The results were clear. The subjects rated their own highly troubling experiences as entailing more coping, more growth value, and fewer permanent negative effects than their partner's. They also felt that their mildly troubling experiences had fewer negative effects than their partner's, although no differences in coping or growth value were claimed.

Hospital Patients vs. Outsider Viewpoints. Two investigations show that patients tend to have a more positive outlook than do others viewing their situation. The first of these (Mason & Muhlencamp, 1976) demonstrated that hospital patients felt less depressed, anxious, and hostile than their medical therapists judged them to feel. The second study (Hamera & Shontz, 1978) showed that the closer the subject is to the position of the patient, the more likely positive effects of a life-threatening illness will be perceived. The order of closeness to the insider position were patients attending an oncology clinic (closest), followed by parents of children with cancer, and nonmedical hospital employees (least close).

General Results on Perspective. To my knowledge, all research bearing on the perspective of insiders and outsiders shows not only that the meaning of the experience differs, but also that the insider is generally more inclined than the outsider to take into account positives in the situation. It seems clear that the context in which the judgments are made differs greatly in the two cases. Insiders place the significance of the handicap or trouble in a life context so that the span of realities connected with it is wide. Only some aspects are negative, others are clearly positive (e.g., coping, identity), and it is this broad context that restrains negative spread. On the other hand, to outsiders the other person's handicap or problem tends more or less to stand alone. In this case, the context is sparse or simplified, and the negativity of the problem dominates the train of thought.

The discussion of context thus far leads to the important conclusion that *both* internal and external factors combine to organize perception and that under certain conditions one or the other of these sets of factors may become supreme.

SPECIAL TOPICS IMPLICATED BY THE FUNDAMENTAL NEGATIVE BIAS

The fundamental negative bias can alert us to a variety of traps in research and clinical work that often lead to misleading and potentially harmful conclusions and applications. Space limitations permit examination of only six problem areas.

The Problem of Relationships with Strangers

We have seen that where the context is sparse the situation is especially vulnerable to the fundamental negative bias. This is the case in stranger relationships, where there is not much to go on other than whatever characteristic of the observed person appears distinctive. Thus, where a disability or other personal attribute is obvious, it readily becomes the outstanding characteristic. Other facts that may be apprehended in passing, such as age and sex, are usually so general that they hardly compete in being given preponderant weight.

Research has shown how easily the fundamental negative bias can take hold in the stranger situation. Two of our studies (Wright, unpublished) have examined the fortune phenomenon from the point of view of strangers and friends. In one, subjects were asked to recall a friend who had a disability. They were then asked to imagine meeting a stranger with the same disability on the street and to rate the stranger and the friend on the fortune scale. Whereas friends were rated average or above on the fortune scale, strangers were frequently rated below average. In the second study, people with disabilities indicated on the fortune scale that strangers would regard them as more unfortunate than would their family and friends.

In another study, the treatment of children with disabilities was compared at home and in school with that of their able-bodied, matched peers (Schoggen, 1978). The data provided "no support for the proposition that the social environment of children with physical disabilities tends in general to be either oversolicitous or rejecting and indifferent" (p. 133). As explanation, it was stressed that these children were observed in situations "where they were well known to nearly all other persons with whom they came into contact. . . . Perhaps interviews, questionnaires, and attitude tests can hardly avoid giving an inaccurate picture, because they almost necessarily isolate disability . . . as the characteristic of special interest or importance" (p. 145).

It is important to realize that most social-psychological laboratory research, in contrast to the preceding ecological study, involves a subject reacting to an unknown person(s), either face-to-face or as a labeled abstraction in paper and pencil tests (e.g., tests of attitudes toward "the disabled," or "blacks"). Unfortunately, the temptation is great to generalize the findings to relationships between people who know each other. A case in point is the frequently cited finding, based on Kleck's research series (e.g., Kleck, 1968), that able-bodied persons feel uncomfortable with a "disabled person" and therefore maintain a greater physical distance and terminate the interaction sooner than when interacting with a nondisabled person. In no case that I am aware of have the interpretations been restricted to stranger relationships!

The thrust of this chapter, stressing as it does the importance of context, clearly makes such overgeneralization unwarranted. Surely relationships between friends, acquaintances, and family members are no less important than stranger relationships! An urgent caveat is in order; namely, that the psychology of disability must not be made equivalent to the psychology of disability in stranger relationships. The same caution clearly applies to the psychology of relationships involving different races, sexes, and so forth. A specific recommendation is that researchers should make explicit, in cases where only strangers served as subjects, that their findings pertain only to stranger relationships.

The Problem of Attitude Tests of Stereotypes

When measuring attitudes toward a particular group, the intent is to get at stereotypes, at attitudes that are tied to the label designating the group. If the label connotes something negative to the respondent, as is often the case in regard to disability or poverty, for example, then the label is likely to give rise to a negative mindset in answering the items, especially because the label is an abstraction, separated from particular people and circumstances.

Contributing to this mindset is a preponderance of negatively focused items that frequently, although not always, characterize attitude tests about groups felt to be inferior in some way. This negative loading may be a manifestation of the fundamental negative bias inasmuch as the test constructor may be led by the group's stigmatized status to formulate items that imply devaluation. It also may be felt to be a way to minimize the influence of what has been called "social desirability," a subject's inclination to respond favorably to items expressing what is socially proper.

In any case, the negative loading can have several unfortunate consequences. First, we should be concerned that a preponderance of negatively worded items orients thinking toward the negative side of possibilities, thereby strengthening a negative-response bias. Also, rejecting a negative statement is not the same, affectively and cognitively, as affirming a positive statement. Rejecting the idea, for example, that a particular group is often lazy or resentful does not imply the opposite belief, that the group is often eager to work or appreciative. Both types of statements are needed to guard against a negative bias as well as to offer respondents the opportunity to express attitudes that reflect genuinely positive, as well as negative, feelings and beliefs.

In addition, an overload of negatively worded items might provide a misguided educational experience, leading the respondent to begin to believe devaluating statements that had not been entertained before. The possibility of this happening is increased by evidence showing that people tend to give more weight to negative aspects of something than to positive aspects (Kanouse & Hanson, 1971). To counteract the excessive weight that might be given to negative items, the most obvious suggestion is to include at least the same number, and preferably a greater number, of positively worded items.

Another concern relates to the nature of stereotyping itself. Although it is understandable that attitude tests avoid differentiations among group members captured by the label, the possible deleterious effects of an ostensible scientific instrument that homogenizes people in this way are of concern. Homogenization flies in the face of decades of research showing that the fact of disability tells us almost nothing about what a person is like. As we know, individuals are unique in their combination of interests, values, abilities, circumstances, and so forth. Because of the nature of stereotypes, however, the tests themselves have to deny this uniqueness. To minimize both the negative-biasing and stereotyping effect of such tests, it is recommended that subjects be cautioned against this possibility during debriefing.

Another urgently needed recommendation is that researchers spend at least as much time searching for and uncovering positive attitudes as they do negative ones. To agree with this recommendation depends on believing that positive attitudes toward disadvantaged groups not only exist, but are *as important as* negative attitudes. They are important for two reasons. (1) Attitudes are frequently (typically?) ambivalent, and when evaluated within this more complex matrix, the perception of the group is likely to change. A telling example discussed earlier is the attitude change that took place toward the delinquent youth as soon as positive traits were brought to the fore. (2) Positive attitudes are also important because it is these attitudes that have to be drawn upon, built upon, and spread in the effort to overcome disparaging beliefs and feelings of one group toward another.

The Problem of Comparison Groups

Consider an experiment in which conditions are held constant in two groups except for the independent variable. This type of between-group design is common and was used in the research example, presented at the beginning of this chapter, in which subjects were interviewed by someone who either had or did not have an obvious disability. An analysis of this type of experimental design in terms of saliency and context from the perspectives of investigator and subject will help us understand why the unwary researcher becomes an easy prey to the fundamental negative bias.

The investigator was seduced into attending to the disability variable as the salient factor, while neglecting context conditions, because "all other things were kept equal." That is, from the vantage point of the experimenter, the controls served to suppress the influence of the context in which the behavior of the interviewer took place. The negative value attributed to the disability, therefore, stood alone in determining the negative flow of thoughts and feelings, leaving the investigator to become trapped by the fundamental negative bias, even to the extent of treating findings favoring the interviewer with the disability as if they were negative.

For the subject, however, the situation was very different. The subject knew nothing about control conditions maintaining equality of interviewer behavior in two groups in which only a physical attribute of the interviewer varied. All the subject was aware of was an interviewer whose status and behavior were positive. Thus, instead of the context being obliterated, the context was decidedly positive. Under these circumstances, response intensification occurred, a response that fits with other research (see p. 7).

The different contexts in which the subjects and experimenter perceived the situation remind one of the difference in perspective between insiders and outsiders. The experimenter, in interpreting ratings made by others (subjects), held the position of an outsider, whereas the subjects were insiders with respect to their own ratings. The conclusion is a compelling indication that two vastly different situations were evaluated, one as perceived by the subject and a very different one by the experimenter. Researchers must become aware of possible differences in perspective between themselves and subjects, especially in terms of issues of the saliency and context of variables under study.

An additional problem involved in some types of comparisons stems from the act of categorizing people. Categorizing requires sorting people according to some variable such as age, sex, race, or disability. The variable, then, with its name or label, becomes the item of interest. The danger is that any differences found between groups will be attributed to the variable under study, with not even a thought given to likely confounding factors. This is what happens when the role of the environment is ignored in accounting for differences between blacks and whites, or boys and girls, or people with and without disabilities. That is, the differences tend to be attributed to the factor of race, sex, or disability alone. Thus, when children attending a residential school for students who are blind or deaf or have emotional problems are compared to "normal" children, frequently the different educational environments, or the fact of living at home versus away from home, are not considered in accounting for the differences found in personality, achievement, or behavior. It is recommended that the investigator always entertain what my esteemed teacher, the philosopher Herbert Feigl (1953), referred to as the "something-else-perhaps" query, in order to avoid "nothing but" interpretations based on a salient, labeled variable. Feigl also reminds us that in replacing "nothing but" by "something else," the investigator must be pressed to discover "what's what."

The Problem of Statistical Significance

The fundamental negative bias has still another ally in the logical precept that a statistical null hypothesis cannot be proven (Fisher, 1955). Thus, similarities between groups are typically regarded as null findings and ignored. Instead, the researcher tries to discover differences between groups, which then become highlighted in the interpretation of results. The consequence for understanding attitudes toward different groups is serious, and in the case of groups that are already disadvantaged, ignoring similarities adds to the disadvantagement.

One reason for this conclusion is based on the Gestalt principle of similarity as a unit-forming factor, previously referred to, and on Heider's balance theory of sentiments (1958). Stated briefly, this theory posits an interdependence between a person's liking for someone (sentiment relation) and the feeling of belongingness with that person (unit relation). There are many factors that give rise to the feeling that two persons belong together in some way, among the strongest of which is the factor of similarity. Thus, different people may be thought of as a unit because of similarity of beliefs, nationality, or religion. The idea is that when a person identifies with someone because of similarity, a tendency for that person to like the other person will be induced. Induced liking toward a group tends also to occur when similarity with the self is perceived. Much research, as well as common everyday experience, supports these propositions.

If perceived similarity induces liking, what about perceived differences? Although the evidence in the former case is much more consistent than in the case of dissimilarity inducing dislike, differences can be perceived in a way that promotes prejudice. Inconsistency of results is seen in the following examples. (1) Perceived dissimilarity may simply lead to an absence of any unifying force, rather than a force moving people apart; the observer can then be said to be indifferent to the dissimilarity. Or (2) dissimilarity may be perceived as complementing oneself, thereby providing a good fit that leads to a positive reaction. However, (3) perceived dissimilarities can also be disturbing, especially when they arouse discomfort, fear, or devaluation; in this case, alienation and disliking are likely to be induced. On these grounds alone, we need to be concerned when differences are singled out for attention and similarities are ignored.

There is still another basis for concern regarding the issue of highlighting differences. The Gestalt principle of part–whole relationships suggests that attending solely to differences creates a different impression of those differences than when perceiving them within a system that includes similarities as well.

Returning to the issue of the null hypothesis, we can ask whether there is any way to use statistical reasoning to uncover similarities between groups.

Researchers traditionally use the .01 or.05 alpha level of significance to refer to the small probability that the obtained difference between groups could be due to chance. I would like to propose that the high end of the probability range could be used to suggest the likelihood of similarity (rather than exact equivalence) between groups. While it is true that the null hypothesis cannot logically be proven, and can "at most be said to be confirmed or strengthened" (Fisher, 1955, p. 73), we should note that large *p*-values do in fact "confirm or strengthen" the hypothesis that group differences are small or nonexistent. In other words, one could conclude that the obtained difference is unreliable as a difference but is reliable as a similarity. The similarity, then, will have to be judged as to whether it is of psychological importance, just as a statistically significant difference has to be so judged. Of course, the size of the sample, as well as the reliability and validity of the measures themselves, also should meet standards of adequacy. Greenwald (1975) presents evidence and argument regarding the detrimental effects of prejudice against accepting the null hypothesis. He also offers a variety of procedures that can help to eliminate this bias.

The important conclusion is that just as not all differences that are *statistically* significant are *psychologically* meaningful, not all statistically *non*significant differences are psychologically meaningless. In fact, the latter may be viewed as psychologically significant when they are judged to represent important similarities. Applying these considerations will force investigators to examine similarities as well as differences between groups in understanding their data. The conclusions drawn can then be expected not only to represent group comparisons more validly, but also to promote positive relationships between groups.

The Problem of Problem-Oriented Clinical Settings

Clinical settings are established to help solve problems—physical, mental, or emotional. And that is part of the problem. Being problem-oriented, the clinician easily concentrates on pathology, dysfunction, and troubles, to the neglect of discovering those important assets in the person and resources in the environment that must be drawn upon in the best problem-solving efforts (Wright & Fletcher, 1982). The example of the counselor at the beginning of this paper demonstrated how easy it is for the fundamental negative bias to take hold when problems are the focus of concern.

A brief example of the efficacy of using assets in the service of managing deficits involves the case of a middle-aged man whose visual-spatial skills were impaired by a stroke (Chelune, 1983). The neuropsychologist was able to demonstrate the potential utility of using the client's intact verbal skills as a means of compensating for the considerable difficulty he had performing such construction tasks as copying a cross. When instructed to "talk" himself through such tasks he was able to do them without difficulty. If only the impaired side of his functioning had been attended to, remediation possibilities would have been limited.

Uncovering hidden environmental resources, though no less important than uncovering personal strengths, tends to be even more elusive in person-centered settings. Since it is the person who is to be treated, attention is focused on the person. The consequence is that assessment procedures are inclined toward the person, not the environment. Adequate attention to resources in the environment is also made more difficult by the fundamental negative bias. Just as the negative train of thought gives short shrift to personal assets, thinking in terms of positive resources in the environment requires an affective shift. It is sometimes easier to ignore the whole environmental problem. Adequate assessment of the environment, however, is mandatory, not only because of its possible role in contributing to problems, but also because remediation outside the clinical setting requires the support of resources in the home and community.

One way to offset the power of the fundamental negative bias in problem-oriented settings is for the clinician to keep in mind that it is of utmost importance to give as much attention to disclosing strengths and resources as to exposing deficiencies and problems with respect to *both* the person and the environment. With this in mind, the clinician can "stop the action" as soon as he or she realizes that the focus has been primarily on deficits and then shift energies toward discovering strengths. The example in the section below demonstrates that it is possible to establish such a mindset and to follow through accordingly.

The Problem of Unsightly and Bizarre Personal Encounters

The discussion of the preceding five topics analyzed how the fundamental negative bias implicates the work of professionals in a variety of research and clinical areas. The sixth topic considers deeply emotional, personal reactions in special cases. Since no one is immune to the fundamental negative bias, including those who are committed to human dignity and respect for others, all of us can be expected to encounter situations in which the conditions for the fundamental negative bias will be overpowering. Who among us has not had the experience of being riveted on some aspect of a person that fills us with aversion or some other form of devaluation? Under extreme conditions, the negative aspect usurps the place of the individual and the person becomes dehumanized.

When this occurs, the recommendation is to *deliberately find the person* by talking to him or her and discovering feelings and thoughts that will restore the individual's personhood. The bizarre behavioral characteristics of some forms of mental illness, or the disturbing physical appearance of some people who are old, ill, or have a disability, can be muted by perceiving a human being. In effect, the saliency of the negative aspect is diminished and a context established that constrains the fundamental negative bias.

One can go even further in helping to assure that personal characteristics will be apprehended within a positive context. I would like to suggest that it is possible to invoke, at will, a constructive way of looking at the nature of problems, even when the negatives loom large. The essence lies in the distinction between what has been designated the *"coping versus succumbing frameworks"* (Wright, 1983). It is proposed that the way in which problems are perceived and reacted to, their very nature, is strongly influenced by these two vastly different orientations.

Briefly, the succumbing framework highlights the difficulties of problems in terms of their devastating impact, not in terms of their challenge for meaningful adaptations. The emphasis is on the limitations of the person, the heartache, suffering, and tragedy. Such a state is viewed as pitiful, and the person as an individual with a highly differentiated and unique personality is lost.

The coping framework, on the other hand, orients the evaluator to scan problems in terms of solutions and satisfactions. The person with the problem is seen as actually or potentially playing an active role in attempting to work toward constructive living, not as being passively defeated by difficulties. The problem of managing difficulties has a double focus. One is geared toward changing those alterable conditions in the environment that add to the person's difficulties, such as architectural or attitudinal barriers. The second focus is directed toward improving the abilities of the person, whether through medical procedures that reduce disability, education and training that lead to new skills, or value changes that facilitate self-acceptance. (See Wright, 1983, pp. 194–211, for further conceptual clarification and implications of the two frameworks.)

That it is possible to switch from the succumbing framework to the coping framework is seen in the following example. A student in training observed an occupational therapist working with a man who had had a stroke. The student had been alerted to the steps that could be taken to counteract the fundamental negative bias in her course work. In reporting her experiences, she wrote:

> The man had one arm paralyzed and the muscles on one side of his face were also paralyzed. Because he had little control over his face muscles, he would continually drool and would take an old, dirty rag to wipe his mouth. When I first saw this, I thought it was "icky" to look at. It was so disgusting. Then I thought I would try to look at it through the coping framework. I drew my

attention to his arm which the O.T. was helping to move and exercise. He was trying so hard, and I realized it was painful for him to move his arm. My whole attitude changed when I concentrated on him as a person, striving to move his arm, and the expression on his face made me aware of his determination! This was a very valuable experience for me (personal communication).

It should not be inferred that the coping framework precludes attention to the suffering and the difficulties themselves. Coping implies coping with problems, not remaining indifferent to them or pretending that they do not exist. Fundamentally, the distinction between the coping and succumbing frameworks provides a way to steer the person, whether insider or outsider, to *constructive views of life with a disability.*

Because of space limitations, many other domains in which the influence of the fundamental negative bias can be detected are not examined here: attempts to change attitudes through simulating a disability, role-playing, educational programs, information, or contact; fund-raising campaigns; health care messages; the semantics of language usage; professional-client relations; motivation; societal factors; and environmental neglect. (These problem areas are addressed in Wright, 1972, 1975a, 1975b, 1978, 1980a, 1980b, 1983.) Having read the present chapter, the reader will be prepared to see specific connections with the fundamental negative bias. In some of the references the principles of the coping framework have been used as guidelines to show how the insidious effects of the fundamental negative bias can be counteracted.

SUMMARY OF CORRECTIVE MEASURES

The basic proposition of the fundamental negative bias states that if, for whatever reason, something is perceived as negative (value aspect), and stands out (saliency aspect) in a sparse context (internal or external), then the psychological events that follow will assume a negative course. In effect, the resulting attitudes are negative. These conditions alert us to the varied snares that lie in wait for the unwary researcher and clinician. The following list of recommendations is based on an analysis of the implications of the fundamental negative bias in a variety of situations. They are offered as ways to guard against being misled by the distorting and potentially harmful consequences of the bias.

1. When social-psychological research involves only subjects who do not know the person(s) to whom they are relating, it is incumbent upon investigators to *explicitly* limit the interpretation of their findings to stranger relationships. This is necessary to prevent extending conclusions

to relationships in which the behavior of the other person is perceived in a very different context.

2. In attitude tests it is important to include at least the same number, and preferably a greater number, of positively worded as negatively worded items, for two reasons: to counterbalance a possibly negative mindset resulting from excessive weight being given to negative items, and to provide respondents an opportunity to express genuinely positive attitudes.

3. To minimize the possible stereotyping effect of attitude tests, the difference between a stereotype and the fact of heterogeneity among members of a group should be stressed during debriefing. Subjects should also be cautioned against the learning of misinformation appearing in test items.

4. At least as much attention should be devoted to searching for and uncovering positive attitudes toward disadvantaged groups as is devoted to negative attitudes, both to avoid a negative bias and to provide a more accurate and comprehensive basis for improving attitudes.

5. When between-group comparisons are made, the context in which the subjects interpret the experimental variable(s) may be different from that of the experimenter, leading the unwary experimenter to false conclusions. The experimenter needs to be aware of this possibility by becoming sensitized to the difference in perspective between the insider (subject) and outsider (researcher). A good precaution in interpreting findings is to ask "What is salient?" and "What is the context?" from the vantage point of both subject and experimenter.

6. In comparing the performance of groups differentiated by a label, it is essential to guard against the tendency to interpret the findings solely in terms of the characteristic indicated by the label. Other factors may be more important in discovering "what's what." A good check is to raise the "something-else-perhaps" query.

7. It is important to seek out and recognize similarities as well as differences between groups. Emphasizing the latter to the neglect of the former not only leads to a distortion of the nature of the groups being compared, but also may lead to a distancing between groups and even to an increase in rejection.

8. Similarities should not be ignored or discounted because the null hypothesis cannot be proven. The high end of the probability range, in conjunction with other precautions and procedures, can be used to point to probable similarities.

9. To check the power of the fundamental negative bias in problem-oriented clinical settings, the sensitized clinician can "stop the action" as soon as it is realized that the focus has been primarily on deficits. The focus can then be shifted to discovering strengths and resources in both the

person and the environment. A good question to ask is, "What does the client have going for him or her?"

10. When unsightly or bizarre behavior leads to disgust and devaluation, the observer can purposely reinterpret the situation by talking to the person, thereby discovering that the person has feelings and thoughts that can restore that person's humanness. In this way, the saliency of the negative aspect is diminished and a context established that constrains the impact of the fundamental negative bias.

11. The distinction between the coping and succumbing frameworks provides a strategy for shifting from a harmful view of problems to one that is more constructive.

In concluding this chapter, I would like to stress that to become sensitized to the conditions and implications of the fundamental negative bias and to become mindful of corrective measures are of extreme importance not only to those whose work impacts the lives of people from disadvantaged groups but, inevitably, to society as a whole.

CHAPTER 2
The Politics of Disability

Joseph Stubbins

The toughest item on the agenda of disability is that modern America has no need for most disabled persons. In the rehabilitation community this conclusion is unthinkable, although such a conclusion is both plausible and real. Even those disabled citizens who lead conventional lives (about one-third) tend to repress their pariah status and the patronizing attitudes of the able-bodied and interiorize the values of the straight world. Autobiographical accounts by Zola (1982, p. 213), Hahn (1983, 1985b), and many outside our field emphasize these insights. Such confessions or revelations are an embarrassment to professionals, since they are reminders of how little progress has been made toward the normalization of handicapped persons. To put it differently: Should handicapped people confront the kind of economic and social life imposed upon them, or should they compromise for the marginal existence available to them? And what should be the roles of rehabilitation professionals in the struggle of disabled persons for a better social and economic existence?

Rehabilitation professionals are inextricably caught in a mesh I am calling *the politics of disability*. We are trapped in power relationships that give us little self-determination vis-à-vis our clients, and yet we wield power over them directly and as surrogates of our agency or employer. Each of us, however, does have the option of reflecting on the politics of disability and coping with the anxieties that it brings to our lives. Or we can choose to avoid such painful decisions, even as many successful disabled people do.

Disability means many things. This multibillion dollar industry provides practitioners, researchers, and academics with fulfilling careers and a respectable livelihood. This is not mentioned to diminish the achievements of those whose careers depend on this sector of the economy, but to focus attention on what most professionals choose to ignore—the sociopolitical aspects of the disabled status. My intention is to explore the hypothesis that those with an economic interest in disabled persons define disability and its remedies differently from those who are disadvantaged by disabilities, a subject explored elsewhere (Stubbins, 1984a). In brief, *professionals define the problems, the agenda, and the social reality of disabled persons in ways that serve their own interests more closely than those of their clients.* Since clients know far less about their helpers than vice versa, most of them are poorly situated to be aware of how their own interests might be compromised. Clients often define what troubles them by interiorizing the attitudes and values of their professional helpers.

Just as there is a culture of professionalism, there is also a culture and ideology, although less clearly articulated, among disadvantaged handicapped persons. The majority of persons everywhere tend to deal with their world as they find it, with little time or inclination to reflect upon it. Others, however, prefer to visualize improved conditions and even utopias. Neither professionals nor disabled persons are automatically locked into their social roles, and this fact opens up vistas for transcending the problems with which this chapter deals.

WHAT IS THE POLITICS OF DISABILITY?

Politics concerns the processes by which scarce resources are authoritatively allocated among segments of the population and the ways in which these decisions are made (Easton, 1971). Changes in the relations between disabled and able-bodied persons are often brought about through a political process, such as the 1973 amendments of the Rehabilitation Act. These amendments for the first time recognized certain rights of disabled persons. In general, power relations between disabled people and various segments of society, including professional helpers, have considerable significance. A clear example of what politics involves is the effort to pass the Equal Rights Amendment, which would, among other things, make equal pay for men and women mandatory.

The politics of disability encompasses far more than what we learned in college courses in political science. To understand the decision processes that affect the lives of handicapped persons, we must seek the help of all the social sciences. The success of such a multidisciplinary approach can be seen in the remarkable progress made in the last 30 years by the advocates and parents of mentally retarded children and adults. Disability problems cannot be comprehended by a single discipline, such as physical medicine, vocational psychology, and so on. Reductionistic attempts to do so can best be guarded against by laymen who have no vested interest in a particular disciplinary perspective. I have been critical of psychological reductionism in rehabilitation; I would not want to settle for political reductionism, either (Stubbins, 1984b).

It would be difficult to visualize the improved status of women without thinking of the political processes that contributed to it. The system of community property for married persons, nondiscrimination between the sexes, and new employment opportunities are end products of politics or the redistribution of scarce resources among men and women. The political science of disability is the study of how to account for the limited resources to which disabled persons, as compared to the nondisabled, have access. For example, Bowe (1983) reported that 65.5% of disabled working-age men and 80.6% of disabled working-age women were not in the labor force. Clearly, most disabled persons are poor; the average earnings of those working are lower than those of nondisabled persons; many are underemployed; they are subject to discrimination in educational opportunity and in housing. Disabled people are a disadvantaged minority, just as women and some racial groups are. This is only the beginning, for the facts reveal nothing about the causes and remedies of the problems they pose—most of which are complex and elusive.

Important as the politics of disability is, no one expects clients and their helpers to cease working on their individual problems until social and political solutions become effective. Rehabilitation is big business, and so there is room for multiple approaches.

THE CHANGING DEFINITION OF DISABILITY

Rehabilitation technologies have largely solved problems of impairments by creating alternative and compensating ways of getting about, of communicating, of self-care, so that only the most severely disabled persons choose to remain in nursing homes (Crewe & Zola, 1983). But much less progress has occurred in enabling persons with deficits to become involved in mainstream social and economic activities. Medical advances have transformed the central meaning of disability from physical survival to the search for meaning when one is socially isolated, unemployed or underemployed, and lacking essential environmental accommodations. Or as Victor Finkelstein (1980) put it: to be disabled is to belong to an oppressed minority.

The essence of disability is the *social and economic consequences* of being different from the majority. Being female rather than male or being black rather than white are symptoms of being disadvantaged. The disadvantages inhere in social relationships.

Disability can be viewed as a particular kind of relationship between a person with an impairment and the social and physical environment. What kind of relationship is this? (1) It is a superordinate–subordinate one; able-bodied persons have power over those with impairments. (2) This power relationship is manifested by the able-bodied population's defining critical words from their perspective, e.g., in saying that disability is *in* the person rather in the relationship, and having control of the environment. (3) The relationship is characterized by the able-bodied person's asserting the right to determine what kinds of rehabilitation services disabled people need.

These characteristics of the relations between disabled and so-called normal persons persist across time, specific individuals, and individual differences. They are role relationships built into the structure of our institutions and our society. Role relations have received little attention from rehabilitation pyschologists and counselors, who have tended to underestimate the stability and resistance to change that role relations imply. The complexity of these roles was detailed by Higgins (1985). This tends to make the subordinate position of disabled persons relatively resistant to change. Since some handicapped persons manage to escape the limits of these role relationships, the way is opened for explaining all the difficulties of the others as due to such traits as lack of intelligence, persistence, and so on.

POWER, TRUTH, AND REHABILITATION EXPERTISE

Power involves a relationship in which one person can constrain, coerce, and/or determine the behavior of the other. The power resources of rehabilitation professionals consist of their control over welfare funds, their credentials, their ideology, their authority, and their roles as experts on disability. Power need not be conceived of only as brute force or only as exercised by the judiciary, the police, and corporate enterprises. It is exerted with increasing degrees of subtlety in the modern democratic state and decreasingly by repression. Michel Foucault's life project was to un-cover all the manifestations of power that had become occluded by moder-nity (Gordon, 1980; Dreyfus & Rabinow, 1982).

Foucault noted that poor people, deviants, and political dissidents in modern times have been treated with less overt constraints than in earlier epochs. Several interpretations may account for the evolution from overt oppression to more circumspect ways of managing people. For Foucault, the preferred one was that *the social science professionals and their technical knowledge have taken the place of brute force.* We can see just such an evolution in the Soviet Union since the Stalin era, when dissidents were disposed of by a shot to the head.

In the modern state, in which the citizenry are literate, an important source of power is the knowledge and techniques generated by the applied social sciences. This kind of power is not easily identified as emanating from economic and monopolistic sources, since it appears as neutral technical and scientific information. Nor are rehabilitation practitioners necessarily aware of how their choice of techniques is tied to power considerations—both by the influence exerted upon them by political and ideological interests and by the influence they exert on their clients in carrying out their assigned mandate. They practice their skills in ways sanctioned by their professions, which combine contemporary wisdom and science. We shall return to this theme in the section on "possessive individualism."

We know that the professional consensus changes over time, but few of us take the trouble to analyze the transformations in practices other than to label them innovation or enlightenment. It is as if the insights of history can teach us nothing about the nature of our professional practices. As a counselor educator, I have observed that few students are interested in developmental accounts of their profession, probably because they do not perceive them as contributing to their clinical skills. At any rate, most of them seem to assume that what is most recent is most valid and proficient. ". . . the sciences provide a particularly promising area in which to explore the role of forces current in the larger society in shaping the evolution of a discipline" (Kuhn, 1971, p. 229). Kuhn was referring to the natural sciences, but his point is even more appropriate to the social sciences. After reading Foucault, one cannot help wondering what would happen if more practitioners could stand back from their daily activities with the anthropological detachment that one might bring to assessing folk medicine as practiced by a remote tribe! Foucault did this with medical practice (1973), insanity (1965), crime (1979), education, and sexuality (1978).

Some years ago, at a regional conference sponsored by advocates for mentally retarded citizens and attended by both professionals and laypeople, it was inspiring to observe how well informed the laymen were. The communication was clean and undistorted by professional patronizing and lay deference. This experience reminded me that information is a power resource that can be used to impress or to empower others. Generally, disabled people know practically nothing about the personnel and agencies where they go for help. But counselors get to know a great deal about the lives of persons with impairments. If professionals and clients had equal access to information about the other, the groups might have more nearly equal power.

Disabled persons are not a self-conscious constituency in the sense that practitioners, researchers, and academics are. Therefore, they very much depend on the latter for information, although there are some notable exceptions. The most important feature of these politically sophisticated groups is their autonomy and freedom to address their needs directly to legislatures and the public, unfiltered by parochial professional interest. For this reason, they tend to attract that minority of professionals who are sensitive to the needs not being met by traditional rehabilitation services. *The technical and practical knowledge needs of professionals and handicapped people are different,* a lesson that the larger community of disabled persons has yet to master. As disabled people gain confidence about this, they will be less distracted and intimidated by technical jargon.

Those rehabilitation personnel who regard their careers as more than a way of making a living are deeply dissatisfied with existing rehabilitation services. The philosophy of science underlying rehabilitation practices would interest these professionals (Stubbins, 1984c). Those with the patience to struggle with the writing style of continental intellectuals will find that the works of Michel Foucault offer many interesting leads by which to pursue the subject.

A NEW ANGLE ON PROFESSIONALISM

Michel Foucault was a generative thinker whose views cannot be captured by the existing labels by which social scientists are classified. He has been called a historian of ideas, a philosopher, a structuralist, a sociologist, and an archaeologist. He had a creative way of relating prevailing professional practices in the management of mental illness, crime, poverty, and education to developments in the contemporary culture. Although other writers have written on one or another aspect of this theme, the sweep of Foucault's erudition and his command of most of the social sciences made him a remarkable philosopher of the social sciences.

Foucault used the term *discursive formation* to encompass the set of practices that give coherence and rationality to what practitioners in the social sciences do at any given historical period. He came by this term through the historical study of social practices, the applied social sciences, for example, the care and treatment of mentally ill persons. Many of the practices that prevailed in earlier periods certainly strike us as strange, superstitious, and quite irrational. Likewise, those that prevail today would have been regarded as irrational by our forebears and no doubt will be so regarded by our descendants. This relativity of rationality in social practices as developed by Foucault contrasts with popular views that regard the past as a period of darkness compared to the present. More importantly, Foucault challenges us to use historical insights to explore the relation between current practices in our field, on the one hand, and prevailing social and economic conditions, on the other.

In the applied social sciences, it is particularly difficult to distinguish those components of practice based on scientific method from those based on habit, custom, values, ideology, and special interests. In fact, all these bases form a blend or compound. For instance, vocational rehabilitation practitioners typically try to make accurate measurements of their clients' aptitudes, interests, and vocational skills; reduce these figures to percentile or other normative scales; and write reports in the objective style of laboratory researchers. But a desk audit would reveal that many of these data are of marginal or no use when it comes to applying them to the tasks of job placement. When finding *any* kind of job for the disabled client is impossible, diagnostic procedures are irrelevant. But the procedures persist because of the pressure to envelop practice with scientific authority.

The clinical model in vocational rehabilitation (Stubbins, 1982; Stubbins & Albee, 1984) can be viewed as a *discursive formation*. This is the term by which Foucault refers to a blend of science and culture that constitutes the wisdom of a particular applied social science. The clinical model as a combination of science and ideology begs for analysis. On the one hand, the technologies by which counselors attempt to match client to job and to make the client more marketable are rooted in scientific rationales. On the other hand, one need only survey a text dealing with vocational rehabilitation to realize that the appraisal and job promotion of clients proceeds on the assumption that they must adapt to an essentially *unproblematic* social and industrial world.

We should consider the possibility, for instance, that the role function of professionals prohibits concern with difficulties generated by industrial policies. A rehabilitation pundit once said that the best remedy for unemployment among the disabled was an industrial policy of full employment. If we had a lower level of unemployment, would the need for professionals in vocational rehabilitation be reduced? Why is so little of our intellectual talent invested in exploring the social and industrial world? Why do we invest so much in diagnosing and shaping our clients to adapt to that industrial world, which presumably lies beyond the scope of our expertise?

Specialists in rehabilitation tend to reduce disability problems to dimensions and procedures that lie within their discipline. For instance, a counselor, sociologist, or economist is competent in some areas and not in others. This is the danger that must be faced and the price that must be paid for the advantages of specialization. Who is to mediate among competing claims to expertise in the area of disability? In practice, it is one profession that has the hegemonic role. Is this leadership and dominance justified in terms of the needs of disabled persons? And who should determine those needs? Who should define the scope of the expertise required to deal with those needs? These questions get to the heart of what the status of being disabled means to those who live it: impairment or social disadvantage, poverty resulting from personal deficit or from social and economic structure, social isolation immanent in deviance or in socially sanctioned meaning, powerlessness or lack of social competence, and so on.

The power of the professions touches all of us, whether disabled or not. I do not wish to create the impression that rehabilitation experts are *the* enemy in this drama. But if we are to sort out the wheat from the chaff of professionalism, we must run the risks of self-examination. Extremists can quote us out of context and use our honest attempts at reorientation to depreciate the valid contributions of, for instance, vocational rehabilitation. We must examine our professional roles simply because they interface with disabled persons, typify how society deals with disabled citizens, and can provide the raw material through which to explore the problem further (Bledstein, 1976; Foucault, 1972; Larson, 1977).

Whatever the origins of the current system of rehabilitation, probably few practitioners had much voice in creating it. However, as experts, they have considerable influence in maintaining and extending it. In the nineteenth century the public regarded the deplorable status of disabled people as a moral problem. But increasingly moral problems have been transformed into technical issues to be resolved by scientists and technocrats.

Rehabilitation experts have power over clients as well as over disabled persons as a group. Rehabilitation experts focus on certain features concerning the problematics of disability and conceal others from public scrutiny. Similar processes have occurred in the areas of medicine, law, national defense, economic policy, and wherever special interests are at stake. However, disability as an economic and social issue has not captured the public's attention to the same degree as medicine and other social issues have.

POSSESSIVE INDIVIDUALISM

This phrase was borrowed from MacPherson (1962), whose classic work is still contemporary in its significance. Power sharing between disabled people and professionals might influence the goals of rehabilitation. Handicapped persons are beginning to see the implications of being assessed and guided in their careers by special counselors. Why shouldn't they receive such help in the same way as able-bodied persons? The promise of making disabled persons more competitive in our nonproblematic industrial world is less and less attractive. There is a widening gap between the ideology and culture of professionals and disabled persons: they disagree about what the problem of disability is.

It may be that dissatisfaction is not articulated in quite this way. My interpretation is an attempt to frame what troubles handicapped persons trying to break out of a depreciated self-concept. Both professionals and disabled persons live in a socially constructed world that impacts them differently, providing them with diverse values. Professionals offer disabled people techniques of winning in the competition for jobs; but disabled people want to change the rules of the game.

Behind these two sets of values lie collectivism, individualism, and the kind of society that features an optimum mixture of the two. These values have always posed a profound contradiction to our national ethos. Americans promote innumerable social causes unrelated to private gain. Such altruism competes with greed and the credo that the general interest is best served by everyone's pursuing his or her own interests. Unbridled individualism, however, is especially promoted by ultra-conservative political interests.

In this brief chapter it is not possible to fully develop the thesis that professionals as clinicians support the individualistic, conservative version of the good society. In another article, I intend to elaborate the social philosophy of possessive individualism and show how fully the clinical model of rehabilitation is impregnated with these values. Clinicians would probably deny that what they do has anything to do with a particular version of social reality. But the clinical model *does* respond to whether the economic plight of disabled persons should be regarded as a private or collective matter. Clinicians operate on the assumption that the disabled individual can be helped as a more or less self-contained entity, which Sampson (1977, 1981) dubbed the greatest invention of American psychology! This preference for reducing disability problems to self-contained individual technical issues has the smell of the new conservatism. Unlike its West European counterparts, the American cutbacks in social welfare programs are made from a lower base, since the percentage of our gross national product devoted to welfare programs has always been lower than in the other democratic countries of the West.

The reduction of spending for social programs and its impact on the bottom 20% of the socioeconomic hierarchy is dramatically detailed by Thomas B. Edsall (1984) in *The New Politics of Inequality*. Edsall analyzed the political and intellectual factors that contributed to the conservative consensus and created changes that were unthinkable only a few years ago.

THE NEW CONSERVATISM

What does conservatism imply for the future of disabled poeple? First, the revival of social Darwinism. This revival has drawn inspiration from the relatively new science of sociobiology (Wilson, 1975), the application of evolutionary principles to the understanding of social behavior. Political conservatives draw inspiration from the new insights into the social life of animals by constructing them into a paradigm of the natural world, even though sociologists disown such extrapolations from their studies. An entirely new conservative cosmology has arisen, designed to justify current government policies as consistent with the natural world, where inequality is more prevalent than equality. The conservative establishment is actively disseminating its cosmology and clothing its special interests in a naturalistic rationale.

Second, technological changes of the postwar period have resulted in the reduction of unskilled and semiskilled jobs, in which a large share of disabled persons previously found employment (Cornes, 1984). Rehabilitation personnel should come to terms with the probability that many, perhaps the majority of, disabled persons will never work (Croxen, 1983). However, the resources for developing alternatives for employment are not good. The number of rehabilitation personnel in the public sector is dwindling, morale is at a low point, and the younger professionals are taking jobs with private consulting firms and with employee assistance programs in industry.

Third, the current difficulty of pressional rehabilitation is not an ephemeral phenomenon generated only by a business cycle, or by rapid technological change, or even by the new conservatism. Rather, the impasse is rooted in the structure of vocational rehabilitation services as defined in the state-federal programs, and in the kind of graduate training mandated for professionals entering those programs. The latter had their beginnings at a time when there were far fewer seriously disabled persons available for work, when unemployment rates were lower, and when SSDI and SSI were not in place. Today, we have the disincentive of a virtual guaranteed annual wage for disabled persons. The impact of welfare programs on vocational rehabilitation is one of these major policy issues which professionals have not addressed (Hahn, 1985a).

Vocational rehabilitation badly needs an affirmative ideology congenial to the unmet needs of disabled persons as a counterpoint to conservatism. The current appeal of rugged individualism, of succeeding against the odds, and of demonstrating that one is superior to the millions of unemployed citizens is increasingly at variance with the world of handicapped people. A rehabilitation ideology must transcend the current divisiveness caused by organizations based on medical diagnoses and must recognize that the *common disadvantaged status of disabled people* is more crucial than their medical or psychological differences. Disabled persons are badly divided by their many national organizations, each pursuing its specific goals and not heeding the collective impact of large numbers.

An appropriate ideology should give proper emphasis to our basic interdependence as members of the species *homo sapiens* (Bellah et al., 1985). There is little in the conservative ideology that takes account of the increasing relational, integral, and complex aspects of modern society and what a smoothly functioning society requires of citizens in the way of cooperation. Part of the success of the women's rights movement can be found in its skill in getting women of diverse ethnic and socioeconomic status to cooperate on issues of civil rights.

The conservative notion that success or failure for handicapped persons is essentially an individual challenge is far from an anomaly peculiar to rehabilitation professionals. Americans generally believe that they are quintessentially the architects of their lives, notwithstanding how much the quality of their living depends on others. This obscuring of the real world is not peculiar to the area of disability and rehabilitation but is rooted in the intentionality of all knowledge. Knowledge is socially conditioned and therefore contains social and political interests (Berger & Luckman, 1966). We should expect that the basic interests of stigmatized persons would differ from those in the mainstream who are already established in their careers. The task of drafting the world as seen by disabled persons has barely begun.

How do professionals get on with the task of modifying professional roles to bring them more in line with the needs of disabled people? To get involved we must identify middle ground between disillusionment and burnout and naive attempts to become change agents in institutions committed to the status quo. If we begin by seeking a more collaborative style with disabled persons we can get ideas and inspiration from those concerned with the developmentally disabled and the many organizations concerned with the civil rights of disadvantaged groups.

SUMMARY

There is an imbalance between the resources devoted to the analysis and remediation of individual deficits and the economic and social dynamics that keep handicapped people in a marginal status. The study of politics might uncover the sources of the social and economic disadvantages experienced by disabled people. Some suggested starting points for further research are the role of professionals in stabilizing the dissatisfaction of disabled people, the dominance of individualism in rehabilitation, and the drafting of an ideology that would provide handicapped persons with more dignity than traditional rehabilitation does.

PART II
Sources of Attitudes

CHAPTER 3

A Dimensional Perspective on the Origin of Negative Attitudes Toward Persons with Disabilities

Hanoch Livneh

A review of the literature on sources of negative attitudes toward individuals with disabling conditions indicates that a variety of systems to categorize these attitudes exist (Gellman, 1959; Siller, Chipman, Ferguson, & Vann, 1967; Wright, 1983). These systems have one thing in common: they all seek to elucidate the possible origins, determinants, roots, or sources of these negative attitudes. In other words, they attempt to provide an answer to the often puzzling question of "Why are attitudes toward persons with physical, emotional, mental, and social disabilities overtly or covertly negative?" Some of the categories utilized to classify these sources include psychodynamic sources, sociocultural sources, historical or childhood-originated sources, disability-related factors, and observer (i.e., nondisabled) demographic and personality factors. These categories are not mutually exclusive; some degree of overlap exists. This is not to say that the present classification efforts are useless; it merely indicates that the origins of attitudes toward disabled groups are complex, intertwined, and do not easily lend themselves to study.

The purpose of the present chapter is to offer an integrated and simplified perspective on the origin of negative attitudes toward persons with

disabilities. The suggested perspective places the sources of negative attitudes toward persons with disabilities along six dimensions, tentatively
termed sociocultural-psychological, affective-cognitive, conscious-un-
conscious, past experience-present situation, internally originated-exter-
nally originated, and theoretical-empirical. It should be pointed out that
the six dimensions are not necessarily categorically exclusive or independent of each other. They are offered as separate entities solely in order to
shed some light on the perceived complexity of attitudinal sources toward
individuals with disabilities. The remainder of the chapter discusses each of
the suggested source dimensions.

SOCIOCULTURAL-PSYCHOLOGICAL SOURCES

The first dimension conceives of the origins of negative attitudes as ranging from those associated with pervasive socially and culturally valued
norms and customs (i.e., transpersonal sources) on one side, to those
stemming from psychodynamic and developmental experiences (i.e., personal sources) on the other side. Examples of sociocultural contributing
factors are society's emphasis on physical integrity, "body beautiful," personal appearance, health, athletic achievements, and so forth (Roessler &
Bolton, 1978; Wright, 1983). Other factors include emphasis on personal
achievement and productivity and the individual's ability to be vocation-
ally competitive and gainfully employed (Safilios-Rothschild, 1970). Finally, sociocultural norms also attach, overtly or covertly, a status degradation to being disabled. Such degradation may be inferred from the social
deviance and stigma associated with being disabled, different, or an outsider (Davis, 1961; Goffman, 1963; Wolfensberger, 1972; Yamamato,
1971). Similarly, the status of the person with a disability is often equated
with that of ethnic, racial, or religious minority groups in terms of marginality status and stereotypical perceptions (Barker, Wright, Meyerson, &
Gonick, 1953; Wright, 1983).

In contrast to the sociocultural factors, the psychodynamic contributing
factors tap sources on a more personal level. Some of these are based on
psychoanalytic concepts. Among the more frequently suggested origins of
negative attitudes are those implicating the requirement of mourning; the
expectation that the person with a disability ought to grieve for the loss of a
body function or part. This serves the non-disabled person's need to
safeguard his or her values regarding the importance of a whole and
functioning body (Dembo, Leviton, & Wright, 1956/1975). A second
psychodynamic source of negative attitudes is explained through the operation of a negative "halo effect," or the "spread phenomenon" (Wright,
1983), whereby a host of unrelated negative attributes are associated with

and generalized from one specific physical or mental characteristic. A third source may be discovered in the operation of the "guilty-by-association" mechanism; the nondisabled person fears that associating socially with a disabled person may be conceived by others as a sign of some personal maladjustment, thereby leading to social ostracism (Siller, Chipman, Ferguson, & Vann, 1967). Another guilt-based mechanism is that of feeling guilty for being "able-bodied" or "able-minded" in lieu of the suffering and injustice experienced by the person with a disability. Dissociating from the latter serves as a protective function and as a guilt-reducing device (Siller, Chipman, Ferguson, & Vann, 1967).

The role of attitudinal ambivalence has also been explored. These theories seem to occupy a more centrally located position on the sociocultural–psychological dimension, since both perspectives are considered. One perspective suggests that individuals with disabilities are construed as objects of ambivalence, triggering momentary, fluctuating favorable and unfavorable feelings of compassion and sympathy but also of aversion and distaste. This state of affairs creates behavioral instability toward the object of ambivalence, which is perceived as being personally undesirable (Carver, Glass, & Katz, 1978; Carver, Glass, Snyder, & Katz, 1977; Katz, Glass, & Cohen, 1973; Katz, Glass, Lucido, & Farber, 1977). The ambivalence is believed to intensify feelings of guilt (and consequently threaten one's self-esteem), which, in turn, are reduced by lowering the perceived worth of the disabled individual (i.e., denigrating his or her status) (Gibbons, Stephan, Stephenson, & Petty, 1980). A final ambivalence model suggests an ambivalence between the desire to explore a novel stimulus, thereby lessening the unpredictability of the environment, and the fear of violating a well entrenched social norm against staring (Langer, Fiske, Taylor, & Chanowitz, 1976). The latter perspective may have its roots in the psychoanalytic concept of unresolved conflict over scopophilia, which stresses the importance of sight and the pleasure of looking at others in early psychosexual stages of development (Blank, 1957). All of the models ascribe negative feelings to the ensuing ambivalence, resulting in avoiding the individual who is perceived to trigger such feelings and derogating his or her social status.

Finally, the psychodynamics involved in associating disability with personal responsibility and punishment for sin should be mentioned. There are several versions of this theme in the literature. The basic premise revolves around conceiving of a disability, or more generally of suffering, as a punishment for personal or even ancestral transgressions. In the same vein, the person with a disability may be perceived as evil—for committing an act of wrongdoing, or as dangerous—if he or she was unjustly punished and now seeks retribution to balance the inflicted injustice (Siller, Chipman, Ferguson, & Vann, 1967; Wright, 1983). Other versions may be found in Gellman (1959) and Thurer (1980).

FIGURE 3-1 Sociocultural–Psychological Dimension

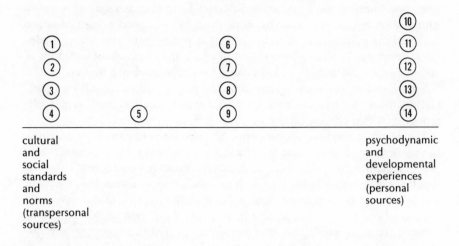

cultural			psychodynamic
and			and
social			developmental
standards			experiences
and			(personal
norms			sources)
(transpersonal			
sources)			

(1) emphasis on physique and beauty; (2) emphasis on health and athletic prowess; (3) emphasis on achievements, productiveness, and employment; (4) disability connotes lower status, social deviance, minority, membership, and marginality; (5) requirement for mourning; (6) ambivalence between favorable and unfavorable feelings; (7) ambivalence–guilt–threat to self-esteem; (8) ambivalence between desire to visually explore and fear of violating social norm against staring; (9) associating responsibility with etiology; (10) "spread phenomenon" operation; (11) "guilty-by-association" mechanism; (12) guilty for being "able-bodied"; (13) disability as a punishment for sin; (14) disabled person as evil and dangerous.

AFFECTIVE–COGNITIVE SOURCES

The second dimension is occupied by emotional reactions (e.g., anxiety, guilt) on one pole and by intellectual reactions (e.g., lack of self-insight, cognitive dissonance, inability to tolerate ambiguity) on the opposite pole. The sources of negative attitudes when approached from an affective perspective include references to aesthetic aversion at the sight of certain body deformities or mental and emotional conditions affecting one's behavior, mobility, or speech (Siller, 1963; Siller, Chipman, Ferguson, & Vann, 1967). Many anxiety-related sources have been reported in the literature. Included are references to anxiety invoked when threat to one's body image or body integrity are anticipated. More specifically, one of the frequently cited sources is a threat to one's intact body image when in the presence of a person with a disability due to the fear that a similar impairment could also happen to oneself (Novak & Lerner, 1968; Roessler & Bolton, 1978; Siller's, 1969, "distressed identification" concept). Other sources implicate the reawakening of archaic castration anxiety in the presence of analogous loss situations (Fine, 1979; Siller, 1984), unresolved infantile separation anxiety from parental figures triggered by the presence of a missing body part or a lost bodily function (Siller, 1964), and the rekindling of death anxiety when interacting with a physically disabled person whose loss of a body part or function is symbolically equated with the loss (i.e., death) of one's ego, thereby denying one's unconscious and infantile sense of immortality (Endres, 1979; Fish, 1981; Parkes, 1975).

The cognitive end of this dimension is occupied by a host of worries, concerns, misbeliefs, and misconceptions regarding the nature of the impairments and disabilities involved. Among the more often encountered sources are those suggesting that an interaction with an individual with a disability parallels a cognitively unstructured situation. This unfamiliarity disrupts the accustomed social rules of interaction, which leads, in turn, to avoidance or withdrawal from the situation. Similarly, the

FIGURE 3-2 Affective–Cognitive Dimension

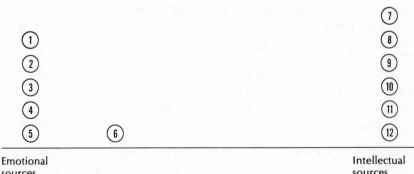

Emotional sources (e.g., anxiety, guilt)

Intellectual sources (e.g., worries, misbeliefs)

(1) aesthetic aversion; (2) threat to one's body image; (3) reawakening of castration anxiety; (4) infantile separation anxiety; (5) death anxiety; (6) fear of mutilation (of physical integrity); (7) unstructured/ambiguous/unpredictable situation; (8) unfamiliarity with physical disabilities; (9) attribution of personal accountability to disability; (10) fear of contamination/inheritance; (11) requirement for mourning; (12) cognitive dissonance/ambivalence formulations.

physically disabled person, being physically different and often unfamiliar to the ablebodied person, is perceived as dissimilar and strange and is therefore disliked (Heider, 1958; Weinberg, 1973; Yamamato, 1971). Another cited source is associating responsibility with the etiology of the disability, thereby attributing personal and moral accountability to the cause of the ensuing condition (Safilios-Rothschild, 1970). This assumption may help explain the prevalent negative attitudes often associated with social and behavioral disabilities (e.g., alcohol abuse, drug abuse, criminal conduct). Fear of, or more properly the myth of, contamination or inheritance also provokes aversive attitudes toward, and avoidance of, certain types of disabilities, especially some forms of cancer and of AIDS.

CONSCIOUS–UNCONSCIOUS SOURCES

Attitudinal roots along this dimension range from these associated with full awareness of the attitudes by the observer at one end, to these of which the observer is presumed to be totally unaware at the other end. Examples of consciously based determinants of negative attitudes include associating personal or moral responsibility with etiology of disability, fear of social ostracism as implied by the "guilt-by-association" phenomenon, and fear of contamination or inheritance through interaction. Unconscious sources, on the other hand, include most of the previously discussed sources. These attitudinal sources include those associated with early childhood influences related to certain childrearing practices and experiences, the opinions on viewing disability as a punishment for sin or fear of imminent punishment to oneself, threats to body image or physical integrity, and the related views on the reawakening of castration anxiety, separation anxiety, and the belief in the parallelism between reactions to the loss (i.e., death) of body parts and life in general.

PAST EXPERIENCE–PRESENT SITUATION SOURCES

The fourth dimension contrasts attitudinal causes stemming from early life influences and experiences with causes believed to be anchored in current situational experiences. Early life influences are associated with childrearing practices, parents' transmittal of cultural, social, and moral beliefs and attitudes, and specific negative personal experiences relating to disease, illness, or disability. The early life experiences that may trigger negative attitudes toward people with disabilities often pertain to parental emphasis on the importance of health and normality.

FIGURE 3-3 Conscious–Unconscious Dimension

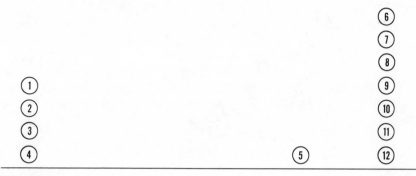

Conscious
sources

Unconscious
sources

(1) attribution of personal responsibility to disability; (2) fear of social ostracism ("guilt by association"); (3) fear of contamination/inheritance; (4) minority-group comparability; (5) threat to physical integrity; (6) early negative childhood experiences; (7) childrearing practices; (8) disability as a punishment for sin; (9) threat to body image; (10) castration anxiety; (11) separation anxiety; (12) death anxiety.

Infringement of health rules is equated with illness, sickness, physical impairment, and long-term disability. The period of childhood is, therefore, fraught with anxiety-laden beliefs and pseudo-beliefs concerning the etiology of a variety of illnesses and impairments. Similarly, the view of suffering and disability as a punishment for early personal, or even ancestral, wrongdoing falls into this category. Again, present consequences (i.e., impairment, disability) are perceived as being caused by previous occurrences (i.e., past transgressions, misdeeds). The opposing belief, that situational experiences determine negative attitudes toward disabled individuals, emphasizes the importance of current events in attitudinal formation. Some of the present-based attitudinal determinants include fear of social ostracism by other nondisabled individuals and the ambivalence triggered when sympathy and caring are invoked simultaneously with aversion and repulsion. Ambivalence may also exist between the wish to reduce unstructured situations by exploring previously unfamiliar objects (i.e., individuals with disabilities) and the fear of violating the sociocultural norm that staring intrudes on others' personal lives (Langer, Fiske, Taylor, & Chanowitz, 1976). Similar to the foregoing views are those associating guilt with ambivalent feelings, which, in turn, leads to denigration of the disabled person so as to reduce the guilt (Katz, Glass, Lucido, & Farber, 1977), and with being "able-bodied," which may result in an attempt to dissociate

FIGURE 3-4 Past Experience–Present Situation Dimension

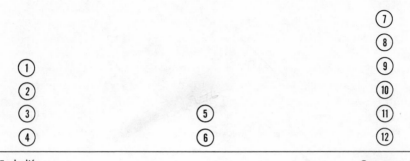

Early life experiences sources		Current situational interactions sources

(1) childrearing practices; (2) early negative personal experiences; (3) parental transmittal of moral–cultural beliefs; (4) disability as a punishment for sin; (5) ambivalence–guilt–threat to self-esteem; (6) threat to body image; (7) un-structured/ambiguous situation; (8) fear of social ostracism; (9) ambivalence between favorable and unfavorable feelings; (10) ambivalence between wish to explore unfamiliar object and fear of violating social norms against staring; (11) threat to physical integrity; (12) fear of contamination.

oneself further from the individual perceived to be the cause of the guilt feelings. Two other situation-based determinants are threats to one's body-image integrity when in the presence of an individual with a physical deformity and fear of being contaminated when socially interacting with impaired or disabled persons.

INTERNALLY ORIGINATED–EXTERNALLY ORIGINATED SOURCES

This dimension contrasts observer (i.e., nondisabled) attitudinal sources with actor (i.e., disabled) sources. The former is associated with those demographic or personality variables of the outside, nondisabled, observer implicated in negative attitudes toward individuals with disabilities. These variables include demographic characteristics such as the sex of the ob-server (i.e., females display more favorable attitudes than males, at least on paper-and-pencil psychometric instruments) and his or her age (e.g., young adults appear to be more accepting of disabled individuals than either adolescents or the elderly) (English, 1971; Harasymiw, Horne, & Lewis, 1978; McDaniel, 1976; Pulton, 1976; Ryan, 1981; Schneider & Anderson, 1980).

Other suggested demographic variables include socioeconomic status and educational level (English, 1971; Harasymiw, Horne, & Lewis, 1978). The amount of previous contact with the disabled individual has also been suggested as affecting attitude; the more one has interacted with members of a disabled population on an equal basis and in a positive manner, the more positive one's attitudes tend to become (Golin, 1970; Schneider & Anderson, 1980).

The list of personality variables presumably influencing attitudes toward individuals with disabilities has grown considerably in the past two decades. The frequently mentioned personality characteristics or traits associated with negative attitudes include ethnocentrism, authoritarianism, dogmatism, rigidity, narcissism, aggressiveness, lack of self-insight, low self-esteem or poor self-concept, ego weakness, lack of body or self satisfaction, anxiety, ambiguity intolerance, interpersonal alienation, and external locus of control (Cloerkes, 1981; English, 1971; McDaniel, 1976; Noonan, Barry, & Davis, 1970; Pederson & Carlson, 1981; Schneider & Anderson, 1980; Siller, 1984b).

The opposite end of this continuum is occupied by characteristics associated with the insider, the disabled, observed individual. Among the variables suggested within this context are prejudice-provoking behaviors (Gellman, 1959; Roessler & Bolton, 1978; Wright, 1983), such as actions manifested by the disabled individual that may be construed as nonacceptable or negative by the nondisabled person. Included are behaviors such as being overdependent, seeking secondary gains and financial disincentives in order not to engage in gainful employment, being insecure, fearful or apathic, and withdrawing from social contact. These behaviors of the "self-fulfilling prophecy" type serve to create and strengthen low expectations of the disabled individual.

A second group of externally originated sources are inherent in disability-connected factors, such as the type of disability (e.g., socially, mentally, and psychiatrically disabled persons are often perceived more negatively than physically or sensorially disabled individuals [Furnham & Pendred, 1983; Harasymiw, Horne, & Lewis, 1976; Safilios-Rothschild, 1970], level of severity, degree of visibility, and degree of cosmetic involvement (Pulton, 1976; Safilios-Rothschild, 1970; Siller, 1963). Also important are the body parts or functions affected by the disability, since they carry both personal and social implications and differentially affect perceptions of the individual with a disability, and the degree of predictability and curability of the impairments involved.

FIGURE 3-5 **Internally Originated–Externally Originated Dimension**

Observer (nondisabled)-	Actor (disabled)-
connected sources	connected sources

(1) demographic variables of observer (e.g., gender, age, educational level); (2) personality characteristics of observer (e.g., ethnocentrism, rigidity, ego weakness); (3) prejudice-provoking behaviors; (4) disability-related factors (e.g., level of functionality, severity, visibility).

THEORETICALLY BASED–EMPIRICALLY STUDIED SOURCES

The final dimension may be perceived as ordering the origins of negative attitudes from those based on theoretical or speculative formulations to those yielded by research findings. The majority of suggested determinants of negative attitudes clearly belong to the former pole. They include the formulations regarding childhood influences and experiences, the variety of developmental and psychodynamic mechanisms implicated, threats to body integrity, and so on. A steadily growing body of research, however, seems to yield evidence of association between negative attitudes toward individuals with disabilities and certain situational and personality correlates.

Examples of empirical findings include correlational studies of the relationship between negative attitudes toward persons with disabilities, using the Attitudes Toward Disabled Persons Scale (Yuker, Block, & Campbell, 1960) and the Disability Factor Scale–General (Siller, 1969), and heightened death anxiety, as measured by the Fear of Death Scale (Endres, 1979; Fish, 1981; Livneh, 1985). Other examples include associating a variety of disability-related factors (e.g., functionality vs. organicity, severity level, visibility) with negative attitude (Furnham & Pendred, 1983; Harasymiw, Horne, & Lewis, 1976, 1978) and, as previously discussed, the association of certain demographic and personality variables (e.g., sex, age, anxiety, defensive style) with rejection of the disabled individual (Siller, 1984b). Finally, studies were reported, mainly in the field of social psychology, where the construct of ambivalence was studied in terms of its effect upon guilt feelings, threat to self-esteem, cognitive dissonance, and their reduction by denigration of the disabled person (Gibbons, Stephan, Stephenson, & Petty, 1980; Katz, Glass, Lucido, & Farber, 1977).

It should be mentioned, parenthetically, that although most of the foregoing studies used correlational and ex-post-facto research designs,

FIGURE 3-6 Theoretically Based–Empirically Studied Dimension

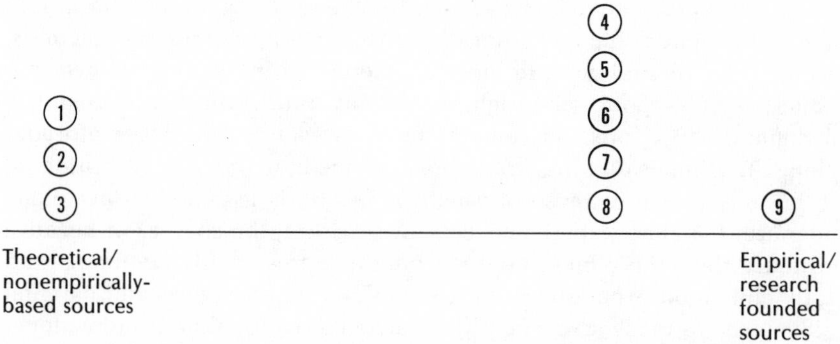

Theoretical/
nonempirically-
based sources

Empirical/
research
founded
sources

(1) childhood experiences; (2) early parental influences; (3) various developmental and psychodynamic mechanisms; (4) death anxiety; (5) manifest, state, trait anxieties; (6) disability-related factors; (7) demographic variables associated with nondisabled observer; (8) personality characteristics of nondisabled observer; (9) ambivalence and its effect upon guilt feelings and threat to self-esteem.

thereby not being able to clearly establish cause-and-effect relationships (i.e., linking disability-related, demographic, and personality variables as antecedents to the formation of negative attitudes toward individuals with disabilities), it is assumed by most authors that such temporal relationships do exist. In other words, characteristics inherent in the disability (e.g., extent of functional limitation, degree of visibility) or in the nondisabled observer (e.g., gender, age, certain personality traits) are viewed as antecedents to and determinants of attitudes, beliefs, and opinions held by the person. The remaining empirical studies, relying in large part on factorial designs, are more appropriately conducive to detecting cause-and-effect relationships. They suffer, however, from two main drawbacks: relying mainly on college-student populations and being confined to controlled laboratory settings. These limit their generalizability to other populations, settings, and types of interactions with disabled individuals.

SUMMARY

This chapter offered a dimensional perspective on determinants cited in the literature concerning the origin of negative attitudes toward individuals with disabilities. Six dimensions were selected for this purpose. (1) Sociocultural–psychological; the origins of negative attitudes along this dimension range from those associated with social and cultural values and norms to those triggered by unique psychodynamic and developmental experiences. (2) Affective–cognitive; the roots of negative attitudes along this dimension vary from those occupied by emotional reactions, such as anxiety and guilt, to those characterized by intellectual determinants, such as poor self-insight, ambiguity intolerance, and cognitive dissonance. (3) Conscious–unconscious; the causes of negative attitudes along this dimension range from those of which the observer is considered to be fully aware to those of which he or she is assumed to be totally unaware. (4) Past experience–present situation; the sources of negative attitudes along this dimension vary from those presumably stemming from early childhood experiences, such as childrearing practices and parental influences, to those associated with current situational and interactional experiences. (5) Internally originated–externally originated; the determinants of negative attitudes along this dimension range from those related to the nondisabled individual observer, such as his or her specific demographic or personality correlates, to those related to characteristics associated with the disabled individual or the disability. (6) Theoretical–empirical; the origins of negative attitudes along the final dimension vary from those based on purely theoretical or speculative formulations to those derived from empirical research findings.

CHAPTER 4
Attitudinal Ambivalence and Behavior Toward People with Disabilities

Irwin Katz, R. Glen Hass, and Joan Bailey

We will review a program of research on attitudes and behavior toward people with physical disabilities. The studies were designed to test a theory concerning the majority's reactions to a range of groups with marginal status in American society. Included in this category, in addition to people with disabilities, are racial minorities, elderly persons, former mental patients, persons with chronic diseases, addicts and alcoholics, and the like. We make the assumption that members of such groups tend to be perceived by others as *deviant*, in the sense of possessing certain disqualifying attributes of mind or body, and also as *disadvantaged*—either by the attribute itself (for example, blindness, illiteracy, inherited poverty) or by the social and economic discrimination that having it entails. This dual perception should tend to generate in the majority group observer contradictory feelings of aversion and even hostility on the one hand, and of sympathy and compassion on the other. That is, attitudes about disabled people and many other marginal groups should often be ambivalent rather than simply positive, negative, or neutral.

Suggestive support for this view can be found in the research literature. In a comprehensive review of early empirical studies, Barker, Wright,

[1]The preparation of this chapter was supported in part by a grant from the National Science Foundation (BNS-8316303) to Irwin Katz and R. Glen Glass.

47

Myerson, and Gonick (1953) concluded that public, verbalized attitudes toward those who had disabilities were favorable on the average, whereas deeper, unverbalized feelings were frequently rejecting. Similar assessments of the research findings have been made by Goffman (1963), Katz (1981), and Wright (1983). Especially noteworthy are the well-controlled experiments that were conducted by Kleck and associates (Kleck, 1968; Kleck, Ono, & Hastorf, 1966). Their findings document the conflicts involved in people's reactions to disabled individuals. In face-to-face encounters with a stimulus person who either was or was not seated in a wheelchair, subjects reacting to the wheelchair condition made greater efforts to be socially agreeable and later evaluated the other's personality more favorably. But in the wheelchair condition subjects also revealed more unease (showed motoric inhibition) and broke off conversations sooner.

AMBIVALENCE AND RESPONSE AMPLIFICATION

Clinical observation suggests that ambivalence creates a tendency toward behavioral instability, in which extremely positive or negative responses may occur toward the object of ambivalence, depending upon how the specific situation is structured. This phenomenon has been discussed by psychoanalytic writers. Freud (1923/1961) used the term *ambivalence* in reference to loving and hating the same person and believed that the conflict could be resolved by a "reactive displacement of cathexis," energy being withdrawn from one impulse and added to the other, opposite impulse. He speculated that an instinct deriving from one particular source could transmit its energy to another instinct originating from a different source.

Making the assumption that attitudes toward mentally ill persons are essentially ambivalent, Gergen and Jones (1963) performed an experiment in which normal subjects displayed amplified positive or negative reactions to stimulus persons described as mental patients when the latter's behavior had either favorable or unfavorable consequences for the subjects. Presumably the stimulus person's behavior "split" the subject's ambivalent attitude, so that one component was suppressed and the other component was enhanced. We believe that the ambivalence-amplification hypothesis that guided the Gergen and Jones experiment also describes the majority's behavior toward physically disabled persons and many other socially marginal groups.

Psychoanalytic theory calls attention to the phenomenon of ambivalence-induced behavioral amplification but it fails to specify either the psychological mediators of this relationship or the conditions under which it is likely to occur. We believe that ambivalence potentiates threat to self-esteem in situations of contact with the attitudinal object or cues associated with the attitudinal object. Specifically, with respect to an encounter with a stimulus person who is a member of a stigmatized group, such as the physically disabled, a majority-group actor may perceive himself or herself as having friendly feelings for a more or less discredited, unworthy other, or as having hostile feelings about someone less fortunate than oneself. Either type of self-referent cognition should pose a threat to the actor's self-image as one who treats others humanely yet with discernment. We believe that this sense of threat gives rise to threat-reductive efforts that are often manifested as extreme behavior toward the attitudinal object, either positive or negative depending upon the structure of the situation.

Further, in a given contact situation, initially occurring stimulus events might accord with one component of an ambivalent disposition but contradict the other, opposite component. For example, the actor might unintentionally help or harm the stigmatized other person or the latter might reveal favorable or unfavorable traits. Such stimulus events should tend to increase the salience of the attitudinal conflict, resulting in heightened efforts at eliminating the conflict. These efforts could take the form of either defense or denial of the discredited attitude. For example, the actor might reinterpret the stimulus events so that they no longer contradict the attitude or might engage in overt actions that compensate for the attitude. Which alternative is used in a particular instance would largely be determined by relative cost and availability and would often be observable as response amplification—that is, as behavior toward the stigmatized person that is more extreme than behavior toward a nonstigmatized but otherwise similar person in the same type of situation. The theory just outlined has been fully presented elsewhere (Katz, 1981). We will now describe some relevant experiments designed to test this theory.

SCAPEGOATING A DISABLED VICTIM OF HARM-DOING

Various studies not involving disabled or other minority-group stimulus persons have documented the fact that people who unintentionally harm another may denigrate the other as a means of justifying the harm-doing. That is, by reducing the victim's worth, the denigration seems to function as a guilt-reduction mechanism for the harm-doer. Our theory states that when denigration is the most readily available means of reducing such guilt, there should be more denigration of a victim who happens to be disabled than of a victim who is nondisabled. In an experiment by Katz, Glass, Lucido, and Farber (1977) women subjects were randomly drawn from a pool of paid volunteers who had filled out a psychological test battery several weeks earlier. Included in the battery was a modified version of Kaplan's (1972) split semantic differential scales for assessing attitudinal ambivalence. The group rated was physically handicapped persons. This instrument consisted of 16 unipolar, six-point (0-5) evaluative scales, of which eight had positive trait labels (e.g.,"warm") and eight had polar opposite labels (e.g., "cold"). An introductory statement explained that one purpose of the scales was to permit people to express duality of feeling when it existed. The ambivalence score reflects the extent to which subjects assign high ratings to the target group on *both* the positive traits and the negative traits.

During the experimental session, subjects were induced to deliver noise signals to a female confederate under the guise of a learning experiment in which the female confederate was the learner and the subject was supposed to punish her for errors. In one condition the female confederate was seated in a wheelchair, apparently disabled, and in another condition she was seated in an ordinary chair, apparently nondisabled. Also, half of the subjects in each condition delivered noise signals that they were led to believe were painful, high-decibel blasts, and the other half of the subjects delivered noise signals they believed to be of mild intensity. Before and after the ostensible learning task, subjects rated the confederate on various personality traits. It was found that before the learning task, ratings of the confederates in all four conditions (i.e., wheelchair/no wheelchair by painful noise/mild noise) were approximately the same. But after the learning task, subjects in the wheelchair/painful noise condition rated the confederate's personality substantially less favorably than did subjects in any of the other conditions. Only in the former condition was the before-after change in ratings significantly negative.

Also, for subjects who had just harmed the apparently disabled confederate, there was a marginally significant relationship ($p < .10$) between the negativity of their personality ratings of the confederate and the amount of ambivalence they had expressed about disabled people in general at the prior session. This relationship was not present in any of the other experimental conditions.

COMPENSATORY HELPING OF A DISABLED VICTIM

In another study, Katz, Glass, Lucido, and Farber (1979) examined the consequences of unintentionally harming a person who was disabled or nondisabled when, instead of being required to evaluate the victim, subjects were provided an opportunity for compensatory helping of the victim. Again, the disability variable was crossed with a harm-doing/non-harm-doing manipulation. Male and female paid volunteers were administered a "personality test," ostensibly for the purpose of standardizing the instrument. A female confederate, posing as a research assistant, administered the questionnaire. For half the subjects she was seated in a wheelchair and for the other half she was apparently nondisabled. After collecting the tests and leaving the room "to score them," the confederate returned and announced that some of the tests were useless because participants had failed to follow instructions. Subjects randomly assigned to the harm-doing condition were privately informed by the confederate that, because they had not filled out the questionnaire correctly, she would have to run additional people on her own time. Those in the neutral, control condition were told that their questionnaires were usable. Later, subjects in all four experimental conditions were given an opportunity to help the confederate by volunteering to participate without pay in her dissertation research for about half an hour.

It was found that subjects who were led to believe they had inconvenienced the assistant in the wheelchair were twice as willing to help her as were subjects in any of the other three experimental conditions. Levels of volunteering were uniformly low in the latter conditions. Unfortunately, it was not possible to measure individual differences in favorable and unfavorable attitudes toward disabled people in general. Hence it could not be shown directly that the enhancement of compensatory helping responses in the wheelchair condition was caused by ambivalence. Nonetheless, the findings are consistent with an ambivalence assumption.

HELPING A DISABLED PERSON WITH POSITIVE OR NEGATIVE TRAITS

In this experiment adults worked at tasks given them by a research assistant who was either disabled or nondisabled and either likeable or obnoxious. Later, the subjects were provided an opportunity to help the assistant by agreeing to be interviewed at another time without pay. It was expected that people would be more willing to help the disabled person than the nondisabled one when both were likeable, but less willing to help the former as compared with the latter when they were equally obnoxious.

More specifically, the subjects were male and female paid participants and were administered the tasks by a young woman who either was or was not seated in a wheelchair. Also, her manner was either pleasant and outgoing (positive condition) or caustic and apathetic (negative condition). For example, after explaining to subjects that the purpose of the session was to pretest cognitive materials for use in future research, the tester mentioned in the positive condition that she did not know much about the tasks because she was a graduate student in history and worked only part-time in the psychological testing program. In the negative condition she merely said that she was employed part-time on the project, adding, "So don't bother asking me any questions, because I don't really feel like answering them, even if I could." To give another example of positive and negative self-presentation, after handing out the test booklets the tester in the positive condition politely requested subjects to read the instructions carefully, adding, "I realize you're not just here for the money, and I hope you'll feel that you've gotten something more out of taking these tests than just that." In contrast, the following comment was made in a sullen voice in the negative condition: "Make sure you read all the instructions very carefully, because there are always some people who manage to screw things up, no matter what. I know you're only here for the money but try to follow the directions."

When the tasks had been completed the tester collected the booklets and left the room, whereupon the "project director" entered and paid the subjects for participating in the study. Then he mentioned that the young woman who administered the tests had asked him to make an announcement on her behalf. He explained that she had another part-time job, with an advertising agency, and needed people to interview about consumer product preferences. Unfortunately, she had no money to pay interviewees. Subjects indicated their willingness to be interviewed by writing their name, telephone number, and times available on a sign-up sheet.

Contrary to the theoretical expectation, subjects in the positive self-presentation condition were three times as willing to help the nondisabled tester as they were to help the tester in the wheelchair, whereas in the negative condition they were just as strongly biased in the opposite direction—that is, in the direction of giving relatively more help to the tester with the disability. Looking at the effect of the self-presentation variation within each of the disability conditions, one finds that when the confederate was in the wheelchair, obnoxious behavior elicited substantially more willingness to help than did friendly behavior; but when the confederate seemed to be nondisabled there was an equally strong helping bias in favor of the pleasant tester.

The unanticipated findings cast doubt on our working assumption that the personal qualities that society finds desirable in most people are also the qualities that are deemed desirable in disabled persons. It appeared that a more appropriate perspective was provided by Goffman (1963), in his discussion of the stigma role that the majority group imposes upon those who are physically disabled. The latter, he argues, must know their place, keep their aspirations and achievements at a modest level, and refrain from testing the limits of the acceptance shown them. The person with an exceptional characteristic is supposed to "fulfill ordinary standards as fully as he can, stopping short only when the issue of normification arises; that is, when his efforts might give the impression that he is trying to deny his differentness" (p. 115). In a similar vein Dembo, Leviton, and Wright (1956/1975) maintain that members of the majority group often want those who are physically different to suffer as a sign that the physical assets they lack are valuable and important. Dembo and associates hypothesize that normal people tend to (1) insist that the disabled person is suffering, even when there is no evidence of suffering, or (2) devaluate the unfortunate person because he or she ought to suffer and does not.

The implication of our experiment is that subjects in the positive self-presentation condition may have become angry or annoyed with the wheelchair confederate because she violated their beliefs about how people in wheelchairs are supposed to behave. That is, instead of seeming to feel inadequate, she was outgoing, competent, and achievement-oriented. This could account for the relatively small amount of helping that occurred in the disabled–positive condition. The stigma-role conception of Goffman and of Dembo and associates can also account for the reversal of the disability effect in the negative condition. There the rudeness and apathy of the tester in a wheelchair could have been seen by subjects as a consequence of misfortune, causing them to feel sorry for her and treat her kindly. In contrast, the noninjured confederate's obnoxious behavior, being taken at face value, led to angry rejection of the helping request. If this reasoning is correct, covert anger should have been relatively high in the disabled–positive and normal–negative conditions, as compared with the normal–positive and disabled–negative conditions. Also, the tester should have been perceived as less happy in the disabled–negative condition than in any of the other conditions. To test these conjectures another experiment was done.

Subjects were exposed to the same manipulations as were used in the first experiment, following which covert anger and perception of the tester's mood state were assessed. The measure of anger was a paper-and-pencil test that required subjects to generate synonyms for neutral and hostile stimulus words, the latter including the word *anger*. The reasoning behind the test was that the higher the state of anger arousal of the person taking the test, the more anger-related responses would be cued by the hostile stimulus words. In addition, subjects rated the confederate's apparent mood on scales such as happy–unhappy and tense–relaxed. The results generally supported the Goffman hypothesis. That is, in the wheelchair condition there were more anger responses when the tester's behavior was friendly as opposed to obnoxious. But, as one would have expected, the nondisabled person occasioned more anger responses when she was obnoxious as compared to friendly. Also, the "nasty" confederate was seen as more unhappy and tense than the "nice" one regardless of whether she was disabled or nondisabled.

It should be noted that in the research just described, the confederate's self-presentation behavior had no particular positive or negative consequences for the subject. That is, the behavior had little hedonic relevance.

Consider now a situation in which the stimulus person's behavior has either rewarding or punitive consequences for the subject. Under these conditions one might expect the ambivalence-amplification process to come into play, so that the subject's unfriendly feeling for someone responsible for an unfavorable outcome would be especially strong if the other person were disabled. Gibbons, Stephan, Stephenson, and Petty (1980) tested this notion experimentally. Undergraduates were matched with a confederate who posed as a fellow subject. The confederate was either disabled (i.e., walked with the assistance of Canadian crutches and mentioned to the experimenter that she had a hip injury) or appeared to be nondisabled. The pair worked together at a cognitive task, ostensibly competing against another two-person team for an attractive reward. In one condition the good performance of the confederate was mainly responsible for a successful outcome, and in another condition this person performed poorly, thereby causing the team to fail. Subsequently, the subject was required to evaluate the personality of the partner. There was clear evidence of an amplification effect; when the team was successful the disabled teammate was evaluated more positively than the nondisabled one, but when the team experienced failure the former was evaluated more negatively than the latter. However, without a measure of subjects' attitudes about disabled people in general, one may not conclude that the amplification effect was necessarily caused by ambivalence.

DEVELOPMENT OF POSITIVE AND NEGATIVE ATTITUDE SCALES

In accordance with our view that most people have more or less conflicting sentiments and beliefs about those who have impairments, we are currently developing Likert scales to measure positive and negative attitudes toward disabled persons. We have already used this measurement approach in the domain of racial attitudes, constructing reliable pro-black and anti-black scales that are virtually independent of each other. However, measuring favorable and unfavorable attitudes toward disabled persons has proven to be a more complex undertaking. Respondents are apparently less willing to express critical, unfriendly sentiments about disabled persons than they are about black persons, even though previous research suggests that at a covert, unconscious level such feelings are commonplace. Furthermore, disability seems to be a much more hetero-geneous social category than blackness, embracing as it does a wide range of functional and cosmetic conditions of varying degrees of severity. Hence there is more diversity in attitudes about the disabled, a fact that makes it relatively difficult to identify clusters of general beliefs.

In developing items for the new scales, we have been guided by the work of Yuker, Block, and Young (1966/1970), as well as other investigations. With regard to positive attitudes, a number of researchers have found that individuals who are physically different are commonly believed to possess many desirable qualities and to be similar in important respects to other people. In several studies disabled persons were rated highly on such characteristics as self-reliance, kindness, persistence, and intelligence (e.g., Comer & Piliavin, 1975; Kleck, 1968; Mussen & Barker, 1944; Siller, Ferguson, Vann, & Holland, 1967). It has also been reported by Siller, Ferguson, Vann and Holland as well as Wright (1983) and others, that those who are physically different are often considered to be deserving of special aid and consideration. On the negative side, there is evidence that the majority associate conditions such as blindness, deafness, and paraly-sis with inferiority and psychological maladjustment (Goffman, 1963; Siller, 1967, Titley, 1969; Wright, 1983).

We are now testing preliminary versions of pro-disabled and anti-dis-abled attitude scales. There are 12 pro items, which deal with (1) civil rights issues (e.g., "Big companies should make special efforts to hire qualified disabled people" and "Disabled people are entitled to equal employment and educational opportunities"); (2) favorable personality attributions (e.g., "Disabled people make good friends because they are sympathetic and caring" and "Some disabled people want to be as self-sufficient and independent as possible"); and (3) the notion that physi-cally disabled persons may be similar to the majority (e.g., "Except for their particular physical problem, some disabled people are the same as anyone else" and "There is no reason why people confined to wheelchairs should not be encouraged to become doctors, lawyers, or teachers if they have the necessary intelligence").

Most of the 18 anti items refer to traditional negative stereotypes of disabled persons. They are described, for example, as overly sensitive, self-pitying, easily discouraged, and expecting special treatment from others. A few additional items refer to the discomfort experienced by nondisabled persons in the presence of people with bodily anomalies (e.g., "Even without meaning to, people with extreme deformities often make me uncomfortable" and "People with severe disabilities sometimes insist on entering situations where they make others feel uncomfortable").

When administered to a sample of 50 college students, the internal consistency of the 12-item pro scale, as estimated by Cronbach's coefficient alpha, was .74; and the alpha value for the 18-item anti scale was .85. The Pearson correlation between pro and anti scores was approximately zero. Thus the data from this small sample encourage us to believe that the scales will prove with further testing to have adequate reliability and to be tapping relatively independent attitudinal dimensions.

The near-zero correlation between pro and anti scores suggests that a motive to express socially desirable opinions was not an important determinant of subjects' responses to the items, inasmuch as adherence to the social norm of kindness toward disadvantaged people would have produced a combination of high pro and low anti scores. Further indication that the attitude scores did not reflect a need for social approval was provided when these scores were compared with the same subject's scores on the Marlowe–Crowne Social Desirability Scale. The correlations were close to zero.

We have also found, in a sample of 84 adults, moderate relationships (r's above .30) between (1) pro attitude scores and scores on a scale of humanitarian value orientation and (2) anti attitude scores and a measure of the individualistic, Protestant-ethic value outlook. These relationships, suggesting that attitudes toward disabled persons are rooted in two core values of American society, are being investigated further.

We also are planning to use the disability attitude scales to examine directly the notion that individual differences in ambivalence toward disabled people mediate the phenomenon of response extremity. To test this hypothesis we will adapt the experimental design employed by Gibbons, Stephan, Stephenson, and Petty (1980), in which subjects are required to evaluate the personality of a disabled or nondisabled teammate who has been responsible for the team's success or failure at an important task. The theoretical prediction is that subjects who, at a prior testing session, obtained relatively high scores on both the pro and anti scales (i.e., who are highly ambivalent) will evaluate the disabled confederate more positively in the success condition and more negatively in the failure condition than will other subjects.

CONCLUDING REMARKS

We have reviewed a theory and described a program of research on people's attitudes and behavioral reactions to individuals with physical disabilities. Thus far the overall pattern of results suggests that the reactions can be extremely favorable or unfavorable depending upon the situation. The findings are generally consistent with the following ideas: (1) the sentiments of many people about persons who are disabled tend to be ambivalent rather than unambiguously hostile or friendly; (2) the pro and anti attitudes tend to be rooted to some extent in two general value orientations, individualism of the Protestant ethic variety and humanitarianism; (3) stimulus events that make salient one's ambivalence about disabled people create a state of psychic tension; and (4) efforts at tension reduction may take a form of extreme behavior toward members of the group in question.

In addition to its theoretical implications, the ambivalence-amplification perspective also has practical ramifications. For example, by calling attention to the conflicting nature of the majority's feelings and beliefs about persons who have disabilities, this approach points up the potential that exists for either support or opposition by the public with respect to government policies for insuring equality of opportunity for disabled people in employment, education, and housing. Insofar as a proposed remedy is perceived as reasonable from the standpoint of costs and benefits both to disabled persons and to the community as a whole, the theory would predict a strongly favorable majority response. By the same token, if the proposal is felt to be unreasonable from the standpoint of net costs and benefits, strong opposition should be expected. The amplification principle implies that these positive and negative reactions would be more extreme than reactions to policies with similar cost-benefit characteristics, but which did not involve the interests of an ambivalently regarded group such as disabled persons.

CHAPTER 5

Intrapsychic Aspects of Attitudes Toward Persons with Disabilities

Jerome Siller

How are we to understand the following experiences that emerged during psychotherapy? A woman in her late twenties described a recurrent fantasy of having a deformed child. A 19-year-old male reported the following dream: "I was in a house all alone, but there was a hunchbacked monster haunting the house and there was much soap on the floor."

In the first situation, the woman was unmarried and fighting strong homosexual conflicts that up to that time had not been acted upon. The associative pattern to this fantasy suggested that she was talking about her own feeling of crippledness due to being a woman and thereby castrated. This was her interpretation, not something imposed upon her by my suggestions.

The second situation was interpreted by me to the dreamer in the form of a question. I asked him whether he had masturbated the evening before. With great surprise he indicated that he had. (At his age and given the state of his sexual affairs, this would not have been a bad guess most anytime, but the assumption was directly related to the manifest dream content.) My understanding of the dream was that there was a projection of ego-alien and detested self-feelings. The dream therefore referred to guilt and self-hate about repeated masturbation that evening, with the monster representing the dreamer himself. The interpretation of the meaning of the dream was confirmed by the dreamer.

Since fantasy and dream material may seem remote from reality and assuming that factor analysis, multidimensional scaling, and experimental designs are truer reflections of what really exists, I will end my clinical illustrations with an experience recounted to me during the course of psychoanalysis. This example is but one of a number of highly emotionally charged experiences with disabled persons that this person reported. The experience was recounted in a highly dramatic manner. At the time of the telling, the woman was 23 years old.

When I was about four or five, my sister took me and some friends to a swimming pool. I was having a very, very good time, fooling around, swimming, and sitting on my sister's shoulders, and all of a sudden, I saw this girl. I told you [at another session] that I remembered her as being a hunchback, but then my sister told me this summer that she really had no arms. But I didn't remember that, I really thought she was a hunchback. I can't even remember what she looked like or anything. But I can remember being on my sister's back and I can remember screaming. Really, I screamed, and I felt as if somebody had just hit me in the pit of my stomach. It was so terrible. It was such a, such a sick feeling. Like nothing could make me feel good. Nothing in the world could make me feel good. Nothing. Nothing could make me feel good after I had seen that girl. You know, I just wanted to get out of there. I couldn't bear anything. You know, everything had suddenly become very horrible. Everybody in the pool was horrible, the sky was horrible, the pool was horrible, everything was horrible. And I said, "We have to leave. We have to leave." And my sister said, "Why? What's the matter?" And I wouldn't tell her. I just said we have to leave. "Call daddy." She said, "We just came, and you'll spoil everybody's fun." I just had to leave. She said, "Well, OK," and called daddy. She said, "He's on his way but it will be a half hour so we might as well swim." And I said, "No, I want to get dressed and wait outside!" I didn't even want to be in the pool, around the place, you know, it was so terrible. And . . . and that's all I really remember, but recently my mother told me when I got home, I wouldn't say a word to anybody. I didn't tell my mother what it was. My sister hadn't told her anything about what I had seen, a girl with no arms. I just went right upstairs and went to bed. I just said "I feel very tired, I feel sick," and went up to bed. That's all I remember.

I introduce this account not to analyze it but as a reminder that there is nothing in the experimental research literature on disability that can even remotely account for this particular reaction. Concepts of stigmatization, marginality, value duality, and other socially dominated explanations can only partly account for it. It is my contention that what makes reaction to physical disablement different in important respects from that of other stigmatized conditions is that it is a *physical* condition. Thus, while sharing many characteristics with other outgroups, persons who are physically disabled possess a unique quality in that the body itself is involved.

In describing the ego, Freud (1923/1961) stated: "The ego is first and foremost a bodily ego; it is not merely a surface entity, but is itself the projection of a surface" (p. 26). In 1927 Joan Riviere, an authorized translator of *The Ego and the Id*, in which this statement appears, appended this with the following clarification: "I.e., the ego is ultimately derived from bodily sensations, chiefly from those springing from the surface of the body. It may thus be regarded as a mental projection of the surface of the body . . ."

The implication of these observations regarding the development of the ego from bodily sensations is profound. The stress upon the reaction to the physical aspect of disability implies that something basic reaching into the core of the self is involved. These processes cannot be fully grasped without considering intrapsychic phenomena. It means that the manner in which the developing person makes the shift can have great relevance for subsequent reactions to physical cues. For example, one might suspect that disturbed development at this point would generate different reactions of greater intensity, such as in the girl's reaction described above, than would a reaction based upon concern about social appearance and acceptability stemming from an already established ego and value system. Different strategies for attitude change would then follow.

It is with this underlying assumption of the distinctiveness of the physical quality in evoking reactions that I, with the aid of my students, have undertaken a research program oriented toward the intrapsychic dimension influencing attitudes of nondisabled persons toward those with physical disabilities. I fully subscribe to the idea that attitudes toward disabled persons, as indicated by Cowen, Underberg, and Verillo (1958), ". . . are undoubtedly multiply caused . . . [by] psychodynamic, situational, sociocultural, and historical determinants" (p. 303). My efforts might be seen as an attempt to introduce some balance through recognition of the neglected aspect of intrapsychic phenomena.

Research and theoretical literature relating intrapsychic phenomena such as self-representation, quality of object relationship, anaclitic and narcissistic object choices, ego defenses, and the like to attitudes toward the disabled are almost nonexistent. There are some references in a generalized way to the obvious possibility of castration anxieties negatively affecting attitudes toward those with disabilities (cf. Follansbee, 1981; Siller, 1984b); and while Barker, Wright, Meyerson, and Gonick (1953) reviewed psychodynamic theories as of that time, systematic research under controlled conditions was lacking. Around 1960, Katz included in his paper on "The Functional Approach to the Study of Attitudes" references to ego-defensive and value-expressive functions, both of which stem from psychodynamic considerations. In the same issue of the *Public*

Opinion Quarterly Sarnoff wrote of "Psychoanalytic Theory and Social Attitudes." His is a sophisticated discussion that describes attitudes in relation to ego defenses, conflict theory, motives, and unconscious processes. As is obvious from the time that it was written, it does not reflect more modern psychoanalytic developments involving the stress on preoedipal developmental factors. Also, neither Katz nor Sarnoff took on physical disablement as a specific focus.

With this background, I would like now to describe the line of research I have been following. But first it might be in order to define a few of the terms I will be using. A *representation* is a psychic impression or image of oneself or another (object). The congruence between the actual features of the self or object in reality and their representation is highly variable. *Object relationship*, a term I will be using a lot, is a self-representation interacting with an object representation under an affective tonus or valence (Kernberg, 1966). Object relationships involve the relation of the subject to an object, not the relation between the subject and the object, which is an interpersonal relationship.

My initial effort (Siller, 1959/1964) was a clinical theoretical one directed toward applying the level of object relations of the nondisabled person to attitudes toward disabled persons. Freud's 1914 paper "On Narcissism" served as my point of departure. Freud distinguished between narcissistic object choice (where similarity is the basis for identification) and anaclitic object choice (which is based on difference and need-gratification value).

Assuming various degrees of maturity of object relationships, it was theorized that acceptance of disabled persons lessens as narcissistic regression increases. I suggested a continuum of object cathexes ranging from purely narcissistic, through anaclitic, and on to mature object relations. For each developmental level or character typology a different quality of attitudes was described. For example, at the most developed level, those who attained mature object relationships, only transient aversion (if any) would occur. Personality insecurities are not activated and really strong identifications with disabled persons as disabled do not occur. This could be contrasted with others who have attained object relationships based primarily on physical appearance and have personalities that are basically anaclitically oriented (Siller, 1959/1964).

Following this line of reasoning, I undertook a major research effort to put these ideas to test. I posited that ego strength and stability of object relationships would be positively related to acceptance of persons with physical disabilities. Using extensive self-report personality measures administered to large groups of college, high school, and junior high students, and a variety of attitude measures, the basic hypotheses were supported. Thus variables such as anxiety and hostility were negatively correlated with acceptance of disabled persons, while ego strength and nurturance were correlated positively. Using projective techniques and a small set of subjects, only permeability of ego boundaries showed a relationship (an inverse one) to acceptance of disabled persons, while hostility, ego strength, impermeability of boundaries, castration anxiety, and dependency failed to correlate significantly. Dissatisfaction with the then-available measures of disability attitudes led me to develop the multidimensional Disability Factor Scales (Siller, Ferguson, Vann, & Holland, 1967).

Since that early work suggesting the relationship of attitudes toward disablement and those with disabilities to levels of narcissistic development, important new concepts pertaining to object relationships have been preoccupying the attention of psychoanalysts. Where for Freud (1914/1957) narcissistic maturity is contingent upon the allocation of libido between self and objects, Kernberg, an eminent contemporary theorist, advances the model that mature narcissism is determined not so much by the degree of self-love as by the quality of the internal self-representation that is loved. Optimal adult narcissism is esteem for a self-representation at the ego-identity level, that is, congruent with reality, capable of empathic, intimate, and reciprocal relationships, and able to maintain differentiation of self from object. Kernberg (1966) describes three phases of internalized object relationships: introjection (the most primitive), identification (a more developed level), and finally ego identity, which is similar to Erikson's concept.

Ann Follansbee (1981), working with me on her doctoral dissertation, attempted to bridge developments in conceptions of narcissism and object relations theory from my early paper and Kernberg's more recent ideas and to apply the enhanced understanding to attitudes toward disabled persons. She investigated the effects of attitudes toward disabled persons of baseline and aroused castration anxiety, as well as mediation of this anxiety by the individual's level of object representation. The research design combined a correlational and experimental study. One hundred males were randomly assigned to either an experimental or comparison group after collection of three dreams from each. A comparison of the experimental (high arousal of castration anxiety through viewing an anxiety-arousing film) and the comparison group (low arousal of castration anxiety) was made. Measures were obtained on the Schwartz TAT Castration Anxiety Index (Schwartz, 1955), Krohn's Object Representation Scale scored for reported dreams (Krohn & Mayman, 1974), and the Disability Factor Scales–General (Siller, 1970). Hypotheses that related castration anxiety and object representation to attitudes toward those with physical disabilities were supported, albeit with weak correlations. A third hypothesis, that the film arousing castration anxiety would negatively affect attitudes toward those with disabilities, did not receive support. This last finding is presently being followed-up in another doctoral research project. Robert Lipkins, using the subliminal psychodynamic activation technique of tachistoscopic presentation popularized by Silverman (1976) in an experimental study, is trying to check whether Follansbee's failure to induce anxiety had resulted from the too-conscious presentation of arousal material. This is a possibility suggested by other work on subliminal activation.

The typical study using castration anxiety as a focus does not come up with startling results. By now I and my students, not to mention those outside my own circle, have done about half a dozen studies using castration anxiety, usually as measured by the Schwartz TAT scoring method. Where we get significant results, as with Follansbee's, they are not strong. Yet there is a point to be made. Despite the obvious measurement weakness, significant findings usually occur. One might then ask: Why encumber oneself with calling it castration anxiety rather than a more neutral descriptor such as "fear of mutilation." A study by Jeffrey Fine and myself (Fine, 1979) suggests the value of having a theoretical rather than an atheoretical approach. Psychoanalytic theory suggests that the period from four to six years of age, the oedipal stage, is a highpoint of castration anxieties. Fine, in a rare study of preschool children's personality and attitudes toward those with disabilities, found that the preschool children with high amounts of castration anxiety (Blacky test) and negative self-concept perceived physical deviance at an earlier age than did other children. Castration anxiety, but not self-concept, was related significantly to negative attitudinal evaluation. The hypotheses of the Fine study were directly derived from the psychoanalytic theory of the oedipal stage of personality development. I do not know what basis there would have been for predicting the relationships found for children of this age using fear of mutilation as our explanatory concept.

In another one of our studies focusing upon intrapsychic factors, Gladstone (1977) built upon psychoanalytic conceptions of ego functioning for maintenance of psychological equilibrium. Psychoanalytic object-relations theory holds that firm ego boundaries reflect a successful separation of self from the object (other person or thing) world. The management of stress and anxiety are seen as a particular function of the ego defenses. Following object-relations theory, more rigidly defended persons have a higher level of general anxiety, tend to use more stereotyped, less adaptive defenses to deal with stress, and are more vulnerable to perceiving the world as threatening and potentially dangerous to their physical and psychological well-being. Using the Defense Mechanism Inventory (DMI), which identifies five patterns of defensive style, a physical pain-tolerance instrument, and the Disability Factor Scales–General, 163 men and women were divided into different defense-style groups on the basis of the DMI. Support was found for the hypothesis that there would be a relationship between defense style viewed as an ego function and aspects of body ego both expressed in a direct form in the experience of physical pain and reflected in an extended or indirect form in attitudes toward physical disability. Rigidly defended persons were more rejecting of those with physical disabilities.

In another study, Caroline Gould and I were interested in entering into the dimensional structure of attitude specified in my previous work in identifying and measuring salient dimensions of attitudes. One of these components of attitudes was labeled "distressed identification" and involves highly personalized reactions to physical disability, with the items exclusively of the self-reference type. For example, "When I see a blind person, I try to imagine what it is like to be blind", "I am sometimes afraid of losing an arm or a leg." We attempted to identify intrapsychic factors that lead a person to being vulnerable or not vulnerable to threat in the presence of physical disability, with distressed identification as an assumed expression of the mechanism of the threat's resolution. The emphasis is on the person's disability as a stimulus that activates anxiety about the respondent's own vulnerability. We tried to explain the attitudinal component of distressed identification by building a "deductive passageway" from the concept to hypotheses appropriate to its empirical evaluation.

The deductive passageway from the observation of the phenomenon labeled distressed identification and measured by our scale of that name back to possible origins was based on the following rationale. Since physically disabled persons are not really directly hurting those high in distressed identification, the disability must represent something threatening. Those with distressed identification are not consciously aware of what the disability symbolizes, so the threat must be on some subconscious level. To unconsciously reject someone because of a threat to oneself involves projection, a defense mechanism of the ego. When one is unable to separate self and one's personal identity from another, ego boundaries must be weak and permeable. These conditions can lead to an overidentification with those with physical disability through the mechanism of projective identification.

Therefore, persons with high distressed identification may be overidentifying with the person with a disability and projecting an unconscious fear onto this stigmatized outgroup. The most salient aspect of the disability is the "crippling" of the body and of the person's self-identity (assumed by the nondisabled). Isomorphically, the most direct counterpart to the physical "crippling" should be the threat to the dissolution of one's own ego identity.

Using the theoretical speculations of Edith Jacobsen, an important contributor to the psychoanalytic theory of the development of object relationships, it was hypothesized that those experiencing distressed identification conceive of their parents as highly dissimilar in terms of their personal qualities and attributes. By being pulled in opposite directions by conflicting parental demands and attitudes, these persons may be unable to synthesize a meaningful self-representation or a unified self-identity. As indicated before, considering the ego as a mental projection of the surface of the body, it was hypothesized that body–ego boundaries are perceived as weak, hazy, vulnerable and are thus more easily penetrated in those with distressed identification.

Another hypothesis advanced was that the greater the perception of parental dissimilarity, the greater the distressed identification. In a correlational study we examined 140 community-college students using the following: for parental similarity/dissimilarity, the Semantic Differential; as a measure of body–ego boundaries, the Fisher–Cleveland Barrier and Penetration scales of the Holtzman Inkblot Technique; and the Disability Factor Scales distressed identification measure. Distressed identification correlated significantly with a total score of the Semantic Differential $(-.17)$, the Evaluative Scale $(-.28)$, and the Potency Scale $(-.16)$ but not with the Activity Scale $(-.12)$. The hypothesis regarding body–ego boundaries was not supported. Interestingly, the parental similarity/dissimilarity and body–ego measures were significantly correlated, with the strongest relationship being between parental evaluation as similar and firm and body–ego boundaries.

A serendipitous finding was that experience with the mentally ill was significantly related $(r = .22, p < .01)$ to distressed identification, where the more unfavorable the experience, the higher the distressed identification. Fear of mental illness in oneself was significantly correlated with distressed identification $(r = -.30, p < .001)$, where the greater the fear, the higher the distressed identification. Since distressed identification is postulated as an overidentification with a stigmatized outgroup by those with a weak self-identity, it is possible that the same unconscious fear of dissolution of one's self-identity could be projected onto the mentally ill (Gould, 1984).

Other equally interesting studies cannot be described due to space limitations. For current reviews of the relation of personality to attitudes toward those with physical disabilities I recommend a paper by Cloerkes (1981) in the *International Review of Rehabilitation Research* and a recent chapter that I wrote in the book *Current Topics in Rehabilitation Psychology*, edited by Golden (1984).

I want to react now to an attitude expressed in various places that by invoking psychoanalytic categories one is adopting a reductionistic approach that reduces attitudes, behavior, prejudices, and the like to certain personality variables, such as authoritarianism or ethnocentrism, and then finally to abstract psychoanalytic terms such as *ego, ego strength*, or *castration anxiety*.

My position in regard to this issue was stated elsewhere (Siller, 1984b):

A reductionist notion of patterns of strata, which in effect makes motivation and personality structure into a "nothing more than" phenomenon, can be juxtaposed with the findings of Gladstone (1977) on the role of ego defense styles, and Follansbee (1981) on castration anxiety and object representation. To say that a flexible defense style or low castration anxiety or more mature object representation are associated with acceptance of the disabled does not reduce the attitude phenomenon to those personality characteristics. Rather, it suggests that such persons are better able to cope with potential stress emanating from the discrimination of a deviant physical state for the following reasons: (1) a more mature level of object relationships (ego identity level) having been attained, the differentiation process of self from body is more secure and their ability to perceive people as people rather than objects is greater than for those at a less developed level of object relationships; (2) the developmental stage where fantasies of threats to body intactness were active having been successfully passed through, this possibility no longer is a source of conflict; and (3) whatever tensions may exist can be tolerated with an ego structure that is characterized by a flexible defensive style. When too direct a relationship between attitudes toward the disabled and one of the more basic personality stratum exists, e.g., separation or castration anxiety, this emphasis reflects a pathological process where the variable is dissociated and acting in isolation or so pervasive as to affect wide aspects of functioning (p. 221).

The vitality of intrapsychic concepts for understanding what on the surface might appear to be socially dominated reactions to those with disability can be shown with the concept of alienation. Descriptors of alienation include such characteristics as isolation, sense of powerlessness, meaninglessness, self-estrangement, and so forth. These qualities come extraordinarily close to modern concepts of the narcissistic personality disorder. To say this does not reduce alienation to a strictly intrapsychic condition, but it certainly suggests why some persons more than others are vulnerable to social currents. For disability this can be an important connection, because alienation has been found to be one of the person-

From: J. Siller (1984). The role of personality in attitudes toward those with physical disabilities. In C. J. Golden (Ed.) *Current topics in rehabilitation psychology*. Orlando, FL, Grune & Stratton. Reprinted with permission.

ality variables most highly correlated with aversive attitudes toward those with physical disability.

Throughout this chapter I have attempted to interest researchers (and practitioners) in following a line of thought that seems to be essentially absent from the current literature. Neither the early somatopsychological orientation based upon phenomenological analysis, nor the current stress upon behavioral analysis, in my estimation, can do the job by themselves. Even when these are supplemented by the increasingly sophisticated psychometric approaches, we find that significant portions of the variance accounting for reactions to those with disabilities remain unaccounted for. The personological variables such as those I have mentioned cannot be expected to add substantially to multiple-prediction equations. However, if we were to rethink our operations along process lines, such that explicit paths following from multidimensional–multilevel reasoning were the subject of our analysis, much could be accomplished. The quotation from my 1984 paper given just above and the discussion of Gould's and my work with distressed identification is a beginning of such a line of reasoning, but it is restricted to the intrapsychic level. I hope some time in the future to coordinate this level with the other important levels (e.g., historical, cultural, social, situational). It would seem evident that even a preliminary formulation of the task must transcend methodological and theoretical parochialism. For our research to be meaningful, the social and behavioral contexts require coordination with experiential and intrapsychic realities. I raise again the challenge made at the very outset of this chapter, to wit, can our customary methods of research and explanation explain the phenomenon described? The answer of "no" still remains true. But it will be less true if intrapsychic elements become a serious part of the explanatory model.

CHAPTER 6

Mindfulness/Mindlessness: A New Perspective for the Study of Disability[1]

Ellen J. Langer and Benzion Chanowitz

The purpose of this chapter is to propose consideration of a new variable—mindfulness/mindlessness—in trying to understand the perception of and behavior toward disabled persons. Although we have just begun to explore how far this concept can take us in this area, at first glance the distance seems to be considerable.

To be perceived as a disabled person is to have been categorized. As such, most attempts at relieving the problems of disabled groups have been implicitly aimed at reducing the tendency people have to categorize other people. Purportedly people should be integrated into one group, and all belong to the category "human being." Yet categorizing is a fundamental and natural part of human activity, and a desirable one (Brown, 1958; Bruner, Goodnow, & Austin, 1956; Rosch, 1978). It is the way one comes to know the world. This suggests almost inevitable failure for any approach to eliminating group biases that focuses on assimilation of minorities into the larger group, into one category. Such approaches, even if they had the desired consequences of reducing prejudices, are not feasible; people will not surrender their categories. When they cease for whatever reason to make any particular categorical distinction among people, they will make

[1]The preparation of this chapter was greatly facilitated by a grant to the first author from the National Institute of Mental Health (1 RO1 MH32946-01 FYS).

another, and so they should. The mindlessness/mindfulness formulation suggests a very different approach to resolving the problems of disabled persons.

PREMATURE COGNITIVE COMMITMENTS

To be mindful is to actively, consciously construct categories, and mindfulness is essentially positive. It is the cognitive state characterized by active distinction-making, in contrast to mindlessness. Mindlessness is a state of reduced cognitive activity in which an individual processes cues from the environment in a relatively automatic manner without reference to the other aspects of those cues. When mindful, one actively constructs categories and draws distinctions. When mindless, one relies on already constructed categories.

Mindlessness is pervasive; yet research with elderly persons, for example, suggests that mindfulness may be crucial to one's physical health (Langer, 1980). The mindlessness/mindfulness formulation suggests that people should make more rather than fewer distinctions among people. To see people as possessing many attributes on which they may be categorized in different situations may eliminate many of the woes now produced by excessive mindlessness with respect to disabled persons. It would do so by preventing one characteristic from dominating the characterization of the individual. It would make the global specific (a disabled person versus a person who cannot do X) and what is now felt to be important (disability) unimportant. It is the purpose of this chapter to show why this would be the case.

Contact with a disabled person typically provokes mindfulness. Mindfulness is provoked by novel stimuli, and disabled people are just such stimuli. Even the rigid stereotypes of disabled persons that others mindlessly respond to were initially created mindfully. That is, the first determination one makes—that people vary according to the number of legs they have, for example—is mindful. The later categorical treatment of a person with no legs as a person who cannot do those activities globally associated with having legs is mindless. Thus, these variables exist in a complex relationship with disability. There are positive and negative consequences of mindfulness and mindlessness for disabled and able-bodied people alike. In this chapter we will explore several of these consequences.

To evaluate the validity of these consequences, it is necessary first to understand what mindfulness and mindlessness are. Thus we will illustrate the causes of mindlessness, then discuss its consequences. In so doing, we hope it will become apparent why increasing mindfulness for disabled and nondisabled people alike could ameliorate many of the difficulties people now experience individually and in interaction with one another. For the moment let us say that many of these difficulties may be a result of the pervasiveness of mindlessness.

For the typical individual, mindfulness is expected to occur only when there is some signal to the individual that the structure of the stimulus is novel. For example, (1) when significantly more effort is demanded by the situation than was originally demanded; (2) when the external factors in the situation disrupt initiation of the mindlessness sequence; (3) when external factors prevent the completion of the mindlessness sequence; (4) when negative or positive consequences are experienced that are sufficiently discrepant with the consequences of prior enactments of the same behavior (Langer, 1979a). Mindlessness may come about in one of two manners. Both will be described to highlight the different ways this variable may be relevant to the study of disability.

Mindless information processing may arise either after many repetitions or, in certain instances, after a single exposure. In the former case, as an individual's experience with a certain situation accumulates, a rigid structure of the situation is formed that represents its underlying "semantics." The appearance of similar cues on subsequent occasions will then trigger a mindless sequence of behavior. Once an activity becomes mindless, the underlying semantics may no longer be available for conscious cognitive manipulation or even examination.

In the latter case of a single exposure, reduced cognitive activity does not result from reliance on cognitive structures built up over time but from reliance on a cognitive structure that one has appropriated from another source. When this occurs the individual does not sufficiently scrutinize the information available at the time and, therefore, does not have that information available for later scrutiny. If on a subsequent occasion adaptive behavior requires examination of the information, the individual may be incapable of this.

The more familiar (but not necessarily more frequent) way of achieving mindlessness is through repeated exposure. With repetition a structure of the situation will emerge, so that when similar situations are encountered it signals to the individual that the situation is familiar and need not be mindfully considered. The original studies of mindlessness were demonstrations of this, designed to show that people in typical situations, in which one might think they were actively thinking, often were not mindfully considering relevant information presented to them. This was shown by presenting subjects with communications that were either oral or written, depending on the study, and observing their responses.

For half of the subjects the communication was presented in a very familiar way, and for half the structure of the communication was novel. We found equivalent responding to semantically sound and senseless information as long as it was presented in a familiar way. This, of course, suggests that subjects in these conditions were responding to the structure or form of the message that had been repeatedly experienced rather than actively considering the content of the communications (Langer, Blank, & Chanowitz, 1978). This suggests that negative outcomes can result when the current situation is only superficially similar to the past, where novel content packed in a familiar structure may be mindlessly received. These negative outcomes of mindlessness can be mild or severe, depending on the circumstances. As an example, consider an executive who daily has to decide whom to assign to what job. Assume she has in her employ many people, one of whom is hearing impaired. What she routinely may do is consider only her most "competent" (hearing) people from this group for important tasks. In essence, the structure she has built is: for an important job choose a competent person. If one of the important jobs that came along required intense concentration in a noisy and distracting environment, for example, we would predict that she would mindlessly send one of her competent hearing employees rather than the hearing-impaired individual, who would be the wiser choice if the decision was made mindfully.

While one may easily infer some of the negative consequences of mindlessness for disabled persons from this illustration, the Langer, Blank, and Chanowitz studies also imply negative consequences from another perspective. After repeatedly interacting with able-bodied individuals, one tends to mindlessly assume uniformities and commonalities that probably exceed those which exist. However, when confronted with a novel structure (physically disabled person) one may be primed to look for differences, for example, differences in competencies, interests, values, and so forth. As we will see later this leads to exaggerated perceptions of the difference between disabled and nondisabled individuals.

The effect of mindlessness achieved through repetition can be even more subtly destructive in terms of its impact on the disabled person's self-confidence. Greater experience with a task may lead one to lose touch with one's own competencies. Unless one is intentionally set on approaching the task anew on every trial, on each repetition the individual components of the task tend to coalesce, forming the emergent structure of the task. The result of the individual task components' coalescing or dropping out of consciousness, phenomenologically speaking, on the positive side is that the activity typically is performed faster. However, if there is reason for the individual to question how the task is performed, a confident answer must be lacking. That answer would be the individual task components. However, if the task is overlearned these components are no longer available. The point is that people performing overlearned tasks know *that* they can perform the task but they no longer know *how* they perform it. This leads to a surprisingly low ceiling to just how confident one may be. Tasks that could lead to confidence are now mindlessly performed and renewed mindful experience of them results in inferior performance: *either the task is imperfectly mindfully being performed or it is performed perfectly mindlessly* (Langer, 1979b).

This relationship between amount of experience and vulnerability to competence-questioning has been tested in research by Langer and Imber (1980). They varied task performance such that subjects had either no practice, a moderate amount of practice, or sufficient practice enough to perform the task in question mindlessly. Then they performed a different task, as bosses or assistants or without a label. When subjects were labeled "assistant," it was expected to lead them to question their competence. Not surprisingly, those assistants who had no practice now performed poorly on a new task. Interestingly, those who were overpracticed also performed poorly. However, the perjorative label had no effect for subjects with a moderate amount of practice. They were the only group for whom the components of the task were still salient, the mindful group.

Thus mindlessness seems to lead to vulnerability to circumstances that may lead one to question one's competence. This occurs because evidence of competence, the individual task components, become inaccessible to consciousness as mindlessness is achieved. To provide further support for this contention, we ran a second study where all of our subjects would be performing an overlearned task. For half of them we made the task components salient, while the remaining half performed the task without this manipulation. Those for whom the components were salient, and who thus had evidence of their competence, did not show a debilitation.

THE PROVOKING OF MINDFULNESS

How are these findings particularly relevant to disabled persons? At least some of them are individuals who must visibly wear their mark and thus are constantly labeled by others. The old and the physically disabled, for instance, clearly fall into this group. It is perhaps easy to see how they would be similar to the "assistants" in the research just described. As such, they probably frequently question their behavior, and when it is over-learned they may erroneously conclude incompetence. But even when the disability is hidden, similar consequences can be expected when the individual labels him- or herself in such a way that self-questioning is provoked. The physical and interpersonal environments constructed for the nondisabled majority (in which the disabled person typically must live) provide enough obstacles to ensure frequent, if not almost continuous, self-questioning. Skills cannot be taken for granted. Other people's reactions must be contended with constantly. Thus, things may not proceed smoothly and effortlessly. Hence, she/he is more mindful. This in general will be good, but in specific instances it may be quite negative. Tasks that could have been performed mindlessly will now be performed more poorly, in the manner just illustrated.

It is hard to imagine that people who are aware of being disabled do not engage in extensive self-questioning of their physical and intellectual prowess. One could easily imagine that this would be especially true in the presence of other people. While this questioning may be self-instigated for purposes of social comparison, it is probably more often reactive. It may be a reaction others have to the mark. In a study by Langer and Abelson (1974) it was shown that even clinicians may fall victim to the effects of labels. Here different labels for the same objective stimulus resulted in differential responding. A patient label provoked judgments of illness, while a neutral label did not. If this effect was found for clinicians, differential responding in the presence of a disabled person by many other people would surely follow.

Whether the stimulus is internal or external, the "typical" disabled adult is likely to experience more mindful self-questioning than the "typical" nondisabled adult and therefore is likely to experience more of this kind of poor performance. It is important to note that we are not simply saying that self-consciousness leads to poor performance. Rather we are specifying the precise circumstances under which it will and will not impede performance. Concretely, what does this analysis mean for the behavior of the disabled person? Typically an overlearned task is performed mindlessly and the individual can go on to other activities. The disruption for the mindful disabled person might impede building upon the task, integrating it into other behavior, and so forth, although it may not impede initial acquisition. Of course there are times when one should mindfully examine an overlearned task and tolerate periods of "disrupted performance" in order to progress. The problem arises when one takes the period of disruption as a sign of incompetence.

Since the mindless/mindful distinction is not typically apparent to individuals, it cannot readily serve as an attribution for behavior. Since it is an unknown cause for poor performance, misattribution for failure is likely to occur (Ross, Rodin, & Zimbardo, 1969; Weiner & Sierard, 1975). The disabled person who performs poorly on a previously overlearned task will probably often blame the disability. This, of course, will lead to even more self-doubt and possibly to giving up. When the nondisabled person questions how to walk, walking is disrupted. The result seems strange. When the person who is crippled questions it, the result may not seem extraordinary, but rather a part of the illness. The disabled person unfortunately may be led unnecessarily to resigning him- or herself to the "disability." In an investigation similar to the Langer and Imber (1979) study, we induced self-questioning by having subjects helped by a confederate. The subjects' (elderly nursing home residents) self-questioning on an overlearned task rendered them incompetent. Their implicit attribution for the poor performance was not that they were given unneeded help, a situation easy to remedy, but rather that they were old (Avorn & Langer, 1980).

This formulation suggests why a person who becomes disabled when she/he is an adult may in some ways have more of a handicap than a person who is born with it. Excessive difficulty in adjusting to the disability may result from a rapid change in status from normal to deviant. The change in competence one experiences may be a function of mindful consideration of mindless performance rather than solely a direct function of the disability.

The prolonged effect for the disabled person of this poor performance should be chronically lower self-esteem than for people who experience themselves as nondisabled. Low self-esteem is not a necessary consequence of being disabled, but it is a likely consequence in achievement-oriented societies. In an achievement-oriented culture, outcome rather than process is the primary value (McClelland, 1961). And an outcome-orientation promotes mindlessness (Chanowitz & Langer, 1980). This is because why and how we do what we do are not considered while we do it. Tasks are repeatedly experienced in the same way to speed up production, at the expense of mindful processing. In this society high self-esteem typically comes from an individual's recognition that she/he has mastered (overlearned) the targeted task and now can easily come up with a product, preferably more products than the next person. And, again, this is done without questioning how the task is accomplished while it is being accomplished; which, we have seen, renders the individual vulnerable to such questioning at a later time.

In a process-oriented society, evaluation would be a somewhat irrelevant dimension. Overlearning of tasks in the service of increased productivity would be less likely. In fact, in that kind of society, where the members would be almost constantly mindful, the notion of disability as a way of defining a person would make no sense. But this conclusion is still premature for this point in the chapter.

Chronically lower self-esteem for the disabled person than for the non-disabled person is certainly not a novel prediction. It may easily be predicted without reference to the mindful/mindless distinction. However, a less obvious prediction is that disabled people are likely to be protected from the lowest levels of self-esteem for several reasons. First, although their greater mindfulness may prove disruptive on overlearned tasks, it is because of their greater mindfulness that disabled people are less likely to overlearn any given task, that is, to take their skills for granted. Yet it is likely that the nadir of self-esteem is reached when basic skills one mindlessly accepts are called into serious question. It is on such occasions that the rug, so to speak, is pulled out from under one, and one may be led to question one's more general competence: "What else can't I do that I thought I could?" The disabled person is less apt to be caught unaware in this fashion.

Moreover, in the case of an unsuccessful outcome, the disabled person has available a self-protective attribution. The disability itself provides a ready explanation for virtually any failure, an explanation that may save the deviant from questioning his/her basic worth. That is, the disabled person can believe that were it not for the disability, this skill would be performed readily. Nondisabled people do not have this ego-saving device so easily at their disposal. The efficacy of such an explanation is testified to by the fact that nondisabled individuals may frequently employ "self-handicapping" strategies, that is, anticipatory self-protective explanations for possible failures (Jones & Berglas, 1978; Jones & Pittman, 1980). However, these fabricated explanations are more apt to have the flavor of a rationalization than the more compelling ("real") handicap of the disabled person.

A positive way of looking at all the self-questioning the disabled person does is to consider him or her as more mindful. Such mindfulness permits continued meaningful interaction with the environment. We assessed this with respect to dyslexia. Essentially, we felt that the disability might prevent people from being comfortable enough to take the world for granted and treat it mindlessly. If one does not know if a "d" will look like a "d" or a "b" the next time one looks at it, one would remain mindful. This is just what we found. Dyslexics in our study used target objects in a novel way. They were more mindful and creative than their "nondisabled" counterparts.

Yet this greater mindfulness creates one more way in which disabled people differ from the majority. Greater mindfulness may lead to perceptions of the world that differ from those of the majority and that the majority may view as bizarre. Yet these perceptions often may be more informed, that is, may result from noticing more distinctions in the world. The issue therefore becomes not simply how we might teach nondisabled persons to be less judgmental, but also how we might get them to value these more creative perceptions and, indeed, to generate them on their own. In view of the negative judgments disabled individuals may receive for the products of their mindfulness, it is not surprising that many disabled people join similar others to affirm their perceptions of the world. (Interestingly, this analysis suggests that these consciousness-raising attempts may be successful in part because they promote mindlessness. By teaching the person that it is okay to be old, black, gay, disabled, and so forth, one relieves the person from questioning his or her competence as a function of membership in that group.) It would seem, then, that although there are the expected, negative consequences of disability, there are also some unexpected positive consequences, ones that might well be instructive for the larger society.

We said earlier that mindlessness may be achieved in either of two ways. Both of these have implications for our understanding of disability. Thus far we have been discussing the effects of mindlessness that come about through repeated experience. Let us now turn to the case of a single exposure. Rather than a rigid structure emerging over time through repetition, the structure may be established on initial exposure to information in the environment. When this happens, people are said to make a premature cognitive commitment to the information. Suppose one were told that people with six fingers on one hand were stupid, insomniacs, and walked funny. Since for most people this information is irrelevant, it will mindlessly be accepted unquestioningly. Why bother carefully considering it if it is irrelevant? A structure representing a rigid relationship between the information and the behavioral response that it calls for may be established. It is the same structure that could have emerged over time with repetition. If a person grows a sixth finger, she/he will now be stupid, an insomniac, and walk funny. Once a rigid structure or premature cognitive commitment exists, the individual responds in a mindless way without recognizing how the information could be viewed otherwise.

Chanowitz and Langer (1981) set up an experiment to mirror the situation in which an individual is given information about the symptoms of a disease at a time when such information is irrelevant, so that it would be processed mindlessly. Irrelevance encourages the uncritical acceptance of the stated relationship between the symptoms and the disease. Other groups initially were led to mindfully process the information. The information later became relevant when subjects in each group discovered they had the disease. The mindful groups performed well on follow-up tests that required abilities related to symptoms of the disorder. However, the mindless group did not; these subjects showed a severe decrement and performed only half as well as the other groups did. They all took in the same information about the disease but they processed it differently, with different consequences.

Many people first hear information about disabled people when it is irrelevant to them. Negative stereotyped information regarding abilities and motivations may be uncritically accepted at that time. What happens if, through an accident, the individual now becomes a member of that class? If she/he had mindlessly accepted a relationship between a physical disability and a mental disability, for example, that person might now display whatever symptoms and deficiencies she/he mindlessly accepted. It would not occur to the person to do otherwise. If the disability became relevant not through personal injury but rather through the injury of a close relative, one's child, for example, the individual might mindlessly respond to the child as if she/he were mentally deficient. One can only surmise what difficulties and unnecessary incompetencies such relating could foster. If, to take another example, one mindlessly accepted information about the "symptoms" of old age, poor memory, for example, it would not occur to the person—to the detriment of elderly persons—to make challenging requests of the elderly adults the person may later come to know.

Thus far we have been considering the relevance of the mindfulness/ mindlessness distinction for disabled persons. This variable also has relevance for able-bodied persons in interaction with disabled persons. We have already suggested one way in which this distinction may be important, and that is with respect to the premature cognitive commitments one has made. These premature cognitive commitments may guide one's response to disabled persons. This may be of consequence to the nondisabled person when she/he needs assistance, relationship, or social comparison (with respect to nondisabled aspects of the disabled person) and it does not occur to the able-bodied individual to consider the disabled person as a viable candidate to fill the need.

MINDFULNESS AND INACCURATE EVALUATIONS

There is another way in which this distinction is relevant for nondisabled people. If one rarely has commerce with disabled individuals, then interaction with them should provoke mindfulness. The presence of the disabled person may result in the able-bodied person's noticing things she/he typically takes for granted. This will be experienced as positive or negative, depending on the content of the mindful consideration. For example, consider research, conducted in part to test the pervasiveness of mindlessness, in which individuals were provoked into mindfulness by a disabled person.

If people are mindless much of the time in their day-to-day interactions, they may have a very abstracted notion of normal. That is, so much repeated experience with normals may result in mindlessness with respect to individual idiosyncracies. We reasoned that disability is novel and novelty breeds mindfulness. Thus, when people interact with disabled people they may conclude that the disabled person is different from normal. But this should occur not because she/he is different or because of biased perceiving. It should occur only because of a faulty comparison. That is, tics, gestures, and other physical characteristics are typically not noticed in a mindless interaction with a normal person. However, thor-

oughly typical characteristics should be noticed in a mindful interaction—
for example, when interacting with someone who is disabled. Thus these
accurate perceptions should be evaluated as atypical, since they typically
go unnoticed.

In this experiment, Langer and Imber (1980) had all subjects view the
same videotape to evaluate it as a medium to be used in a dating service.
They expected to see a target person who was either a millionnaire, a
homosexual, a former mental patient, a cancer patient, a divorced person,
or an unlabeled person. Thus positive and negative deviances were compared to a normal condition. To support further the assumption that it is
the mindless/mindful asymmetry that causes the difference, rather than
any deviance *per se*, the normal group was divided in half. The mindless
group was asked to watch the TV, the mindful group was asked to think
about the target person's (the person on the videotape) physical characteristics. The prediction was that there would be no difference among the
mindful groups—positive deviance, negative deviance, or normal mindful—but that they would be more accurate in their perceptions of the
person on the videotape and would evaluate all that they noticed as
extreme in comparison to the normal mindless condition. That was what
happened. On virtually each measure, the mindful groups noticed a
greater number of typical characteristics than the mindless group, and in
each case they evaluated them as extreme. This occurred even when the
mindful subjects were viewing a target person they had initially presumed
to be normal.

While this work shows that initial mindfulness leads to perception of
disability, other work on the novel-stimulus hypothesis (Langer, Taylor,
Fiske, & Chanowitz, 1976) suggests that when subjects have to mindfully
consider ways of interacting with disabled persons and are allowed sufficient time to accustom themselves to the disability, interactions proceed
normally.

Thus the belief that disability is globally different is perpetuated by
inappropriately evaluating the typical as atypical. The similarity in subjects' responses to positive and negative deviances, and the similarity of all
of those groups to the normal mindful condition, suggests that the role of
mindlessness in the perception of disability may be considerable. Erroneous mindful evaluations can confirm hypotheses that may be used as
rationales for prejudicial treatment. Evidence from the normal-mindful
condition suggests how individuals mistakenly labeled may be seen as
deserving of the label.

These results also may explain all or part of the guilt by association
people fear when befriending someone who is different. That is, if the
disabled person provokes mindfulness in the observer, then mindful examination of the person with whom she/he may be seen is likely. Again, since

mindlessness is the rule, this person who is now mindfully considered will appear atypical. Thus there may be more than a little truth to support the fear.

IMPLICATIONS

To summarize, we have just discussed three ways in which the mindlessness/mindfulness distinction is relevant for able-bodied persons in interaction with disabled persons. First, the able-bodied person's premature cognitive commitments may lead him/her to inappropriately overlook the disabled person and thereby ignore whatever competence that person may have brought to the situation. Second, disabled persons typically provoke mindfulness in the nondisabled. And third, this mindfulness, because of its atypicality, may result in the nondisabled person's making inaccurate evaluations of disabled and nondisabled persons alike.

While most disabled groups may be mindful, this is not true of all. The physical environment created for some disabled groups in society, elderly persons, for example, may make their world so small that they may experience the most mindlessness. Groups like the elderly might also choose to withdraw into a familiar world to avoid fighting what may seem an impossible environment to negotiate. Research we have conducted with elderly persons (Langer, 1980) points to the conclusion that excessive mindlessness may result in physical disability and premature death. It is likely that some of the problems encountered by elderly persons stem from the fact that they did not always belong to this disabled group.

The mindlessness/mindfulness formulation results in predictions that there are important differences between congenital disability and acquired disability. Specifically, congenitally disabled persons will be more mindful with respect to their disability and with respect to their environments. First, because beliefs related to their disability were always relevant to them, they would be less likely to make premature cognitive commitments to beliefs that might later prove debilitating (e.g., negative beliefs about competencies). Second, because the disability requires the individual to negotiate the environment differently, they are less likely to view and interact with it in the standard fashion and are more likely to consider alternative functions for objects, alternative strategies for accomplishing things, and so forth.

Nondisabled persons who become disabled may see their new, more limited environment as impoverished, for they have formulated rigid categories that now restrict their perceptions. Take, for example, the farmer who makes numerous distinctions about wheat (Whorf, 1956). A city dweller who finds her- or himself on the farm will not see the same things in the wheat and even with prolonged residence on the farm may never think to look for them. If both had only this wheat as food for thought, the city dweller would starve and the farmer would not. One tends to make finer discriminations the more relevant the issue, but whether the category is broad or narrow, once the distinctions are made, the elements are rarely recategorized.

What are the implications of the results of the studies on mindlessness for social change with respect to disability? Clearly one would not want to find ways of increasing the mindlessness of deviant persons so that it is equal to that of normal persons, since the negative consequences of mindlessness may be profound. Further, as is probably clear by now, programs designed to teach people, particularly children, not to categorize people in the first place are probably doomed to failure, and well they should be. Mindfulness relies on distinction-making and categorizing, and being mindful may have important psychological and biological significance. Thus categorizing may be inevitable. Since people probably cannot be taught not to categorize people—the most salient aspects of their environment—teaching them how to use these categories mindfully rather than mindlessly may be the most effective means for reducing or preventing prejudice.

It makes no sense to speak of physically disabled people as a category. To add the particular activity in which one might be less competent to the description of the person would reduce the globalness of the handicap. With this approach we would soon see that we are all disabled. At present, disability is a category that typically relies for its definition on another category with which it is mutually exclusive. To have no arms or one leg, to be "too fat" or "too thin," suggests more than just another categorical distinction. To be disabled is to *not belong* in the statistically larger group. As such, evaluative judgments are essentially built into the system, and so are all the difficulties endemic to that state of affairs. One can drink one's coffee "black" or "without milk." The former reflects a category unto itself, the latter does not. Instead it says that milk's presence in the coffee is the natural state and the other, the aberration. While the state that is presumed to be natural may change, the implicit negative evaluation for the disabled person is inevitable.

This mindful approach would teach that we are all deviant with respect to some of our attributes and not to others (number of freckles, size of fingers, lengths of nails, size of nose, the way we eat, dress, walk, talk, etc.), where each attribute or behavior lies on a continuum. Once we categorize people, we arbitrarily treat this continuity as discontinuous. Those in one group are seen as normal and those in the other are seen as abnormal. The other differences ("abnormalities") within the larger group receive little attention. The individual in the deviant group becomes stigmatized.

We conducted one last study to see if one could, indeed, reduce prejudice by increasing mindfulness. We assessed the effectiveness of training children in mindfulness on responses to a "handicapped" target (Langer, Bashner, & Chanowitz, 1985). Children given this training evidenced less prejudice and were better at finding multiple explanations for the behavior of others as well as themselves. Subjects in the high-mindfulness group were asked to give several answers or solutions to each question asked, while, for the low-mindfulness group, the more typical single answer was requested for each question asked. For example, a slide was shown of a man, supposed to be a newscaster, who either was or was not in a wheelchair. The high-mindfulness group was asked for four reasons why he might be good at what he does and four reasons why he might be bad. The low-mindfulness group was asked to list only one good and one bad reason. Several questions on different topics were included. For half of the subjects the questions referred to the person depicted as disabled and for half they did not. Teaching children to be more mindful, especially when bolstered by explicit references to disabled persons, resulted in the view that *disabilities are function-specific and not people-specific.* Children in this group were less likely to discriminate inappropriately for or against the disabled person. That is, we decreased prejudice by increasing discrimination. Moreover, subjects in this group were less likely to avoid a disabled other (Langer, Bashner, & Chanowitz, 1985).

CONCLUSION

We have been arguing for measures that increase mindfulness as a new means for dealing with the difficulties that have been considered as endemic to disability. Interestingly, we teach a course in everything but how to actively think, how to be mindful. For any question, students are handed *the* answer. For any phenomenon, they are given *the* explanation. Just making people aware of how often they may be mindless, and what the consequences of that may be, could go a long way toward ameliorating the situation. While the specifics as to the best means to these ends are as yet unclear, what should *not* be done is clear. Programs intent on leading people not to categorize the most salient and important aspect of their environment—people—would, even if successful, cause more problems than they would resolve. What is called for instead is *more* categorization, but categorization of a creative and constructive—a mindful—nature.

CHAPTER 7

Media and Disability: A Discussion of Research

E. Keith Byrd and Timothy R. Elliott

The effects of media presentations depend on such variables as the characteristics of the audience, the message content of the presentation, and when and how the effects are measured. This chapter focuses on content. It discusses research performed by the authors that describes disability portrayal in television, film, popular literature, and literary classics.

TELEVISION

Three studies have been conducted that describe the frequency of disability portrayal in television. The initial study (Byrd, Byrd, & Allen, 1977) described prime time television in 1976. Two judges read program descriptions in *TV Guide*, each being responsible for one half of the programming year. Both judges held graduate degrees in rehabilitation counseling. Chi-squares were calculated. Significant results at $p < .01$ are reported for network, program type, and disability. The largest frequency of disability-related programs appeared on the Public Broadcasting Service and were news documentaries. Mental illness was portrayed most frequently by the private networks, and the largest portion of programming portraying disability was of a dramatized or comedic nature.

A second study (Byrd, McDaniel, & Rhoden, 1980) compared 1967–68 and 1977–78. The largest number of programs were on NBC in 1968. However, in 1978 the greatest number occurred on the Public Broadcasting Service. A partial explanation may be increased numbers of programs on PBS overall and their traditional concern with public interest and service programming. The commercial networks historically have been in the business of entertaining; they portray disability in that format as well.

Movies headed the list of programs dealing with disability in 1968; however, in 1978, dramatic series and children's programming headed the list, followed by news documentaries and telethons. Paraplegia occurred most frequently in 1968, followed by mental illness, drug addiction, and emotional disability. In 1978 mental illness was at the top of the list, followed by alcoholism, emotional disability, and physical handicaps. Paraplegia in 1968 occurred most frequently in the program "Ironside," which featured a paraplegic detective. Mental illness and emotional disturbance seemed to be consistent targets over the decade for popular programming in prime time.

Elliott, Byrd, and Byrd (1983) investigated the presentation of disability on prime-time television in 1980 by incorporating direct observation and ratings by trained judges. Four judges were trained to review portrayals of disability. They were instructed to make judgments regarding the presence of disability without a list of disabilities for reference. A list was not provided so that the judges had the freedom to note all instances of conditions that might be interpreted as disability. A disabled person was defined as any character with a major difference (other than racial and socioeconomic differences) from the average character portrayed on television.

Data collection and analysis were designed to answer two research questions. What are the relative frequencies of disability portrayal on programs, commercials, and public service announcements? And what is the judged depiction and judged effect of disability portrayal? Forms were constructed for programs, commercials, and public service announcements. Each time a disability was portrayed the judge completed the appropriate form. Each judge was assigned one of the three major networks or the Public Broadcasting Service. Judges viewed the assigned network from 7:00 P.M. to 10:00 P.M. the week of October 25 through 31, 1980. The broadcasting of the presidential election debates took place during this week, with simultaneous coverage by the three major networks. Chi-squares were calculated. That week, a total of 74 commercials portrayed disability, 54 programs depicted a disability, and 15 public service announcements concerned a disability.

Variables in which there was no statistical difference for commercials were network and time slot. Variables where there was no statistical significance for programs included network, program time, program length, and title of program. Insufficient data prevented the calculation of chi-squares for variables observed in public service announcements. Independent *t*-tests were calculated between the ratings of judged depiction of disability on commercials and programs. Dependent *t*-tests were calculated between the rating of judged effect and depiction for commercials and programs. Critical values of t for the independent tests were non-significant. Critical values of t for the dependent tests were significant at $p < .02$.

Based on the results of the chi-square analyses, a significantly greater number of commercials depicting disability aired on Sunday and Monday (43%) night utilizing a dramatic format. Old age (50%) was the primary disability portrayed in commercials.

The judged effect and accuracy of portrayals in the commercials were considered neutral by the raters. Movies (22%) and situation comedies (22%) had larger frequencies of disability than other types of programs. The accuracy of these depictions was rated by the judges as very realistic or neutral in a significant number of programs. Old age (19%) was again the primary disability portrayed in programs; another major category was mental illness (13%). The ratings of judged effect and depiction in commercials and programs were significantly different, suggesting an accurate portrayal of the disability despite a neutral context.

Of interest in these results is the presentation of individuals who are elderly in commercials. Apparently aging conveys credibility to an advertiser and connotes experience and wisdom that could enhance the attractiveness of a product to an audience. Several commercials concerned with the impending presidential and senatorial elections used a presentation of aging to express a plea for a return to more fundamental political ideals and traditional values. Depictions of elderly persons were used to sell political ideology as well as household products on the basis of a supposed credibility that accompanies aging.

Aging and mental illness appeared in prime time programs. Movies and situation comedies were program types depicting disabilities. Presumably aging and mental illness portrayals were incorporated into the story lines and plots of these movies and comedies to entertain or add suspense. Although the negative effects of associating suspense with disability have been noted in the literature (Elliott & Byrd, 1982), there appears to be no conclusive evidence regarding the association of disability with humor on television (Bernotavicz, 1979).

The contrasting results between the ratings of judged effect and actor's depiction indicate that depictions of disability have attempted to be more realistic. Actors have trained for particular roles portraying disability in an attempt to accurately encompass all facets of the character into the role (Jankey, 1978). The neutrality of the judged effect may be attributed to the context of the medium itself, which has been considered by some researchers to be too general and passive to disseminate specific and accurate information about disability to an audience (Bernotavicz, 1979). It is encouraging, however, to note that there may be a trend toward providing realistic depictions of disabled characters in prime time programs and commercials.

DISABILITY PORTRAYAL ON TELEVISION

Byrd (1979c) rated programs depicting disability during prime time (7:00 P.M. to 10:00 P.M.) in July 1977. They were selected from program descriptions in *TV Guide* and Home Box Office program listings. The seven raters were assigned two to four programs each to rate on seven variables: mobility, communication, self-care, self-direction, work tolerance, work skills, and social attitudes. Six of these variables appeared in federal regulations (*Federal Register*, 1974) for use in selecting severely disabled clients for vocational rehabilitation services. Social attitudes were added as a seventh variable because it was felt to be important in adjustment to disability. Ratings were made on a Likert-type scale, with a value of one assigned to "disability presented unrealistically" and a value of five assigned to "disability presented very realistically." A value of three was assigned the "uncertain" response. A record of disability, program type, and network was kept. Total score and means were calculated for the three variables.

Twenty-four portrayals of disability appeared during prime time in July 1977. Spinal-cord injury was the most realistically portrayed disability. Alcoholism and multiple disability were depicted unrealistically according to the raters. All other disabilities were positively rated. All program types were given a positive rating and all networks received a rating of average or better. Drama specials and news documentaries were rated most positively, along with the Public Broadcasting Service and Home Box Office.

None of the variables yielded statistically significant results. It appears that all disabilities were treated essentially the same in terms of the extent of their realistic portrayal. Program type did not discriminate between realistic and unrealistic portrayal. Networks did not treat the portrayal of disability much differently from one another.

A grand mean of 25.8 placed the portrayal of disability approaching a somewhat realistic level. Favorable implications from the results should be guarded, since ratings were barely positive. The analysis suggests that no real leaders exist in the portrayal of disability. Networks and program producers should pay attention to how they portray disability. Misinformation *can* be avoided. Television producers can pay attention to these depictions and work toward the most realistic portrayal possible for each disability.

Elliott and Byrd (1983) conducted an attitude-change study. Subjects for this study came from an eighth-grade class, selected because of the high level of television viewing expected. "The Dukes of Hazzard" and "Dallas" were the most popular programs reported by subjects. Subjects were randomly assigned to one control and two treatment groups. Experimental Group 1 viewed an episode from "Mork and Mindy" selected by the researchers as nonstereotypic. The actor in reality was blind, and the character he portrayed was independent in mobility and personal adjustment, was employed, and appeared to be assertive in his behavior. This character was nonstereotypic as described by Leonard (1978). Experimental Group 2 viewed a professional film developed by the American Foundation for the Blind titled *What Do You Do When You Meet a Blind Person?* The control group viewed another episode of the "Mork and Mindy" series with no depiction of disability. Subjects in each of the groups were administered Form A of the Attitudes Toward Disabled Persons Scale (ATDP) (Yuker, Block, & Younng, 1966/1970), then given the treatment followed by Form B.

Experimental Group 1 and the control group experienced no significant differences between pretest and posttest. Experimental Group 2 exhibited an increase in the means between pretest and posttest at $p < .05$. An analysis of variance on the pretests yielded no significant differences between any two groups. A significant difference occurred between Experimental Group 2 and the other two groups in the analysis of variance on the posttests. A Scheffe procedure identified Experimental Group 2 as significantly different from the other two groups at $p < .05$. Attitudes toward disabled persons were not altered significantly by viewing a depiction of disability in the television program studied here. However, the experiment did yield evidence that attitudes were altered by viewing a professionally produced film designed to educate relative to disability.

The professionally produced film appeared to facilitate short-term positive attitude change as measured by the ATDP. This may be attributed to the novel presentation of disability in a film versus a more commonplace presentation on television. The subjects may have been more receptive to the direct information provided in the film. It should be reiterated that the particular program presented in the treatment of Experimental Group 1 had a nonstereotypic depiction of disability. Whereas past research has indicated that stereotypic portrayals foster negative attitudes based on misinformation, this study was designed to detect if nonstereotypic portrayals could facilitate positive attitudes.

Donaldson (1980) stated that negative attitudes can occur after video presentations in which the audience does not have equal status with the portrayal and characters involved and experiences some degree of discomfort while viewing the presentation. A teacher functioning as a monitor in

Experimental Group 1 behaved autocratically and may have contributed to subject anxiety. Another aspect concerning the results of Experimental Group 1 relates to the position of Bernotavicz (1979), who regarded mass media as having too broad and general an approach to provide the accurate information necessary for a specific audience to experience a change in existing attitudes. Whereas the professional film *What Do You Do When You Meet a Blind Person?* provided concise and specific information regarding disability, the television program portrayed reactions and adjustments of main characters to the disability of an individual. Also, the program employed comedy while depicting the reactions and adjustments of the characters. In addition, subjects' expectations may have been influenced once the television series was recognized, thereby inhibiting the reception of information that may have been available in the program. If the television program had altered attitudes positively, there would be a rationale for recommending production of additional programs using a similar approach. On the other hand, if the television program had altered attitudes negatively, there would be a rationale for recommending the elimination of such programming.

Elliot and Byrd (1984a) utilized male college students in assessing attitude change. The study sample consisted of male college students living in a residence hall at a large southern university in the United States. Students were randomly divided into three groups to allow for two experimental groups and one control group. The Attitudes Toward Disabled Persons Scale, Forms A and B (Yuker, Block, & Younng, 1966/1970), was used. Fourteen persons participated in the control group, and the two experimental groups each had sixteen participants. After the subjects filled out Form A of the ATDP, each group viewed an audiovisual presentation. Experimental Group 1 viewed the same episode previously mentioned of the ABC television series "Mork and Mindy" featuring a depiction of blindness considered nonstereotypic by the researcher. Experimental Group 2 viewed the film *What Do You Do When You Meet a Blind Person?* The control group viewed an educational film on time management. The subjects were then administered Form B of the ATDP.

Analysis of covariance (Pedhazur, 1982) was used to analyze the data. The Form A pretest was the covariate. The F test to determine the effect of the treatment conditions while holding the covariate constant resulted in a significant F ratio ($F = 9.13$, $p < .01$). The General Linear Models Procedure indicated both experimental groups to be significantly different from the control group on the posttest.

The experimental group viewing the educational film produced by the American Foundation for the Blind scored in a significantly positive direction on the posttests, consistent with the results of the study by Elliott and Byrd (1983) that utilized the same film. The balance of an emotional and rational appeal and the relevance of material in a visual presentation are considered by Bernotavicz (1979) to be critical in modifying attitudes toward disabled persons. By providing specific rather than general information about a particular disability (blindness), the film may reduce anxiety that would be detrimental to interaction with a person who is disabled (Donaldson, 1980). It also appears to address many concerns of the nondisabled person regarding blindness and offers insights and suggestions that could enhance interaction. These qualities may impact a viewer's *behavioral intentions*—toward those with blindness, a term Threlkeld and DeJong (1982, 1983) consider more dynamic and indicative of a person's future behavior than the often nebulous construct of attitudes—toward blind persons.

Results from the ANOVA procedure, consistent with past studies, indicate that the film produced by the American Foundation for the Blind could serve as an efficacious agent for modifying attitudes toward disability. The experimental group that viewed the television program appeared to be influenced by the nonstereotypic portrayal of blindness, and the treatment was significantly different from that of the control group. Yet the small increase in mean scores implies the television program did not result in a large attitudinal shift.

Elliot and Byrd (1984a) utilized video depictions plus discussion as a treatment. The study sample consisted of volunteer undergraduate students enrolled in two sections of a human relations class in the counselor education department and graduate students enrolled in a rehabilitation course in the same department at Auburn University. One of the undergraduate classes ($N = 17$) and the graduate class ($N = 16$) were assigned to experimental treatments and the other undergraduate class ($N = 13$) served as the control group. Each individual subject was assured that participation was voluntary and given an opportunity to decline.

The Attitudes Toward Disabled Persons Scale (Yuker, Block, & Younng, 1966/1970) was used for assessing possible changes in attitudes. Form A was used as the pretest, Form B as the first posttest, and Form 0 as the follow-up posttest. Experimental Group 1 then viewed a videotaped segment from the "Mork and Mindy" television series featuring a nonstereotypic depiction of blindness. After the episode was seen once in its entirety, the researchers replayed the episode, stopping the videotape to discuss certain incidents and characterizations in the program with the subjects. Feedback and reactions were elicited from the subjects and processed. At the end of the second viewing, subjects were requested to describe common misconceptions and stereotypes of disabilities that may be reflected in media presentations. Subjects were divided into small discussion groups to generate separate listings, which they later presented to the researchers. These listings were shared with the total group. Following this exchange of ideas, subjects were administered Form B.

Experimental Group 2 viewed the film *What Do You Do When You Meet a Blind Person?* These subjects were given Form B of the ATDP immediately following the film. The control group ($N = 13$) received the pretest and received no treatment. Two days later at the next class meeting, the control group was given Form B as a posttest measure. Five weeks after each group was administered the questionnaires, a follow-up posttest was administered.

The results of the analysis of variance conducted on the pretests indicated no significant differences between any two groups. The analysis of variance conducted on the Form B posttests yielded a significant difference between the groups. The analysis of variance conducted on the Form 0 posttests yielded no significant difference between any two groups. Dependent t-tests on the Form A pretests and Form B posttests revealed significant differences within Experimental Group 1 and Experimental Group 2; both groups experienced an increase in scores on the ATDP. The control group remained unchanged.

The Scheffe procedure detected a significant difference on the Form B posttests between Experimental Group 1 and the control group at $p < .05$. No differences between groups occurred for the Form A pretests or the Form 0 follow-up posttest by the Scheffe procedure.

These results demonstrate a substantial increase in positive attitudes on the ATDP scales by both experimental groups. The group that viewed and discussed the television portrayal of blindness was significantly different from the control group on the Form B posttest, as detected by a conservative *post hoc* procedure. The second experimental group exhibited the most pronounced within-group increase in mean scores on forms A and B; this group had viewed the film from the American Foundation for the Blind. A lack of between-group differences on the Form 0 follow-up posttests may prompt suspicions concerning the long-term effects of either treatment, but these remain speculative without within-group comparisons. Active participation, as recommended by Bernatovicz (1979), with nonstereotypic television depictions of disability appears to facilitate an atmosphere wherein individuals can explore their own misperceptions and assimilate information from others concerning disability.

Two important implications stem from this research, one of which concerns the broadcasting industry. Combined with discussion, accurate depictions of disability may positively influence attitudes of viewers toward persons with disabilities. These results imply that the mass media can play an important role in the formulation of informed, positive attitudes among the public by depicting accurate characterizations of persons with disabilities.

FILM

Byrd and Pipes (1981) described the incidence of disability portrayal in feature films. A two-year sample (May 1977–April 1979) of films produced in the United States was reviewed using the *Monthly Film Bulletin.* A total of 287 films depicting disability appeared in the sample. Chi-square analyses for disability and the dichotomous rating of above or below average (a judge's evaluation of a critic's review) yielded nonsignificant results, indicating that there is no difference in the expected frequencies of different disabilities and that the frequency of above- and below-average ratings is equal.

Thirty-six disabilities were portrayed. The largest percentages of these were mental illness, alcoholism, and drug addiction. Interestingly, mental illness ranked first in both 1976 and 1978 in television (Byrd, Byrd, and Allen, 1977; Byrd, McDaniel, and Rhoden, 1979). Alcoholism ranked second in the 1978 television study. Drug abuse was first, with alcoholism and mental illness tied for second, in the study of popular literature and disability (Byrd, 1979a). Apparently mental illness and alcoholism were favorite themes for television, popular literature, and major film productions. However, the chi-square analysis in this study was not significant; no disability was portrayed significantly more often than any other. Apparently the film industry finds a fairly diverse group of disabilities interesting for portrayal on film.

Of the 33 films depicting disability, 12 (36%) were rated equal to or above average by the researcher based on the professional film critic's review; 21 (64%) were rated below average. It should be kept in mind that the critic's evaluation (and hence the researcher's ratings) were based on the overall quality of the film and not on the actor's depiction of disability. The chi-square value was nonsignificant, suggesting that film critics do not evaluate films portraying disability either positively or negatively. As an example of the potential discrepancy between the rated quality of the film and the quality of the portrayal of disability it can be noted that Jon Voight received an Academy Award for his acting in *Coming Home,* despite a poor evaluation of the film by a professional critic.

The results of this study support the idea that the film industry utilizes a variety of disabilities in its dramatizations. The most popular categories were mental illness, alcoholism, and drug addiction. However, perceptual and physical disabilities were depicted as well. There is a possibility that disabilities selected for depiction by film producers are those that are conveniently integrated into the story line and will, in the view of the director, add an element of interest; physical disabilities are perhaps not as easily suited to this process as are such disabilities as mental illness. There appear to be fewer films that deal specifically with a physical disability when that disability is the central focus of the film. Two notable exceptions are *Coming Home* (paraplegia) and *Today Is Forever* (cancer).

A number of well-known performers have portrayed disabled persons, including Jon Voight (paraplegia), Henry Winkler (mental illness), Anthony Hopkins (mental illness), James Caan (mental retardation), Peter Falk (cancer), Jill Clayburgh (leukemia), David Carradine (blindness), and John Savage (amputation). Although the percentage of films portraying disability is relatively small, the fact that well-known performers do at times play the role of a disabled person means that attention is drawn to the area of disability.

Byrd and Elliot (1985) expanded the earlier study by Byrd and Pipes (1981). Films reviewed in volumes 43 through 50 of the *Monthly Film Bulletin* (May 1976 to September 1983) were selected. Four research questions were asked:

1. What percentage of feature films depicted disability?
2. Did one disability receive more attention than another?
3. Were women or men depicted as having a disability?
4. Did film critics evaluate films depicting disability positively or negatively?

Thirty-one critics reviewed the films. The researcher rated the films as positive or negative based on the professional critic's review. A second judgment of the critic's review and the incidence of disability in films reviewed in the *Monthly Film Bulletin* was made independently by another judge to yield information regarding interrater reliability. The judge sampled one additional review from each issue of a film in which no disability was depicted, in order to ascertain a baseline of positive versus negative reviews of films.

Additionally, viewers' ratings of a portion of the films in the sample ($n = 36$), as reported by *Consumer Reports*, were counted to further test the reliability of the researcher's and judge's ratings based on the film critics' reviews in the *Monthly Film Bulletin*. A five-point scale that ranges from better to worse was used by *Consumer Reports*. Those movies with an average rating of at least better than average (ratings highest or next to highest on the five-point scale) were assigned a positive rating.

A total of 1,051 films were reviewed in the *Monthly Film Bulletin* from May 1976 to September 1983. Of that total, 11.4% ($n = 120$) contained portrayals of disability. Of the 120 films, there were three discrepancies on the incidence of disability between the researcher and judge. There were 15 discrepancies between the researcher and judge on their rating of films, based on the film critics' reviews in the *Monthly Film Bulletin*. Discrepancies between the researcher and judge were not discussed, and analysis was based on the researcher's data. There were 15 discrepancies (41.7% of the sample) on film ratings between the researcher and judge on the one hand, and the ratings based on the 36 viewer surveys done by *Consumer Reports* on the other hand; this suggested a large discrepancy between the critics' opinions and public opinion.

A total of 154 disabilities was depicted in the 120 films. The largest number depicted "psychiatric disorder," a category made up of characters described in the film reviews as possessing some emotional/behavioral disorder (e.g., schizophrenic, affective, anxiety, and personality disorders). This category occurred significantly more often than other categories ($p < .001$).

Characters who were disabled were predominantly male ($n = 104$) rather than female ($n < 44$) in those depictions for which sex of the character could be determined from the reviews ($p < .01$). Significantly larger frequencies of films were judged to be negative ($n = 98$) than positive ($n = 22$), based on the researcher's judgments of the critics' reviews ($p < .001$). The baseline data for critiques of films depicting no disability yielded 67 negative and 15 positive. Of the surveys conducted by *Consumer Reports*, 15 were positive and 12 negative.

It is interesting that the high frequency of psychiatric disorders in this study parallels results found in similar studies of portrayals of disability on television programs (Byrd, Byrd, & Allen, 1977; Byrd, McDaniel, & Rhoden, 1980). Apparently disabilities of this type appeal to both film producers and television script writers. The realistic quality of the portrayals could not be surmised in this study, and this area warrants further investigation. Many of the descriptors used by film critics in their reviews may suggest stereotypic presentations of these conditions (e.g., "psychotic killer"). These emphasize the distorted and bizarre, which perhaps fit well into dramatizations that require suspense and action to elicit audience anxiety. Comedies might also attempt to capitalize on these misconceptions to depict slapstick humor and buffoonery.

The overwhelmingly negative reviews by film critics may have implications for the quality of films produced generally and the resulting effect on disability portrayal in films. While it may be that disability portrayals may be effective even in the context of poor overall quality, it is more likely that the viewing audience dismisses the disability portrayals along with the films. Ultimately that decision is made by the viewer. The viewer's rating of a film may be different from that of the film critic, as noted above.

POPULAR LITERATURE

Byrd (1979a) investigated magazine articles and disability. Of the 15 magazines with the greatest circulation in 1977, the 10 included in the

Reader's Guide to Periodical Literature were selected for review. They included *Reader's Digest, National Geographic, Better Homes and Gardens, McCall's, Ladies Home Journal, Good Housekeeping, Redbook, Time, Newsweek,* and *Senior Scholastic.*

Eighteen disabilities listed as severe by the *Federal Register* were selected for review: alcoholism, amputation, arthritis, blindness, cerebral palsy, cosmetic disability, deafness, diabetes, drug abuse, epilepsy, heart disease, kidney disorder, mental illness, mental retardation, multiple sclerosis, muscular dystrophy, paraplegia, and stroke. Disabilities listed and cross-referenced by the *Reader's Guide to Periodical Literature* were searched and a tally sheet maintained, with categories including magazine, disability, issue, and title of the article. Frequencies were computed and chi-square calculated on these categories.

A total of 59 articles were listed in the 10 magazines, yielding a 5.9 mean number of articles per magazine. The chi-square analysis yielded results at $p = .02$ for magazines. *Newsweek* contained the greatest frequency of articles on disability, followed by *Time* and *Good Housekeeping.* The periodicals with basically news content had the greatest number of articles, which may be due to a trend toward informing the public about dangerous substances and major health hazards. Although *Good Housekeeping* is directed more toward family and household concerns, it appears that it also is attempting to cover major health hazards and resulting disability.

Drug abuse was covered more frequently than other disabilities, followed by alcoholism, heart disease, and mental illness. It should be noted that mental illness and alcoholism were the most frequent disabilities covered by television in prime time (Byrd, Byrd, & Allen, 1977). This study resulted in heart disease and drug abuse being ranked 7th and 14th, respectively. The public's concern about substance abuse (especially alcohol) and emotional disturbance may account for the high frequency of these topics when dealing with disability. It may be argued that the media create the effect of concern in the public rather than responding to it.

The data in this study seem to reflect appropriate coverage by the popular literature. It is encouraging that the two magazines that have news content and format were leaders in the frequency of articles regarding disability. It also is encouraging to see a 5.9 mean for the 10 magazines. Apparently, there is interest regarding disability on the part of the public as perceived by editors in popular literature. This interest may come from a concern for one's own health and potential hazards to health. The motivation for writing these articles may be to inform and to appease the public regarding this threat. In any event, the public appears to be becoming more aware of disability and its effect. An outcome of this coverage may be a somewhat better understanding of disability. It is doubtful, however, that popular literature will change attitudes enough to affect one's level of interaction with a disabled person.

A study conducted by Giles and Byrd (1986) tallied disability in popular literature. The 10 publications with the largest circulation in 1981 were surveyed. A five-year time span was used (July 1, 1978, to June 30, 1983). Data were collected by reviewing the content sections of the magazines. Disabilities were collapsed into three categories: chemical abuse ($n = 46$; 25.4%), mental illness ($n = 89$; 49.2%), and other ($n = 46$; 25.4%) for purpose of analysis. These data support the Byrd (1979a) data with regard to the prevalence of mental illness and chemical abuse coverage in popular periodicals.

Byrd, Williamson, and Byrd (1986) studied literary characters who are disabled. Descriptions of literary characters in the *Cyclopedia of Literary Characters* edited by Magill (1963) provided the data base for this research. This resource was selected because of its comprehensiveness and organization. Index cards were used to gather and tabulate the data. Only disability that represented a chronic condition over a significant portion of the character's life and was considered to interact with the story presented was included.

Frequencies were calculated for disability categories, 50-year periods of time from 1550 to 1950, and for authors with a minimum of five disability depictions. Frequencies of works depicting disability by author and in the 50-year time periods were compared with total frequencies of works. Physical disability was the most frequently portrayed, psychiatric disorder the least frequently portrayed, disability. The most frequent portrayal of disability took place in the first half of the twentieth century, the least during the first half of the seventeenth century. Authors with the most frequent depiction of disability are listed in Table 7-1. Charles Dickens headed the list with fourteen works depicting disability. Some of Dickens's works that depict disability include *A Christmas Carol* (orthopedic), *The Old Curiosity Shop* (giantism, amputation), *David Copperfield* (dwarfism), *Pickwick Papers* (deafness), *A Tale of Two Cities* (alcoholism), and *Oliver Twist* (alcoholism).

Physical disability headed the list, with alcoholism second. Previous research found alcoholism the most frequently portrayed disability in films (Byrd & Pipes, 1981), television (Byrd, Byrd, & Allen, 1977; Byrd, McDaniel, & Rhoden, 1980) and in popular literature (Byrd, 1979a). It is interesting that physical disability ranked higher in this study. This may be a function of the visibility factor associated with many physical disabilities, as opposed to the essentially hidden nature of alcoholism. Physical disability can be dealt with in literature, where readers can construct their own image of a particular disability, perhaps minimizing its less attractive nature. Alcoholism, on the other hand, provides an interesting element to

TABLE 7-1 Authors with Most Frequent Disability Portrayal

Author	Author's works portraying disability: frequency	Total frequency of literary works	Percentage
Charles Dickens	14	16	87.5
Thomas Hardy	6	8	75.0
Fyodor Mikhailovich Dostoevski	4	7	57.1
Emile Zola	3	6	50.0
Leo Tolstoy	3	7	42.9
William Faulkner	3	9	33.3
Euripedes	5	16	31.3
William Shakespeare	6	36	16.7

From Byrd, E. K., Williamson, W., & Byrd, P. D. (1986). Literary characters who are disabled. *Rehabilitation Counseling Bulletin.* Copyright © AACD. Reprinted with permission. No further reproduction authorized without permission of AACD.

characters depicted on television and film, while not posing explicit physical abnormalities. It is interesting that such a large portion of the sample falls into the twentieth century, suggesting the existence of a more open fictional forum for the introduction of characters who are disabled.

The data in this study indicate alcoholism is a popular topic for nearly all forms of media. It adds interest and entertainment value to a story plot. Physical disability, however, has been given more exposure in literature, perhaps because the reader is able to decide what form that disability takes on visually. It is noted that the authors who most frequently portrayed disability are recognizable.

CHAPTER 8

The Impact of Cultural, Ethnic, Religious, and National Variables on Attitudes Toward Persons with a Physical Disability: A Review

Esther Zernitzky-Shurka

Negative attitudes toward persons with a physical disability pose a significant obstacle to the successful completion of rehabilitation. These societal attitudes oblige persons with a physical disability to cope with rejection by elements of their environment in addition to possible difficulties in personal adjustment to the disabling condition (English, 1971). In the rehabilitation literature dealing with attitudes toward persons with a physical disability, it is frequently suggested that they have a social status comparable to that of minority groups (Friedson, 1966; Gellman, 1959; Wright, 1983). Furthermore, prejudice against persons with a physical disability has been found to be associated with cultural norms that attach great importance to health and physical appearance (Jaques, Linkowski, & Sieka, 1968; Schneider & Anderson, 1980), and also to the degree of cultural modernity (Jordan & Friesen, 1968).

The purpose of the present chapter is to examine and compare the attitudes toward persons with a physical disability of different cultural, ethnic, religious, and national groups in Israel. In addition, this chapter will compare these attitudes to attitudes of other societies in the world. The first part of this presentation will review the literature and research relating to the Jewish population, with its cultural and ethnic composition; the second part will review the literature and research relating to the Arab population, with its religious composition; the third part will compare the Israeli Jewish and Israeli Arab populations with other cultural groups.

JUDAISM, ISRAELI JEWISH SOCIETAL STRUCTURE, AND ATTITUDES TOWARD PHYSICAL DISABILITY

The traditional approach of the Jewish religion to physical disability is essentially negative. According to the book of Leviticus a person with a blemish or disability could not serve as the Lord's priest. Furthermore, even an animal with a physical deformation or blemish could not be used as a sacrifice to the Lord. Thus, it may be reasonable to suggest that physical disabilities were interpreted as an expression of rejection and displeasure of the Lord. Epstein (1960) contended that the traditional approach of Judaism sees physical disability as a divine retribution for sinful deeds, as purification for the hereafter, or as a test of a person's faith.

An additional variable that may be significant in research involving the Israeli Jews is their societal structure. Although sharing similar religious beliefs and practices, the Jews, who are the majority group in Israel, have a pluralistic value system based on various cultures (Peres & Katz, 1980). The massive immigration from over 70 countries with extreme differences in cultural background has led to the creation of multicultural patterns, with no single culture as a dominant one (Florian & Katz, 1983; Weisman & Chigier, 1965). However, the Israeli Jewish population can be divided into two ethnic groups: (1) Jews of Eastern origin, consisting of Israeli Jews who were born (or whose parents were born) in Balkan, Middle-Eastern, or North African countries (mainly Arab and Islamic), and (2) Jews of Western origin, consisting of Israeli Jews who were born (or whose parents were born) in North or Central America or Eastern or Western Europe (mainly Westernized countries).

According to the professional literature, the Jews of Eastern origin have a fatalistic approach to physical disability, which is seen as a punishment from heaven or resulting from unnatural forces (Chigier & Chigier, 1968; Palgi, 1962). Florian and Katz (1983) further contended that in Eastern cultures physical disability is perceived as unchangeable by medical means and that therefore the attitudes of these cultural groups is one of passive acceptance of fate, as well as pity toward persons with a physical disability. Furthermore, primarily because of the emphasis placed on the "whole" body by this cultural group, they perceive persons with a physical disability as inferior. Persons with a physical disability further need to deal with the problem of finding a "respectful"spouse. The presence of a person with a physical disability may also affect the family's social status and may interfere with the ability of other members of the family to find a spouse.

The Jews of Western origin, being more exposed to Western values and modern conceptions of equality, thus emphasize the importance and value of human life over the physical disability (Rofe, Almagor, & Joffe, 1980). Florian and Katz (1983) contended that, according to Western cultural values, persons with a physical disability are expected to be able to fulfill societal obligations, to contribute to society, and to adapt to the non-disabled life style as much as possible. In other words, the Jews of Western origin have adopted the modern ideas of equality among social groups and equal opportunities for all.

Thus it may be reasonable to assume that the differing cultural values of Eastern and Western Jewish groups will have a direct and/or indirect influence on attitudes toward a family member with a physical disability. A review of studies that compared Israeli ethnic groups, families, and individuals from various cultural backgrounds found support for this assumption. Rofe and associates (1980), in studying attitudes toward physical disability and ethnic origin, found that the attitudes of Jews of Eastern origin were significantly more negative than attitudes of Jews of Western origin, measured by the Attitudes Toward Disabled Person scale (ATDP) developed by Yuker, Block, and Campbell (1960). Weisman and Chigier (1965) studied the attitudes of parents of cerebral palsied youth and found that parents of Eastern origin had more fatalistic attitudes and were more ashamed of the disabled youth than parents of Western origin, who had more realistic attitudes. Mandel, Palgi, Pinkis, and Greenberger (1969), in their research on the attitudes of parents of children with cerebral palsy, found that parents of Western origin tended to blame medical negligence for the child's condition, while the parents of Eastern origin tended to blame fate or themselves. Adler, Shanan, and Adler (1968) studied hemiplegic patients' wives of Eastern and Western origin. They found that spouses of Eastern origin were more rejecting of their disabled husbands after a cerebrovascular accident than spouses of Western origin.

On the other hand, Palgi (1962), studying Jewish parents of children with physical disabilities from different countries of Eastern origin (Iraq, Yemen, and Morocco), found the Iraqi families tended to view physical disability as a curse for the disabled child and his family and as punishment from God for the sins of a family member; Yemenite parents believed that the disability was caused by demons or God's will, the family not being blamed and there being no shame attached; and Mococcan parents had a fatalistic attitude toward the physical disability, which was perceived as caused by unnatural power, the "evil eye," or bad luck and therefore entailing no family stigma.

The above review supports the assumption that there is a difference in attitudes between Jews of Eastern and Western origin toward persons with a physical disability. Cross-cultural studies in Israel reveal that the Jews of Western origin appear to have less negative attitudes toward disability and disabled persons compared to Jews of Eastern origin (Adler et al., 1968; Mandel et al., 1969; Rofe et al., 1980). However, McDaniel (1976) and Florian and Katz (1983) contended that variables such as socioeconomic and educational level are significant in attitude determination. In general, the Jews of Eastern origin in Israel are of lower socioeconomic status and have a lower level of education compared to Jews of Western origin (Florian & Katz, 1983). Thus although differences in attitudes toward physical disabilities exist between Jews of Eastern and Western origin, these difference may not be simply culturally biased, but rather the result of an interaction among various demographic variables.

Generalizations based on the previously mentioned assumption may be limited. For instance, Palgi's (1962) study of families from various Eastern countries identified a differentiation within the group of Eastern Jews and resulting attitudes toward a person with a physical disability. Thus it would be erroneous to consider Jews of Eastern origin as a homogeneous group rather than as a group consisting of a variety of cultural entities. It may be reasonable to assume that such a contention is equally applicable to the Israeli population of Jews of Western origin.

ISRAELI ARABS' RELIGIOUS COMPOSITION, CULTURAL VALUES, AND ATTITUDES TOWARD PHYSICAL DISABILITY

The Arab minority group in Israel is divided into a large group of Muslims, a relatively small number of Christians, and a still smaller number of Druze (Florian & Katz, 1983). The Muslim religion sees disability as a punishment from God for sins committed, as a result of the "evil eye," or as an arbitrary consequence of divine will (Hamza, 1964). Thus disabled persons are perceived and treated as physically and spiritually weak individuals who do not contribute to society and who deserve pity. Arab Christian attitudes are influenced by the biblical notion that disease and physical disability are punishments sent by God for sins or immoral behavior. Sick and disabled persons deserve to suffer for having sinned. Although some of these ideas continue to exist, they have been found to be counterbalanced by church teachings that encourage charity and care of sick and disabled persons and emphasize that all human beings are equal in the sight of God (Weinberg & Sebian, 1980). The Druze religion, an offshoot of Islam, is shrouded in secrecy. Its religious leaders refuse to, and indeed are not allowed to, reveal its basic tenets. However, according to Makarim (1974), it is known that predestination is a basic concept of this religion. The believers have to accept the word of God and must thank him for what has been provided, even if they suffer as a result of it.

Despite the differing religious beliefs of these three subgroups, they are culturally influenced by the norms, customs, and values of the Arab tradition (Florian & Katz, 1983). Furthermore, they use the same language, live in the same geographical areas, and are affected by similar behavior norms (Samoocha, 1980). While undergoing a continual process of modernization, the Arabs in Israel may still be characterized as a relatively homogeneous, traditional society (Sharabi, 1975). In professional literature the Arab family has been described as an authoritarian extended familial framework in which the proper roles of members are clearly defined (Antonovski, Meari, & Blanc, 1978; Kramer, 1985). Taking a sociological perspective, Patai (1973) analyzed the basic characteristics of Arab societies and concluded that in spite of differences among them, these societies share some values related to social relations: courage-bravery, hospitality-generosity, honor-dignity, and the Islamic identity. Bravery refers to the individual's readiness to take great risks in order to save his fellows, while courage refers to self-control in situations of physical and/or emotional stress. Hospitality is required for gaining social reputation and respect, while generosity refers to giving to others even if individual or familial sacrifices are required. Honor and dignity in the Arab society are generic concepts that imply unlimited loyalty to the family, defense of the individual's social image, conformity to social and traditional norms, and preserving the "good name" of the women of the family. The Islamic influence is expressed through determinism and the belief in the omnipresence of God. This may have a positive consequence—helping the individual in dealing with life's difficulties; alternatively, it may lead to a negative consequence—fatalism, a pessimistic view of the individual's ability to change life conditions, and avoidance of taking responsibility for one's behavior, all of which may lead to submissiveness.

It may be assumed that characteristics of Arab societies will have an impact on the attitudes toward persons with a physical disability. Florian (1977) studied the attitudes of 655 eleventh- and twelfth-grade Israeli Arab students toward disabled persons, as measured by the ATDP. Significant differences were not found among Muslim, Christian, and Druze subjects. On the other hand, Shurka (1983), in her study of attitudes of Israeli Arabs toward the mentally ill, found that Christian respondents expressed fewer negative attitudes than Muslem respondents. A possible explanation for the differences between these two studies may be due to the fact that in Florian's (1977) study subjects were high school students, while in Shurka's (1983) study subjects were a random sample of the Arab population between the ages of 20 and 50 with different levels of education. Indeed, Shurka (1983) found that subjects with higher levels of education revealed more positive attitudes. Furthermore, in Florian's (1977) study subjects were asked to relate to physical disabilities, while in Shurka's (1983) study the subjects were asked to relate to mental illness. Thus the gap between the studies may be a result of the different stimuli (physical vs. mental disability) as well as the differences in the age and education levels of the subjects. Since most of the studies carried out on the Arab population have been cross-cultural in nature (comparing Arab and Jews) a more detailed review of these is given in the next section.

CROSS-CULTURAL STUDIES OF ATTITUDES TOWARD PERSONS WITH PHYSICAL DISABILITIES

Probably one of the most interesting and exciting areas of research in rehabilitation is the examination of how different cultures relate to persons with physical disabilities. Israel may provide an excellent background for a comparative study of attitudes toward persons with a physical disability in modern and traditional societies. Israel is a society that continues to absorb Jewish immigrants from various cultural backgrounds. This same society also includes a national minority group of Arabs with various religious beliefs and practices.

Florian (1977), in the study mentioned earlier, found a significant difference between Israeli Arab and Jewish students' attitudes toward disabled persons, Arab students revealing more negative attitudes. Since both groups were of comparable socioeconomic level, Florian concluded that the cultural variable appeared to be the dominant one in influencing these attitudes. Tseng (1972), using the ATDP, reported that American students showed significantly more positive attitudes toward persons with physical disabilities than did Asian students at West Virginia University. Tseng concluded that this confirmed the hypothesis that since minority groups consist of members of traditional and less modernized cultures, they show more negative attitudes toward persons with a physical disability than do cultural majority groups. Contrary to these findings, Shurka and Katz (1978), studying similar populations, found no significant differences between Israeli Arab and Jewish attitudes toward the person with a physical disability. A possible explanation for the differences may be due to the fact that in Florian's (1977) and Tseng's (1972) studies the subjects related to disability in general, while in Shurka and Katz's (1978) study the subjects related to a specific person with a physical disability.

A further interesting finding by Florian (1977) was that Israeli Arab and Jewish students who perceived themselves as not religious revealed more positive attitudes than students who perceived themselves as religious. This finding, taken together with the lack of significant differences among the three Arab religious groups (Muslem, Christian, and Druze), may indicate that the level of religious belief plays a significant role in influencing negative and positive attitudes toward persons with a physical disability.

Feldman (1976), in her study of Arab and Jewish community leaders' attitudes toward rehabilitation and disability, found similar results. In groups of both Israeli Arabs and Jews, subjects who considered themselves as not religious revealed more positive attitudes. However, the variable of degree of religious belief needs to be viewed with caution, since it is often confounded by such other variables as subject's age, gender, and educational level. Examination of Feldman's sample of Arab leaders revealed that the religious leaders were generally older, less educated, and had less contact with persons with a physical disability than their Jewish counterparts. In addition, Feldman found that the female leaders who had the highest level of education showed the most positive attitudes toward the disabled. These women were also younger and less religious than the men. The question that arises here is whether the positive attitudes were a function of the gender of the evaluator, the level of religious belief, the level of education, age, or an interaction among these variables.

In order to understand the source of the differences between Arabs and Jews there is a need to evaluate attitudes not only as a function of national entity, but also in interaction with other sociodemographic variables. Florian (1977) found a significant interaction among three variables: national group, family contact with the disabled, and type of disability. He found that the variables of contact and type of disability had no significant main effects on attitudes toward persons with a physical disability. However, Jewish subjects with "family contact" revealed more positive attitudes than Jews who did not have a disabled relative. The opposite was found for the Arab subjects. For the variable of type of disability, Florian reported that Jewish subjects had more negative attitudes toward amputation than other disabilities. A person seated in a wheelchair was evaluated most negatively by Arab subjects, while the Jewish subjects evaluated him most positively. An additional datum was that in both populations blindness did not receive the most negative attitudes, as found by researchers in the United States (Gowman, 1957; Grand & Strohmer, 1983; Pascal, 1954; Whiteman & Lukoff, 1965).

Several cross-cultural studies have examined the influence of these two variables, contact and type of disability, on attitudes toward a person with a physical disability. For example, Jordan (1971), in his study involving several ethnic groups in seven nations, reported that parents of deaf children did not score most favorably in their attitudes toward the deaf. Florian and Shurka (1981) and Shurka and Florian (1983) compared Arab and Jewish Israeli parental attitudes toward their child with a physical disability. These authors concluded that the cultural variable appeared to influence these parents' coping styles and perceptions of their child with a disability. They furthermore contended that the cultural variable was related to the issue of traditional versus modern family structure, with Arab families complying more with traditional family structure and attitudes and Jewish families with modern Western family structure. Concerning this point, it is interesting to note that Jordan and Friesen (1968), in their study of professionals from special-education and rehabilitation services, found that disabled persons were viewed more positively in modern societies than in the traditional societies.

The cultural influence on attitudes toward types of disabilities has been studied by Richardson and associates (Richardson, Goodman, Hastorf, & Dornbusch, 1961; Richardson, Goodman, Dornbusch, & Hastorf, 1963). In the initial research, white, black, and Puerto Rican lower- and middle-class boys and girls aged 10 and 11 were found similar in their ranking of five physical disabilities. The rank of order of preference from the most to the least favorable was: a child with no physical handicap, a child with crutches and a brace on the left leg, a child sitting in a wheelchair, a child with the left hand missing, a child with facial disfigurement, and an obese child. In the later study of Jewish and Italian students of low socioeconomic status, the results showed a difference in ranking assigned to physical disabilities by the two groups. The Jewish preferential order was: a child with no physical handicap, a child with facial disfigurement, a child with the left hand missing, an obese child, a child with crutches and a leg brace, and a child seated in a wheelchair. The authors explained these findings as a reflection of the value placed on food in the Jewish culture and the presence in that culture of an association between feeding and affection. Using the same method applied by Richardson and associates, Chigier and Chigier (1968) tested a heterogeneous sample of Israeli students. They found in their sample of 1,333 children, aged 10 and 11 years, that the rankings of physical disabilities were similar to those of Richardson's Jewish group, but not other American groups. Horne (1978) studied the cultural effect on attitudes toward labels of bilingual Hebrew, Italian, and Spanish fourth-grade students, with black and monolingual comparison groups. Her results showed only minimal support for the effect of culture on attitudes toward types of disabilities and, when compared with previous findings, suggested the existence of a stable hierarchy.

Grand and Strohmer (1983) compared black and white students' evaluations of disabled persons as measured by six semantic differential scales (Osgood, Suci, & Tannenbaum, 1957). They found that black students gave significantly higher ratings to persons with a physical disability than did white students. The authors explained this finding on the basis of interpersonal attraction theory and group membership status of social deviance and stigmatization. However, both groups gave the highest ratings to individuals seated in a wheelchair, which were significantly different from those given to visually impaired and cerebral palsied individuals.

The discrepancies among the above-mentioned research results may be due to the differing research groups, measurement procedures, and stimuli of disability. A feasible solution to this research dilemma may be found in the comparison of similar methodologically designed studies independently undertaken in Israel and the United States.

In a cross-cultural study in Israel of the influence of contextual variables on attitudes toward persons with a physical disability, Shurka and Katz (1982) found that attitudes of both Arab and Jewish high school students were related to whether the disability occurred in a civilian or a military framework. Disabilities portrayed as the consequence of war injuries were less stigmatized than those that were portrayed as resulting from a civilian accident. For the Jewish adolescents the effect of this contextual variable was strong enough to reverse the usual negative valence of the disability, so that a veteran with a physical disability was evaluated more positively than a nondisabled individual. In addition, the study demonstrated that persons described as having been responsible for their disability through negligence or disobedience to authority received lower evaluations than persons who were described as having no control over the cause of their disability. The last finding is consistent with research results reported by Shurka, Siller, and Dvonch (1982) on American white, native-English-speaking New York college graduates. Furthermore, it is congruent with Wright's (1983) contention that societal attitudes toward persons who are perceived as being not responsible for their disability are more favorable than toward persons who are held accountable for their disability.

Katz, Kravetz, and Karlinsky (1986) replicated Shurka and Katz's (1982) study. Using an American sample of high school students in Berkeley, they found that, in contrast to the Israeli sample, the attitudes of the American sample toward persons with a physical disability were more positive than toward nondisabled persons. Katz and associates explained the positive evaluations toward persons with a physical disability as a consequence of social desirability. They also offered a plausible alternative explanation for their "unusual" findings in the possibility that there had been a change of attitudes as a result of the extensive exposure of the nondisabled population to a large number of persons with a physical disability living independently in the Berkeley community. Another difference between the American and the Israeli samples may have been due to the attribution of responsibility to the person with a physical disability, which did not have a statistically significant impact on the American sample. It is possible that responsibility for the disability had more impact in Israel, where attitudes toward the disabled were negative but, because of social desirability, may have been more difficult to express. According to this explanation, when persons are deemed responsible for their disability they may be evaluated without any pangs of conscience. In the American study subjects displayed positive attitudes and therefore did not require justification for their attitudes. In addition, the American study was motivated by the assumption that, due to the Vietnam war, military service was less valued than in Israel. Therefore the positive effect of the military framework uncovered in Israel was expected to be reversed or reduced in the United States. However, since the American study did not reveal the expected negative attitudes toward disability, its results do not provide clear-cut support for the above assumption.

CONCLUSIONS

Review of the studies on attitudes toward persons with a physical disability in Israel appears to indicate differences in attitudes: Israeli Jews of Eastern origin (mainly from Arab and Muslim countries) appear to have more negative attitudes toward persons with a physical disability than Jews of Western origin, and Israeli Arabs appear to have less positive attitudes toward persons with a physical disability than Israeli Jews. One explanation for these negative attitudes may be that members of a traditional and less modernized culture show more negative attitudes toward disabled persons than members of modernized Western cultures (Florian, 1977; Jordan & Friesen, 1968; Tseng, 1972).

A plausible alternative, but not necessarily unrelated, explanation for these negative attitudes may be based on the characteristics of guilt and shame societies. Ausubel (1955) contended that anthropologists see guilt as a unique property of persons who as children experienced the kinds of relationships with parents allowing for "superego" formation that is typical of individuals growing up in cultures adhering to the Judaeo-Christian tradition, that is, Western society. Different studies, carried out in Western society, portray mothers' relationships with their disabled children as characterized by the mothers' guilt feelings (Burton, 1975; Doernberg, 1978). Guilt constitutes a most effective watchdog within each individual, serving to keep his/her behavior compatible with the moral values of the societies in which he/she lives (Ausubel, 1955). These guilt feelings may limit the influence of the "spread-effect" (Wright, 1983), which is often at the core of negative attitudes toward persons with a physical disability. On the other hand, Hamady (1960) and Patai (1973) contend that one of the main differences between the Arab and Western personality is that in the Arab culture shame is more pronounced than guilt. What pressures the Arab is not guilt but shame, or, more precisely, the psychological drive to escape or prevent negative judgment by others, what Patai (1973) refers to as honor and dignity. Hamady (1960), in discussing that aspect of Arab life, which she called "shame society," came to the conclusion that the main concern of the Arab in performing an action or refraining from it is whether he/she would be ashamed if people knew about it and what people would say is the main reason for his/her choice. Ausubel (1955) defined shame as an unpleasant emotional reaction by an individual to an actual or presumed negative judgment of him/herself by others, resulting in self-depreciation vis-à-vis the group.

Extrapolating from the above dichotomy, the negative attitudes expressed by persons of Arab cultural background may be more comprehensible. It may be that sensitivity to what others might say predisposes people to more negative attitudes toward persons who display deviant behavior and deviant body characteristics. However, this conclusion needs to be viewed with caution since other variables may provide plausible alternative explanations or confound the data in some of the studies cited. Such variables could include gender, age, educational level, socioeconomic status, and level of religious belief of the nondisabled; contact with disabled persons; and type and source of the disability. In addition, none of the studies reviewed attempted to look at such personality variables as anxiety, locus of control, and so forth, and their impact on attitudes toward persons with a physical disability in different cultural and ethnic groups. Finally, it should be remembered that Arabs in Israel constitute a religious, ethnic, and national minority group who, because of Israel's security situation and warring condition with its neighboring Arab countries, hold a unique status. Thus it is possible that the attitudes of Israeli Arabs toward disability and disabled persons are not representative of the attitudes of Arabs in other countries.

The important question to be answered by cross-cultural investigations is whether there is a common human element that forms the basis of attitudes toward persons with a physical disability that transcends cultural, ethnic, religious, and national influences.

PART III
The Measurement of Attitudes

CHAPTER 9

Methods to Measure Attitudes Toward People Who Are Disabled

Richard F. Antonak

The scientific study of attitudes was initiated in Germany in the 1850s with the investigation of people's responses to certain classes of stimuli (Triandis, Adamopoulos, & Brinberg, 1984). L. L. Thurstone led the work in the United States in the late 1920s with his pioneering article titled "Attitudes Can Be Measured" (Thurstone, 1928). In this article Thurstone presented his method of equal-appearing intervals for the construction of an attitude scale. To decrease the complexity, reduce the laborious scale-construction procedures, and circumvent the tenuous statistical assumptions of Thurstone's method, Rensis Likert (1932) proposed an alternative technique, which has been used thousands of times by researchers around the world to construct the ubiquitous summated rating attitude scale. If we add to these the subsequent methodological contributions of E. S. Bogardus (1932), Louis Guttman (1944), William Stephenson (1953), Charles E. Osgood (Osgood, Suci, & Tannenbaum, 1957), H. G. Gough (1960), and C. H. Coombs (1964), we have the measurement methods that account for nearly all attitude measures: social distance scales, linear deterministic scaling, Q-methodology, semantic differential scales, adjective checklists, and the unfolding technique, respectively.

Investigation of attitudes toward people who are disabled has concerned researchers for more than half a century, since the pioneering work of social psychologists such as Strong (1931) and Barker (1948). Although the designs of recent studies are more sophisticated and the statistical methods used to analyze the attitude data have changed substantially from simple descriptive statistics, the attitude instruments do not differ much from the three-option checklist used by Strong. They are for the most part designed for specific research situations and often used only once, without formal validation or detailed psychometric analyses. There are notable exceptions, including the scales of Linkowski (1971), Yuker and his colleagues (Yuker, Block, & Campbell, 1960; Yuker, Block, & Younng, 1966/1970), and Siller (1969).

Research concerning attitudinal barriers to the rights of disabled people to participate in society requires psychometrically sound instruments. The collection of data using these instruments will allow researchers and policy makers to answer questions concerning the formation, structure, correlates, and modification of attitudes toward disabled people. It is the intention of this chapter to assist researchers in the selection of an attitude-measurement method by presenting summaries of the basic methods available to measure attitudes, including both indirect and direct methods.

PURPOSE OF ATTITUDE MEASUREMENT

The purpose of attitude measurement is to convert observation of a respondent's behavior into an index that represents the attitude presumed to underlie the behavior. In this chapter, I will use Triandis's (1971) definition of attitude as "an idea charged with emotion which predisposes a class of actions to a particular class of social situations" (p. 2). The class of social situations will be known as the referent; this may be an object, a person, an event, or a construct. The researcher measuring attitudes must begin with a set of assumptions about the respondent's internal state, the referent toward which the respondent directs his or her behavior, and the relationship between the respondent's internal state and external behavior. The methods available to accomplish this measurement task can be classified as either indirect or direct methods.

INDIRECT AND DIRECT METHODS

In some cases, the researcher may select or devise an indirect measurement method in which the respondents are unaware that they are being measured or observed. For example, the researcher may create a situation in which the respondent, who is seated on a bench awaiting a bus, is joined by three confederates of the researcher. A woman (another confederate) who is obviously physically disabled—she is walking with a peculiar gait and using crutches—then approaches the bench. The respondent presumably may select any one of a class of personal actions in this situation. The respondent may ignore the woman and remain seated, as the confederates do; or may remain seated but ask the woman what happened to her legs; or may get up and offer the woman a place on the bench. Each of these behaviors can be preceded, accompanied, and followed by facial expressions, gestures, and vocalizations, which can be noted.

Other indirect measurement methods are: (1) those in which the respondents are aware that they are being observed or measured but are unaware of the purpose of the measurement; (2) those in which they are purposefully deceived as to the purpose of the measurement; and (3) those in which they are inactive participants, as in physiological measurements.

In most situations the researcher cannot observe a respondent's behavioral reactions to the attitude referent. The researcher may not be able to devise a situation in which the behavior will be evident, such as in an investigation of attitudes toward capital punishment. The researcher may not have the resources to commit to an experiment, such as hiring confederates, arranging props, or purchasing and operating a video camera. Or the researcher may not have time to observe the behaviors of respondents when interested in the attitudes of a specific group of respondents, such as fourth graders' attitudes toward the integration of physically handicapped children into public school classrooms. In these and other cases, the researcher will typically select a direct measurement method.

The researcher may ask respondents to react to a contrived situation and to report what they would do or how they feel about certain actions. For example, the researcher may ask respondents to view a videotaped vignette depicting a physically handicapped woman approaching a bench full of people seated waiting for a bus, and then ask the respondents what they would do in that situation. Or the researcher may ask the respondents to read a description of a woman who is physically disabled and then state how they would act in various situations (would they offer her their seat on a crowded bench?), or how they feel about certain characteristics of the woman (are physically disabled people helpless?), or how they feel about certain societal provisions for the woman (should at least one seat on all bus benches be reserved for disabled people?).

The researcher may select a direct measurement method in which the respondents are asked to read a list of 12 types of disabling conditions and select those conditions in which, if they knew that a person had that condition, they would be willing to offer that person their seat on a crowded bus bench. Alternatively, the researcher may ask the respondents to rank the 12 conditions in the order that represents their willingness to surrender their seat to people with those conditions. Finally, the researcher may ask the respondents to express their willingness to surrender their seat to a person with each of 12 handicapping conditions on a six-point continuum from very unwilling to very willing.

WHICH METHOD TO SELECT?

The type of measurement method that the researcher selects to study attitudes must be determined by the question that the researcher hopes to answer and by the parameters of the research situation. Among these parameters are time, cost, availability of respondents, and the researcher's competence and motivation. Some researchers are commited to only one type of measurement method, using it to answer all research questions— or rather, asking only those questions that can be answered by the measurement method. Another researcher may avoid a particular type of measurement method—perhaps because this method has not traditionally been a part of the researcher's professional discipline—even if it is the best method to answer the research question. It is Lemon's (1973) contention, as well as mine, that "the crucial question must always be whether a given technique constitutes an adequate operational definition of the underlying theoretical assumptions. If it does, then substantive conclusions can be drawn from it. If it does not, then the whole enterprise becomes a charade" (p. 27).

To assist the researcher in selecting an attitude measurement method that can provide the data needed to answer the research question, I have organized 14 different measurement methods into two categories. Ten of these are direct methods of measuring attitudes, and the remaining four are indirect methods. This taxonomy is a synthesis of the classification systems of Dawes (1984), Horne (1980), Lemon (1973), and Shaw and Wright (1967). Although this taxonomy is a comprehensive collection of attitude-measurement methods, it is not exhaustive. I have not included descriptions of Coomb's (1964) unfolding technique nor certain phenomenological and multidimensional scaling methods. The researcher who wishes to learn more about these methods is referred to Carroll (1980), Fishbein (1967), Kruscal and Wish (1978), Lemon (1973), or Summers (1970).

DIRECT METHODS OF ATTITUDE MEASUREMENT

Direct methods of attitude measurement are those in which the respondents are aware that they are participating in an attitude-measurement experiment. These are by far the most widely known and most used in measuring attitudes toward disabled people. Ten methods will be examined: opinion surveys, interviews, rankings, Q-methodology, sociometrics, adjective checklists, paired comparison scales, semantic differential scales, probabilistic rating scales, and deterministic rating scales.

Opinion Surveys

Opinion surveys ask the respondents to express in writing their beliefs, attitudes, feelings, or intentions toward some referent by responding to a list of questions. These methods are obtrusive and reactive measures, because the respondent is aware of the purpose of the research. Respondents may change their responses in an effort to protect their privacy or to provide the researcher with the data they think the researcher wants. Opinion surveys may be structured (closed) or unstructured (opened).

In a structured opinion survey, respondents are asked to select from among a set of responses the one (or ones) that they agree with, or that they endorse. An unstructured opinion survey permits wider latitude in the type of response they can provide and frequently asks that the respondents provide a justification for the answer. Comer and Piliavin (1972) explored the reactions of physically handicapped respondents in interactions with physically handicapped and physically normal interviewers using an open-ended question format. In an investigation of the reactions to disabilities of a group of 462 undergraduates, Linkowski, Jaques, and Gaier (1969) used an unstructured opinion survey in which the respondents were asked to list those disabilities they considered to be the most and least severe and why they thought so. To analyze the resultant responses, the researchers used thematic analysis. It was suggested that insights from these analyses be tested in subsequent research.

Interviews

Interviews require that the researcher interact directly and orally with the respondent, although the interview may take place over the phone or through field assistants who are carefully trained to conduct the investigation with many respondents in various locations. Although the interview may be conducted with more than one person at a time (for example, the parents of a disabled newborn may be interviewed together), typically a single respondent is the subject of the interview.

Structured interviews are organized to include a fixed set of questions of various types (agree–disagree, select those which apply, open-ended), called the interview protocol or schedule. The protocol is established in advance by the researcher and used in a fixed sequence with all respondents. Branching within the protocol may allow the researcher to skip over certain questions in the sequence, depending on the respondent's answer to an earlier question, or to ask more detailed questions to investigate a particular response. In an unstructured interview, the researcher is free to explore the respondent's attitudes and opinions in any way that presumably will contribute insight to the question being investigated (Williamson, Karp, Dalphin, & Gray, 1982).

Lyth (1973) used a semistructured interview protocol to investigate the attitudes of employers toward the employment of disabled people, while Philips (1975) used an unstructured interview procedure with employers to explore similar attitudes toward deaf people. Other examples of research using interview methods are Barngrover's (1971) investigation of educators' views about the efficacy of special classes for mildly handicapped children and Mercer's (1966) investigation using open-ended interviews to explore the attitudes, feelings, and motives of a group of parents of previously institutionalized mentally retarded children.

Rankings

Ranking methods require the respondent to arrange a small set of objects or statements (typically 20 or fewer) into an order according to some specified criterion. For example, Abroms and Kodera (1979) asked a group of 138 college students in introductory courses in special education to rank order a collection of 15 disability category labels according to the acceptability of the disability to them. Ranking methods have been used many times to compare the attitudes of various groups of respondents (e.g., Barsch, 1964; Orlansky, 1979).

It should be noted that ranking methods can use other than paper-and-pencil responses so that the method may be suitable for young respondents and for respondents who may not be able to read the scale or record their rankings in writing. For example, Richardson, Goodman, Hastorf, and Dornbusch (1961) used drawings of children with various types of levels of physical disabilities (e.g., a child seated in a wheelchair or one who was obese) to study the attitudes of handicapped and nonhandicapped young children of various races and religions. Jones and Sisk (1967) also used a set of pictures to assess the attitudes of children between the ages of two and five years toward children with orthopedic handicaps.

Q-Methodology

Q-Methodology, developed by William Stephenson (1953), requires that a respondent sort a set (typically 50 to 150) of attitude statements, written on separate cards, into an ordered collection of piles according to a criterion such as favorability, intensity of agreement, or descriptiveness. The number of piles is specified (typically, nine or fewer), and the number of items that the respondent may put in each pile is also specified.

The sortings of different respondents may be compared and analyzed to derive clusters of respondents with similar orderings. The content of the items in each pile for different clusters of respondents is examined in order to characterize the respondents. That is, the judges are clustered, not the items. The researcher may then assign a respondent to a group of similar respondents by comparing the respondent's orderings with those obtained in previous research. The clusterings may be examined before and after some event or intervention to discern changes in respondent's attitudes. For example, Shaver and Scheibe (1967) used Q-methodology (among other methods) in a pre- and posttest design to investigate the influence of an intensive camp experience on the attitudes of college students toward people with chronic mental illness.

If the items to be sorted are written to represent a particular theoretical perspective, the method can test that theory. An early study by Barker (1964) used Q-methodology to test a theoretical model of disability groupings. Barker found that sorters used a bivariate model to sort the disabilities, with organic (physical) disabilities in one set (e.g., cancer, malaria, blindness) and functional (mental) disabilities in another set (e.g., alcoholism, neuroses). An early review of investigations using Q-methodology in psychiatric research is provided by Block (1961).

Sociometrics

Sociometric techniques are designed to determine how a person behaves or intends to behave toward a particular attitude referent when given a choice of behaviors. It is important that the respondents believe that their choices may have consequences for the referent or that their choices may affect themselves. If not, the respondent's stated intentions will differ little from a self-report questionnaire. The types of choices offered must be typical choices for the situation, such as asking school children who they want to eat with, play with, sit near, or date. The respondent may be presented with a roster of the people in his/her class or group and asked: "Which of your classmates on the list below do you most like to sit with in the lunchroom? . . . next most? . . . least?"

The resultant data can be analyzed to yield a sociogram of the number of times a child, or group of children, is nominated or selected in various situations. The study by Jones and Sisk (1967) mentioned previously used a sociometric method in which the selections of orthopedically disabled children as playmates and companions of 230 children between the ages two and six were obtained and analyzed. Sociometric techniques have been widely used to determine which variables influence the integration of disabled children in schools and adults in communities and workplaces. Jay Gottlieb, a prolific contributor to research on attitudes toward disabled people, provided an excellent review of sociometric research techniques and results concerning mentally retarded people (Gottlieb, 1975). Mac-Millan and Morrison (1984) discuss sociometric research with a variety of other groups and areas within special education and rehabilitation.

Adjective Checklists

The original Adjective Check List (ACL) was constructed by Gough (1960) for the investigation of personality and self-concept. A list of 300 adjectives arranged alphabetically was presented to respondents who were asked to select those adjectives that they felt described themselves. Factor and cluster analytic investigations led other researchers to derive a variety of scales from the ACL, presumably measuring aspects of such personality as achievement, autonomy, self-confidence, and personal adjustment. Cleland, Manaster, King, and Iscoe (1975) used the 300-word ACL to determine differences in perceptions of mentally retarded people.

Typically a subset of the ACL items is arranged alphabetically on a scale, and the respondents are asked to select those that they feel characterize different groups of disabled people. Siperstein, Bak, and Gottlieb (1977) used 34 positive and negative adjectives in children's everyday lexicon to investigate differences in children's attitudes toward their handicapped peers. The Personal Attribute Inventory (Parish, Bryant, & Sherazi, 1976), which was derived from the ACL, has been used in a number of studies of the attitudes of respondents of various ages to types of handicapped people. Recently Williams (1986) used a modified adjective checklist procedure to investigate college students' perceptions of people who are mentally retarded. Goldstein and Blackman (1975) used an 84-item checklist, originally used to study attitudes toward ethnic groups, to study attitudes toward other devalued groups: the mentally retarded, the mentally ill, criminals, alcoholics, and the physically disabled. A review of research using adjective checklists is provided by Gottlieb, Corman, and Curci (1984).

Paired Comparison Scales

The method of paired comparisons requires that the researcher present the respondents with all possible pairs of items that the researcher wishes to scale. The respondents are asked to select the item in each pair that they would rate higher in terms of a criterion presented by the researcher. As opposed to the ranking or Q-sort methods discussed previously, the respondents are required to compare all items to each other and to state a preference. The resultant data are analyzed to yield an ordering of the items. Typically all possible pairs are presented twice, the second time in reverse order, to determine the consistency of the respondent's selections. Because the method requires a total of n times $(n-1)$ pairs, the method is usually reserved for a small sample of items.

Jones, Gottfried, and Owens (1966) presented 13 group labels (11 handicapped labels, plus "gifted," and "nonhandicapped") to high school students in order to scale their rankings in seven social situations (as a neighbor, as a visitor, etc.). Wicas and Carluccio (1971) investigated the attitudes of counselors toward the culturally different, ex-convict, and former mental patient by presenting these three group labels in a modified paired comparison arrangement in each of 25 situations (employability, trust, etc.). Janicki (1970) used 66 paired comparison dyads to investigate the attitudes of hospital employees to 12 disability groups.

Semantic Differential Scale

The semantic differential method was developed originally by L. L. Thurstone in the late 1920s but has come to be most closely associated with Osgood and his colleagues (Osgood, Suci, & Tannenbaum, 1957). In this method, a single concept (e.g., mental retardation) is presented on the top of a page anchored at each end by bipolar adjectives connected by a line marked in intervals, or by a series of blanks or boxes (generally seven blanks or boxes or points are used). Respondents are asked to check the box or mark the line at a point that represents their rating of the concept on each scale.

In Osgood's original work, three clusters of scales emerged regularly from analysis of an original set of 50 items. He termed these evaluative, potency, and activity scales. Other researchers, using different scales and different concepts, have derived dimensions in addition to the original three. The data obtained are the ratings of the concept on each scale, as well as the mean rating or the sum of the ratings of the concept on all of the scales. A respondent's scores can be analyzed to determine their relationship to respondent characteristics, or they can be compared before and after an intervention, or they can be compared across concepts. The scores of different groups of respondents to different concepts can also be compared.

Golin (1970) used 11 seven-point semantic differential scales to study the attitudes of respondents who were asked to read fictitious stories about disabled people. Other studies that used semantic differential ratings of groups of disabled people were conducted by Panda and Bartel (1972) and by Rapier, Adelson, Carey, and Croke (1972). Begab (1970) used the technique to measure the change in attitudes of students following training, Jaffee (1972) studied changes before and after team conferences concerning mentally retarded children, Sadlick and Penta (1975) studied changes in nurses' attitudes after training using television, and Stude (1973) studied changes in rehabilitation counselors' attitudes toward people with epilepsy following training.

Probabilistic Rating Scales

These rating scales require that the respondents indicate the strength of their agreement or disagreement with each item in a collection of items concerning the attitude referent. Because respondents are free to use any rating category as many times as they wish, the rating assigned to one statement theoretically does not have any influence on the respondents' ratings of any other statement. The ratings may be tallied to derive a frequency distribution for each item and a crude ordering of the items or respondents. To obtain more precision in the orderings, researchers assign numerical values to the points on the item response continuum and then calculate the median response of a set of respondents to each item. Because the rating scale data are ordinal data, the calculation and use of median index values is defensible. The calculation of a mean index value, however, requires interval data, which is clearly not the case. The precision obtained from interval data index values, and the statistical manipulations that can be performed on interval data, but not nominal (category) or ordinal (rank) data, led to a search for measuring methods that would yield interval data index values from rating scales.

Summated Rating Scales. In Likert's model (1932), the items that comprise the universe characterizing the attitude referent are assumed to be arrangeable on a monotonic continuum determined by the probability that a respondent who holds the attitude will endorse or agree with the item. The respondents are asked to indicate the extent of agreement with each item, and numerical weights are assigned to each response category (successive integers, typically 1 to 6, or − 3 to +3). The highest numerical value is usually reserved for the response category representing the strongest endorsement of the item. The score for each respondent is determined by summing the weighted responses to the items.

While many Likert-format scales have been used in research on attitudes toward disabled people, in most cases these scales are not summated rating scales. Although the items are in the appropriate form, they have not been rigorously selected according to Likert's procedure and may be of dubious quality. They do not provide the interval data required for the analyses subsequently performed by the researcher. The results of any study using a Likert-format scale for which item and scale development information is not provided should be treated with extreme caution. Perhaps the confusions and contradictions noted in the literature by reviewers such as Gottlieb (1975) may be explained by the failure of researchers to adhere to the psychometric requirements of summated rating scales.

The granddaddy of all summated rating scales is the Attitudes Toward Disabled Persons scale developed by Harold Yuker and his colleagues (Yuker, Block, & Campbell, 1960; Yuker, Block, & Younng, 1966/1970). (The 1960 publication used the singular "attitude," the 1966 publication used the plural "attitudes," while other publications use both. I choose to use the singular because Yuker argues that the scale is a unitary measure of attitude toward the disabled considered as a group.) Examples of other scales which have been carefully developed are the Scale of Attitudes Toward Disabled Persons (Antonak, 1981a, 1981b, 1982, 1985a, 1985b), and the Opinions About Mental Illness scale (Cohen & Struening, 1959, 1960).

Consensual Location Scaling. Basing his work on psychophysical methods, Thurstone (1928) sought a method of attitude scaling in which an index value could be assigned to any item characterizing the attitude referent. The respondent's attitude is estimated from the median of the index values of those items that he or she endorsed. This model assumes that the dispersion of responses to any item is normal and that the item's index value is the true index value for the item. The researcher constructs a scale by selecting a small number of items of suitable dispersions and index values, covering the continuum from complete agreement to complete disagreement.

Consensual location scaling requires that the researcher collect 100 to 150 items concerning the referent and submit them to a large number of judges (typically 100). Each judge is asked to sort the items into piles (typically 9 or 11) or to rate each of the items on a scale (of 9 or 11 points), representing the degree to which the item expresses favorability to the referent. Note that the judges are not asked to rate the items on the extent of their agreement with them. The dispersion of the judges' ratings is obtained, the median is calculated, and items (30 to 50) with values that cover the full continuum are selected for a second-stage analysis. The items are presented on a second scale to a second sample of judges, and the dispersion of their responses to the items is analyzed for consistency (minimum variability). Approximately 20 items are retained, with index values fairly equally spaced along the continuum (hence, the other name for the method, equal-appearing intervals) and randomly arranged on the final scale.

In 1970, Tringo combined the work of Bogardus (1932) with a new set of items expressing social distance from people who are disabled, analyzed the resultant data according to Thurstone's method, and created the nine-item Disability Social Distance Scale. Horne (1978), using Thurstone's method, created the Perceptions of Social Closeness Scale to measure pupil and teacher attitudes toward other class members. These scales have been used in a number of studies of attitudes toward different disability groups (e.g., Harasymiw, Horne, & Lewis, 1976; Hollinger & Jones, 1970; Rickard, Triandis, & Patterson, 1963). Other scales have been developed that did not use Thurstone's method and generally do not report the scale development and analysis data necessary to inspire confidence in their validity and usefulness. Many of these so-called social distance scales are essentially self-report questionnaires of dubious quality.

Deterministic Rating Scales

Some rating scales are based on a deterministic model in which it is assumed that the response to any item on the scale is completely determined by the latent attitude of the respondent. Hence, any respondent's attitude toward the referent can be measured by presenting a set of items of known index values to the respondent and locating the one item that he or she is willing to endorse. This method requires both the assumption of no error or inconsistency in responding and the assumption that a set of items of known index values can be written.

The most widely used deterministic scaling method is scalogram analysis (Guttman, 1944), used to determine whether a set of items comprise a unidimensional linear scale. Recently, Bart and his colleagues (Bart & Krus, 1973) have proposed a method of ordering-theoretic data analysis to generate multidimensional and nonlinear scales of items.

Guttman Scaling. The task for the researcher who wishes to use a Guttman scale to measure attitudes is to select items that, as a group, form a unidimensional continuum spanning the range of favorability to the attitude referent. Based upon a respondent's score on the scale, it will then be possible, with a perfect scale, to reconstruct the respondent's responses to each item. Endorsement of one item in the scale implies endorsement of all other items lower in the ordering; conversely, failure to endorse an item implies failure to endorse all items higher on the linear scale. The respondent's score (the number of items he or she endorses) is a measure of the respondent's attitude toward the referent. The researcher places the respondent on the continuum of favorableness to the attitude referent by determining where in the ordering of people the respondent falls. All people who present an identical endorsement pattern are considered to hold an identical attitude toward the referent.

A perfect scale is one in which all responses are completely predicted from the score. This is rarely found in practice because there are typically one or more endorsement patterns in which the stringent rule does not hold, so that the resultant ordering matrix of the items and people is inconsistent. A coefficient of reproducibility expresses the degree to which the scale items present perfect ordering. A coefficient of .85 or better is generally considered to indicate a satisfactory Guttman scale.

There are several limitations of Guttman scaling. For example, the coefficient of reproducibility may be adequate, but the unidimensionality of the items may be questionable. That is, the items may not be a homogeneous set of characteristics of the attitude referent. The construct validity of the scale must be carefully examined to determine if the items represent a homogeneous set of items. In addition, it is extremely unlikely that a researcher can obtain a reproducible scale with more than eight items (there are 40,320 possible different orderings of eight items, and over 1.3 trillion different orderings of 15 items!). Scalogram analysis has been extended to several dimensions (Lazarsfield & Henry, 1968; Lingoes, 1963); however, the constraints of a small item pool and a large sample, and the issue of what is an acceptable coefficient of reproducibility, still limit its use.

Few examples of Guttman scaling in research on attitudes in general, and research on attitudes toward disabled people in particular, are available. Several investigations have used the method to analyze data from Bogardus's social distance scale to study prejudice toward various groups (Triandis & Triandis, 1965). Cohen (1963) used the scalogram technique to investigate attitudes of employers toward hiring mentally retarded people. Yamamoto and Dizney (1967) constructed the Tolerance Scale to order respondents on a continuum of tolerance to different disability groups. Yamamoto and Wiersma (1967) later used this scale in a study of the relationship of self-concept to tolerance of disability.

Ordering Theory. Ordering theory is a deterministic measurement model that extends scalogram analysis to include nonlinear item orders in unidimensional as well as multidimensional configurations (Airasian & Bart, 1973; Bart & Krus, 1973; Krus & Bart, 1974; Krus, Bart, & Airasian, 1975). Using Boolean algebraic analysis methods (Krus, 1975, 1977), the ordering-theoretic analysis of bivalued response patterns identifies prerequisite relationships among a set of items.

To overcome the limitation, shared with other deterministic measurement models, of dealing with random error in the item-response patterns, ordering-theoretic data analysis identifies a prerequisite relationship between two items only if the frequency of disconfirmatory response patterns is less than or equal to the frequency of such response patterns established by an error tolerance level selected by the researcher. All possible 2×2 item response tables are constructed from the respondent data and examined to specify the relationships among the items. It should be noted that different item hierarchies are constructed for different tolerance levels. As the level approaches zero percent, fewer prerequisite relationships are found and the resultant hierarchical ordering becomes compressed into fewer dimensions.

An example of the use of ordering theory in attitude research is Antonak's (1979) ordering-theoretic analysis of data from the Attitude Toward Disabled Persons scale. The resultant hierarchical orderings were examined and insights were suggested for experiments concerning attitude formation and modification. In an investigation of the ordering of statements expressing attitudes toward the school integration and community integration of 11 groups of exceptionality and the normal, Antonak (1980) showed that attitudes toward the integration of disabled people are multidimensional and involve separate factors for different disability groups.

Ordering-theory can also be used to confirm a theory of attitude structure. A set of items is composed that are derived from the theory, and the presumed relationships among the items are specified. Respondent data are then examined to determine if the hypothesized hierarchical ordering can be established. Antonak (1985c) used ordering-theoretic data analysis as a follow-up to a multivariate statistical test of data from a questionnaire given to service providers. The research question was whether, as predicted from Finkelstein's (1980) conceptualization of the problems faced by people who are impaired, service providers endorse the premise that society contributes to the disablement of people with impairments. The resultant orderings showed the endorsement of the premise for different impairment groups. Ordering-theoretic methods can also be used to generate higher-ordered multidimensional scales from clusters of attitudes scales derived from factor analysis or latent partition analyses (Antonak, 1985b).

INDIRECT METHODS OF ATTITUDE MEASUREMENT

The direct methods of attitude measurement considered in the previous sections of this chapter are all subject to several threats to their validity. Direct measures may sensitize respondents to an attitude domain of which they have a nebulous view and, therefore, create nonexistent attitudes that the researcher interprets as significant in some way. Gottlieb and Siperstein (1976) discussed a related phenomenon in their study of the effects of attitude referent specificity on attitudes toward people who are mentally retarded.

Other potential weaknesses of direct methods of attitude measurement are the biasing influences of response sets. The respondent may show an acquiescent response set (Couch & Keniston, 1960) in which all the items are answered "agree" or "yes" (the "yeasayers") or all the items are answered "disagree" or "no" (the "naysayers"). Similarly, the respondent may endorse only those items on the attitude scale that he or she considers to represent the socially appropriate or sanctioned response, a tendency referred to as social desirability (Edwards, 1957). Or the respondent may only (or never) select the most extreme response alternatives (Nunnally, 1978).

To overcome these weaknesses, indirect measurement methods have been proposed to measure attitudes. Four methods will be examined in this section: projective techniques, disguised measures, behavioral observations, and physiological methods.

Projective Techniques

The literature on projective techniques in the measurement of personality, interests, and attitudes is vast. The common feature of these techniques is the presentation of an essentially unstructured task with vague or ambiguous stimuli and only brief instructions for responding. The assumption is that the way in which the respondent perceives and responds to the task stimuli will depend upon his or her inner feelings and emotions. The respondent "projects" his or her attitudes onto the attitude-measurement task, which the trained researcher can then interpret or score.

Projective techniques can be organized by the type of task stimuli that are presented or, alternatively, by the response that is required. Among the most widely known of these techniques are the verbal responses to inkblots, verbal or written responses to ambiguous pictures, word association or free association tests, sentence completion tests, drawings of common objects, and other expressive or dramatic products such as role-playing, psychodrama, and children's play with toys.

While projective techniques have been used for the investigation of the psychological aspects of disability and the personality functioning of disabled people (Plummer, 1976), their use for the measurement of attitudes toward disabled people is limited. An example is the research of Billings (1963), who used sentence completion and pictorial stimuli to investigate the attitudes of elementary school children toward physically handicapped children. Ford, Liske, and Ort (1962) used a sentence completion technique to study attitudes toward people with chronic illnesses. Moed, Wright, Feshbach, and Sandry (1963) developed a picture response projective test for their study of children's attitudes toward disability.

Disguised Measures

In disguised techniques the respondent is not aware of the true purpose of the investigation, or the respondent may actually be told that the purpose of the investigation is other than what it is. These techniques differ from the projective techniques because they have an inherent structure to the task. Some of these tasks present the respondent with no clear criterion for success or no clear purpose. For example, the respondent may be asked to sort a random sample of photographs of people into two groups, those who are liberals and those who are conservatives. Some of these photos may be of disabled people in various activities.

Other disguised techniques do present a clear criterion for success. For example, the respondent may be asked to select an answer from among three provided to a set of questions presented as a test of knowledge about some concept. In fact, all of the answers are wrong, but they are written by the researcher in such a way as to reflect varying degrees of favorableness or unfavorableness to the attitude referent. These so-called error-choice tests may include real items in order to disguise the nature of the investigation.

In a memory distortion procedure, the respondent is first shown a picture or asked to read a vignette and then asked to recall details or answer questions, some of which are about events that were not presented. For example, a picture of a classroom of children during free play may be shown to the respondent and the question may be asked, "What was the child in the wheelchair doing?" when there was no such child in the picture.

Although these disguised techniques appear to hold promise for research into attitudes toward disabled people, no studies using them were located in the research literature.

Behavioral Observations

The most direct operationalization of the respondent's attitude is the behavior that he or she displays in natural settings with reference to the attitude referent. Of course, it is true that all of the techniques presented so far are in fact samples of the respondent's behavior, albeit within the standardized conditions of the scale's administration.

Several studies using behavioral observations to measure attitude toward disabled people have used innovative research situations in natural settings. Pomazal and Clore (1973) placed a person with or without a knee brace and arm sling on the side of a highway next to a car jacked up with the spare tire laid out beside it. Similarly, a hitchhiker with and without a knee brace and arm sling was used as the attitude referent. Baker and Reitz (1978) used as a foil a person using the phone in their investigation of attitudes toward blindness. Willis, Feldman, and Ruble (1977) investigated experimentally the amount of money that children aged five and nine years donated to charities for disabled children and adults. Pancer, Adams, Mollard, Solsberg, and Tammen (1979) used a woman crossing the street with and without groceries, who was presumable physically handicapped or not. Carver, Glass, and Katz (1978) used the bogus pipeline technique (Jones & Sigall, 1971) to study attitudes toward handicapped people. Subjects are led to believe that they are being connected to a machine that measures physiologically the direction and intensity of attitudes toward the referent of a series of questions asked by the experimenter. In fact, it does no such thing. It is thought that respondents will give a more accurate self-report of their attitudes in this situation.

Other behavioral observation techniques include the study of written records (e.g., the voting records of local or state politicians on bills concerning the attitude referent), analyses of laws and public policies, reviews of media presentations, and naturalistic observations of behaviors in various settings (e.g., Gottlieb & Budoff, 1973).

Physiological Methods

Physiological methods purport to be beyond the control of the respondent; they measure some autonomic function of the respondent's body, such as skin conductance, heart rate, blood pressure, perspiration, pupil dilation, or voice pattern. For example, VanderKolk (1976a) studied vocal patterns and modulations using the Psychological Stress Evaluator to analyze respondents' recorded readings of a list of 11 impairments. Wesolowski and Deichmann (1980) used galvanic skin response and heart rate as measurement methods with groups of respondents who viewed vignettes of people who were disabled or nondisabled, and of neutral scenery.

In general, physiological measures propose an interesting line of inquiry, but their reliability has not been conclusively demonstrated, except perhaps in extreme cases. They should be considered as experimental methods until reliability and validity data can be accumulated.

SUMMARY

This chapter has presented a taxonomy of 14 methods for the measurement of attitudes toward disability and people who are disabled. Ten are direct methods and the remaining four are indirect methods. The discussion should assist the researcher in selecting an attitude-measurement method that can provide the data needed to answer the research question.

The concept of attitudes toward people who are disabled is complex, and the measurement of attitudes is not a simple task. Far too often researchers investigating attitudes have been responsible for perpetuating the myth that this area of research is simple. It is easy to create a useless instrument and to collect useless data. Nor is there any doubt that the report of such useless research can be published if the researcher looks hard enough for a publication source that looks the other way on issues of psychometric adequacy of the measurement instrument. Researchers in university settings must also share the criticism for instruments created by students pursuing graduate degrees.

The investigation of the formation, structure, correlates, and modification of attitudes toward disabled people requires measurement methods yielding psychometrically sound instruments that are reliable, valid, and multidimensional. Without such instruments, it will not be possible to obtain conclusive answers to important research questions concerning the relationship between these attitudes and the improvement of programs and services for the education, rehabilitation, and community integration of people who are disabled.

CHAPTER 10

Multidimensional Perspectives in the Perception of Disabilities

Liora Pedhazur Schmelkin

This chapter raises the question: What are the perceptions that people have of disabilities? Answers to this question will enable us to gain a better understanding of people's attitudes and resultant interactions (Jones, Farina, Hastorf, Markus, Miller, & Scott, 1984). The categories that are used with regard to disabilities and persons with disabilities, the stereotypes that are held, the organizational structure that governs perceptions will affect (and be affected by) such things as attitudes, behaviors, expectations, interactions, treatment, and attributions that are made. Additionally, the particular perceptions held by people with or without disabilities may have profound effects on the adjustment of those with disabilities (Bartel & Guskin, 1971; Bowe, 1978; Siller, 1976b; Wright, 1983). The presentation that follows first briefly defines what is meant here by perceptions. This is followed by an overview of traditional approaches to perceptions of disabilities. The final section presents a relatively newer methodology, multidimensional scaling, and summarizes some of the findings that have resulted from its use in the study of perceptions of disabilities.

PERCEPTIONS

Various theoretical frames of reference have been used in the study of perception. Orientations have differed, among other ways, in the scope of the stimuli studied, ranging from the very narrow, such as the perception of size or weight of objects, to the broader and more abstract stimuli of social perception. Furthermore, approaches have placed differential emphases on varying aspects of the perceptual process, some being concerned primarily with the objects of perception, the stimuli and their structure, while others have focused more on the perceiver and/or the situation. (For some representative presentations of perception in general, and social perception in particular, see Allport, 1955; Berkowitz, 1975; Bruner, 1964; Erdelyi, 1974; Haber, 1969, 1974; Postman, 1951; Schneider, Hastorf, & Ellsworth, 1979; Solso, 1973; Tagiuri, 1969; Warr & Knapper, 1968.)

> Perception is not a simple, iconic, direct apprehension of external reality, but a process involving the interpretation and encoding of information. We do not respond directly to the social, or even the external physical world, but to our image of it. This 'internal representation,' 'cognition map,' 'mental configuration,' or 'schema' includes the person . . . and the social structure (Coxon & Jones, 1978, p. 18).

In an attempt to simplify an otherwise overly complex world, individuals impose structure, stability, order, and meaning by actively attending to different aspects of stimuli, be they people, groups, objects, or events. This perceptual process relies heavily upon "the construction of a set of organized categories in terms of which stimulus imputs may be sorted, given identity, and given more elaborated, connotative meaning" (Bruner, 1964, p. 251). The perceived stimuli derive part of their meaning from the categories in which they are placed.

Individuals organize and categorize stimuli primarily on the basis of their perceived similarity on various dimensions. Categorization heightens the perception of similarity within categories and sharpens the perception of differences between categories. In a general sense, dimensions can be viewed as similar to factors in factor analysis, namely, the constructs, or "causes," that underlie the relations among a set of variables. More specifically, dimensions reflect the kind of criterial attributes and characteristics of the stimuli that people rely on when they make similarity judgments among stimuli.

When the objects of perception are social groups such as disability groups or ethnic groups the classification is based on internalized conceptions, or stereotypes, of these groups. Much has been written about stereotypes since Lippmann first introduced the term in 1922. Some of the issues that have been raised concerning stereotypes include whether or not they are (1) inherently bad, (2) essentially erroneous, (3) individual or consensual beliefs, (4) characteristics of groups or attributes that differentiate target groups from other groups, as well as (5) the functions they serve (for reviews and elaborations see Ashmore & Del Boca, 1981; Brigham, 1971; Cauthen, Robinson, & Krauss, 1971; Fishman, 1956; Hamilton, 1981; Vinacke, 1957).

Three major orientations have been used in the study of stereotypes: sociocultural, psychodynamic, and cognitive (Ashmore & Del Boca, 1981). The focus in this chapter is on the cognitive approach, which views stereotypes as "generalizations about social groups that are not necessarily any more or less accurate, biased, or logically faulty than are any other kinds of cognitive generalizations" (Taylor, 1981, p. 84). (For examples of the other two approaches within the disability literature, see Tringo, 1970 (sociocultural) and Siller, 1976b (psychodynamic).

Viewing stereotypes as cognitive generalizations that aid in the categorization process leads to the following question with regard to perceptions of disabilities: What organizing categories or dimensions are used in the perceptions of disabilities? This question is purposely stated in the plural form to highlight the fact that perception is multidimensional in nature and that, therefore, the methodology used needs to take this multidimensionality into account; this point is taken up again later in this chapter.

As an example of the multidimensional nature of perceptions of disabilities, consider the following six critical dimensions of stigma proposed by Jones and associates (1984) in a review of the research on social stigma in general (with primary emphasis on disabilities):

1. *Concealability.* Is the condition hidden or obvious? To what extent is its visibility controllable?
2. *Course.* What pattern of change over time is usually shown by the condition? What is the ultimate outcome?
3. *Disruptiveness.* Does it block or hamper interaction and communication?
4. *Aesthetic qualities.* To what extent does the mark make the possessor repellent, ugly, or upsetting?
5. *Origin.* Under what circumstances did the condition originate? Was anyone responsible for it, and what was he or she trying to do?
6. *Peril.* What kind of danger is posed by the mark and how imminent and serious is it? (p. 24).

In addition to these six major dimensions, Jones and associates propose that other dimensions (e.g., kind of mark, nature of interaction, varying areas of functioning, individual characteristics, situational circumstances) may play a role as well.

Perceptions, however, cannot be viewed in a vacuum. As in the remarks made by Yuker and others in this volume, there is the realization that perceptions and attitudes are dependent on a variety of things, including perceiver characteristics, stimulus characteristics, and the situation, context, or interaction within which they take place. Perception, in general, relies heavily on past experiences, language, present motivational states, values, needs, and goals for the future. The effects of past experiences on the perceptions of disabilities is an issue closely related to the effects of contact on attitudes toward persons with disabilities. While there are no clear-cut and definitive answers regarding this issue (see Yuker, Chapter 19 of this volume), with respect to perception, it seems reasonable to suggest that familiarity and contact lead to the use of more categories and, hence, greater complexity (Taylor, 1981). Speaking of the effect of experience on the perception of different groups, Berkowitz (1975) states:

> Obviously, the less experience people have with any given category, the broader and more diffuse it will be. Those persons who have little contact with, say, Jews or Africans, are not likely to make distinctions and erect subclasses within these particular categories. Everyone (or everything) belonging to these large classes will be regarded as being virtually alike. That is, the less familiar we are with a particular group and the less we know about it, the more likely we are to think about the group in terms of a simple social stereotype (p. 105).

TRADITIONAL APPROACHES TO THE STUDY OF PERCEPTIONS OF DISABILITIES

An examination of the literature dealing with disabilities reveals that there have been two basic approaches to the study of perceptions of disabilities. The first (and by far the most prevalent) approach has focused on only one or two disabilities at a time in order to try to arrive at the stereotype of a particular disability.

For example, a lot of work has been done in the area of mental retardation (Begab, 1970; Blatt, 1960; Clark, 1964; Edgerton, 1967; Gottlieb, 1975; Gottlieb & Corman, 1975; Gottwald, 1970; Greenbaum & Wang, 1965; Guskin, 1963b, 1963c; Hollinger & Jones, 1970; Siperstein & Gottlieb, 1977; Willey & McCandless, 1973). In general, the stereotypes of persons who are mentally retarded have been found to be mainly negative, particularly when contrasted with the stereotype of "normal." Among the aspects used in differentiating between individuals who are retarded and those who are not are cognitive capacity, social competence, and behavior; the cognitive capacity factor being perhaps the most important determiner of this differentiation. It should be noted that the term *disability* usually conjures up the image of physical handicaps. It is, therefore, not surprising that perceptions of mental retardation also include references to physical disabilities, despite the fact that children who are classified as educable mentally retarded (the largest group in terms of mental retardation) do not differ significantly in physical attributes from average children.

Research has also been directed at other disability groups, including blindness (Baker, 1974; Kang & Masoodi, 1977; Whiteman & Lukoff, 1962, 1965), deafness (Blood, Blood, & Danhauer, 1978; Horowitz & Rees, 1962), mental illness (Farina, Allen, & Saul, 1968; Farina & Ring, 1965; Farina, Thaw, Felner, & Hust, 1976), emotional disturbance and learning disability (Foster, Ysseldyke, & Reese, 1975; Ysseldyke & Foster, 1978). While this approach has contributed to our knowledge of the content of stereotypes of individual disabilities, one can only conjecture about any commonalities that may exist in the perceptions of varying disabilities.

The second major approach has attempted to study a wider group of disabilities. The majority of studies have focused primarily on attitudes rather than on perceptions or stereotypes *per se*. This state of affairs is reflective of the ambiguities and disagreements that exist in defining attitudes and perceptions. Some researchers view perception as the cognitive component of the tripartite definition (i.e., cognitive, affective, behavioral) of an attitude; some seem to imply that perception and attitudes are distinct, though related, constructs; others fail to address themselves to this issue.

Some conclusions as to organizing dimensions are possible. Representative of this approach are studies by Abroms and Kodera (1979); Antonak (1980); Badt (1957); Baker (1974); Grand, Bernier, and Strohmer (1982); Harasymiw, Horne, and Lewis (1976); Jones (1974); Jones and Gottfried (1962, 1966); Jones, Gottfried, and Owens (1966); Kingsley (1967); Kvaraceus (1956); MacDonald and Hall (1969); Panda and Bartel (1972); Semmel and Dickson (1966); Shears and Jensema (1969); and Tringo (1970). Some of the organizing or contrasting dimensions suggested by this line of research include: organic (stressing medical and physical), functional (psychoeducational, psychosocial), sensorimotor, visibility, interference in communication, social stigma, reversibility prognosis, extent of incapacity, difficulties in daily routine, normal versus exceptional.

By focusing on a large number of disabilities a more comprehensive picture of disabilities is possible. Still, most of the research has relied on relatively simplistic methodologies that obscure the complexity of the subject matter. The heavy reliance on unidimensional scaling approaches often leads to conclusions that the resulting perceptual structure is unidimensional. For example, studies (e.g., Badt, 1957; Tringo, 1970) that rely primarily on rank ordering techniques to create single hierarchies imply that the underlying structure (of social distance, of acceptance, etc.) is unidimensional. Yet that structure may result because the particular method forced *a priori* acceptance of unidimensionality.

An additional concern in both approaches involves the particular types of measuring instruments commonly used (e.g., adjective checklists, semantic differential; see Antonak, Chapter 9 in this volume, for a review). A major shortcoming is that they depend on the researchers' *a priori* conceptions of the relevant dimensions. For example, respondents are restricted to a preselected vocabulary when using adjective checklists and to a preselected set of scales in the use of the semantic differential. "Any stimulus dimension not represented in the scales will not emerge from the semantic differential analysis even though it is important for differentiating stimuli" (Cliff, 1973, p. 486).

In consequence it is not possible to determine what part of the perceptual structure is due to the respondents' perceptions and what is due to the constraints placed on them. Relevant to this issue is a study of stereotypes of ethnic groups (Ehrlich & Rinehart, 1965) in which responses to an adjective checklist were compared with responses to an open-ended format. The two formats produced different lists of traits. In addition, those responding to the adjective checklist assigned more traits to the various ethnic groups and exhibited greater consensus than did the respondents who used the open-ended format. It is evident, therefore, that the method used to elicit the responses affects the resulting pattern and structure. Because it is less constraining, the method of response elicitation in multidimensional scaling seems to be closer to "real-life" situations (Cliff & Young, 1968).

MULTIDIMENSIONAL SCALING

Multidimensional scaling (MDS) techniques are designed to explore the internal representation or psychological structure underlying a set of stimuli; to determine whether, in fact, that structure is unidimensional or multidimensional; and to discover the dimensions in as unconstrained a way as possible. Answers to two basic questions are sought:

1. How many dimensions best or most appropriately describe the perceptual space? The decision as to the appropriate number of dimensions depends on statistical, theoretical, and pragmatic considerations. In terms of perceptions of disabilities, how many dimensions are necessary to account for perceived similarity among the disabilities?

2. What is the nature of these dimensions? In other words, how are the organizing structures or contrasting categories to be interpreted? What are the major categories that are used in perceiving similarity among disabilities?

Methods of eliciting responses are designed to be as unconstraining as possible so as not to impose the researcher's conceptions on the subjects. For example, the simplest response method consists of pairing every stimulus with every other stimulus and asking subjects to rate each pair on a similarity scale. Subjects are told to use their own frame of reference in arriving at a similarity rating. The fundamental assumption underlying MDS is that judged similarity between pairs of stimuli is reflected by their proximity in the resulting configuration. An additional advantage is that the solutions that are retained as most appropriate can then be presented graphically, greatly enhancing the interpretations.

Numerous variations exist in MDS methodology aimed at, among other things, different approaches to obtaining the responses, different assumptions about the nature of the data, varying methods of analysis, individual differences approaches, and preference mapping approaches. (For discussions of various MDS methods, their assumptions, and representative applications, see Davison, 1983; Kruskal & Wish, 1978; Romney, Shepard, & Nerlove, 1972; Schiffman, Reynolds, & Young, 1981; Shepard, Romney & Nerlove, 1972.)

Applications of MDS to the study of perceptions of disabilities are a recent development; the majority of studies being conducted in the 1980s. Brief descriptions of most of these studies are presented below, followed by general conclusions. The study by Livneh (1983), using smallest-space analysis, a form of MDS, is not reviewed here since it deals more centrally with attitudes than with the cognitions that are of primary concern in this chapter.

The first use of MDS in this area was by Guskin (1963a), who presented subjects with all possible pairings of the following groups: normal or typical, feeble-minded, developmentally defective, educationally inadequate, autistic, emotionally disturbed, unpopular, delinquent, of low social class, physically handicapped. The MDS analysis revealed four dimensions underlying the judged similarity of the groups. The major dimension that emerged reflected a contrast between the normal and the deviant. The remaining dimensions described more specific contrasts of the various deviations, such as mentally versus socially deviant, threatening versus fearful, tough versus weak (physically).

Schmelkin conducted a series of studies aimed at investigating the perceptual structure of disabilities and the effects that various forms of presentation have on this structure. The first of these (Schmelkin, 1982) utilized 13 concepts as stimuli: behavior disorder, brain injury, communication disorder, emotional disturbance, exceptionality, health impairment, learning disability, mental retardation, multiple handicaps, normal, physical disability, slow learning, and social maladjustment. Two different forms consisting of all pairwise similarity ratings were constructed, one providing labels only, the other consisting of labels and definitions. Three groups of subjects were used—special educators, regular educators, and noneducators.

> The major finding was that the perception of disabilities was multidimensional, reflecting differentiations among behavioral-emotional, cognitive, and physical disabilities, as well as a generalized contrast between normal and disabilities. These important dimensions underlying perceptions of disabilities appeared in all the solutions. The nature of the specific contrasts between types of disabilities and/or the order of their importance, however, differed among the groups. At least two variables may have led to some of the differences among the groups. First, the perceptual spaces differed for groups with varying experience with the disabled. . . . Second, perceptions of disabilities were also dependent on the manner in which the stimuli were presented (i.e., defined versus undefined). [pp. 173–174]

Using a larger, more comprehensive stimulus set, Schmelkin (1985) asked respondents to sort 35 disability labels (e.g., cancer, mental illness, deafness, mental retardation, cerebral palsy) into as few or as many categories as they saw fit, depending on whether they thought the disabilities belonged together. As subjects were provided with no other frame of reference, this task closely parallels the implicit process of classification and categorization used when one is confronted with large numbers of varied stimuli. An MDS analysis yielded four dimensions: (1) physical disabilities, (2) behavioral-emotional versus cognitive disabilities, (3) specific versus diffuse disabilities, and (4) visibility.

Utilizing a different approach, Schmelkin (1983) presented subjects with 20 disability labels that they were to rate on each of 10 rating scales (mild disability/severe disability, dangerous/not dangerous, educable/not educable, no impairment in social relations/severe impairment in social relations, no intellectual impairment/severe intellectual impairment, visible/not visible, sick/healthy, segregated/integrated, no physical impairment/severe physical impairment, normal/abnormal). An MDS analysis that placed both disabilities and rating scales in the same perceptual space yielded three dimensions, which were interpreted as (1) physical, (2) severity, and (3) visibility.

Lieberman (1983) explored another aspect of the effect of differing stimulus presentation. She constructed four forms, each consisting of pairwise similarity ratings of 14 disability conditions. The forms differed in terms of how the information relevant to the disabilities was presented to subjects: (1) labels only, (2) unlabeled behavioral descriptions, (3) labels followed by behavioral descriptions, and (4) behavioral descriptions followed by labels. Results indicated that the solutions for all four treatments were three-dimensional in nature, although the particular dimensions differed. The greatest differences were found between the label-only group and the unlabeled-behavioral-descriptions group. Differences were also found between the labels-only group and each of the two groups that consisted of both labels and behavioral descriptions, although these differences were not as great as those between the labels-only group and the one that received unlabeled behavioral descriptions. It was concluded that some type of recency effect seems to be operating when labels are followed by descriptions.

Exploring the effects of familiarity and contact on the perceptions of disabilities, Garvar (1986) presented 30 disabilities to four groups: regular class teachers, special-education teachers, principals, and special-education administrators. Participants were asked to sort the disabilities, according to instructions similar to Schmelkin (1985). While it was concluded the separate MDS solutions were most appropriate, some commonalities in specific dimensions were evident across the four groups (e.g., each solution consisted of a dimension contrasting disabilities that are perceived to be physical in nature with the remaining disabilities).

Britton (1983) utilized multidimensional preference mapping to investigate 11 disabilities in terms of their ability to be mainstreamed. First the disabilities were scaled in terms of how suitable each was for mainstreaming; learning disabilities were considered the easiest to mainstream and autism the most difficult. Then the dimensions underlying the mainstreamability of these disabilities were explored yielding two dimensions: severe–mild and physical–mental.

Using MDS in a reanalysis of Tringo's (1970) hierarchy of social distance preference toward 21 disabled groups, Schmelkin (1984) concluded that the structure underlying these preferences was multidimensional. The three dimensions focused on the visibility of the disabilities, the organic versus functional nature of the disabilities, and an element of ostracism.

Rounds and Neubauer (1986) explored the perceptions of disabilities of rehabilitation counselors using pairwise similarity ratings of 12 disabilities. An MDS analysis yielded three dimensions, which were interpreted, with the aid of external analyses, as normality, severity, and controllability. Embedded in the normality dimension is a contrast between psychodevelopmental disabilities at one end and physical disabilities at the other. Additionally, the severity dimension seems to highlight terminal versus sensory/motor disabilities.

CONCLUSIONS

The research reviewed above highlights the multidimensional nature of perceptions of disabilities. While differences are evident in the specific nature of the various dimensions found by the differing studies, there is a great deal of commonality in the major dimensions that appear to exist. A cataloguing of the different dimensions reported indicates that four organizing structures appear consistently across much of the research:

1. *Physical.* The most prevalent dimension emerging appears to be some type of emphasis on the physical nature of the disability or a contrast between those disabilities that are considered physical in nature and other types of disabilities (e.g., cognitive impairments). This type of dimension was cited by Guskin (1963a), Schmelkin (1982, 1983, 1984, 1985), Lieberman (1983), Britton (1983), and Garvar (1986), and alluded to by Rounds and Newbauer (1986).

2. *Cognitive.* A cognitive dimension either contrasting cognitive impairments to their absence or contrasting cognitive impairments to some other type of impairments (e.g., physical versus cognitive) was reported by Guskin (1963a), Schmelkin (1982, 1985), Lieberman (1983), Britton (1983), and Garvar (1986).

3. *Behavioral-Emotional.* This third type of contrasting dimension, highlighting behavioral-emotional disorders, was found by Guskin (1963a), Schmelkin (1982, 1985), Lieberman (1983), and Garvar (1986).

4. *Normality.* In addition to the above three dimensions emphasizing a particular type of disability, a dimension highlighting some aspect of "normality" or lack of deviance or disabling condition was reported by Guskin (1963a), Schmelkin (1982), Lieberman (1983), and Rounds and Neubauer (1986).

Other dimensions emerged with less frequency. These include: visibility (Schmelkin, 1983, 1984, 1985); severity (Britton, 1983; Rounds & Neubauer, 1986; Schmelkin, 1983); specific–diffuse (Garvar, 1986; Schmelkin, 1985); sensory impairments (Garvar, 1986; Lieberman, 1983; Rounds & Neubauer, 1986); communication disorders (Garvar, 1986); and controllability (Rounds & Neubauer, 1986).

All of the above dimensions are consistent with those suggested by the more traditional approaches reviewed earlier. The dominant differences are (1) an overt recognition that perception is multidimensional and (2) a methodology that enables one to obtain these dimensions from a more direct appraisal of subjects' responses rather than from a primary reliance on researchers' preconceptions.

Two types of variables appear to account for some of the differences that are evident among the various research studies using MDS. The first relates to the way the stimuli are presented to subjects, with emerging differences dependent on whether the stimuli are defined versus undefined (Schmelkin, 1982) or presented with behavioral descriptions versus without them

(Lieberman, 1983). Additionally, the emerging perceptual space is somewhat dependent on the particular stimuli that are included within the set, with larger, more comprehensive data sets yielding distinctions that would not necessarily be evident with a smaller set of stimuli. These presentation effects have implications for various intervention strategies. If we accept the premise that perceptions will affect attitudes, expectations, and behaviors, then different perceptual sets may have differential effects that need to be explored.

A second important variable appears to be familiarity and contact, with differences apparent in the cognitive maps of groups with varying degrees of knowledge and experience with persons with disabilities (Garvar, 1986; Schmelkin, 1982). As a general conclusion, it seems that contact with persons with disabilities increases cognitive complexity in the perceptions of disabilities.

Applications of multidimensional scaling methods to the study of perceptions of disabilities have demonstrated the utility of these techniques. Many questions remain unanswered, however, and deserve continued research efforts. Most of the research to date has been within the educational realm, using as subjects teachers and others involved in education. While the continued study of teachers is warranted because of the important role they play in educating and interacting with all individuals (those with and without disabilities), other subject groups need to be researched as well. Various MDS approaches could be easily adapted for use with children, enabling researchers to examine perceptions of disabilities developmentally. MDS can also be applied to various sociometric studies that attempt to examine group structure. Additionally, the perceptual structure of persons with disabilities has not received any attention. Finally, individual differences in perception need to be explored more fully and related to attitudes and behaviors.

PART IV
Attitudes of and Toward Specific Groups

CHAPTER 11
Another Perspective: Attitudes of People with Disabilities

Nancy Weinberg

The general public tends to believe that people with disabilities have suffered a terrible tragedy and are forever bitter about their misfortune (Weinberg, 1976; Wright, 1983). How accurate are these perceptions? Do people with disabilities feel they have suffered a great tragedy, and are they continually bitter about it? The purpose of this chapter is to review several studies that have examined how people with disabilities feel about their lives and about being physically disabled.

HAPPINESS AND LIFE SATISFACTION

The first major study to examine how people felt about their lives as disabled individuals was done by Cameron, Titus, Kostin, and Kostin (1973). These researchers asked 145 physically disabled individuals (64 with paralysis, 37 with muscular difficulty, 16 with a deformed limb, 12 with a missing limb, 11 with visual impairments, and 4 with hearing impairments) and a similar number of nondisabled individuals of the same sex, age, and status (i.e., hospital inpatient or college student) to rate their life satisfaction, frustration with life, difficulty of life, and happiness. No differences were found between the two groups on their ratings of satisfaction, frustration, or happiness. The only difference was found on ratings of the difficulty of life. People with disabilities judged their lives to be more difficult and more likely to stay that way. However, the degree of difficulty, in and of itself, did not increase their feelings of frustration with life or lower their feelings of satisfaction or happiness.

A more recent study by Freedman (1978) focused specifically on the relationship of health and happiness. Based on data from over 90,000 mail-in questionnaires and over 9,500 one- to two-hour interviews, he concluded that although we think of good health as a prerequisite to happiness, the relationship between health and happiness is rather weak and shows up mainly in extreme cases, when someone is critically ill. It appeared to Freedman that it is only at the stage when poor health becomes associated with death or fear of death that it makes happiness difficult or impossible.

In fact, Freedman found that many people with chronic, but not fatal, health problems not only seem to be quite happy, but even seem to derive some happiness from their ability to cope with their difficulty. As an example he cited the case of a woman with kidney disease. She reported, "Naturally, it makes many things in life very hard and interferes with lots of activities. Suffice it to say that I'm quite pleased with my ability to cope with this health problem and lead a worthwhile and happy life in spite of it or perhaps partly because of it" (Freedman, 1978, p. 122). At age 19, this woman was living with a boyfriend, was a graduate student in psychology, was happy with her friends, and was optimistic about the future. Her kidney problem had made her childhood very difficult, but now she was managing to cope with it.

The findings of both of these studies suggest that we need to question the assumption that physical limitations are directly related to happiness. Instead, it may be that many people with disabilities find happiness despite their disabilities, even though the able-bodied public would not always expect this.

THE WISH QUESTION

In our first study in this area (Weinberg & Williams, 1978) we focused on how people with disabilities felt about their condition. Judy Williams and I asked 88 persons with various physical disabilities (spinal-cord injuries, cerebral palsy, muscular dystrophy, multiple sclerosis, visual impairments, and auditory impairments)—all attendees at the Illinois White House Conference on the Handicapped—to fill out a survey. One item on the survey asked: "If you were given one wish, would you wish that you were no longer disabled?" We asked this question because we assumed that if disability is viewed as a tragedy, and if people with disabilities are unhappy about their condition, they would wish to be able-bodied. Our results went counter to this expectation. Only 43 people (49%) said they would use their wish to remove their disability; the remaining 45 people (51%) said they would not use their wish to remove their disability. Thus half of the sample did not feel that their life was so difficult or unhappy that they would use their wish to become able-bodied.

Another item on the survey asked respondents if they thought of their disability as: (1) a fact of life, (2) an inconvenience, (3) a cause of frustration, (4) a terrible thing that happened to them, or (5) the worst thing that ever happened to them. Respondents could check as many of these choices as they thought applied to them. In response to this item 53 people (60%) indicated that they thought of their disability as a fact of life, 44 people (50%) thought of their disability as an inconvenience, and 17 people (19%) said their disability was a cause of frustration. Only 10 of the respondents (11%) viewed their disability as a terrible thing that happened to them, and only 7 (8%) saw it as the worst thing that ever happened to them. Thus, again counter to society's perception, only a small percentage of our sample thought of their disabilities in extreme or tragic terms, as either a terrible thing or the worst thing that had ever happened to them.

When we informally shared the findings of this study with able-bodied individuals, they did not believe that people with disabilities would not prefer to be able-bodied. Surely, they argued, nearly all people with disabilities, if actually given the chance, would choose to be able-bodied. Those who responded otherwise are being defensive or do not wish to be pitied. They just want to convince others, and perhaps themselves, that they are not defeated by their disabilities. Others who found the results hard to believe suggested that only half the people would use their wish to become able-bodied because they were saving their one wish for other things, such as health for another family member or for greater personal wealth.

THE WISH QUESTION REEXAMINED

Since all of these were plausible alternative explanations, we decided to conduct another study. In this new study we offered the disabled person only the opportunity to be able-bodied; we did not offer them a free wish. Furthermore, we tried to find out why some people with disabilities apparently would want to remain disabled when they could become able-bodied. In other words, we wanted to discover the reasons they would give to justify such a choice. Did they have reasons for wanting to be disabled, or was their rejection of the idea of becoming able-bodied a defensive reaction or a dishonest response?

The sample for this research included 30 adults with physical disabilities, 19 females and 11 males (Weinberg, 1984). Twenty-three members of the sample were orthopedically disabled (8 had cerebral palsy, 8 had spinal-cord injuries, 3 had congenital limb deficiencies, 1 had spinal muscular dystrophy, and 3 had polio), 2 were deaf, and 5 had severe visual impairments. The sample was obtained in the following manner. The author knew 11 of the respondents through her work at the University of Illinois. These 11 interviewees nominated other persons with disabilities who could be interviewed. All of the people approached for an interview were willing to participate.

The procedure involved intensive interviews that lasted from two to 16 hours and took place over two to six sessions. The interview was semistructured, with interviewees responding to questions on a wide variety of topics. It included the following question: "If there were a surgery available that was guaranteed to completely cure your disability (with no risk) would you be willing to undergo the surgery?" After interviewees responded, they were asked why they answered as they did. The interviews were tape-recorded, transcribed, and data were coded from the transcripts.

In analyzing the data, we found that the 22 individuals who had been disabled from birth or by age seven responded differently from the eight persons who had been disabled later in life. Information provided by persons congenitally disabled or disabled by age seven will be discussed first.

GOALS

Fifty percent of the persons disabled early in life said they would choose the surgery, while the other fifty percent would not. These results thus replicated the findings of our previous study.

Why would some choose the surgery while others would not? The 50% who would opt for surgery did so because they felt that their disability substantially interfered with their achieving desired goals. For example, Richard, who has cerebral palsy, longs for a sexual relationship, a desire he feels is out of reach because of his disability. Another respondent, Lois, whose job involves the supervision of teachers, said that her inability to observe classrooms on the second floor of her school building is an obstacle in her effectively carrying out her present position as well as a hindrance to her chances for promotion.

In contrast, the 50% who would not want surgery felt that they could reach satisfying goals without it. On the whole, those who would not want a cure were not achieving more things than those who would wish to be cured, but they were more satisfied with what they were achieving. For example, two women we interviewed both used wheelchairs to get around and had similar life situations. Both were college-educated, both were single and lived alone in their own apartments, both drove their own cars, and both had steady, fairly well paying jobs. Yet one woman was satisfied with her life and would not want the surgery, and the other was dissatisfied and would opt for the cure. The first was delighted that she had achieved so many of her goals, while the other was disappointed because she had hoped to be further ahead in her job, to have married, and to have had children.

What distinguished these women had nothing to do with either their disabilities or with what each was able to achieve. What distinguished them was how they construed their situations—what they set as their goals and whether they considered themselves capable of reaching these goals. This is no different from one middle-class family that is discontent because they are unable to be upper class, while another middle-class family is delighted to be economically secure.

PERSONAL IDENTITIES

Along with achieving valued goals, those who would not choose to be able-bodied liked their personal identity. Indeed, a primary factor in their hypothetical decision against surgery was fear that they would no longer be the same person. Those who were congenitally disabled noted that this was the body they were born with, grew up with, and could cope with. No longer being disabled would mean becoming a new person, and they did not want to lose the person that they now were. Even those who were injured in childhood thought it would be strange to be no longer disabled. The disability had denied them many things, but it had also given them the opportunity to become who they now were. Changing bodies, they feared, might change their present identity, a thing they did not wish to do.

In expressing his hesitancy to undergo the hypothetical curative surgery, Bill, who has severe cerebral palsy, noted "I am psychologically adjusted rather than resigned. I have established my own values and identity with respect to effectively interacting with society and would not want this disrupted." Another respondent simply noted, "I am unique, I don't want to change that."

Naturally, our data do not indicate what people would do if they were actually given the opportunity to be cured. However, there were real-life instances we learned of, when individuals did not try to be as able-bodied as they could be. Jill provided a good example of this. In her case, even her physicians and parents underestimated her ability to accept, cope with, and develop a positive feeling about her disability.

Jill was born with no legs and only one arm, which ended at the elbow. As a child she was forced by her parents to wear prosthetic arms and legs. Doctors assured her that she would get used to wearing them; all she needed was to develop the habit. Physical therapists worked intensively with Jill to teach her to use the devices. By Jill's evaluation she was quite proficient in using the prosthetic arms, and although she could not walk very well on her prosthetic legs, they served an aesthetic function while she was in her wheelchair.

Jill's doctors and parents assumed that it was best for her to appear and to function as much like an able-bodied person as she could. Yet Jill was continually resistant to using her artificial limbs. Her parents decided that at age 16 she could decide for herself what to do; as soon as she was of age, Jill rejected the use of her artificial limbs and faced the world with only one limb, an arm that ended at the elbow with a protruding thumb.

Jill regrets that during her first 16 years, despite her requests, no efforts were made to teach her to do things with the physical resources that she did possess. It was only at 16, when she went, as she described it, "natural," that she could prevail upon medical staff to help her. Other people, she felt, viewed her as only part of a person and wanted to make her whole. But from her perspective, she was already whole. Having artificial limbs made her feel like an octopus. She was satisfied with herself, with her identity, and with her body just as it was.

Finally, in addition to the disabilities' being part of their personal identities and compatible with their achieving desired goals, some who rejected hypothetical cures thought of their disabilities as an integral part of their social identities. Three people were married to disabled persons and felt that alterations in their physical states might disrupt their relationships. Others had disabled friends or were part of organizations for the disabled and were apprehensive that if they were no longer disabled this might disturb the harmony that now existed in their social activities.

NEW VERSUS OLD GOALS AND IDENTITIES

The data from the eight people who had been injured either during late adolescence or during adulthood were different from those who had been disabled early in life. First, all these individuals reported that if they had been offered a curative surgery when they were newly disabled, they definitely would have taken it. Many had, in fact, undergone procedures with relatively high risks and few guarantees in hopes of regaining whatever functioning they could. During this early period they were willing to try anything to become able-bodied once again.

Now, at least six years since their injury, a more varied response was found. Three of the traumatically injured individuals were still actively looking for a cure and instantly said "yes," they would take it. Two others said "no" to the hypothetical surgery. The remaining three were undecided. The three who would want the surgery were unhappy with their current lives and felt that only if they were once again able-bodied could they do what they wanted to do. The two who would not want the surgery felt they had benefited from the injury in terms of personal growth and maturity; they would not want to risk losing their improved selves by becoming physically able.

The remaining three who could not give a definite "yes" or "no" said their decision would be dependent on additional information. For them the surgery would have to meet certain requirements before it would be acceptable. For example, they wanted to know how long the procedure would take. Specifically, how long would they need to be hospitalized, and how long would it take them to recuperate from surgery? In addition, they wanted to know how much time they would have to spend in physical therapy. Financial considerations were also raised. How much would the operation cost? Would their insurance pay for the surgery or would they have to pay the bill? It became clear that they were weighing their desire to be no longer physically disabled against other goals they had. One person indicated that she would be willing to pay as much for an operation as she would to buy a new car. If it cost much more than this, she thought it would not be worth it; she could spend the money on other things she wanted.

Money, time, and energy were all important considerations for those who were undecided because they had already spent a long time being operated on and being rehabilitated. Now they had other things they were trying to accomplish. Establishing a marriage, having children, finishing their education, or working at a job were their current goals, and they were not willing to see these objectives interfered with too radically. In general, these respondents were making progress toward or had already established a satisfying lifestyle, and maintaining or advancing their present life was as important or more important than the goal of becoming once again able-bodied.

Thus it appears that a number of people with disabilities had specific reasons for preferring to remain disabled. They felt they had been able to achieve important objectives, and they wanted to preserve their current lifestyle and their current personal and social identity.

ATTITUDES TOWARD DISABILITY

In a third study we tried to more specifically define and label the types of attitudes people have about their disabilities. In this study data obtained from three different sources were combined, including (1) additional material collected as part of the 30 personal interviews that were discussed in the previous section, (2) published autobiographies by people with disabilities, and (3) published essays by and interviews with people with disabilities. Multiple data sources were used so that the views of a large number of people with disabilities could be sampled.

To obtain the autobiographical data my research assistants and I read and analyzed for content autobiographies by disabled authors. The idea for using autobiographies as a source of data came from the work of Wright (1960). Since there is not a single listing of autobiographies by people with disabilities, in order to identify such autobiographies we surveyed numerous information sources, including: (1) *Subject Guide to Books in Print* (New York: R. R. Bowker Co., 1948 through 1981); (2) *Biographical Books* (New York: R. R. Bowker Co., 1950 through 1980); (3) *Cumulative Book Index* (New York: H. W. Wilson Co., 1957 through 1980); (4) Kaplan, L., *A Bibliography of American Autobiographies* (Madison: University of Wisconsin Press, 1961); and (5) *Library of Congress Catalogs* (subject catalogue, 1950 through 1960).

Next, we searched card-catalogue entries in the public libraries of Seattle, Los Angeles, Chicago, New York, Champaign–Urbana, Santa Monica and in the libraries of the University of Illinois at Urbana–Champaign and the University of California at Los Angeles. Librarians in the following specialized libraries and information centers also conducted searches for us: the National Rehabilitation Information Center, the National Library Service for the Blind and Physically Handicapped, the Illinois Regional Library for the Blind and Physically Handicapped, the Washington State Regional Library for the Blind and Physically Handicapped, and the Library of Congress.

Through these methods we identified 121 autobiographies, which we read and analyzed. A listing of these autobiographies is available from the author. Fifty-three authors were female and 68 male. With respect to disability, one author had a facial scar, 36 had visual impairments, 7 had auditory impairments, and the remaining 77 had orthopedic disabilities (21 had cerebral palsy, 14 had spinal cord injuries, 13 had limb amputations, 17 had polio, and 12 had other conditions such as muscular dystrophy, arthritis, or osteogenesis imperfecta). In the autobiographies we took note of any comments that revealed how the individuals felt about being disabled and how they felt they had coped with their disabilities.

Our third data source was published essays by, or published interviews with, people with disabilities. These were located in periodicals and in volumes edited by Brightman (1984), Cassie (1984), Corbet (1980), Henrich (1961), and Hunt (1966). Through this third source, information was gathered on 77 males and 45 females, including six with cosmetic disorders, 11 with hearing impairments, 13 with visual impairments, and the rest with orthopedic disabilities (51 with spinal-cord injury, 11 with cerebral palsy, two with spina bifida, one with osteogenesis imperfecta, four with amputations, four with multiple sclerosis, three with muscular dystrophy, 11 with polio, three with arthritis, two with other orthopedic disabilities.) In these sources we again looked for material that indicated how the individual felt about being disabled and how he or she adapted to his or her condition.

Combining the findings from these three sources the following results emerged. People's feelings about being disabled varied along a continuum. At one end were people who were very bitter about being disabled and continually regretted that they were not able-bodied. In the middle were a number (the largest number) of people with disabilities who neither liked nor despised their condition but simply accepted it as a condition of life that they had to live with. At the other end were people who enjoyed being disabled and embraced their disabilities.

Although these groups represented three distinct points along a continuum, people could be placed all along the length of the continuum. Furthermore, a person's place on the continuum did not appear to be fixed. During some phases of life a person could feel very positively about his or her disability and at other times, quite negatively. On the whole, it appears from our data that attitudes go from one extreme to the other, with the middle ground being most densely inhabited.

FOREVER BITTER AND UNHAPPY

The first group, as noted, felt very bitter. This group fit with the way society believes most people with disabilities feel. They believed that disability was the worst thing that had happened to them, and they were bitter. The feelings of the people in this group were epitomized by the statement of one traumatically injured interviewee, "I was very bitter and I still am." People with this attitude saw their disability as a tragedy. They were continually bothered by the extent of their limitations, which they felt prevented them from doing the things they wanted to do.

Author Bill Kiser (1974) has cerebral palsy and seems to feel this way. During the lifetime discussed in his book, he was never able to live on his own, never able to marry, and never able to get steady employment. Although he actively worked at each of these goals, he never met his objectives. In his autobiography he describes his ongoing unhappiness:

> I am angry—no, damned mad—most of the time every day. This should not have happened to me—there is no reason, no fairness to the way I am. I have to accept my condition, but nobody's going to make me like it. I hate it, and much of the time I hate everyone: those more fortunate than me, because they are, and those as badly or worse off, because they remind me of my own

state. I am no cheerful Tiny Tim, with a sweet nature developed by affliction, I am bathed in anger almost always. Don't worry, I won't leap out of my wheelchair and run amok. If I could, I wouldn't need to be angry (Kiser, 1974, p. 204).

RESIGNED AND ADAPTING

In contrast to these individuals, people in the middle group viewed their disabilities as facts of life without feeling either excessive bitterness or special joy. The disability was perceived as an inconvenience that could usually be mastered. Occasionally they did become bitter, but this was an infrequent rather than an everyday occurrence. Their anguish was sparked when the disability directly or indirectly blocked a goal. One man with cerebral palsy expressed it in this manner, "Though 98 percent of the time I view my 'handicap' as an 'inconvenience' and seldom allow it to stop me from doing what I want to do or going wherever it is important for me to go, 2 percent of the time I think it's a fucking drag!" (Brightman, 1984, p. 37).

The people in this group generally felt that disability was a limitation that needed to be coped with, just like other limitations. In essence, they perceived living with a disability as no different from living with other types of human deficiencies. They often pointed to similarities between their lives and the lives of other people. One person we interviewed put it this way:

I realize, as perhaps no one else does, that I may never be able to do many things I should like to do, but in that predicament I would seem to be a member of the majority of people and my disability thus becomes something of a symbol of normality.

A similar response came from a university student we interviewed who had had polio as a child. It had left him paralyzed from the waist down and with limited upper-body movement. When asked what being disabled meant to him, he emphasized that he was not basically different; that he had all the restrictions of life that plague nondisabled persons, complicated by some special ones. Not being able to do certain things, he felt, was the same for him as for others. Imagine, he said,

that everybody is going to go ice skating and you are not so hot on ice skates. So you don't go. Everyone goes out and ice skates and you are there all by yourself, and it kind of depresses you because you can't ice skate. But it is not an overwhelming thing. It is like, if you had money, you could go on a trip to Florida or the Bahamas, but you don't, so you can't do it, but you will get over it.

EMBRACING THE DISABILITY

At the far end of the continuum was the third group, which consisted of individuals with attitudes many people might find startling. Here we found a group that most people do not realize exists. Here were people who embraced their disability. Carolyn Vash, a psychologist who is orthopedically disabled, first recognized this group in her book, *The Psychology of Disability* (1981). She noted that people in this group recognize that without their disability they would be different from what they are, and they have no desire to be different. They have an appreciation that disability, like all other life experiences, can be construed as an opportunity or gift that has positive features.

Some people who embraced their disability saw the disability as a challenge, and meeting that challenge provided them with an extra feeling of satisfaction and confidence. Others who embraced their disability believed the uniqueness of the disability allowed them to do things that would not have been possible if they were able-bodied. For both types the disability was not struggled against, but instead experienced with positive regard.

Since this particular attitude has not been given much attention I would like to give three examples of people who appear to embrace their disabilities. The first of these is Joni Eareckson (1976). On a hot July day, Joni, aged 17, dove into the murky waters of Chesapeake Bay. Her head struck something hard and unyielding, and her body sprawled out of control. She had broken her neck and severed her spinal cord. For many bitter months she struggled to accept and to adjust to being a quadriplegic. During this time she was very bitter and very angry. But, finally, she did adjust.

In fact, as time went by Joni came to see her disability as a special gift from God and as something she felt positively about. She felt so positively that when a teenage girl asked her if she was happy, Joni replied that she was very happy and she would not change her life for anything. She felt privileged that God had intervened in her life and helped her to see what was really important. Joni came to embrace her disability because it had a special spiritual meaning for her. Although Joni embraced her disability for religious reasons, we found that others embraced their disabilities for other reasons.

The second example is Kitty O'Neal, who is deaf but is also a Hollywood stuntwoman. She has drowned, caught on fire, and had a car careen over her head. She has made frequent appearances on such TV series as "Baretta" and "Police Woman." Kitty has been totally deaf since infancy. She learned to lip read and speak from her mother, a Cherokee Indian, who was instrumental in founding the School of Listening Eyes in Texas. When asked if her deafness ever caused any problems, she answered, "No, it helps a lot. It really gives a lot of advantage because I have the power of concentration. I'm happy to be deaf. Being deaf is not a handicap. Rather, it is a challenge to conquer, like being called on to do a difficult stunt" (*Accent on Living*, Summer, 1980, p. 440).

A final example of an individual who appears to embrace his disability is Michael Petruciani, who was born with osteogenesis imperfecta, a disease marked by a calcium deficiency that makes bones brittle and retards growth. When Michael was growing up, his bones were so fragile that he had 160 fractures. In recent years Michael has had fewer fractures because his bones have stabilized. The disease, however, has left a visible mark: he weighs about 50 pounds and is about 3 feet tall (McMurran, 1985, p. 113).

Michael has gained recognition as a jazz piano virtuoso. His philosophy is to never let anything stop him from doing what he wants to do. Unfulfilled wishes spur him on. Michael says "I would like to write a symphony and make music for films. . . . As a child my dream was to become who I am now. Sometimes I think someone upstairs saved me from being ordinary" (McMurran, 1985, p. 113).

In sum, it appears that persons in this group are satisfied with who they are and are able to reach their life goals despite or even because of their disabilities. They are happy just the way they are. While society tends to view disability as a continuing tragedy, we found that attitudes of disabled persons seem to be the same as those of any group of individuals who try to adapt to a difficult situation. As in any other instances of difficult conditions, a few people view it very negatively, a few find something positive in it, and the majority fall in between.

IT'S NOT THE WORST THING THAT EVER HAPPENED

This idea—that people with disabilities perceive their situations in much the same way as anyone else with a crisis would—may be difficult for the majority of able-bodied people to accept. Adjusting to a physical disability is typically seen as the hardest adjustment a person would ever be called on to make. People have been known to say, "I would rather die than be blind, or paralyzed, or grossly disfigured." People do not usually say, "I would rather die than be poor, or lonely, or depressed." However, many people with disabilities who have adjusted to their situation feel that a physical disability is not the worst thing that can happen to a person.

It was noteworthy that some of the individuals we interviewed and read about pointed out that disability was neither their biggest problem nor the most traumatic thing that had ever happened to them. Within their own lives, worse things had sometimes happened. One woman who felt this way has a spinal-cord injury and uses a wheelchair; she is married to a man who also has a spinal-cord injury and uses a wheelchair. She and her husband have been married 14 years, but a few years ago they separated for 16 months, subsequently getting back together. According to the wife, the emotional trauma and the pain of the marital breakup and separation was far worse than breaking her neck or anything else she had had to live through because of her disability (Corbet, 1980).

Another individual, who had been blind from birth, reported a similar type of feeling. The most difficult part of her life had come when her husband requested a divorce while she was pregnant with their third child. As outsiders, we expect people to be able to adapt to divorce crises more easily than to visual limitations and spinal-cord injuries. However, from the insider's point of view it may be quite different.

Finally, Jim provides a dramatic example of a more difficult adjustment. He had served in Vietnam and had returned physically unharmed. After being home a short while, he was blinded in a chemical explosion on his family's farm. He had to learn new ways of coping. He learned to read using braille, learned to type using a braille typewriter, and learned to move about with the help of a cane. He adjusted his social life and his self-image. All of these were major adjustments. Yet from Jim's perspective they were not the hardest adjustments he had to make in his life. His most difficult adjustment by far, according to him, has been to his war experiences. All loud noises still bother him, and he still wakes up in the middle of the night from nightmares about the war. Comparing Vietnam and blindness, he believes that blindness was the easier experience to adjust to.

Thus it may be most appropriate to see disability as a difficulty that imposes limits and problems in much the same say that other facets of life impose difficulties. Life has elements of a struggle for everyone, and the struggle of the disabled person is not so different from the struggle of others. Disability is a problem and a difficulty, but it is not the only one. Furthermore, people with disabilities, like those who are nondisabled, have the full range of ways of seeing their situation and adapting to it.

CHAPTER 12

Teacher Attitudes Toward Children with Disabilities: An Ecological Analysis

Mary Elizabeth Hannah

Sally has spina bifida. She uses a wheelchair and has not developed bowel or bladder control. Jeff is blind in one eye but has partial vision in the other. Mike is very shy and withdrawn. He never talks or plays with other children; at recess he runs around making a noise like a motor. Twenty years ago students like Sally, Jeff, and Mike would have been excluded from school or educated in separate educational facilities. However, through court decisions and legislation, students with disabilities have established their right to an education in the least restrictive environment. This mandate, commonly known as mainstreaming, refers to the fact that students with disabilities are to be educated to the maximum extent possible with nondisabled students. Consequently, greater numbers of children with disabilities are being placed in regular education classrooms than ever before.

When considering whether or not to mainstream children with disabilities the focus is typically on the child and his or her intellectual, academic, and behavioral characteristics. Frequently overlooked is the classroom teacher's attitude toward the disabled child. Martin (1974) has stated that should mainstreaming be unsuccessful, it can most likely be attributed to the "attitudes, fears and anxieties and possible overt rejections which may face handicapped children, not just from their schoolmates but from the adults in the schools" (p. 151). Research with normal children, which may be generalizable to those with disabilities, indicates that teachers have different attitudes toward various kinds of children without disabilities. These attitudes lead to different patterns of interaction (Good & Brophy, 1972). For example, Silberman (1971) found that teachers had fewer and more negative interactions with students they would prefer not to have in their classes. In contrast, those students they would like to teach for another year received frequent praise and positive interactions. Since positive attitudes toward a child with a disability may facilitate the child's functioning and negative attitudes may compound the difficulties, familiarity with this area is particularly vital.

To date, research has focused either on teacher attitudes toward children with various disabilities or the teacher characteristics that influence such attitudes (see Hannah & Pliner, 1983). Less emphasis has been given to the ways in which school characteristics influence teacher attitudes toward children with disabilities. The intent of this chapter is to review the research related to teacher attitudes within a broader frame of reference: the premise that a person's behavior is a function of characteristics of the person and of the environmental context in which the person is functioning (Sarason, 1967). To understand behavior, it is imperative to consider both individual and environmental factors. Applying this reasoning to teacher attitudes toward children with disabilities, attitudes are viewed as a product of teacher and environmental characteristics. Relevant aspects of the environment can be divided into those related to the school in which the teacher works and those related to the disabled child who is the target of the attitude. First, the literature on teacher attitudes toward children with disabilities will be summarized.

GENERAL STRUCTURE OF TEACHERS ATTITUDES

The research on teacher attitudes toward children with disabilities has frequently treated attitudes as a unitary concept, with researchers measuring one dimension and assuming that the results would apply to the other dimensions. In an attempt to rectify this situation, the first section of this chapter discusses a tripartite conception of attitudes and focuses on each component separately.

Cognitive Component

The cognitive component of an attitude consists of the categories used to classify stimuli and the attributes and beliefs associated with each category. Factor-analytic research (Abroms & Kodera, 1979; Jones, 1974) indicates that persons with disabilities are not only conceptually distinct from individuals without disabilities, but also that they tend to be categorized into physically, sensorially, intellectually, and psychologically disabled persons. Using multidimensional scaling with regular and special-education teachers, as well as a sample of nonteachers, Schmelkin (1982b) found that all three groups made distinctions between persons who are normal and those who are disabled. Furthermore, persons with disabilities were perceived as falling into a tripartite classification of cognitively, physically, and behaviorally-emotionally disabled persons.

The general category "disabled" has been investigated through the use of the Attitudes Toward Disabled Persons (ATDP) scale. According to the authors (Yuker, Block, & Younng, 1966/1970), the ATDP measures the extent to which the respondent believes that persons with disabilities are the same as normal individuals or whether they are different and need special treatment. In a study by Conine (1969), teacher scores on the ATDP (Form 0) did not differ significantly from those of the general population. Similar results on the same scale have been reported by a number of other researchers for a variety of teacher groups: TMR teachers (Skrtic, Sigler & Lazar, 1978), undergraduate teaching majors (Drake, 1977; Schmelkin & Lieberman, 1984) and special-education teachers (Sigler & Lazar, 1976). Thus it appears that teachers of varying types and stages of professional development hold beliefs about disabled persons similar to those held by the general public.

Research with teachers has often focused on the attributes and characteristics that teachers associate with a particular disabling condition, with retardation, learning disabilities, and emotional disturbance being the most frequently investigated conditions. Teachers are given a list of characteristics and asked to check those that apply to a child with a particular disability. Using this method, teachers have expressed the belief that children with retardation are low in academic performance, unable to work with abstraction or remember, and are docile, trusting, and dependent (Keogh, Tchir, & Windeguth-Behn, 1974; Moore & Fine, 1978). In contrast, teachers appear to view children who are emotionally disturbed as unmotivated to learn, unfriendly, impolite, dishonest, unhappy, aggressive, unable to relate to others, in great need of professional help, and as manifesting hallucinations, tics, compulsions, and phobias (Boucher & Dino, 1979; Carroll & Repucci, 1978; Casey, 1978). Children with learning disabilities are perceived to have characteristics attributed to both children with retardation and with emotional disturbance. Such descriptions as aggressive, disruptive, angry, hostile, socially distant, frustrated, and low in academic performance are frequently attributed by teachers to children with learning disabilities (Boucher & Dino, 1979; Bryan & McGrady, 1972; Moore & Fine, 1978). Children with physical disabilities are perceived to require considerable teacher time, to generate anxiety in the teacher, and to require medication (Frith & Edward, 1981; Nader, 1984). Thus while teachers have distinct conceptions regarding children with certain kinds of disabilities, beliefs about children with other conditions—for example, deafness or blindness—have yet to be investigated. For the most part, these conceptions have negative connotations. Since there is research (Palardy, 1969; Rist, 1970; Rosenthal & Jacobsen, 1966) indicating that expectations may have an effect on student learning and behavior, the negative conceptions that teachers have of children with disabilities may well have a detrimental effect on their functioning.

Affective Component

The affective component involves feelings of liking or disliking and is typically assessed through questionnaires. Using the semantic differential, Hughes, Kaufman, and Wallace (1973) asked teachers to rate six labels commonly applied to children with disabilities in schools. Teachers reacted most favorably to the labels *learning disabled* and *educationally handicapped*, and most negatively to the labels *emotionally disturbed* and *behaviorally disturbed*. Similar results were obtained by Hannah and Doherty (1982). On the evaluative dimension of the semantic differential, elementary school teachers had significantly more positive feelings for nondisabled children and children with learning disabilities than they did for those with emotional impairments. Lange (1986) found that both male and female teachers had significantly more positive feelings for shy, withdrawn students than they did for acting-out, aggressive students. In a comprehensive study using the evaluative dimension of the semantic differential, Panda and Bartel (1972) found that the terms *normal* or *gifted* were evaluated significantly more favorably than all other terms. The terms *blindness* and *deafness* were reacted to more positively than other disabling terms. Further, the terms *crippled*, *mentally retarded*, and *speech-impaired* evoked more positive feelings than the terms *epileptic*, *culturally deprived*, *emotionally maladjusted*, or *delinquent*.

Similar results have been obtained with the Personal Attributes Inventory, an instrument designed to measure affect by noting the number of negative adjectives selected as characteristics of the target group. On this instrument teachers reacted significantly more favorably to the phrase *physically handicapped children* than to the phrases *educably mentally retarded children* or *learning-disabled children* (Parish, Eads, Reece, & Piscitello, 1977). In a related study using the same instrument with a group of teachers, aides, and ancillary personnel, the phrase *gifted children* evoked significantly more positive feelings than the phrase *normal chil-*

dren, while the phrases *mentally retarded children* and *severely multiply handicapped children* were reacted to most negatively (Green, Kappes, & Parish, 1979).

While there are differences in the results due to the different techniques, number of disabling conditions investigated, and labels used in the studies, it does appear that teachers have more positive feelings toward children with certain kinds of disabilities than others. Children with emotional disturbance or mental retardation elicit consistently negative affect and children who are gifted, consistently positive affect.

Behavioral Component

The behavioral component of attitudes comprises a predisposition toward a particular action in regard to a subject and has been investigated through the use of social distance scales or behavioral preference rankings. The former method presents a continuum on which the respondent indicates which relationship he or she would be willing to enter into with an individual with a particular disabling condition. Social relationships vary in degree of intimacy from very intimate (would marry) to very distant (would keep out of my country). Behavioral preference rankings with teachers require that they rank a list of labels or series of descriptions of children with disabilities from most to least preferred to teach. Both techniques appear to assume that the respondents will act in accordance with their stated intentions, overlooking the role that social norms, pressures, habit, and/or situations may play in modifying the behavioral intention.

A frequent and consistent finding has been that teachers, not unlike the general public, say they would interact closely with certain kinds of disabled individuals, but not other kinds. Using a social distance scale, Harasymiw, Horne, and Lewis (1976) found that their sample of over 2,000 people, which included teachers, said they would interact most closely with individuals with physical disabilities (e.g., diabetic, crippled), followed by people with sensory handicaps (deaf, blind), than those with psychological disabilities (e.g., mentally retarded, mentally ill), and finally those with disabilities due to social conditions (e.g., drug addict, ex-convict). Tringo (1970) obtained similar results. People with physical disabilities were most acceptable to teachers for close interpersonal relationships, followed by the sensorially disabled. Individuals with disabilities due to social conditions were placed at the greatest social distance.

On a social distance scale more applicable to teachers—which requires that the respondent indicate where a child should be placed in school, with choices ranging from full-time in regular education (most intimate) to not suitable for public schools (least intimate)—Morris and McCauley (1977) found that teachers placed children with emotional disturbance and learning disabilities in regular education with resource-room support, while children with mental retardation were placed in special-education classes for most of the school day. These teachers were more willing to instruct children with emotional disturbance and learning disabilities than children with mental retardation. Williams and Algozzine (1977) asked teachers to indicate the amount of time students with various disabilities should spend in regular education classrooms. Results indicated that teachers were more willing to teach children with physical handicaps and learning disabilities than those with emotional disturbance or retardation. Antonak (1980) asked undergraduate majors in education to indicate the extent to which children with a variety of disabilities could be integrated into regular education. Based on ordering theory, the results indicated that children with physical disabilities, chronic illness, sensory disabilities, and communciation disorders were seen as better able to benefit from mainstreaming than those manifesting behavioral disorders, mental retardation, and severe or profound retardation.

The kinds of children with disabilities that teachers would instruct has also been investigated through studies wherein teachers were asked to rank labels referring to disabling conditions. Teachers in a study by Murphy, Dickstein, and Dripps (1960) ranked labels of disabilities from most to least prefer to teach as follows: gifted, emotionally impaired, physically handicapped, speech impaired (all tied); slow learner; hearing impaired; visually impaired; and delinquent. Kveraceus (1956) asked teachers to rank order eight disability labels in terms of teaching preference. Again, the gifted, emotionally disturbed, and physically disabled were ranked high, with mental retardation, blindness, and deafness ranked low. A similar preference ranking was obtained by Warren and Turner (1966).

Thus there seems to be some degree of consistency across studies between types of disability and the social relationships that teachers would enter into, as well as the relationships teachers want with children with different kinds of disabilities. In a discussion of the social relationships the general public are willing to enter into with people with disabilities, Harasymiw, Horne, and Lewis (1976) theorized that persons with disabilities are ranked according to the work ethic. People who are deaf or crippled and presumably have a greater capacity for productivity are more likely to be admitted into close social relationships than individuals who are mentally retarded and presumably not productive. This theory also seems applicable to schools. For teachers, the child's ability to achieve academically may be a key variable in determining whether or not a teacher wants a student with a disability in the classroom. The disabilities falling toward the bottom of lists of teaching preferences include those conditions in which learning is impaired (e.g., retardation) or those in which specialized teaching techniques or material are perceived necessary for the child to progress academically (e.g., blindness).

General Conclusion

The degree of congruence between the cognitive, affective, and behavioral components of teacher attitudes toward the handicapped is difficult to evaluate, since different researchers have used different labels and/or descriptions to elicit reactions and since no study has assessed all three components. However, it appears that there may not be much congruence among these components. For example, emotionally disturbed children elicit negative feelings and have negative adjectives attached to them (Boucher & Dino, 1979; Hannah & Doherty, 1982), but they are ranked relatively high in terms of teaching preferences (Kveraceus, 1956). Similarly, deaf and blind children rank low in teaching preference (Warren & Turner, 1966), but they evoke somewhat positive feelings (Panda & Bartel, 1972). Research assessing and comparing all three components for common disabling conditions is needed to clarify the relationship.

TEACHER CHARACTERISTICS

The preponderance of research regarding teacher characteristics has sought to determine the relationship between these characteristics and attitudes toward children with disabilities. Characteristics directly associated with teaching, such as grade level, as well as characteristics related to the teacher, such as age, have been investigated.

Grade Level

Considerable attention has been given to the relationship between grade level taught and teacher attitudes toward children with disabilities. Elementary teachers were shown to hold more positive attitudes (Morris & McCauley, 1977); they placed children with disabilities in less restrictive environments than did secondary teachers. Similarly, Larrivee and Cook (1979) found that teachers in grades one through three were most willing to mainstream children with disabilities, junior high school teachers were least willing, while high school teachers and those in grades four through six fell between the other groups. Stephens and Braun (1980) reported that primary and middle-grade elementary school teachers were more willing to mainstream students with disabilities than were seventh- and eighth-grade teachers. Hirshoren and Burton (1979) found that elementary

school teachers were more willing to teach students with mental retardation and emotional disturbance than were secondary school teachers.
However, there were no differences between the groups in their willingness
to mainstream students with visual, hearing, and orthopedic disabilities.
Using the Attitudes Toward Disabled Persons scale, Sigler and Lazar
(1976) did not find a relationship between grade level taught and beliefs
about the persons with disabilities. Similarly, Oliphant (1982) found no
difference between elementary, junior, and senior high teachers' beliefs
about children with learning disabilities.

Since the Sigler and Lazar (1976) and Oliphant (1982) research focused
on beliefs and the other studies dealt with intended behavior, it is possible
that teachers at different grade levels have similar beliefs about children
with disabilities but differ in their willingness to teach them. One explanation for this difference may be the secondary school teachers' focus on
curriculum content rather than interpersonal issues, in combination with
the fact that they teach larger numbers of students. These factors may
make integrating disabled students into secondary classes more difficult
than it would be at an elementary level.

Teacher Knowledge

Much research has been devoted to exploring the relationship between
knowledge of children with disabilities and attitudes toward them.
Teachers in regular education have repeatedly voiced their need for knowledge in this area. Both undergraduate and graduate students considered
knowledge about mainstreaming students with disabilities to be vitally
important to teachers (Schmelkin & Lieberman, 1984). Most teachers do
not feel competent in this area (Horne, 1983; Hudson, Graham, & Warner,
1979; Nader, 1984). In a recent survey of teachers in New York and
Massachusetts, Knoff (1985) found that 80% of the New York teachers and
68% of the Massachusetts teachers felt that teachers in general did not have
the skills to teach children with disabilities. Particular concerns center
around planning instruction, managing classroom behavior, and working
with other professionals as well as parents (Guerin, 1979; Schultz, 1982).

How does knowledge relate to attitudes? Equating knowledge with col-
lege-level courses on children with disabilities, Jordan and Proctor (1969)
found that teachers with extensive college credit in this area were more
willing to teach such children than teachers with no courses of this type.
Stephens and Braun (1980) reported that for their sample of over 900
teachers, willingness to integrate children with disabilities into regular
classrooms increased as the number of special-education courses increased. Mandell and Strain (1978) found that previous coursework in
special education increased teachers' willingness to teach children with mild

disabilities. Johnson and Cartwright (1979) found that information obtained in a course on children with disabilities was as effective in improving the behavioral component of attitudes as was a combination of information and experience with children with disabilities.

Similar results are obtained when more subjective measures of knowledge are used. Murphy, Dickstein, and Dripps (1960) found that children with hearing impairments were among the least preferred to teach, but also the group about which teachers said they knew the least. Kveraceus (1956) found significant correlations between preferences for working with children with various kinds of disabilities and stated knowledge about the condition. In the same vein, Smart, Wilton, and Keeling (1980) reported that teachers who did not refer children with mental retardation for placement felt they had the knowledge to teach these children. While informational campaigns have not been particularly successful in improving the general public's attitude toward persons with disabilities (Yuker, 1976), it does appear that teachers who have more information about disabling conditions are more willing to teach students with these conditions. However, whether knowledge leads to positive attitudes and a concomitant willingness to teach children with disabilities or whether a positive attitude leads teachers to seek out knowledge and be willing to teach children with disabilities remains a difficult empirical question.

Contact with Disabled Persons

Several researchers have investigated attitudes as a function of contact or experience with individuals who manifest disabilities. Panda and Bartel (1972) surveyed teachers with and without experience with children with disabilities. Using a semantic differential failed to find a significant difference between the groups on the affective component of attitudes toward persons with disabilities. In terms of beliefs, Conine (1969) found no significant difference in scores on the Attitude Toward Disabled Persons scale (Form 0) for teachers with and without a reported relationship with a person with a disability. Similarly, Combs and Harper (1967) found that experience did not seem to be related to teachers' beliefs about children with learning disabilities, mental retardation, or emotional disturbance. On the other hand, Warren and Turner (1966) did find positive relationships between educator's preferences for working with children with various disabilities and stated experiences with the disabling condition. Casey (1978) also found significant relationships between teachers' contact with children with disabilities and their perceived social acceptability. However, no such relationship was found for the social acceptability of children with mental retardation. That experience with children with disabilities can also lead to negative attitudes was demonstrated by Shotel, Iano, and McGettigan (1972), who reported that after a year's experience teaching children with disabilities, regular education teachers were less willing to have these children in their classrooms.

Although experience with children or adults with disabilities appears to have an inconsistent relationship with the components of attitudes, such a conclusion may be erroneous. In these studies insufficient control was provided regarding the quality of the contact. Since other research (English, 1977) has pointed out that positive contact or interaction can have a favorable impact on attitude, it may be that teachers who manifest positive attitudes are those who have had pleasant interactions with individuals who are disabled. Conversely, those teachers with more negative attitudes may have been involved in interactions that were perceived as unpleasant.

Gender Differences

Whether men or women are more positive toward persons with disabilities is a question that has often been addressed. Several studies indicate that women have more positive attitudes than men toward children with disabilities. For example, Conine (1969) found that female teachers scored significantly higher than male teachers on the Attitudes Toward Disabled Persons Scale (ATDP), indicating more positive beliefs about persons with disabilities. However, nonsignificant differences between men and women were obtained by Sigler and Lazar (1976), using the Attitudes Toward Handicapped Individuals (ATHI) Scale, a version of the ATDP, and Skrtic, Sigler, and Lazar (1978), using the ATDP Form 0 with teachers of children with retardation. Conflicting results have been obtained on the behavioral component. For example, on a social distance scale, Tringo (1970) found that females were more willing than males to interact with persons with disabilities. In a similar vein, Harasymiw, Horne, and Lewis (1976) found females were more willing than males to enter into close social relationships with persons with disabilities. In terms of mainstreaming disabled students, neither Stephens and Braun (1980) nor Ringlaben and Price (1981) found any gender differences. However, Aloia, Knutson, Minner, and Von Seggen (1980) reported that female physical education teachers were more willing than male ones to integrate students with disabilities into their classes.

In sum, it seems premature to associate women with more positive beliefs about or a greater willingness to interact with persons with disabilities. When gender differences do occur, as Yuker (1976) has noted, they may be attributed to the influence of other variables, such as information or contact.

Age of Teacher

Teacher age has also been investigated as a critical variable in attitudes toward persons with disabilities. Using the Attitudes Toward Disabled Persons Scale, neither Sigler and Lazar (1976) nor Conine (1969) demonstrated a significant relationship between age of teacher and beliefs about persons with disabilities. Teachers of different ages in Casey's (1978) study held similar beliefs about children with various kinds of disabilities; regardless of age, they used similar adjectives to describe them. While Harasymiw and Horne (1975) reported that younger teachers were more willing to interact with persons with disabilities, Hughs, Kaufman, and Wallace (1973) found that older teachers were more positive in their feelings. Interestingly, Plas and Cook (1982) found that although age was not predictive of willingness to teach adolescents with special needs, the respondents' perception of their ages as a facilitating or hindering factor in teaching these children was related to willingness to teach.

Given these conflicting results, the most prudent conclusion is that age itself is not related to differences in attitude. Differences should be attributed to other variables.

Personality Factors

Other researchers have investigated the relationship between personality variables and attitudes toward persons with disabilities. Using students, Siller (1963; 1984a) concluded that acceptance of persons with disabilities is related to such personality characteristics as ego strength, security, and affiliation, while rejection is related to anxiety, hostility, and rigidity. Similarly, Stephens and Braun (1980) found that teachers' confidence in their ability to educate students with disabilities was strongly predictive of their willingness to have a student with a disability in their classrooms. On the other hand, a generalized personality trait such as social adjustment did not relate to acceptance of persons with disabilities by teachers in training (Lazar, Houghton, & Orpet, 1975). Neither locus of control nor degree of self-esteem was predictive of scores on the ATHI for 139 regular and special-education teachers (Sigler & Lazar, 1976). Frericks and Adelman (1974) found that dogmatism was not related to beliefs about low-achieving students. Because personality variables and attitudes have not been widely investigated with teachers, firm conclusions are difficult to draw. However, it does appear that pupils with disabilities are most positively perceived by teachers who are confident of their teaching ability and believe they can handle these children.

Conclusions

There appears to be a relationship between some teacher characteristics and certain components of attitude toward children with disabilities. First, elementary school teachers are more willing to teach children with disabilities than are teachers at the secondary level. Second, teachers who are more knowledgeable about children with disabilities are more willing to have these children integrated into their classes. Further, while personality traits do not seem to be related to beliefs about persons with disabilities, teachers who are confident about their teaching ability seem to be more willing to instruct children with disabling conditions. It may be that positive contact with persons with disabilities impacts favorably on attitude. Lastly, neither age nor sex appears to be related to any component of attitude.

SETTING

While ecological psychologists have indicated the importance of the environment in determining a person's behavior, little attention has been directed toward the role that environmental factors play in teacher attitudes toward children with disabilities. While potentially the attitudes of significant others, such as administrators or other teachers, could impact on teacher attitudes, these variables have rarely been investigated. Research has focused on the presence of support personnel, in-service training, and classroom size.

Support Personnel

When children with disabilities are mainstreamed, the primary responsibility for the child's education lies with the regular education teacher. Since teachers often express doubt over their ability to instruct and manage such students, the provision of support to teachers is vital. Most often such support takes the form of provision of consultants to the teacher or resource-room assistance to the child.

Research in this area has focused on teachers' views of existing resource programs and their beliefs about which components of such programs are most valuable when educating children with disabilities. In one study Speece and Mandell (1980) found that providing materials and suggestions to the regular classroom teacher as well as directly instructing the child with a disability were highly valued components of the program. Lack of such support results in concern. Schultz (1982) surveyed elementary school teachers to determine their concerns about mainstreaming. Having the appropriate materials and equipment and working with a specialist were among the most common concerns. Similarly, of the teachers surveyed by Hudson, Graham, and Warner (1979), 38% felt that materials for the mainstreamed child were inadequate, while 58% felt they did not receive adequate support services. Both Larrivee and Cook (1979) and Mandell and Strain (1978) found that the presence of support services in the form of consultants, resource rooms, or counselors had positive impact on teacher's willingness to mainstream students into their classrooms.

In-Service Training

In-service training is designed to improve the competence and knowledge of teachers. With the advent of mainstreaming, many school systems implemented programs designed to increase teachers' abilities to instruct and manage children with disabilities in regular education classrooms.

In one of the most soundly designed studies, Harasymiw and Horne (1976) investigated the effects of in-service training, along with consultant services, to regular education teachers. The researchers found that, when compared to teachers in similar schools without such a project, teachers in the project schools were more willing to teach students with disabilities and saw these students as more manageable within the regular educational environment. Similarly, Singleton (1978) combined in-service training with consultant services for students currently mainstreamed into the teachers' classrooms; posttesting indicated that teachers became more positive about mainstreaming and more optimistic in their expectations for disabled students. Brooks and Bransford (1971) involved teachers in a summer workshop in experiences such as planning for and teaching students with disabilities, observing, and sensitivity sessions. Based on pre–post testing with the semantic differential, the researchers concluded that the experience impacted positively on teacher feelings. Also in a summer workshop, Glass and Meckler (1972) combined experience with students with disabilities with information about such students. At the conclusion of the program, teachers were more positive about mainstreaming and more confident of their ability to teach pupils with disabilities. More recently, a program that combined information with experience also impacted positively on teachers' willingness to have mainstreamed students in their classrooms (Finn, 1980).

The effects of intensive versus monthly in-service training was examined by Larrivee (1981). Teachers in the intensive training group attended a four-week summer workshop and weekly in-service meetings, as well as receiving classroom consultation, while the teachers in the nonintensive group only attended monthly in-service meetings. Posttesting indicated that teachers in the intensive group were more willing to teach disabled students. Those in the nonintensive group were not different in their attitudes from a group that had received no training. Some in-service programs, however, have not obtained positive results. For example, Bradfield, Brown, Kaplan, Rickert, and Stannard (1973) found that in-service training aimed at helping teachers individualize instruction and improve attitudes had no effect or a slightly negative effect on teachers' feelings toward children with disabilities.

While in-service training seems to have a favorable impact on teacher attitudes, research is needed to isolate the critical elements in such programs. The question of whether information, contact, simulations, or classroom consultation need to be included remains an empirical one.

Class Size

Since teachers often believe the presence of a disabled child in their classrooms will require more teacher time and attention, several researchers have investigated the relationship of class size to teacher attitudes toward children with disabilities. In one study Mandell and Strain (1978) found that teachers with 17 to 25 children in their classes were most positive toward mainstreaming. In contrast, Larrivee and Cook (1979) did not find any relationship between class size and teacher attitudes toward mainstreaming.

Other evidence, however, suggests that teachers may be more willing to teach children with disabilities if class size is controlled. Buttery (1978) found that teachers in training were more receptive to mainstreaming when only one child with a disability would be integrated into their classrooms. Jamieson (1984) noted that teachers' unions have advocated the use of "weighing formulae" in mainstreaming children with disabilities. Such formulae are designed to decrease class size by a particular number of students for every mainstreamed child. This position suggests that teachers would be more positive toward mainstreaming if class size were reduced. Taken together these studies suggest limited support for the position that children with disabilities will experience greater acceptance from teachers with a small as opposed to a large number of students in their classrooms.

CHILD CHARACTERISTICS

Relatively neglected in research on teacher attitudes toward children with disabilities has been the characteristics of the child apart from the label that describes the child's condition. Since these characteristics can serve as an additional stimulus to teacher attitudes and behavior, the elucidation of this area seems vital. Research with children without disabilities has indicated that such child characteristics as gender, level of school performance, interpersonal behavior, socioeconomic status, race, and physical attractiveness can influence teacher attitudes. However, only the first three variables have been explored as they influence teacher attitudes toward children with disabilities.

Gender

Research regarding teacher gender preferences for nondisabled students yields inconsistent results. Some research indicates that teachers have more positive attitudes toward female students (Brown & MacDougall, 1973; Kehle, Bramble, & Mason, 1974). In contrast, neither Mertens (1976), using written descriptions of students, nor Stake and Katz (1982) or Good and Brophy (1972), using observations in classrooms, found evidence of teacher preference for either gender. Observational studies, however, found some differences in teachers' responses to male and female students. Using 16 first-grade teachers, 8 white and 8 black, Simpson and Erickson (1983) found that male students received more praise as well as criticism from white teachers than did female students. No differences were evident for the black teachers. Similarly, male first-grade students received more criticism than females (Davis, 1967).

Scant research has investigated the presence of a gender bias in attitudes toward children with disabilities. Hannah and Doherty (1982) presented elementary school teachers with disability labels expanded to include a child's age and sex. Results calculated on teachers' responses to the semantic differential and a social distance scale indicated no evidence of gender preference in feelings toward or willingness to teach students with disabilities. Investigating secondary school teachers' attitudes toward emotionally impaired students, Lange (1986) presented teachers with vignettes of acting-out and shy, withdrawn students. While no gender bias was evident in willingness to teach these students, female students, regardless of behavior, elicited more positive feelings. That gender interacts with behavior to impact on attitude was the primary finding of Martin's (1972) research. Matching male and female students in terms of behavior and observing second-grade teachers interacting with the students, Martin found that teachers interacted more with male than with female students with behavior problems.

In sum, it appears premature to assume that teachers have more positive attitudes toward males or females with disabilities. When such differences do occur, they might best be attributed to the effect of other variables (e.g., interpersonal behavior).

Achievement Level

With populations not manifesting disability, academic achievement has been shown to be a powerful influence on teacher attitudes toward and interactions with students. A series of studies (Good & Brophy, 1972; Everton, Brophy, & Good, 1973) reported that teachers interact less with low-achieving than with high-achieving pupils. Furthermore, when asked which children they would like to keep in their classes for an additional year, 75% of the students nominated were high achievers. Similar results have been observed in some reading groups (Martin, Veldman, & Anderson, 1980); but in others (Weinstein, 1976; Alpert, 1974), low achievers received more contact and support.

Applying this research to children with disabilities in schools, Pliner and Hannah (1985) sought to determine the role that achievement plays in teacher attitudes toward children with disabilities. Based on vignettes of children with mild disabilities, where mainstreaming would be a possibility, and varying the level of achievement of the child, teachers were asked to indicate the degree to which the pupil should be integrated into regular education classes. Results indicated that an achieving child with a disability was recommended for placement in a regular education classroom with support services to the teacher and/or child. In contrast, low-achieving children with disabilities were recommended for placement in a significantly more restrictive environment, for example, a half day in special education. Using children with more severe disabilities, however, Barber (1985) did not find that level of achievement affected teachers' willingness to mainstream students. Thus it appears that level of achievement plays a crucial role in teacher willingness to teach *mildly* disabled students.

Student Behavior

As previously discussed, teachers react differentially to children with diverse disabling conditions. However, research also indicates that teachers react differently to different kinds of pupil behavior. In a longitudinal study Rubin and Barlow (1978) had teachers rate the behavior of 1,500 elementary school students. Of pupils who received separate ratings by six teachers, 60% were considered disturbed by at least one teacher. This finding supports Algozzine's (1980) contention that teachers vary considerably in the behaviors they find disturbing. In one study in which more than 1,900 teachers were asked to indicate the degrees to which they considered various behaviors disturbing, only limited consensus was obtained, and then only in the extreme categories (Olson, Algozzine, & Schmid, 1980). Other research has indicated that teachers find acting-out behaviors the most disturbing. Lindsey and Frith (1983) asked elementary school teachers to rank various child behaviors. Most detrimental were (1) not following directions, (2) lacking motivation, and (3) not paying attention. Of least concern were (1) being withdrawn, (2) lacking confidence, and (3) not attending school. Coleman and Gilliam (1983) reported that teachers reacted most negatively to aggressive behavior and least negatively to withdrawn behavior. Similar results were obtained with a variety of educational personnel (Algozzine, 1977), with secondary school teachers

(Norales, 1982), and with special-education teachers (Algozzine, 1980). It appears that teachers consider acting-out, aggressive behaviors as most disturbing and react most negatively to children who exhibit such behavior.

CONCLUSIONS

The research reviewed above indicates that teachers are not overwhelmingly positive in their attitudes toward children with disabilities. While there is some variation among conditions, teachers generally have negative beliefs about and feelings toward these children, as well as being somewhat reluctant to enter into teaching relationships with them. A complex of teacher and environmental characteristics appears to be related to teacher attitudes toward children with disabilities. In the former area, grade level taught, degree of knowledge and amount of self-confidence all seem to be predictors of attitude. The quality of a person's contact with persons with disabilities also may affect attitude. In terms of school-setting variables, class size, the presence of support personnel, and in-service training about children with disabilities appear to be related to attitudes. Yet to be investigated is the role that the attitudes toward persons with disabilities held by other school and community personnel play in determining the attitudes of teachers. In the realm of child variables, the degree of disturbingness of the child's behavior and his or her level of achievement affect teacher attitudes toward the child. At present, the role that the child's gender plays in determining attitude is unclear. While race, socioeconomic status, and physical attractiveness of children not manifesting disabilities have been shown to be related to the ways in which teachers react to the children, these variables have not been investigated in terms of children with disabilities.

In sum, this chapter has presented evidence in support of the position that teacher attitudes toward children with disabilities may be related to both teacher and environmental variables. Methodologically sound investigations are now necessary to isolate which variables or complexes of variables are indeed related to teacher attitudes in this area. The practical consequences of such work include the development of intervention strategies to insure that children with disabilities are in fact educated in an accepting environment.

CHAPTER 13

Students with Physical Disabilities in Higher Education: Attitudes and Beliefs That Affect Integration

Catherine S. Fichten

Attitudes can be a vital ingredient in the success or failure of students with a disability and in the overall success of the mainstreaming effort in post-secondary education. Attitudes of nondisabled students, faculty, the administration, and student services personnel, as well as those of other students who have a disability, can all have profound effects on the social and educational integration of disabled students into the college community (Nathanson, 1979). The purpose of this chapter is to provide a summary of the attitudes of these groups and of the ways in which these attitudes translate into behaviors that facilitate or hamper the integration of college students who have a physical disability. Efforts to change attitudes in the college context are also reviewed. The goal is to summarize the trends and, where possible, draw implications for the successful integration of college students with a disability, rather than to comment on the methodological and statistical adequacy of individual studies.

IMPORTANCE OF COLLEGE EDUCATION FOR PEOPLE WITH A PHYSICAL DISABILITY

A college education for people who have a physical disability is important for the same reasons as it is for nondisabled people: it helps in fulfilling personal goals, allows for effective competition in the job market, and contributes to independence and financial security. There is one difference, however; the data indicate that a college education is *more important* for those who have a disability. Asch (1984) cites 1983 census data indicating that while the employment figures for college graduates with a disability is approximately 60% of that of nondisabled graduates; the corresponding figure for all people with a disability is only about 30%. There is also evidence to show that once people who have a disability enter college, they graduate at approximately the same rate (47%) as do able-bodied students (52%) (Lonnquist, 1979). Lonnquist's study also shows that the employment rate of graduates with a disability (79%) is considerably greater than that of disabled college dropouts (52%). These figures are similar to employment rates of nondisabled college attendees (i.e., 89% and 63%, respectively). But a college education has been shown to meet other than economic goals. For example, Helten's findings (cited in Perry, 1981) indicate that college graduates with a disability experience greater job satisfaction, remain in their positions longer, and spend less time finding employment than do dropouts, who, in turn, fare better than those who never went to college.

While the employment picture for college graduates with a disability is by no means rosy, since at all educational levels the jobless rate for people with a disability is higher than for the nondisabled population, the data on the effects of a college education are encouraging. From society's point of view, having extra taxpayers rather than welfare recipients is desirable.

GROWING NUMBER OF STUDENTS WITH A PHYSICAL DISABILITY

Statistics on the percentage of college students with a disability are notoriously vague. It has been estimated that between 1970 and 1980 anywhere from 1% to 6% of college students had a physical disability (Kirchner & Simon, 1984a; Perry, 1981).

For a variety of reasons, including changes in the law, the civil rights movement, increased public awareness, better public school education, advances in medical technology and rehabilitation engineering, and the growing number of middle-aged and elderly college students, the number of students with disabilities appears to be increasing in institutions of higher education. Informal statistics, such as those provided by Perry (1981), document the increase. He indicates that the University of North Dakota has experienced a change from 11 known students with a disability in 1970 to 360 such students in 1980. Kirchner and Simon (1984a) cite data showing increases in the number of college students who have a visual impairment, and White, Karchmer, Armstrong, and Bezozo (1983) document increases in the number of students with a hearing impairment. Enrollment statistics from my own institution, Dawson College, show a growth from 24 students with disabilities in 1984 to 50 in 1987. Of course, these enrollment figures cannot be taken at face value. Statistics are more likely to be reported by those institutions that provide good services and facilities for students with a disability and, thus, are likely to host a disproportionate number of such students. Nevertheless, since more institutions are providing services today than 10 years ago, one can assume that the percentage of students with a disability in American and Canadian colleges and universities is, indeed, on the rise.

ATTITUDES OF VARIOUS GROUPS

Attitudes Of Nondisabled Students

This section deals primarily with the attitudes of nondisabled students who are, at best, casual acquaintances of students who have disability. While friendship formation and interaction between students with a disability and their able-bodied friends are among the more important areas that need to be researched in the future, at present there appear to be no studies that have investigated these issues.

There are very few surprises in the data on attitudes of able-bodied college students. Generally, these are somewhat more positive than attitudes of other age groups and certainly more positive than those of high school students (Ryan, 1981). That college students have more liberal attitudes concerning most minority groups, especially when attitudes are measured using paper-and-pencil instruments, is a well-documented finding. Indeed, Minnes and Tsuk (1986), among others, report that scores on a social desirability scale and the Attitudes Toward People with Disabilities scale (ATPD) were positively related. Thus, it is hardly surprising that education and social science students have been found to have more favorable attitudes than business and engineering students (Auvenshine, 1962, cited in Kelly, 1984). As for sex differences, data indicate either no differences (Semmel & Dickson, 1966) or differences that favor females (Stovall & Sedlacek, 1983).

Positivity (Sympathy) Bias and Response Amplification. As Chapter 4 (by Katz, Hass, and Bailey) in this book clearly shows, much of the data can be understood through an appreciation of the positivity or sympathy bias, on the one hand, and of response amplification, on the other. Many studies have shown that students evaluate certain stigmatized others, such as blacks, the elderly, and those with a physical disability, more favorably than nonstigmatized individuals. There are data showing that this holds across a variety of contexts and physical disabilities (Belgrave, 1985; Carver, Glass, & Katz, 1978; Carver, Gibbons, Stephan, Glass, & Katz, 1979; Gibbons, Stephan, Stephenson, & Petty, 1980; Mitchell & Allen 1975; Scheier, Carver, Schultz, Glass, & Katz, 1978; Tagalakis, Amsel, & Fichten, in press).

What distinguishes studies showing positivity bias from those demonstrating response amplification (i.e., the tendency to make more extreme evaluations in both the negative and positive directions) is the personal relevance of the situation. In situations where there are no personally relevant consequences involved, a positivity bias predominates. In those situations where the actions of the person with a disability are relevant and important to the evaluator (Gibbons, Stephan, Stephenson, & Petty, 1980), or where ambivalent attitudes are legitimized for subjects (Carver, Gibbons, Stephan, Glass, & Katz, 1979), response amplification prevails.

But what happens when the favorable or unfavorable consequences to oneself of the disabled person's actions are not "preprogrammed," when he or she is presented in an ambiguous light? The data here are reasonably clear-cut but not nearly as optimistic as the numerous positivity bias studies would suggest.

Social Distance. Data from studies investigating social distance show that for relatively distant or transient situations, attitudes are generally favorable. For closer, more permanent, and intimate situations, attitudes become progressively more negative (Semmel & Dickson, 1966; Stovall & Sedlacek, 1983).

There is currently much debate about the invariance or the situational specificity of preference for people with particular disabilities (Richardson & Ronald, 1977; Yuker, 1983). In the college environment, there appears to be only one study that has attempted to systematically assess students' preferences as a function of situational context. This study shows that the nature of the interaction situation affects attitudes toward people with specific disabilities, with wheelchair users preferred over blind students in academic situations, and blind students favored over wheelchair users in social situations (Stovall & Sedlacek, 1983). Given the multidimensionality of attitudes toward people with disabilities (see Schmelkin, Chapter 10 in this book), this is hardly surprising.

Affect. In the area of affect the data are not encouraging. Generally, the findings show that college students are less comfortable with their disabled than with their nondisabled peers (Fichten, 1986; Fichten, Amsel, Robillard, & Judd, 1987; Robillard & Fichten, 1983). During interaction with a person who has a disability, students experience higher anxiety (heart rate) than during interaction with a nondisabled student (Marinelli & Kelz, 1973).

Interaction Behavior. Again, the findings are not encouraging when one examines actual behavior. Data show that when students are faced with a clear choice—to interact with a student who has a physical disability or one who does not—they feel duty bound to interact with the person who has the disability. However, when it appears as though there is a socially acceptable reason to avoid contact, students will avoid the person with a disability (Snyder, Kleck, Strenta, & Mentzer, 1979). This avoidance of people with a physical disability is also apparent in Eberly, Eberly, and Wright's (1981) study on vocational rehabilitation students; while these students showed the usual positivity bias in their ratings of potential clients with a physical disability, when asked about their preferences concerning which client groups they wanted to work with, they indicated a clear preference for nondisabled clients.

Able-bodied students have also been shown to prefer greater physical distance between themselves and a student who has a disability (Kleck, 1969). While the pioneering work of Kleck and his colleagues (Kleck, 1968; Kleck, Ono, & Hastorf, 1966) on interaction behaviors has shown numerous differences between the behaviors of able-bodied people when they interact with individuals who have a disability and when they interact with nondisabled people, no such behavioral data on college students exist. Clearly there is a need for studies that investigate actual behavior in typical college interaction situations.

Attitudes Uncontaminated by Positivity Bias or Sympathy Effects. What are attitudes toward students with a disability when attitude measurement is not contaminated by positivity bias/sympathy effects? To avoid sympathy effects, four studies used a response prediction paradigm to assess attitudes toward students with a disability. In the study by Babbit, Burbach, & Iutcovich (1979) it was found that students' self-reported attitudes are significantly more favorable than their ratings in a response prediction condition, in which they indicate not their own attitudes but those they believe to be the attitudes of other college students. These findings are consistent with the results of the other three studies, in which it was found that the response prediction paradigm overrides the positivity bias and that students with a disability are evaluated considerably more negatively than able-bodied students on a variety of characteristics (Fichten & Amsel,

1986a; Fichten, Amsel, Robillard, & Judd, 1987; Robillard & Fichten, 1983). These data, considered together, suggest that nondisabled students, while denying that they themselves are prejudiced, believe that those around them are.

What Accounts for the Negative Attitudes?

What Accounts for the Negative Attitudes? If one excludes the positivity bias results from consideration, the data suggest that able-bodied college students have negative attitudes toward their peers who have a physical disability. They also feel uncomfortable with such students and will avoid them if there is a socially acceptable reason for doing so. In order to facilitate integration, it is necessary to examine what factors account for these attitudes. In the research Rhonda Amsel, Claudia Bourdon, and I have been doing for the past five years, the goal has been to understand the reasons for the negative attitudes, social anxiety, and avoidant behavior.

Part of the explanation for the negative attitudes toward students with a disability is that nondisabled students believe that their disabled peers are very different from themselves. For example, Linkowski, Jaques, and Gaier (1969) demonstrate that able-bodied students believe that a physical disability has adverse consequences for self-esteem, independence, and social relationships. Our own studies, as well as that of Weinberg (1976), demonstrate that able-bodied students believe that students with a disability not only possess negatively valued characteristics, but also that in virtually all domains of interpersonal life they are very different from themselves. For example, while able-bodied students are seen as dominant, extraverted, and calculating, students with a disability are seen as being the opposite—submissive, introverted, and unassuming. While able-bodied students are seen as talkative and sociable, students with a disability are seen as helpless and dependent (Fichten & Amsel, 1986a). Able-bodied students are also quite uncertain about the sociability of students with a disability (Fichten, Compton, & Amsel, 1985). In addition, they believe that male students with a disability are less masculine and females less feminine than their able-bodied counterparts, and that students who have a disability are more socially anxious and less likely to be dating than nondisabled students (Robillard & Fichten, 1983).

In other words, students with a disability are seen as very different in areas important for college-age students. Given the impressive data on the effects of similarity on liking and attraction (Byrne, 1969), it is hardly surprising that able-bodied students do not generally seek out students with a disability as prospective friends and acquaintances. But this explains only part of the problem. The rest—that is, lack of comfort and avoidance of students with a disability—must also be accounted for.

What accounts for lack of comfort and avoidance? While studies from a variety of theoretical orientations have been carried out (Siller, 1984a; 1984b), most do not deal directly with college students. Our own research, conducted from a cognitive-behavioral perspective, has tried to examine the effects of two factors found to cause anxiety and avoidance: poor social skills and faulty cognitive appraisals.

The first topic we explored was the role of social skills, since it was plausible to assume that anxiety in interpersonal encounters between able-bodied and disabled students may be due to able-bodied students' not knowing what to say or do during interaction. Hundreds of subjects and two studies later (Fichten & Bourdon, 1986), we found that able-bodied students *do* know what to say or do in frequently occurring interaction situations. However, we also found that they underestimate the appropriateness of their behaviors, suggesting that negative self-evaluation, self-consciousness, and low self-efficacy expectations may be implicated in the lack of ease that characterizes interaction between able-bodied and disabled students.

These findings prompted us to explore the role of cognitive factors. Results to date show that the thoughts, both about oneself and about the person with a disability, that students have concerning interaction with individuals who have a physical disability and those who do not, are clearly different. This is especially true of negative thoughts about the other person, which are also strongly related to lack of comfort during interaction (Fichten, 1986; Fichten & Amsel, in press). Research that further explores the nature of the thoughts that influence comfort during interaction is presently in progress in our laboratory. In this current investigation we intend to examine the nature and content of thoughts that are associated with high and low anxiety. Our study of self-efficacy expectations also suggests that cognitive factors constitute an important dimension (Fichten, Bourdon, Amsel, & Fox, in press). That study reported that weak expectations of being able to interact effectively with people who have a physical disability are related to discomfort, lack of knowledge about appropriate behavior, and negative attitudes toward disabled people.

Attitudes of Professors

There is relatively little research on attitudes of professors toward students with a physical disability. What little research exists suggests that professors have moderately favorable attitudes toward disabled students on campus, but their attitudes are somewhat less positive about having such students in their own department. Experience teaching students with a disability, however, generally results in more positive attitudes and greater comfort with disabled students.

Admission Policy. One way of inferring professors' attitudes is to examine their views on the admission of students with a disability to their institutions and departments. A study by Newman (1976), which sampled a large number of professors, shows that 78% of them said the university should have an unrestricted admission policy. However, when admission to their own departments was at issue, only 60% said that an unrestricted admission policy was desirable. In other words, as with the able-bodied students, the greater the social distance, the more favorable the attitudes, while the lesser the social distance, the more negative the attitudes.

Why do professors not favor an unrestricted admission policy? Newman's (1976) study showed that 48% of professors indicate that there would be problems with the admission of students with a disability to their departments. While they believe that orthopedic problems, including amputations, cerebral palsy, and paralysis, would cause some difficulties, a hearing impairment is considered to be moderately handicapping, and blindness is seen as the most serious disability for academic work. The assumption that a visual impairment constitutes a major handicap for scholarly work is similar to the beliefs of the able-bodied students in Stovall and Sedlacek's (1983) study. In our own studies (Fichten, Amsel, Bourdon, & Creti, in press; 1986) it was also found that professors have a clear hierarchy of preference, orthopedically impaired students being most preferred. The ratings of visually impaired, cerebral palsied, and hearing-impaired students are different, however, for professors who have not taught students with the disability in question; they believe that hearing impairment and cerebral palsy were the most undesirable disabilities for academic work. Interestingly, professors who have experience teaching students with the disabilities in question believe that a hearing impairment is less of an academic handicap than a visual impairment or cerebral palsy. We also found that professors, especially those who have not taught disabled students, are uncomfortable with students who have a disability.

Effects Of Contact and Experience Teaching Students with a Disability.
Given professors' lack of ease with students who have a physical disability, it is important to know what can be done to alleviate discomfort and make professors more interested in teaching disabled students. The available research on this topic focuses on the effects of contact and experience. Three investigations (Fichten, Amsel, Bourdon & Creti, in press; Fonosch & Schwab, 1981; McQuay, 1978) show that professors with contact or experience with disabled students have more favorable attitudes than those who have no such experiences. The study by Fonosch and Schwab also found that female professors and those in education and social science programs hold more positive attitudes. The study by Fichten and colleagues found that experienced professors are more willing to teach students with a disability in the future and more comfortable with disabled students in general.

Another study (Walker, cited in Emerton & Rothman, 1978) found that experience with hearing-impaired students resulted in more negative attitudes among Rochester Institute of Technology (RIT) professors, contradicting the results of the studies described above, even though one of these (McQuay, 1978) focused exclusively on professors' attitudes toward hearing-impaired students. Perhaps the methodology of the Walker study, which assessed pre–post changes, and the design of the other investigations, in which differences between groups were evaluated, can explain the discrepancy. Or perhaps professors who elected to teach at RIT, an institution with a large hearing-impaired population, were idealistic about students with a hearing impairment before they started teaching. As suggested by Emerton & Rothman (1978), with time they might have revised their attitudes from idealism to realistic classroom practice. Whatever the reason for the discrepancy, more studies are needed to evaluate the effects of experience teaching students with various physical disabilities.

Attitudes of Student Services Personnel

In general, findings from noncollege contexts suggest that while clients with a physical disability are rated favorably when it comes to behavior, people with a disability are not preferred clients (Eberly, Eberly, & Wright, 1981). In the college context, a study by Kelly (1984) evaluated the attitudes of coordinators of services to students with disabilities. She found that the attitudes of these individuals are more favorable than those of other populations, that female coordinators and those under age 40 are more positive, and that frequency of daily contact is unrelated to the favorability of attitudes. Palmerton and Frumkin (1969) found that while amount of contact makes no difference, more favorable attitudes are held by those counselors who find it difficult to avoid contact with disabled students and also enjoy the experience. Thus, expected future interaction coupled with pleasant experiences may contribute to favorable attitudes.

Attitudes of Students with a Disability

The findings concerning attitudes of disabled students are not clear-cut. On the one hand, students generally minimize problems related to their disability and wish no prominence as a disabled student (Newman, 1976). On the other hand, they believe attitudes toward them held by others are negative.

Attitudes Toward Able-Bodied Students. Data on attitudes of disabled students toward their peers suggest that they are comfortable with nondisabled students and have as many nondisabled friends as do their able-bodied peers (Fichten & Bourdon, 1986). However, they also believe that the greatest obstacles to integration on campus are others' values and lack of knowledge and that social isolation is a serious and significant problem (Penn & Dudley, 1980). Students with a disability also believe that able-bodied students hold more negative attitudes toward them than they themselves do or than able-bodied students *appear* to hold (Babbit, Burbach, & Iutcovich, 1979; Schroedal & Schiff, 1972).

The situation is not clear. Do students with a disability experience a misconception about the attitudes of other students, or do they perceive the situation accurately? I tend to believe the latter, that students who have a disability are accurate in their assessment of the beliefs their able-bodied peers hold, especially where interpersonal behavior is concerned and the positivity bias no longer operates.

Attitudes Toward Self and Other Students with a Disability. Data on disabled students' attitudes toward other students who have a disability reveal many ambiguities. Some studies found that attitudes both about oneself (Fichten, Amsel, Robillard, & Judd, 1986; Weinberg-Asher, 1976) and about others with a disability are quite favorable—as favorable as are able-bodied students' attitudes, which presumably include the positivity bias (Babbit, Burbach, & Iutcovich, 1979). Other studies, however, show that disabled students' attitudes are more negative (Fichten & Bourdon, 1986; Schroedal & Schiff, 1972).

The inconsistent results in this area may be due to methodological factors, such as the nature of the measurement instruments used, the duration of the disability, and whether attitudes toward oneself, others who have the same diisability, others who have different disabilities, or the disability *per se* are measured. Thus while data show that disabled students are more comfortable with others who have the same disability as they themselves do than with people who have a different disability, and while their self-attitudes are positive, their attitudes toward others with both similar and different disabilities are somewhat negative and stereotyped (Fichten, Amsel, Robillard, & Judd, 1987). It appears the students are caught between adopting the perceived views of the majority and adopting the civil rights movement's ideology.

Attitudes Toward Professors. Another important area of investigation is disabled students' attitudes toward their professors. Data on attitudes toward able-bodied professors show that students with a disability are as comfortable with their professors as the professors are with them and that students are reasonably pleased with the treatment accorded them by their teachers. They also believe that most professor-initiated behaviors toward them are reasonably appropriate; however, they underestimate the appropriateness of student-initiated behaviors (Fichten, Amsel, Bourdon, & Creti, in press). This finding is consistent with results reported by Babbit,

Burbach, and Iutcovich (1979), which show that students with a disability believe that professors hold more negative attitudes toward disabled students than do the disabled students themselves.

There appear to be no data concerning attitudes toward professors with a disability or about the types of professors or professor behaviors that result in favorable attitudes by disabled students. Indeed, the only related data on this topic are provided by Yuker, Block, and Campbell (1960), who report that the attitudes of able-bodied students toward people with a disability are more positive after they have been taught by a disabled professor.

Attitudes Toward Institutional Practices and Student Services Personnel. There are no available data on the attitudes of students who have a disability toward institutional practices or toward coordinators of services to disabled students. The only available data on college professionals show that students with a disability prefer a disabled counselor, but only for educational/vocational counseling (Strohmer & Phillips, 1985).

Institutional Attitudes

Perhaps institutional attitudes are the most important ones. Institutions that discourage students who have a disability from applying, that place insurmountable physical and admissions barriers to them, and that do not provide services needed by the students or by the professors who teach them can cause the most damage by communicating to the college community the message that students with a disability are not welcome on campus.

In both the United States and Canada there are minimal legal safeguards against discriminatory admissions policies. In essence these forbid institutions from asking about the presence of a disability. However, many students who have a disability contact the college prior to application, and a number of departments and faculties have preadmission interviews. In such cases, one can only hope that the spirit of the law prevails.

What about programs that specifically require either sensory or physical abilities? Can a student with a visual impairment become a doctor or an electrical technician? Can a hearing-impaired student or a wheelchair user become a nurse? In spite of numerous documented instances of success, many colleges and universities are struggling with these issues.

Institutional attitudes can be evaluated by examining whether the college or university is providing needed services (e.g., a coordinator of resources for disabled students, assistance with transportation, audiotaping, sign interpreters, note takers, emergency procedures, academic advisors, financial aid), equipment resources (e.g., tape recorders, FM systems, magnifying equipment, computer adaptations), architectural and physical facilities (e.g., ramps, tables and lab benches appropriate for wheelchair users, amplified telephones, raised lettering on office and classroom doors), and whether there is any attempt to train staff and faculty, conduct sensitization programs, or help set up a student organization (Fichten, Bourdon, Creti, & Martos, 1987). Of course the speed with which needs are met is also vital.

The literature suggests that most institutions have made an effort to accommodate students with disabilities and that various beneficial changes have taken place. A number of studies have reported on available services in post-secondary institutions (e.g., Kirchner & Simon, 1984b; Marion & Iovacchini, 1983). Stilwell, Stilwell, and Perrit's (1983) investigation provides comparative data on policy and on social and architectural barriers in 1971 and 1980. This study shows that there has been some progress, although it has been uneven. The results indicated that while special services such as admissions and orientation programs for students with a disability are now generally being provided, housing for disabled students is still an unmet need and the physical needs of visually and hearing-impaired students have not received adequate attention. There is still work to be done in making colleges and universities fully accessible to students who have a physical disability.

WHAT HAS BEEN TRIED TO MODIFY ATTITUDES?

In the college context attempts to change attitudes fall into four categories: contact alone or in combination with information, sensitization via role play exercises, tips for the student who has a disability, and institutional changes.

Information and Contact

Providing information about disabilities or about the people who have them, by itself, appears to be an ineffective means of changing attitudes (Anthony, 1972). Contact between able-bodied students and people who have a physical disability has variable effects; some studies have found that contact has some beneficial effects on attitudes and behavior, others have found deterioration, while others still have found no relationship between these variables (Anthony, 1972; Antonak, 1981b; Cloerkes, 1979; Emerton & Rothman, 1978; English, 1971; Fichten & Amsel, in press; Fichten, Compton, & Amsel, 1985; Minnes & Tsuk, 1986; Robillard & Fichten, 1983; Semmel & Dickson, 1966; Yuker, Block & Campbell, 1960). Certainly contact *per se* does not appear to be a powerful means of making people more comfortable or reducing prejudice and discrimination.

Several rehabilitation researchers (Anthony, 1972; Bender, 1981; Yuker & Block, 1979) have suggested that the ambiguous results may be attributed to differences in the extent and type of contact studied. They argue that the best means to increase understanding, reduce prejudice, enhance comfort, and facilitate interaction between able-bodied individuals and those who have a disability is to provide able-bodied people with educational information and to have them experience extended close contact, on an equal-status basis, with people who have a disability.

In the college context, findings on the effects of information plus equal-status contact are mixed. While Anthony and Carkhuff (1970) and Rounds and Neubauer (1986) found that advanced students in a rehabilitation counseling program had more positive attitudes than did beginners or those who were not accepted into the program, testimonials to the beneficial effects of information plus contact, Rowlett (1982) found that students in a residence hall who were given information about disabilities and who had contact with disabled students who lived on the same floor did not differ from students who had only contact, although both groups had more favorable attitudes than a no-contact control group. That extended contact, rather than the combination of contact plus information, is the key variable is also suggested by Weinberg's (1978) findings. In her study, students who lived in segregated dormitories, integrated dormitories, or who shared a room with a student who had a disability served as subjects. The results show that as extent of contact increased so did the favorability of attitudes, with students who shared a room with a disabled student having the most positive view. Emerton and Rothman (1978), however, found no difference, at the Rochester Institute of Technology, between hearing students who lived in an integrated residence and those who lived in nonintegrated housing. However, there were communication difficulties between disabled and nondisabled students in this study, since the hearing-impaired students used sign language for the most part.

The contradictory nature of these studies further illustrates the need to evaluate what types of contact are beneficial. As Yuker's chapter in this book suggests, a thorough evaluation of the characteristics of the able-bodied and of the disabled students, as well as of the nature of the situation, is certainly needed. Nevertheless, studies from other areas of prejudice reduction suggest that the following deserve a try: equal-status contact, a relation that is seen to be continuing and that provides opportunities for reciprocal helping, and a "superordinate" group goal that requires cooperation between the student with a disability and other group members.

There appears to be no research on the effects of cooperative work tasks and assignments in post-secondary education. In public school education, the meta-analysis by the Johnsons and their colleagues (Johnson, Maruyama, Johnson, Nelson, & Skon, 1981; Johnson, Johnson, & Maruyama, 1983) have shown that cooperative working conditions result not only in increased achievement and productivity but also in greater interpersonal attraction and liking. Similarly, in the area of prejudice reduction, Aronson and Asherow (1980) found that cooperative learning results increased liking across ethnic and racial groups. Certainly the effects of cooperative working conditions are worthy of investigation in the college context.

Sensitization via Role-Play Activities

The popular "wheelchair day" types of role-play, when able-bodied students simulate being blind, deaf, or wheelchair-bound, have been shown not only to be ineffective but also "to contribute to disabling myths about disabilities" (Wright, 1980a, p. 174). As the studies evaluating this type of activity show (Clore & Jeffery, 1972; Wilson, 1971; Wilson & Alcorn, 1969), generally there is little, if any, attitude change. There is a lot of new negative affect, however, with participants learning mainly about the frustrations, difficulties, and limitations of having a disability. Of course, this pity orientation is thoroughly undesirable for the integration of students with a disability.

But other types of role-play, those with a *problem-solving set*, could be effective (Wright, 1978, 1980a). Examples that hold promise are Pastalan's (1974) architecture students who role-played having various sensory disabilities with a focus on how to design helpful environments; Williams's (cited in Wright, 1978) assertive role-play concerning how people with a disability could attain rights denied them, and Wright's (1975a) own work on role-play of helping situations with a problem-solving set, where the task is to discover how the giving and receiving of help could be improved. The problem-solving set approach, and what Langer, Bashner, and Chanowitz (1985) have called teaching "mindfulness" are, at the behavioral level, compatible formulations and should be explored further in the college context.

Tips for Students Who Have a Disability

What can students who have a disability do to promote beneficial attitude change? A series of studies from the social-psychological literature shows that there are a variety of things they can say or do to make interaction more comfortable and more likely to occur. Some of these revolve around how best to acknowledge the disability, while others involve the demonstration of similarity between disabled and nondisabled students.

Acknowledge the Disability. Tactics that have been shown effective include making the other person more comfortable by being the first to acknowledge the disability, legitimizing curiosity, and suggesting that it is appropriate to use terms related to the disability (e.g., *walk, see, hear*). For example, Hastorf, Wildfogel, and Cassman (1979) found that a person with a disability is better liked if he acknowledges the disability than if he does not do so. Belgrave and Mills (1981) and Mills, Belgrave, and Boyer (1984) found that if a person makes reference to his or her disability, this is best done after a request for help, and Bazakas (cited in Siller, 1984a) found that presenting oneself as both coping and openly acknowledging the disability results in more favorable evaluations than either of those components alone. Similarly, Evans (1976) found that disclosures that legitimize the other's curiosity, stress some positive elements of having the disability, and indicate acceptance of terms such as *walk, see,* and *hear—* all of which suggest what is and is not appropriate behavior—result in favorable outcomes.

Similarity. Another approach is to demonstrate that one has attitudes and values similar to those of nondisabled students. For example, it was shown by Belgrave (1984) that expressing interest in the other person or discussing one's participation in typical college activities (e.g., athletics, buying tickets for a performance, partying, studying for exams) results in favorable impressions.

The results of such studies suggest that if the only available strategy for attitude change is to provide information, this should be done by portraying individuals with a disability who follow the above mentioned tips, that is, make able-bodied students comfortable and demonstrate that they are similar to their nondisabled peers. Indeed, Donaldson and Martinson (1977) found that giving information in the form of a panel discussion by young disabled adults talking about various aspects of their lives was effective in changing attitudes. That this method of providing information was effective may have been due to the type of information conveyed and the means by which it was delivered.

What Institutions of Higher Education Can Do

Institutions can also effect beneficial changes. Not surprisingly, when institutional attitudes are favorable, the attitudes of able-bodied students are also positive. This has been suggested by the results of two studies (Fonosch & Schwab, 1981; Genskow & Maglione, 1965), which showed that attitudes on campuses where there were service programs for students with disabilities were more favorable than on those where no such services were available. While one would expect that problem-solving workshops for faculty might also be helpful, there appears to have been no empirical investigation of this topic.

CONCLUSIONS

The literature shows some positive trends in the attitudes of various groups in post-secondary education. There are also a number of promising avenues of research and practice: investigation of attitudes toward professors, college professionals, and staff who have a disability; examination of interpersonal behaviors both before and after attempts at attitude change; and the study of the types of contact and experience that facilitate interaction between students with a disability and their nondisabled peers and professors. There is also a need to investigate the dynamics of friendship formation. Studies of attitudes that control for the positivity or sympathy bias also need to be carried out. The effects of different types of problem-solving role-play also deserve exploration. Finally, there is a need for studies that not only recognize that in casual or first encounters the disability is the most salient feature of the person, but that also capitalize on this salience for attitude and behavior change.

Findings on employment and job satisfaction suggest that it is extremely important that people with a disability be encouraged to attend colleges and universities. This includes paying attention to the receptiveness of educational institutions and to the attitudes of people who advise high school students who have a disability.

CHAPTER 14
Attitudes of Health Care Personnel Toward Persons with Disabilities

Mary Anne Geskie and James L. Salasek

The public seems to believe that behaviors can be used to infer attitudes, while researchers have been attempting over the years to identify the extent to which attitudes can be used to predict behavior. For the most part these approaches assume simple models of human behavior and attitudes, that is, that a single attitude, when properly assessed, corresponds to a single behavior and vice versa.

Recent definitions of attitude rely on a multidimensional approach. Attitudes are seen as being comprised of three major components: belief, affect, and behavior. An attitude, then, is a positive or negative reaction to an object, accompanied by specific beliefs that tend to impel the individual in a particular way toward an object (Yuker, 1976). Assuming this, the multidimensional approach broadens the parameters of what constitutes an attitude and necessitates a more complex approach to their assessment.

ATTITUDE MEASURES

Standard attitude measures generally consist of written items representing single statements about feelings, beliefs, or knowledge with respect to a particular object. Verbally oriented measures are seen as tapping either the affective and/or cognitive components of the targeted attitude.

Measures have been developed to assess attitudes toward individuals with mental disorders in a variety of ways. Gilbert and Levinson's (1957) Custodial Mental Illness Scale (CMI) uses 20 Likert-type statements to assess a respondent's ideological orientation, ranging from custodialism to humanism. Baker and Schulberg's (1967) Community Mental Health Ideology Scale (CMHI) is a 38-item measure that assesses the respondent's endorsement of beliefs thought to reflect three general concepts of the modern community mental health movement. Morrison's (Morrison & Becker, 1975) Client Attitude Questionnaire (CAQ) has two forms, both 20-item true/false questionnaires developed to measure endorsement of either the medical model or a psychosocial orientation toward mental disorders. This measure was specifically developed to assess the influence of mental health ideology on attitudes, in addition to measuring changes in attitudes as a function of in-service training seminars. One final bipolar measure is the Attitude Toward Disabled Persons Scale (ATDP) (Yuker, Block, & Younng, 1966/1970). Three forms of the ATDP exist, one 20-item and two 30-item scales of Likert-type format that are considered general measures of attitudes toward disabled persons, including those with mental disorders.

In response to the perceived need for a more detailed measure to assess attitudes toward mental disorders, Cohen and Struening (1962, 1965) developed the multidimensional Opinions About Mental Illness Scale (OMI). The 51 Likert-type statements assess opinions about the cause, treatment, and prognosis of mental disorders. Five relatively independent factors are scored: authoritarianism, benevolence, mental health ideology, social restrictiveness, and interpersonal etiology. These factors have shown stability over time (Allon & Graham, 1970; Dielman, Stiefel, & Cattell, 1973). Despite some reported shortcomings, the OMI is still the most widely used instrument for assessing attitudes toward individuals with mental disorders (Rabkin 1972).

Another area of interest to investigators has been the attitudes of hospital personnel toward patient care and treatment. An instrument developed by Souelem (1955) has two forms, consisting of 36 items with a dichotomous format of agree–disagree. Although originally used to assess mental patients' attitudes toward hospitalization, it was later used to assess the attitudes of professional groups who dealt with inpatients. Rice, Berger, Klett, & Sewell (1966) developed the Staff Opinion Survey (SOS) to assess the attitudes of hospital personnel toward patient care and treatment. The 61 Likert-type items provide scores in six areas: patient control, provisions for a human environment, protective isolation, patient–staff communication, reduction of patient dependency, and restriction of personal property. Substantial occupational differences were obtained on each factor and for each occupation when compared across hospitals. Ellsworth

(1965) utilized the SOS in conjunction with the OMI to create a new instrument with 16 factors, most of which involve assessing authoritarian restrictive control issues. Barrell, DeWolfe, and Cummings (1965) developed the Philosophy of Treatment forms (POT) to assess the attitudes of hospital personnel toward patient care. The 144 items provide scores in seven areas. The POT was first used with personnel from a general medical and surgical hospital, later with personnel from a psychiatric hospital, and finally on a national sample of personnel from ten Veterans Administration hospitals from various geographic areas of the United States. Differences on several of the factors were obtained based on occupation and the type of ward personnel worked on, but no differences were obtained between hospitals.

Elstein and Van Pelt (1966, 1968) assumed that conceptions the staff formed about patients influenced staff-patient interactions and contributed to the prevailing atmosphere of the hospital milieu. They developed two Q-sorts, a behavioral set and an interpersonal characteristics set, in addition to a 63-item rating scale to investigate the salient dimensions the staff employed when forming perceptions about relevant information about patients. The dimensions identified were: need for control; patient prognosis and suitability for available therapies; dependency on staff for structure, comfort, and caring; patient mood; and a favorability rating. Staff members rating the patients agreed along these dimensions less than 50% of the time. The authors concluded the individual styles the staff utilized in organizing perceptions about patients interfered with communicating about those patients.

Several other scales have also been developed, such as Middleton's (1953) Prejudice Scale, Reznikoff's (1963) Multiple Choice Attitude Questionnaire, and Wright and Klein's (1966) Mental Illness Questionnaire. Each of these has been used primarily by its author(s) and has not received widespread use.

ATTITUDES OF TREATMENT PERSONNEL TOWARD DIFFERENT DISABILITY GROUPS

Investigators studying the attitudes of health care professionals usually examined occupational subgroups separately. The findings consistently indicate distinct attitudinal patterns for the various occupational groups, regardless of the attitude measure used. The different profiles obtained cannot be attributed solely to occupational status, since factors such as age, gender, education, and socioeconomic status influence occupational choice. An area receiving considerable attention has been the attitudes of personnel working with individuals with mental disorders.

Cohen and Struening (1962, 1965) extensively investigated the attitudes of mental health professionals. They identified four occupational clusters with different profiles, using their Opinions About Mental Illness Scale. One cluster, "blue-collar workers," including psychiatric aides and kitchen workers, held authoritarian, restrictive attitudes toward persons with mental disorders. The cluster "white-collar workers," including technicians, nurses, dentists, and nonpsychiatric physicians, was differentiated by a pattern low in authoritarianism and high in benevolence. Psychologists and social workers comprised another cluster, whose pattern was high on mental health ideology and interpersonal etiology and low on authoritarianism and social restrictiveness. The fourth cluster comprised the clergy, with a pattern similar to but not as extreme as the psychologists and social workers. Psychiatrists did not fit into any cluster. They resembled both the clergy and the psychologists and social workers, but were not as extreme.

Psychiatric aides have been extensively studied. The attitude pattern aides endorsed on the OMI is reflected by high scores on authoritarianism and social restrictiveness (Cohen & Struening, 1962; Ellsworth, 1965; Lawton, 1964). This profile is considered nontherapeutic because it is thought to reflect an orientation toward patients based on control through coercive handling. However, the profile may be a reflection of job requirements and not an indication of personality characteristics.

Baker and Schulberg (1967) found the attitudes of psychologists more positive than psychiatrists as related to mental health ideology. Durfee (1971) reported that graduate students in psychology had more positive attitudes than social work and medical students, but these results were only for female students. The contrasts in the above findings make one wonder whether basic ideology toward mental disorders is the primary factor here. Morrison and his colleagues believe endorsing the medical model of mental disorders yields attitudes similar to those held by psychiatrists, while ascribing to the psychosocial model reflects attitudes similar to psychologists and social workers.

Authoritarianism also seems to play a role in the attitude endorsed by individuals. Canter and Shoemaker (1960) and Canter (1963) reported that nurses high on authoritarianism showed a more negative attitude toward patients with mental disorders. In addition, the former study showed that individuals who hold strong authoritarian attitudes are less likely to alter their attitudes than persons low in authoritarianism.

Meyer (1973) compared junior nursing students with their university peers and found the nursing students more authoritarian, a trend that decreased as education increased. Morrison, Yablonovitz, Harris, and Nevid (1976) compared senior nursing students with their university peers in psychology and education in regard to their attitudes toward mental disorders. Nursing students' attitudes were found to be moderate, falling between those of the other groups. This may have been due to the psychology courses the nursing students were exposed to.

Rosenbaum, Elizur, and Wijsenbeek (1976) investigated the attitudes toward mental disorders and role conceptions of psychiatric staff members. Mental disorders were viewed by nurses and aides in relation to their beliefs about how the hospital should function and to the role definitions of the other staff members. The authors reported that the more staff members viewed patients as "abnormal, dangerous and unpredictable," the more the patients were seen as sick and the staff's role as custodial in nature.

Rehabilitation professionals as a group have received attention with regard to attitude research. Goldin (1966) indicated that rehabilitation counselors preferred working with patients who had certain types of disabilities. Patients with mental disorders were among the least preferred cases. This may reflect the difficulty of placing these patients in employment and the desire of professionals to work with individuals with whom they will be successful.

In summary, the attitudes toward persons with mental disorders endorsed by treatment personnel is influenced by the individual's occupational group, level of education, authoritarian belief system, and the model of mental ideology ascribed to.

ATTITUDES TOWARD MENTALLY RETARDED PERSONS

Carroll and Repucci (1978) studied the meanings professionals attach to labels for children. Their findings indicate that mental health workers attached more negative meanings to children labeled mentally retarded than to those labeled emotionally disturbed, delinquent, or average. They also found that deviant behavior displayed by retarded persons was not considered atypical, although it would have been had the same behavior been displayed by nonretarded children. This suggests there is an expectation that retarded children will behave in more deviant ways and could partially explain the negative attitudes toward the group.

Kelly and Menolascino (1975) reported that although physicians were frequently expected by parents and other professionals to recommend services for retarded children, they often had limited knowledge regarding services, and instead of recommending community-based programs recommended those requiring institutionalization. The authors suggest that such behavior may reflect poor attitudes toward this disability group. It is also suggested that treating retarded persons may frustrate the physician's goal to heal, since these persons cannot be cured.

Differences in the desire to segregate retarded persons were found to exist based on level of nursing education (Lillis & Wagner, 1977). Baccalaureate nursing students were less willing to segregate retarded persons than diploma or associate nurses. It was also found that the baccalaureate and diploma nurses expressed less of an authoritarian attitude toward retarded persons than nurses educated at the associate-degree level. This finding was thought to reflect the fact that nurses in the baccalaureate and diploma groups had received more course work in areas related to the retarded than the nurses at the associate level. The authors suggested that more exposure of the baccalaureate students to general studies and behavioral science courses may account for the differences in attitudes.

Apparently some health care professionals endorse attitudes that encourage segregation of retarded persons, while others believe this is not appropriate. Authoritarian beliefs, level of education, and expectations associated with retarded persons all produce differential effects on the perceptions of professionals.

ATTITUDES TOWARD PHYSICALLY DISABLED PERSONS

Armstrong (1975) found that treatment teams on an adolescent dialysis unit responded to patients in a manner characterized by anger, anxiety, and a sense of intolerance. The author suggested these findings were the result of constantly being faced with the threat of loss plus the tremendous demands that adolescent dialysands make on the staff.

Chronically ill patients seem to prefer staff members who assume authority over patient care and involve the patient less (Barrell, DeWolfe, & Cummings, 1967). Patients endorsing this preference were more likely to be those not expected to make medical progress over the next year. It was hypothesized that a treatment team with this approach would hold negative attitudes toward patients, since patients would be more dependent and not fulfilling an acceptable adult role in society.

Bell (1962) found that the attitudes of rehabilitation staff members dealing with physically disabled patients were no different than those of members of the general hospital staff. The author expected to find more positive attitudes held by the rehabilitation workers, since they had such close personal contact with disabled individuals. However, recent research in the area of contact suggests that equal-status contact is required for positive attitude formation (Amir, 1969; Langer, Fiske, Taylor, & Chanowitz, 1976; Rapier, Adelson, Carey, & Croke, 1972). That the rehabilitation setting does not present an equal-status situation may help to explain Bell's findings. Attitudes held by pediatric residents toward handicapped children and their parents were more positive following completion of a course designed to change their attitude (Richardson & Guralnick, 1978). After the course the residents were better able to view the children as more positive and capable individuals.

Sadlick and Penta (1975) found a positive change in nurses' attitudes after they had taken a course in dealing with disabled persons. The nurses were able to overcome their sense of helplessness and hopelessness, feelings experienced by some nurses at times when they work with disabled individuals. Perhaps this is a reflection of the frustration the nurses feel when they cannot help a patient attain a total state of health. This may be similar to what was previously reported for the physicians working with disabled populations.

In summary, it seems that the attitudes held by a variety of treatment personnel toward different disability populations vary but are consistently less positive than expected. Education, type and extent of contact, and authoritarian belief systems seem to be variables involved with these findings.

FACTORS INFLUENCING ATTITUDE FORMATION TOWARD INDIVIDUALS WITH MENTAL DISORDERS

A number of factors have been identified as affecting the pattern of scores obtained on the OMI: age, gender, occupational classification, education, general knowledge regarding mental disorders, years of experience working with individuals with mental disorders, and level and nature of staff training. Occupational classification was addressed earlier in this chapter, with the conclusion that there are distinct attitudinal patterns for the various occupational groupings.

Education, a factor related to socioeconomic status, has been found to affect attitude formation. Middleton (1953) found that hospital personnel who were less educated or of lower intellectual functioning were more prejudiced than others toward patients with mental disorders. A weak but significant relationship between educational level and opinions regarding the etiology and prevention of mental disorders was reported by Freeman and Kassenbaum (1960). Clark and Binks (1966) found that less-educated individuals tended to endorse a set of beliefs indicating individuals with mental disorders are irrational, potentially dangerous, and unlikely to recover. Authoritarian beliefs also are related to educational level; Cohen and Struening (1962) found a sharp negative correlation between authoritarianism and education on the OMI.

What an individual knows about a disability has been shown to influence attitudes. Lieberman (1970) reported those most tolerant of individuals with mental disorders tended to be best informed about them. Gelfand

and Ullmann (1961) found that a decrease in authoritarianism scores among nursing students was associated more with an increase in theoretical knowledge than with clinical experience. A decrease in authoritarian and socially restrictive attitudes has been associated with increased mental health knowledge among aides following completion of a basic training course (Pryer & Distefano, 1977).

Gender has also been studied in relation to attitude formation. Gender differences have not usually been reported due to the limited number of males in the studies. However, Costin and Kerr (1962) did find differential effects for females on posttest scores on the OMI authoritarianism scale after they completed an abnormal psychology course. Chesler (1965), Freed (1964), and Yuker, Block, and Campbell (1960) have reported that females score higher on the ATDP than males.

Age shows a strong positive relationship with rejection of persons with a mental disorder according to Clark and Binks (1966), Lawton (1964, 1965), and Murray (1969). Cohen and Struening (1962) indicated that social restrictiveness shows a trend toward increasing with increasing age.

Years of service working with persons with a mental disorder has also been shown to have an effect upon attitude development; older and more experienced aides endorsed more prejudicial attitudes than workers with less experience (Middleton, 1953). Perry (1974), using a modified OMI completed by psychiatric aides, reported that unfavorable attitudes, such as social restrictiveness and authoritarianism, increased with age and years of experience, while favorable attitudes, such as benevolence and mental health ideology, decreased.

Level of training influences attitudes. Student nurses' attitudes toward persons with mental disorders changed in a positive direction as a result of psychiatric affiliation experience (Hicks & Spaner, 1962). Johannsen, Redel, and Engel (1964) concluded that psychological changes took place during a psychiatric nursing affiliation because the students were confronted and forced to interact with patients, which helped the students deal with their own conflicts, anxieties, and insecurities. Walsh (1971) reported an inverse relationship between levels of anxiety and attitudes toward persons with a mental disorder. In contrast to these findings is the work of Canter and Shoemaker (1960), who reported that nursing students with initially high authoritarian attitudes were, as a group, less likely to change their negative stereotypes of persons with a mental disorder following a 13-week psychiatric affiliation. Canter (1963) found similar results and concluded that individuals with high authoritarian scores on the OMI were very resistant to change on this attitude dimension. Jaffe, Moaz, and Avram (1969) concluded that classroom experience alone was not sufficient to change attitudes and stereotypes endorsed by nursing students.

Their findings indicate that practical experience involving direct patient contact is the most potent method for modifying attitudes. However, the environment in which this contact occurs is also crucial; students placed in a university training hospital reduced their stereotypes and negative attitudes, while students placed at a state-affiliated facility increased their unfavorable stereotyped attitudes.

Geskie (1985) incorporated several of the above-mentioned variables using a sample of professional nurses to study the relationship between attitudes toward disabled persons, empathy, and level of nursing education. Professional nurses who were female members of the American Nurses Association were randomly selected from the organization's total membership. They had three different levels of education: a bachelor of science degree in nursing, an associate degree in nursing, or a diploma in nursing. The nurses were mailed the ATDP (Yuker, Block, & Younng, 1966/1970), Hogan's Empathy Scale (Hogan, 1969), the Contact with Disabled Persons Scale (Yuker, 1983), and a background questionnaire.

Geskie found that nurses with a bachelor's degree had more positive attitudes toward disabled persons than nurses with an associate degree, as well as higher levels of empathy than the other two groups. This finding agrees with the work of Lukoff and Whiteman and the work of Roeher (both cited in Yuker, Block, & Younng, 1966/1970), which indicated that more positive attitudes were found with higher levels of formal education. Another finding was that nurses who had taken four or more social science courses had significant positive correlations between the attitude scale and number of social science courses. This result lends support to the Morrison and associates (1976) hypothesis that nurses' attitudes may be affected by the social science courses they are exposed to in their college programs.

Siller (1964) indicated that individuals with a tendency to see themselves as insightful, a quality called intraception, seem also to have more positive attitudes toward disabled persons. In Geskie's (1985) study, nurses with four or more social science courses had more positive attitudes toward disabled persons and also higher levels of empathy, which may well agree with Siller's findings, if intraception can be seen as similar to being empathic. Nurses with more than 11 years of professional practice were less empathic than nurses with less than 11 years of nursing practice.

In summary, the factors that have been consistently shown to influence attitudes toward individuals with mental disorders and other disabilities are gender, education, knowledge about disabilities, occupational classification, years of experience working with disabled individuals, and the level and nature of staff training. These factors must be controlled for to allow for more meaningful research results to be obtained.

THE RELATIONSHIP OF ATTITUDES TO
PATIENT INTERACTION

The importance of studying the attitudes of mental health professionals toward individuals with mental disorders is based on the assumption that these attitudes significantly influence patient–staff interactions and are indirect, easily obtainable measures of staff effectiveness. Rabkin (1975) states, "Staff members' attitudes toward mental illness in general, the expectations regarding the patients they work with and the extent to which their personal attitudes coincide with the prevailing treatment philosophy of their place of work, inevitably play a role in the success of the therapeutic effort" (p. 432). Staff attitudes have also been found to influence the roles mental patients adopt, as well as their views on the etiology of mental disorders (Manis, Houts, & Blake, 1963; Rosenbaum, Elizur, & Wijsenbeek, 1976).

Costin and Kerr (1962), Dixon (1967), Graham (1968), and Morrison and his associates (Morrison, 1976; 1977; Morrison & Becker, 1975) provided evidence that didactic presentations of material concerning mental health information and concepts related to diagnosis, treatment, and outcome can modify attitudes. The attitudes modified tend to be those closely associated with the specific information provided. The underlying assumption made by these and other authors (see Distefano & Pryer, 1975; Hall & Mueller, 1968; Pryer, Distefano, & Marr, 1971; Twomey & Keifer, 1972) is that changes in attitudes produce a corresponding change in behavior, an assumption not supported by the research (Fishbein & Ajzen, 1972; Wicker, 1969). In addition, several factors have been identified that influence attitude change through in-service training, including the length of training, the method of presentation, the stability of the work environment, and the ease of identification with the presenter. Most of these issues are not consistently addressed, nor are they controlled across studies to allow relevant comparisons of outcome.

It is assumed that certain attitudes are "better" or more therapeutic than others. Cohen and Struening (1965) lent support to this belief with findings that patients from hospitals characterized by an authoritarian and restrictive atmosphere spent less time in the community after admission to the hospital than patients from hospitals with less authoritarian and restrictive atmospheres.

Several criticisms of utilizing attitude profiles as measures of staff effectiveness have appeared in the literature. Certain attitudes appear to be class-bound. Individuals from the working class tend to score higher on measures of authoritarianism and restrictive control regardless of the instrument used, and they generally endorse the belief that mental patients are qualitatively different from "normals." In addition, those from the working class are more critical of behaviors they categorize as deviant and more rejecting of those that engage in it.

Several investigators (Cohen & Struening, 1962; Ellsworth, 1965; Foster, McClanahan, & Overly, 1974; Rabkin, 1975) have suggested that the attitudes of hospital personnel, particularly psychiatric aides, are more a reflection of the situational demands and job responsibilities of maintaining security and order on the ward than an indication of a deep-seated personality characteristic. Another explanation offered for the differing attitude profiles was provided by Bowen, Twemlow, and Boquet (1978) and Stotsky and Rhetts (1966), who postulated that different attitudes are in part due to the respondent's adherence to mental health concepts popular among age-specific cohorts.

Edelson and Paul (1976, 1977) and Rabkin(1975) offer two additional objections to the use of attitude profiles as indicators of staff effectiveness. First, conclusions of cause and effect have been drawn from correlational data. Second, factors previously identified as affecting attitude scores, such as demographic variables, were not controlled for, nor were characteristics of the treating units, such as ward size and type of patient population.

A strong objection to the use of profile scores to measure staff effectiveness arises from the lack of objective assessment of staff attitude–behavior relations (Engel & Paul, 1981). Although Ellsworth (1965) and Lawton (1964) reported obtaining correlations between staff attitudes and behavior, the methods utilized to measure staff behaviors were based on ratings of social desirability and not objective assessments of behavior. In Lawton's (1964) study physicians and nurses were asked to rank how valuable aides were, in addition to rating them on ease of supervision, how conscientious and neat they appeared, and how informed they appeared on principles of mental health care. In the Ellsworth (1965) study patients were asked to rate staff on such dimensions as "cool and reserved," "suspicious and skeptical," "sensitive and understanding," "cold and unfeeling."

Ellsworth, Bryant, and Butler (1960) investigated the relationship among attitudes toward mentally ill persons, job satisfaction, and objectively assessed behaviors. The staff were from wards where the personnel were either stable or changing frequently. All subjects took part in an eight-week in-service program. Each group discussed topics of specific relevance to them over the eight-week period. Scores were obtained for each subject on the CMI, a measure of job satisfaction, and the seven-category Aide Behavior Rating Scale (ABRS). Large changes in patient-contact behavior occurred among the staff from the stable ward, while those from the unstable ward were rated as being less self-centered. Those from the stable ward scored higher on the humanitarian pole of the CMI, while those from the unstable ward became more authoritarian. The results of the study highlight the importance of stability in the job setting as an influence on the attitudes and behavior of staff members.

Engel and Paul (1981) investigated the relationship between staff attitude-effectiveness profiles and on-the-floor behaviors. The Staff Resident Interaction Chronograph (SRIC), a behavior rating scale with 21 staff behavior categories and five patient behavior categories, was utilized to obtain objective measures of staff performance. Two groups of aides, one with OMI effectiveness profiles and one with OMI ineffectiveness profiles, were matched on such demographic variables as age, gender, years of service, and education. The OMI effectiveness group showed greater instances of activity and a greater number of activities within contacts with patients; they had a higher proportion of activities with patients. The OMI ineffectiveness group had a higher proportion of activities in job-relevant, but nonpatient, interactions. Neither group differed in the amount of time spent in job-irrelevant, noninteractive activities. Attitude and behavior changes of staff were found to follow, but not predict, patient behavior. This supports results reported by Kellam, Durell, and Shader (1966), who found that marked changes in nursing staff attitudes and feelings occurred with a decrease in ward patients' psychotic symptomatology.

In a similar type of study, Paul, McInnis, and Mariotto (1973) investigated the effect of training approaches on the behavior of aides. Two groups of 14 aides received training in milieu and social-learning principles. One group received traditional, sequential academic training followed by on-the-job training, while the other group received the same content through abbreviated academic training integrated with on-the-job training. Behaviors were rated using the SRIC. While academic instruction increased the understanding of theoretical principles for both groups, those in the integrated approach showed "better" on-the-floor performance than those in the sequential training group.

Salasek (1985) studied the influence of occupation, hospital setting, and in-service training content on the attitudes and behaviors of hospital aides and psychiatric nurses toward individuals with mental disorders. Nurses and aides from private and public psychiatric facilities with similar patient populations and length of stay volunteered to participate in a six-week in-service training program. They were randomly assigned to one of three treatment conditions: seminars based on Morrison's (1977) demythologizing approach, seminars based on traditional abnormal psychology content, and a no-treatment control group. Staff variables shown in the past to be correlated with attitudes such as age, gender, education, and years of service were statistically controlled. All subjects completed the OMI, the CAQ, and the ATDP prior to the start of the seminars, after their completion, and in a three-month follow-up. In addition, the behaviors of all subjects were rated by trained observers, using the 19-item Staff Behavior Checklist (SBC) during each of the three periods.

The results of the study showed a lack of relationship among the attitude scales. Three factors emerged, an authoritarian–restrictive dimension, a dimension attributing the etiology of mental disorders to early childhood experiences, and a dimension endorsing the belief that individuals with mental disorders are qualitatively different from others. With the previously mentioned demographic variables covaried, occupational differences emerged between nurses and aides, with aides obtaining higher scores on measures of authoritarianism and social restrictiveness. Hospital setting was found to have an effect only when the dependent variables were in combination. There was no effect of in-service training on attitudes or behaviors. There was, however, an increase in the amount of knowledge specific to the in-service content, knowledge that decayed from completion of the seminars to the three-month follow-up. These results are in keeping with the pessimism Cohen and Struening (1962) expressed regarding the effectiveness of in-service training to modify the attitudes of hospital personnel. Further, it highlights the complexity of the attitude–behavior relationship.

Rabkin (1975) stated that it should be no surprise when discrepancies occur between attitudes and behavior, considering the number of attitudes each individual has for a particular object, the situational factors operating, and the methodological issues involved with identifying and measuring the salient dimensions of attitudes. The question should not be whether there is an attitude–behavior relationship, but under what set of circumstances one occurs. Fishbein and Ajzen (1972) suggested we are more likely to predict specific acts of behavior if the instrument utilized measures the subject's attitude toward engaging in such an act rather than assessing the subject's attitude toward the object in question. Additionally, Fishbein and Ajzen (1974) have emphasized the need to shift away from the use of a single-act criterion to the utilization of multiple-act criteria in determining the relationship between individuals' verbally expressed attitudes and their patterns of behavior.

SUMMARY

This review covers the literature of the attitudes of various treatment professionals toward different disability groups, with primary emphasis on attitudes toward individuals with mental disorders. The complexity of attitude research is highlighted by the diversity of definitions of attitude, the multiplicity of methods and measurements employed to assess attitudes, the numerous dimensions and factors identified as influencing reported attitudes, and observations regarding the relationship between behavior and attitudes toward individuals with mental disorders. Several consistent findings have been reported in the literature. Distinct attitudinal patterns have been identified for the various occupations, but the results are confounded by demographic variables such as age, gender, education, occupation, and years of experience with individuals with a disability, as well as the type of setting, job role or function, and the level and type of training received. Mixed results are reported regarding the ability to modify and maintain attitude change through academic or practical experience.

PART V
Attitude Change

Modifying Peer Attitudes Toward the Handicapped: Procedures and Research Issues[1]

Marcia D. Horne

Public Law 94-142 has led to the mainstreaming of handicapped pupils, who now receive all or part of their educational program in regular classrooms. The hope is that positive interactions between handicapped and nonhandicapped pupils will occur. But there is abundant evidence that handicapped pupils are rejected in regular classrooms and that being assigned to a low status may have a negative influence on handicapped students' social, emotional, and intellectual development (Horne, 1985). Thus negative peer attitudes represent a significant barrier to mainstreaming.

However, data suggest that positive attitudes can be facilitated through various interventions. These include: (1) providing personal contact with disabled students and/or knowledge about handicapping conditions, (2) organizing small-group, nonacademic experiences to facilitate disabled student acceptance, (3) using team and cooperative learning experiences to promote student interactions, and (4) improving the social skills of disabled students. Other seemingly useful mechanisms for inducing change are role-playing, peer tutoring, bibliotherapy, game playing, and use of the mass media and educational materials. Still other variables, such as the organization and climate of the classroom, may affect the attitudes and interactions of disabled and nondisabled children.

---

[1]Adapted in part from: Horne, M.D. (1985). *Attitudes toward handicapped students: Professional, peer, and parent reactions.* Hillsdale, NY: Lawrence Erlbaum Associates, Inc. Copyright 1985. Reprinted by permission.

This chapter will review programs designed to modify peer attitudes toward school-aged handicapped children and also will consider possible directions for future research.

ATTEMPTS TO CHANGE PEER ATTITUDES

This section opens with a discussion of a controversial issue: the relative importance of personal contact with handicapped students versus knowledge about their handicapping conditions in promoting change. Then attempts to modify peer attitudes using small-group experiences, team and cooperative learning approaches, and training in social skills are considered.

Contact

Some studies have suggested that merely exposing nonhandicapped students to handicapped students will result in more positive attitudes toward handicapped individuals. For example, Towfighy-Hooshyar and Zingle (1984) found that the attitudes of students in grades two, four, and six were significantly influenced by contact with multiply handicapped peers. Rapier, Adelson, Carey, and Croke (1972) found third-, fourth-, and fifth-graders were more positive toward physically handicapped students after an orthopedically handicapped unit opened on the school's grounds. In another study elementary school children who had the most contact with severely retarded and multiply handicapped children expressed the most positive attitudes toward them; these findings also were evidenced one year later (Voeltz, 1980, 1982). Similar results have been reported for preadolescents (Sheare, 1974) and adolescents (Furnham & Gibbs, 1984; Ladd, Munson, & Miller, 1984).

Other studies have reported contradictory findings. Harper and Wacker (1985) reported that although there was a trend for elementary-aged children who had contact experiences to be more positive toward physically disabled peers, contact alone was insufficient as an attitude modifier. Goodman, Gottlieb, and Harrison (1972) found that educable mentally retarded students (EMR) who were mainstreamed into a nongraded elementary school were more rejected than segregated EMR students. Nor did the attitudes of seventh-grade students in nonacademic classes with mainstreamed EMR students differ significantly from those of seventh-graders in schools where EMR students were segregated (Strauch, 1970). Barton, Snart, and Hillyard's results (1985) indicated there was not a significant relationship between the integration of multiply handicapped students and a change in the attitudes of first-, third-, and fifth-graders.

Similarly, integration did not influence the attitudes of fourth-, fifth-, and sixth-graders toward trainable mentally retarded students (Sandberg, 1982).

Other investigations have demonstrated that contact with handicapped persons can produce a negative attitudinal shift. For example, taking high school students on a tour of an institution resulted in more negative attitudes (Cleland & Chambers, 1959; Sellin & Mulchahay, 1965). And elementary school students who had no contact with retarded students had more positive attitudes than students who had contact with retarded peers (Gottlieb, Cohen, & Goldstein, 1974).

Although the evidence regarding the effect of contact on students' attitudes toward handicapped peers is inconclusive, it appears that the findings may reflect the impact of the conditions of contact. Yuker (1983) reviewed the literature and concluded, "the precise nature and duration of the interpersonal relationships involved must be specified before conclusions are drawn" (p. 100). Yuker suggested that contact with a disabled person is more likely to produce an attitudinal shift if the two individuals: (1) share equal status, (2) are working toward common goals, (3) experience more intimate rather than casual contact, and (4) experience a pleasant or rewarding contact. A positive change in attitude is unlikely to occur if the nonhandicapped persons regard themselves as having higher status than the handicapped persons.

Information

Research on the effect of information about disabilities on attitudes has focused on providing nonhandicapped students with information about the causes, characteristics, and learning problems of handicapped students. Findings for the informational procedure are inconclusive.

Sometimes information has a positive effect on attitudes. Gottlieb (1980) found that showing third-graders a videotape of a mentally retarded student followed by a discussion of the causes and characteristics of mental retardation resulted in more positive attitudes. In other studies, however, the effect of information has not been demonstrated (Miller, Armstrong, & Hagan, 1981; Westervelt, Brantley, & Ware, 1983; Westervelt & McKinney, 1980).

More insightful studies are required to understand the relationship between information and attitudes toward the handicapped. Since informational procedures often have involved showing a film, it seems appropriate to develop a better understanding of how the content of films may relate to attitudinal change. For example, will films that consider the same variables Yuker (1983) felt important in a contact experience be more likely to produce an attitudinal shift? It appears that an attitude change is more likely if the viewing is followed by activity. Teacher-led discussion seems to be important. The effects of undirected discussion may be negative (Siperstein, Gottlieb, & Bak, 1977); discussion outcomes also may be related to the type of handicapped condition at issue, as well as the characteristics of the discussants.

Contact and Information

A review of the research on efforts to change adult attitudes toward the physically and mentally disabled led Anthony (1972) to conclude that:

> The attitudes of nondisabled persons toward persons with a disability can be influenced positively by providing the nondisabled individual with an experience which includes contact with disabled persons and information about the disability. Neither alone is sufficient, significantly and consistently to have a favorable impact on attitudes toward disabled persons. It appears that without information contact has only a limited positive effect or may even reinforce existing attitudes. Similarly, information without contact increases knowledge about the disability only but appears to have little or no effect on attitudes (p. 123).

Programs that have provided both contact and information usually have been more successful in modifying participants' attitudes toward disabled peers than either alone.

Programs containing contact and knowledge have been quite different. For example, a program designed to modify the attitudes of elementary-aged gifted students toward the disabled consisted of two major activities (Lazar, Gensley and Orpet, 1971): (1) a unit on creative Americans including those who were handicapped and (2) handicapped guests presented weekly discussions. Students evidenced significant positive attitudinal changes.

In one program (Jones, Sowell, Jones, & Butler, 1981) elementary-aged students were exposed to two two-and-one-half hour activity sessions. They (1) observed and experienced the needs and abilities of handicapped persons; (2) engaged in experiences using orthopedic devices; (3) observed and interacted with a retarded adolescent; (4) conversed with a blind college student; (5) experienced the use of braille; (6) performed games and activities while blindfolded; and (7) watched a film of blind people participating in sports. Brief discussions followed each activity, children engaged in creative writing activities about their experiences, and these activities were followed by a summary discussion. Posttesting showed significant positive attitudinal changes.

A project to modify attitudes of junior and senior high school students included five specific activities: (1) discussion of special-education terminology, legislation, barriers, and problems encountered by handicapped persons; (2) preparation of a research report on a specific disability, including causes, characteristics, and effects on learning and social adjustment; (3) viewing of a film about handicapped children and answering questions about their feelings; (4) participation in three or four simulation activities to experience a handicap; and (5) a personal interview with a blind student. In this study, the evaluation component required that students assess their own attitude change; 82% of the 20 students completing the self-evaluation said they had become more positive and accepting (Handlers & Austin, 1980).

But even when the elements of contact and knowledge are included in an attitude modification program there is no guarantee that a positive change will occur. Simpson, Parrish, and Cook (1976) compared the effects of information versus information plus contact. In this study the informational component presented to regular class, primary-grade students included showing of a filmstrip about handicapped students; discussions with professionals in the area of special education; and a visit to an empty special-education classroom, where another discussion of the special classroom and its enrollees was held. The sessions were held once a week for four weeks. Students in the information plus contact group spent an additional hour per week visiting and interacting with students in a self-contained class for emotionally disturbed children. Posttesting did not demonstrate a significant change in either group.

Newman and Simpson (1983) compared the effects of information versus information plus contact on the attitudes of elementary-aged students toward severely emotionally disturbed children. First, all the students were presented with six one-half-hour informational sessions, which included factual presentations and discussions about: (1) the concept of exceptionality and the nature of different handicapping conditions; (2) similarities and differences between handicapped and nonhandicapped persons; (3) how to interact with handicapped students; (4) methods used to instruct handicapped students; and (5) well-known persons who are handicapped. Students also engaged in simulations of handicapping conditions. Then students in the information plus contact condition were given specific information about the emotionally disturbed pupils enrolled in their school's special classes. Next the students were involved in three one-half-hour nonacademic structured experiences with the emotionally disturbed children in the special class setting. Observational data collected during recess periods indicated that the students in the information only group demonstrated significantly more positive behavioral interactions with the disturbed children than the information plus contact group. The authors speculated that the finding may have been due to (1) an inadequate amount of contact, (2) anxiety and fear experienced by the students in the structured activities or, (3) a discrepancy between the appeal of cognitive knowledge about handicapped persons and the actual experience of interacting with the emotionally disturbed pupils.

The literature on modifying pupil attitudes toward their handicapped peers is characterized by conflicting findings. Although differences in the design and implementation of extant studies make specific recommendations difficult, it seems reasonable to conclude that information combined with contact experiences is desirable.

Small-Group Nonacademic Experience

It has been hypothesized that "if the frequency of interaction between two or more persons increases, the degree of their liking for one another will increase, and vice versa" (Homans, 1950, p. 112). Similar hypotheses have been formulated by Allport (1954) and Zajonc (1968). Thus small-group experiences that require normal and handicapped students to work together have been designed to increase peer acceptance of handicapped students. Lilly (1971) required low-status students to work with high-status students in a filmmaking project outside of the regular classroom for 20 minutes a week for five weeks. Acceptance increased for low-status students after the treatment; the gains were not maintained over time, however.

On another project (Ballard, Corman, Gottlieb, & Kaufman, 1977) small groups contained an educable mentally retarded (EMR) student and four or five nonhandicapped peers. Teachers attended a two-day in-service workshop and were given a manual to help them instruct children in small-group work. The groups were small, structured, and "minimally academic." Each session lasted 40 minutes a day for eight weeks. Students were more accepting of EMR classmates four weeks after the treatment ended.

Small-group experiences have also been developed to increase the status of handicapped students in a special class. In one study (Chennault, 1967) two low- and two high-status mentally retarded students were involved in the planning, rehearsal, and presentation of a play. Testing immediately after the presentation showed a significant improvement in the peer acceptance scores for the low-status students. Rucker and Vincenzo (1970) designed a similar program for unpopular EMR students. Students with the highest and lowest acceptance scores met twice weekly for two weeks in 45-minute sessions to prepare a class carnival. Posttesting three days after the carnival showed significant gains in peer group acceptance for the low-status students; these gains were not maintained one month later, however.

Team and Cooperative Group-Learning Approaches

Horne (1985) described several approaches for conducting small-group experiences using teams or cooperative instructional groups. Initially developed as mechanisms for increasing cross-racial friendships, cooperative group-learning approaches show promise as mechanisms to increase interactions among handicapped and nonhandicapped students. Cooperative learning, an approach espoused by Johnson and Johnson (1975), has been explored somewhat more extensively in relationships to handicapped and nonhandicapped student interactions and thus is discussed in greater detail in the following section.

Cooperative Versus Competitive and Individualistic Classroom Instruction

Teachers may structure classrooms to achieve their instructional goals (Deutsch, 1949, 1962). In a cooperative classroom learning approach, the goals for individuals are linked, so that a student only can obtain his or her individual goal if other students in the group obtain theirs. Students work together and the rewards are given to the group (see Johnson & Johnson, 1975, for the steps followed in the cooperative teaching approach). This is in contrast to the competitive approach, wherein each individual is rewarded for achieving; an individualistic approach does not promote a relationship among the goals of individuals, since a student is rewarded for his/her own performance. According to Johnson (1980), while the cooperative structure provides for the greatest amount of student interaction, the competitive situation "promotes cautious and defensive student–student interaction" (Johnson, 1980, p. 134), and in the individualistic situation there is no interaction. In the ideal classroom situation all three structures would be used. Students would experience working together, competition, and learning on their own.

Cooperative instruction has been proposed by Johnson and Johnson (1980) to increase nonhandicapped students' acceptance of handicapped students:

> A direct consequence of cooperative experiences is a positive cathexis in which the positive value attached to another person's efforts to help one achieve one's goals becomes generalized to that person. Thus, students like each other regardless of their individual differences, self-esteem increases, and expectations toward rewarding and enjoyable future interactions between nonhandicapped and handicapped students are built (p. 94).

In contrast to cooperative instruction, competitive or individualistic structures are viewed as promoting the rejection of nonhandicapped peers, since in competitive situations students are concerned about outperforming their peers and in the individualistic structure they tend to ignore and avoid other students.

Efficacy of Cooperative Instruction

Numerous studies explored the effects cooperative versus competitive and individualistic teaching have on students (see reviews by Johnson & Johnson, 1974; 1979; Johnson, Johnson, & Maruyama, 1983; Johnson, Maruyama, Johnson, Nelson & Skon, 1981). Efficacy studies of the effect of cooperative instruction on handicapped and nonhandicapped student interactions are a more recent trend. When cooperative versus competitive and/or individualistic instruction has been used to teach academic and nonacademic skills to emotionally disturbed, learning-disabled, and mentally retarded students, findings have indicated that significantly more interactions occurred among both the handicapped and nonhandicapped students in the cooperative situation (Cooper, Johnson, Johnson & Wilderson, 1980; Johnson & Johnson, 1981; 1983; Johnson, Johnson, DeWeerdt, Lyons & Zaidman, 1983; Johnson, Johnson, Scott & Ramolae, 1985; Martino & Johnson, 1979; Rynders, Johnson, Johnson, & Schmidt, 1980; Yager, Johnson, Johnson & Snider, 1985).

The efficacy of team-learning approaches as a mechanism for increasing interactions among handicapped and nonhandicapped peers requires more study. Even with the often-employed cooperative learning situation proposed by Johnson and Johnson (1975), more confirming evidence seems necessary because of the different student populations studied and the varied methodologies used to measure social outcomes of increased peer status, interpersonal attraction, and peer interaction. Furthermore, cooperative instruction has been primarily studied with learning-disabled, emotionally disturbed, or mentally retarded students. Thus future research should examine the influence of cooperative instruction on peer acceptance of students with other handicapping conditions.

Other variables also must be considered. Some learners may be cooperatively, competitively, or individualistically inclined, thereby influencing the outcomes of team or small-group learning (Owens & Barnes, 1982). Similarly, group composition with respect to ability and personality may affect the ensuing interactions among students (Webb, 1982). Differential effects on intra- and interpersonal behaviors of male and female students have also been demonstrated for different learning environments (Cosden, Pearl, & Bryan, 1985; Crockenburg, Bryant, & Wilce, 1976). Also, student and teacher training in small-group interaction alone may affect the outcome (Swing & Peterson, 1982; Talmage, Pascarella, & Ford, 1984). Furthermore, according to Sharan (1980), team methods may differentially affect students' attitudes, their achievement, and their relationships. Consequently, all of the procedures must be studied more extensively to understand how they might affect handicapped students and attitudes toward them.

Training in Social Skills

Social skills have been variously defined. According to Foster and Ritchey (1979), social skills are "those responses which, within a given situation, prove effective or, in other words, maximize the probability of producing, maintaining or enhancing positive effects for the interactor" (p. 626). Social skills are situation-specific, learned verbal and nonverbal responses that elicit and/or reinforce behavior (see Van Hasselt, Hersen, Whitehill, & Bellack, 1979, for a further discussion of definitions of social skills).

Numerous studies have pointed out that a deficiency in social skills may be responsible for assignment of handicapped students to a low social status by peers. Misbehavior (Baldwin, 1958; Johnson, 1950; Johnson & Kirk, 1950), deviant behavior (Hutton & Roberts, 1982; Morgan, 1978), and problems in verbal communication skills (Bryan, Donahue, & Pearl, 1981; Cartledge, Frew, & Zaharias, 1985) are among the social skills that are likely to interfere with positive relationships among handicapped and nonhandicapped students. But more subtle attributes also should be considered, such as role-taking (Affleck, 1975) and assertive behavior (Hughes & Hall, 1985; Macklin & Matson, 1985). Further study must be devoted to identifying the relative influence of the multiplicity of social skills (e.g., recreation skills, conversation skills, eye contact, posture, empathic responding, social cue interpretation) on interactions among handicapped and nonhandicapped individuals. Furthermore, in addition to the type of handicapping condition, other variables may influence the relationship of social skills to social status among different subgroups of students. As Schloss and Schloss (1985) pointed out, age seems to be one of the variables to consider. For example, the ability to demonstrate appropriate assertive behavior may have more or less influence on a handicapped student's social status, and the relationship may be different for a blind child than for a deaf child, depending upon the age of peers. Responses rewarded in the student's environment may be studied to learn which social skills should be trained (Matson, Rotatori, & Helsel, 1983; Vidoni, Fleming, & Mintz, 1983). Student gender, social class, and the situational context are also important factors to consider in deciding the relative importance of behaviors in determining social status. In turn, these factors have implications for deciding the order in which these skills ought to be introduced into a social-skills training program designed to increase the social status of a handicapped student. Not to be overlooked is the importance of training nonhandicapped students to interact effectively with their exceptional peers (Strain & Odom, 1986).

Although much of the research dealing with training in social skills has utilized preschool or nonhandicapped populations (see reviews by Cartledge & Milburn, 1978; Gable, Strain, & Hendrickson, 1979; Gresham,

1981; Strain & Shores, 1977; and Van Hasselt, Hersen, Whitehill, & Bellack, 1979), reports are emerging on the efficacy of teaching social skills to school-aged handicapped students. But it is not clear whether these changes have resulted in greater peer acceptance, because frequently peer status changes were not assessed. Furthermore, when changes in peer status have been measured, the subjects have often been in specialized or isolated settings (Cooke, & Appolloni, 1976; La Greca & Mesibov, 1979; Lancioni, 1982). Yet there is evidence that using behavioral procedures to eliminate the undesirable behaviors of handicapped students can increase their status in regular classrooms (Csapo, 1972; Drabman, Spitalnik, & Spitalnik, 1974).

POTENTIALLY EFFECTIVE PROCEDURES FOR MODIFYING STUDENT ATTITUDES

This section discusses additional procedures that may be useful for inducing a change in a student's attitudes and interactions. These include (1) role-playing, (2) peer tutoring, (3) bibliotherapy, and (4) game playing. Consideration is also given to the role of media and educational materials in attitude change.

Role Playing

Researchers distinguish between role-taking ability, role-taking activity, and role-playing. Kitano, Stiehl, and Cole (1978) defined role-taking as "a covert cognitive process of predicting another person's perspective" (p. 61). Role-taking ability is "the individual's cognitive capacity to anticipate another person's perspective when it differs, or is independent, from one's own" (p. 61). In contrast, role-taking activity "concerns the individual's employment of role-taking ability in a particular situation" (p. 61). A further distinction may be made between cognitive role-taking and affective role-taking. Enright and Lapsley (1980) defined cognitive role-taking as "the child's ability to think about what the other is thinking,"; affective role-taking as "the child's ability to understand another's internal subjective or feeling state" (p. 649). Finally, role-playing is "the overt enactment of the role attributes (characteristics and behaviors) of another person" (Kitano, Stiehl, & Cole, 1978, p. 61).

Role-taking ability and activity have been described as social skills that may be important for positive peer interactions. Handicapped children may be deficient in these skills, but the research on role-taking using handicapped populations is limited. Their review of the literature led

Kitano and associates (1978) to conclude that further research is necessary to clarify the ability of a nonhandicapped person to take a handicapped person's role and that there may be a gap between a nonhandicapped student's ability to take a handicapped student's role and his/her
use of that ability or role-taking activity. These authors suggested that role-
training interventions might be developed in which handicapped students
are trained to anticipate the perceptions of others about their actions. At
the same time, training nonhandicapped students to perceive the feelings
and needs of handicapped classmates might facilitate more positive interactions in the classroom.

Role-playing or simulation activities (the terms are used synonymously
in the literature to refer to activities in which nonhandicapped individuals
act out the part of a handicapped person) are frequently part of a series of
activities comprising a program of attitude modification (Handlers & Austin, 1980; Jones, Sowell, Jones, & Butler, 1981); but the technique has also
been effective when used by itself. For example, Clore and Jeffrey (1972)
used direct and vicarious emotional role-playing. One group of college
students, told to imagine that they had been involved in an auto accident
that had resulted in paraplegia, was required to take a 25-minute wheelchair trip around campus; another group of vicarious role players walked
20 feet behind them and observed. After returning, participants wrote a
description of their experience and completed several attitudinal scales.
Results indicated significantly more positive attitudes on the immediate
posttesting and on a four-month follow-up measure for both groups. In
another investigation (Marsh & Friedman, 1972) simulation activities had
a positive influence on high school student attitudes toward blind peers.

But in some experiments role-playing did not result in any attitudinal
changes (Margo, 1983; Wilson, 1971; Wilson & Alcorn, 1969). Furthermore, Wright (1978) carefully examined the findings of several role-playing studies (Clore & Jeffrey, 1972; Wilson, 1971; Wilson & Alcorn, 1969)
and expressed concern about the possibility that role-playing could contribute to or reinforce a participant's stereotype of handicaps if the experience is not a constructively guided one. From this standpoint, role-
playing would involve not only exposure to the disability, with its inherent
losses and difficulties, but would also focus on the "possibilities for personal adaptation and change" (p. 181). Wright also recommended "assertive role playing" in which disabled and nondisabled participants play out
antagonistic roles. For example, in an enacted confrontation between a
blind person and an office manager who refuses to hire him, the blind
simulator must respond, argue his competency for the position, and ne-
gate the arguments presented by the employer about incompetencies
related to the disability. Wright also advocated use of role reversal, wherein

both participants play each role and then discuss the experience from a helping standpoint.

Further research should be directed toward clarifying the effect of constructively guided role-playing. Since role-playing may help bridge the gap between role-taking ability and role-taking activity (Kitano, Stiel, & Cole, 1978), it is particularly important to achieve a greater understanding of how to conduct the procedure.

Peer Tutoring

The use of students as tutors for other students was common practice in one-room schools during the nineteenth and twentieth centuries, and the 1960s and 1970s generated a renewed interest. Numerous studies have demonstrated the positive effect of peer tutoring on the academic performance of both tutors and tutees. Students also accrue a variety of psychosocial benefits, such as improved motivation, self-concept, school attitude, and interpersonal skills. Although not all the findings are positive, and although data on the effects of such variables as age, sex, characteristics of the tutors and tutees, their training, and the training situation must be more systematically gathered, peer tutoring seems to be an advantageous procedure for student tutors and tutees. (For reviews of the literature on peer tutoring, see Allen, 1976; Cohen, 1986; Cohen, Kulik, & Kulik, 1982; Delquadri, Greenwood, Whorton, Carta, & Hall, 1986; Gartner, Kohler, & Reissman, 1971; Paolitto, 1976.)

Recently, peer tutoring has been suggested as a mechanism to facilitate mainstreaming, because handicapped students may receive more individualized help (Bradfield, Brown, Kaplan, Rickert, & Stannard, 1973). When nonhandicapped students have tutored their handicapped peers, achievement as well as behavioral gains have been evidenced (Maher, 1984; Mandoli, Mandoli, & McLaughlin, 1982; McHale, Olley, Marcus, & Simeonsson, 1981). Furthermore, evidence suggests that peer tutors are as effective as teachers especially trained to work with handicapped students (Russell & Ford, 1983). Investigations of the academic and behavioral gains exhibited by handicapped students tutored by handicapped peers have also yielded positive findings (Drass & Jones, 1971; Epstein, 1978; Kane & Alley, 1980; Lazerson, 1980; Parson & Heward, 1979; Scruggs & Osguthorpe, 1986; Stowitscheck, Hecimovic, Stowitscheck, & Shores, 1982).

Peer tutoring is a logical procedure for promoting positive interactions among handicapped and nonhandicapped students (McCarthy & Stodden, 1979). Prejudice exists among handicapped groups (Horne, 1985); peer tutoring may help to develop more positive attitudes. There is limited support for these notions. Donder and Nietupski (1981) trained seventh-grade nonhandicapped volunteers to teach age-appropriate playground skills to moderately mentally retarded peers. The program was designed to facilitate positive peer interactions between retarded and nonhandicapped students. Substantial increases were observed. Fenrick and Petersen (1984) determined that nonhandicapped students' negative attitudes toward moderately and severely mentally retarded peers became more positive after a structured tutoring program. Recently Osguthorpe, Eiserman, and Shisler (1985) explored the social efficacy of having handicapped students tutor their nonhandicapped peers. Elementary-aged educable mentally retarded students enrolled in self-contained special classes trained regular class agemates in sign language. Results indicated that the experience resulted in an increase in the positive interactions among the handicapped and nonhandicapped students during lunch and recess. When interviewed, most tutees indicated they had acquired a more positive attitude toward mentally retarded students.

The effects of peer tutoring on student attitudes are not clear-cut. Indeed, in a recent review of tutoring experiments involving behaviorally disordered students as tutors or tutees, Scruggs, Mastropieri, and Richter (1985) concluded that tutoring experiences may result in more accepting attitudes; however, extant data on social benefits is open to question. And in a review of studies involving learning-disabled students as tutors or tutees, Scruggs and Richter (1985) concluded that the benefits of tutoring experiences with learning-disabled students are equivocal. According to the results for other programs incorporating experience and knowledge (seemingly inherent to peer tutoring), positive attitudinal changes could very likely be produced. Peer tutoring is a component of team-learning approaches; since this method holds promise for increasing peer interactions, peer tutoring seems to have further substantiation. But the procedure must be more thoroughly investigated and studied with diverse populations (e.g., visually, hearing, and physically disabled students). Since perceptions of competence and prestige are fostered by the tutor role (Bierman & Furman, 1981), this could lead to further devaluation of the handicapped tutee; it seems worthwhile to explore this attitudinal aspect of peer tutoring as well.

Bibliotherapy

Bibliotherapy involves three steps: identification, catharsis, and insight. Readers or listeners may identify with the character in the story and vicariously experience the motivation, conflicts, emotions, and so on of the character, leading to a catharsis. Identification and catharsis lead to insight; when nonhandicapped students listen to or read stories about handicapped children, the insights they develop may lead to more positive attitudes and interactions. However, there have not been many reports on the efficacy of using children's literature to modify attitudes toward handicapped persons, and the results are equivocal.

Salend and Moe (1983) demonstrated that just reading books about handicapped persons did not alter student attitudes; but when the reading activity was combined with discussions and simulations, a change was evidenced on an attitudinal measure. Leung (1980) showed that texts and discussion may lead to a verbal expression of attitude change on the part of nonhandicapped students, but no change in the number of social interactions among handicapped and nonhandicapped classmates. Recently, Bauer, Campbell, and Troxel (1985) reported that reading and discussing a text about a handicapped person was more effective in producing an attitude change than a film and discussion or a combination of a book, film, and discussion.

Bibliotherapy seems more likely to be effective when it is used in conjunction with a discussion that includes explanations about handicapped persons. It is interesting to note that reading texts may be more effective than films in changing attitudes. Given that texts are probably more accessible to teachers than are films, the procedure merits further study. But the content of books written about handicapped children must be scrutinized, since texts may present stereotypes as well as inaccurate information (Sapon-Shevin, 1982). Researchers studying the effects of bibliotherapy also should consider using observational data of peer interactions as well as attitudinal measures.

Game Playing

Recently, athletic activities have been advocated to facilitate interactions among handicapped and nonhandicapped students. According to Marlowe (1979), because retarded students are more like nonhandicapped ones in the area of motor skills, motor-related activities represent a particularly viable method for facilitating interactions between these groups. In the games analysis procedure (Morris, 1976), games are structured to take into consideration the individual motoric skill differences evidenced by players and to facilitate particular social and/or emotional goals. Marlowe (1979) used this procedure to increase the social acceptance of an integrated, but socially rejected, 10-year-old mentally retarded student. Classmates were taught how games could be played in an adapted form and then played together. Observational data indicated positive interactions with nonhandicapped peers increased; sociometric data supported a significant increase in peer status three weeks after the program ended. The games analysis procedure was also used by Marlowe (1980) with a gender-disturbed 10-year-old who was the least accepted male in the class. After seven weeks of playing adapted games, sociometric testing indicated a significant gain in peer status, which was maintained eight months later.

Other types of game playing may be useful for increasing interactions among handicapped and nonhandicapped students. For example, in one experiment (Aloia, Beaver, & Pettus, 1978), playing a Bean Bag Game together facilitated interactions among integrated educable mentally retarded children and their nonhandicapped classmates. Another study (Stainback, Stainback, Hatcher, Strathe, & Healy, 1984) demonstrated that use of small-group games increased the interaction between high-status elementary-aged students and low-status mentally retarded students. One study (McHale & Simeonsson, 1980) required second- and third-graders to play with autistic children. The nonhandicapped students were simply told that the autistic children did not know how to play, that they should teach them, and that they could engage in any activities they chose. Pre- and posttesting indicated that the students were initially positive toward the autistic group and that these positive attitudes were maintained.

One hopes that future game-playing experiments will clarify the extent of their usefulness as a mechanism for modifying attitudes. Possibly these strategies will be more useful when they are coupled with an informational component for the nonhandicapped or with social-skills training for the handicapped participants. Evidence with preschool students suggests that the type of materials, toys, and activities employed can influence social behavior. For example, Quilitch and Risley (1973) categorized "social" and "isolate" toys, finding that when children were provided with social toys there was a dramatic increase in the number of prosocial interactions. Structured play experiences have been used to increase interactions between handicapped and nonhandicapped preschoolers (Odom, Jenkins, Speltz, & DeKlyen, 1982; Strain, 1975; Strain & Wiegerink, 1976). Similar experiments with older students might be a good idea.

Media Presentations

Video and film media have been shown to be useful components of projects designed to modify peer attitudes. Although investigations have been initiated to understand the relative merits of live presentations by handicapped individuals versus video- or audiotaped presentations on the attitudes of adult populations, the comparative efficacy of using different types of media approaches to change the attitudes of school-aged individuals has been largely ignored.

It is also not clear how television programming might influence children's attitudes toward handicapped persons. Since it has been demonstrated that changes in children's racial attitudes may result from television viewing (Bogatz & Ball, 1971; Gorn, Goldberg, & Kanungo, 1976), it is important to explore the use of television as a medium to modify children's attitudes toward handicapped group members. Storey (1980) demonstrated that when television viewing is combined with discussion, elementary-grade students may demonstrate more positive attitudes toward a variety of handicapping conditions. Another study (Elliott & Byrd, 1983), with eighth-graders, indicated that a professional film had a positive effect on their attitudes; viewing a television episode did not. The results were attributed to the audience's receptiveness to the direct information provided in the film versus the indirect information that characterized the television episode. It is clear that further research is necessary; studies must consider the issue of content characteristics and the desirability of different types of follow-up activities, as well as the impact different presentations may have on diverse audiences. Such investigations seem to be particularly important given that studies concerning the depictions of disabled persons on television programs indicate that handicapped persons are often inaccurately and unrealistically described and often cast in negative roles (Donaldson, 1981; Elliott & Byrd, 1982). Given the widespread popularity of television viewing, the potential efficacy of designing television programs for children that consider the development of positive attitudes toward handicapped students cannot be overlooked.

Educational Materials

Commercial materials are available for teachers to use in providing students with information about handicaped peers, including films, filmstrips, videotapes, and audio presentations, as well as books about individual disabilities. There are also comprehensive media productions designed to promote student acceptance of a variety of handicapping conditions (see Litton, Banbury, & Harris, 1980, for a list of materials). But there are few reports on the influence these materials have on student attitudes. Hazzard & Baker (1982) examined the attitudinal effect of a nationally marketed multimedia disability awareness program that uses films, activities, discussions, and texts with third- through sixth-graders. Results indicate that participants in the program were more knowledgeable about the characteristics of disabled persons; but on measures of social distance and a scale designed to measure willingness to interact with handicapped peers, there were no significant differences. The authors concluded that media programs may prepare children for interacting with the handicapped "by altering misconceptions and alleviating initial anxiety so that children are more likely to initiate interaction in the presence of a disabled peer" (p. 260), but that more actual contact with handicapped persons may also be necessary. Another program, The Kids on the Block

(Aiello, 1979), uses several large puppets characterizing children with different disabilities (see Aiello, Chapter 16 in this volume, for a discussion of this program). Although research does not clearly indicate whether commercial materials modify peer understanding of, or interactions with, handicapped students in the classroom, an increasing amount of such material is being published. Given the availability of these materials and their potential for widespread use in classrooms, it is important that research efforts be directed toward understanding the influence these programs may have on attitudes toward disabled persons. It is also imperative that these programs be studied under conditions in which children are provided with contact with handicapped peers. Currently there are no reliable guidelines to determine how student characteristics will interact with a particular program.

Possible Influence of Classroom Organization and Climate

A variety of classroom organizational characteristics have been shown to affect the attitudes and interactions of peers in regular classroom settings. However, the effects of such variables as class size, seating arrangements, and so forth usually have not been explored in relationship to the effect they might have on nonhandicapped peer attitudes toward, and interactions with, handicapped students. Understanding the influence of a variety of environmental conditions on student attitudes and interactions must be considered carefully in future research. These variables are briefly reviewed in the following paragraphs. The reader is cautioned that these variables have been assessed in some cases in one or just a few studies and are reported here because of their potential implications. Inadequate replication mitigates against overinterpreting.

Class Size. The number of students in a classroom may affect the nature and number of interactions that occur among classmates. For example, Hallinan (1979) reported that in larger classes children form more "best" friendships and that there are fewer isolates or unpopular students than there are in small classes.

Seating Arrangement. The seat assigned to a student may affect how the student is perceived by his classmates. Schwebel and Cherlin (1972) found that students assigned seats in the front of the class were more positively perceived by their peers.

Classroom Social Structure. The characteristics of classmates may affect classroom interactions. Findings by Rosenfield, Sheehan, Marcus, and Stephan (1981) indicated that group equality in terms of social class and achievement level, as well as the percentage of minority-group members present in a group, contribute to the amount of interaction that will occur among students.

Classroom Organization. Whether a classroom is organized multidimensionally (students work individually on different tasks) or unidimensionally (students are grouped to work on tasks) may affect student perceptions of peers (Rosenholtz & Rosenholtz, 1981; Simpson, 1981). The amount of teacher-directed classroom activity may influence the positivity of peer interactions (Huston-Stein, Frederich-Cofer, & Susman, 1977). In highly structured classrooms where activities are largely teacher-directed, students may be more likely to engage in less prosocial behaviors toward peers, including cooperation, helping, and empathy. Recently Burstein (1986) found that classroom organization had a differential effect on handicapped and nonhandicapped preschool children. For handicapped students structured settings did not facilitate peer interaction; informal settings seemed to be helpful but did not adequately encourage peer interactions. Nonhandicapped students interacted similarly across settings.

Teacher Management Skills. In classes where teachers have good management skills students may exhibit less deviant behavior (Borg, Langer, & Wilson, 1975). This may, in turn, affect peer perceptions of handicapped students, since it appears that the deviant behaviors they exhibit contribute substantially to their rejection by peers. Teachers may require training in group processes to facilitate peer interactions (Schmuck, 1968).

Open Versus Traditional Schools. Open schools can have positive effects on the social and psychological development of students (Giaconia & Hedges, 1982; Horwitz, 1979). It appears that open classrooms affect the pattern of student friendships such that there are fewer social isolates and a more even distribution of popularity; on the other hand, it appears that students in traditional classes have more friends (Hallinan, 1976). In the few studies that have attempted to study the effects of open class attendance on handicapped student status, the results have not been encouraging (Goodman, Gottlieb, & Harrison, 1972; Gottlieb & Budoff, 1973; Scranton & Ryckman, 1979).

CONCLUSIONS

This chapter has described several procedures for modifying student attitudes toward handicapped peers. Unfortunately, there is no specific procedure that is unequivocally supported by research as effective in producing positive attitude changes among students. Rather, some procedures seem to have more or less influence on student attitudes than others. Many unanswered questions surround the task of attitude modification. Future research must be directed toward understanding what types of experience and knowledge should be incorporated into programs for students. Given a particular classroom situation, which method might prove to be most useful for modifying student attitudes? Might some approaches be better for modifying attitudes toward specific handicaps?

Individual differences in attitudes before treatment must also be considered. The interaction of such variables as age, gender, ethnicity, social class, cognitive ability, and attitudinal predisposition deserve further exploration. Livneh (1982) reported on a variety of personality variables associated with adult attitudes toward disabilities, including ethnocentrism, authoritarianism, aggression, self-insight, anxiety, self-concept, ego strength, body- and self-satisfaction, ambiguity tolerance, and social desirability. Such correlates should be explored in relationship to attitude-modification projects designed for school-aged populations.

It is important to investigate whether attitudinal changes demonstrated at immediate posttesting are maintained over time. Do students continue to exhibit positivity? Usually post-posttesting has not been undertaken. When it has, the results have not been encouraging (Lilly, 1971; Rucker & Vincenzo, 1970; Westervelt & McKinney, 1980). Although Ballard and associates (1977) found that the gains in social status of mentally retarded students who participated in a small-group experience were demonstrated after four weeks, it is important to know if they were maintained for the school year, or at least for some significant portion of time.

The generalization of positive attitudes toward different exceptionality groups must be examined. If students become more accepting of mentally retarded students, will they also be more accepting of learning-disabled pupils? Is there a relationship between the severity of a handicap and generalizability? An overriding limitation of extant data on student attitude change has to do with the populations studied; to a considerable extent, researchers have focused on studying the social status of learning-disabled, emotionally disturbed, or mentally retarded students. Approaches efficacious for modifying attitudes toward these groups of students may be more or less effective in modifying attitudes toward those with sensory or physical handicaps. But we do not know. It is important that strategies for changing peer attitudes be tested in relationship to a variety of handicapping conditions.

Most attitude-modification studies have used either an attitudinal scale or sociometric procedure to demonstrate their effectiveness. Future research must aim toward clarifying the relationship of expressed positivity on these measures and actual behavioral changes on the part of peers in the classroom. Observational data such as is commonly gathered for behavioral interventions, and which has been used in efficacy studies for cooperative classroom instruction, is suggested. When observational data are recorded, there is also a need to collect maintenance data; follow-up observations must also be undertaken to explore the durability of change effected when behavioral strategies and cooperative classroom procedures have been carried out.

Finally, although this chapter focused on procedures that may be used to modify nonhandicapped students' attitudes, it may be helpful to consider the ways in which handicapped students might elicit more positive interactions from their peers. How can handicapped students play a more active role in determining the nature of their interactions? Can students with different types of handicapping conditions be taught strategies that will influence the attitudes of nonhandicapped persons toward them?

CHAPTER 16

The Kids on the Block and Attitude Change: A 10-Year Perspective

Barbara Aiello

The Kids on the Block are a group of disabled and nondisabled puppets designed to teach children who are not disabled to accept and appreciate those who are. Puppet characters represent children with a variety of disabilities, such as cerebral palsy and mental retardation; medical conditions, such as cancer, epilepsy, and diabetes; and social concerns, such as physical and sexual abuse, teenage pregnancy, and divorce. They have been in existence for nearly 10 years. Our initiation into the field of special education was in direct response to Public Law 94-142, and over the last 10 years our work with children and adults and attitude change has parallelled efforts at implementing the law.

Today the Kids on the Block program forms a growing network of more than 900 community-based organizations in 49 states and 14 countries. All kinds of persons, from teachers, nurses, and parents, to retirees and college students, use some or all of The Kids on the Block puppets to educate children about disabilities and differences and to emphasize that rather than detracting from a person's selfhood, differences enhance individual personalities and the lives of those around them.

The first Kid on the Block was "Mark Riley," who was developed in response to a desperate situation I faced as a special-education teacher. It is said that necessity is the mother of invention; in this case, a frustrating situation with one of my students—the necessity that he be mainstreamed—led to the invention of the puppets. "Anthony" was a 12-year-old boy with cerebral palsy who was the first special-education student to leave the segregated setting of my class for the "physically disabled" and be mainstreamed into the regular program. The regular school into which Anthony would be placed was just across the street from the special school, so the geography of mainstreaming was amenable to the impending change.

As I contemplated the placement, I did what many of my colleagues did in the early days of the mainstreaming movement. I spoke with the regular class teachers, gathered the appropriate books and workbooks, and for the first six weeks of the 1977 school year prepared Anthony to function academically in the regular fifth-grade class. When we determined that he was up to grade level in the key subjects of math, science, and language arts, I wheeled him across the street. Two weeks later I checked with the teacher and asked how Anthony was doing in his new environment. She reported that he was doing beautifully, "getting A's, B's, and one hundreds, every time I turned around!" Her enthusiastic response prompted me to muse that "this mainstreaming stuff is a cinch and what is everybody complaining about?"

I found out how difficult mainstreaming is when, nearly five weeks after Anthony's "successful" mainstreaming, he appeared at the door of my special class. Even before I could praise his great academic accomplishments, Anthony informed me that under no conditions would he return to his "regular" class. When I asked why, he told me that although his teacher was nice and the work was fun, "Nobody will play with me, nobody will talk to me, and nobody will even eat next to me in the lunchroom." Anthony went on to say that he loved his old class and his old teacher, and he demanded to be part of special education once again.

"The horns of a dilemma" barely describes the state I was in. I have since learned that, as a special educator and part of the group referred to as the helping profession, there is much psychological gratification earned from loving the kids that we think nobody loves and teaching the kids that we feel others cannot or will not teach. There is a large investment on the part of the special-education community, among others, to keep kids dependent and to keep our charges in great need of the services we "special" people provide.

So, I had to decide. By accepting Anthony back into special education, I could provide the warm and supportive environment I knew would make him a comfortable learner. Yet my charge, as is the charge of any educator, regular or special, is that I prepare my students to be functional and competitive citizens of the world—and for disabled children, that means a world where the majority of the contacts and competitors are able-bodied, "regular" folks.

I let Anthony back into my class, but only for two weeks. I promised him that during that time I would think of some way to make the children in the fifth grade more accepting of his differences. At the time I had no idea what I might do, but soon "Mark Riley," the first Kid on the Block, was born.

Mark was made to look, act, and sound like Anthony. That is, Mark, the puppet, used a wheelchair (made of garden hose and right-angle welds), had red hair, wore head gear, and spoke with a noticeable speech difference somewhat common among persons with Anthony's type of cerebral palsy. Mark and I went to the fifth grade, and Mark talked to the kids. He told them about CP, about using a wheelchair, about sports, favorite foods, and television shows. When Mark asked if there were any questions, hands shot up:

"How do you get upstairs?"

"Can you, like, you know, go to the bathroom?"

"Why do you talk like that?"

"How did your Mama feel when she found out that her baby would have trouble doing things and just growing up?"

I was amazed. Were these the same children who walked the other way when Anthony, the real kid with CP, wheeled into the cafeteria? And since they were, why were these same children so open and sensitive with a representation of a person with a disability when they had the chance to ask these same questions to "the real thing"?

Much later I realized why what seemed to be magic had happened. In a shopping center with my daughter, we saw a young woman pushing three strollers joined together. My daughter announced, "Look, Mama, three twinny babies!" I agreed that this was a most unusual sight and that we might go over and chat with the mother and have a better look. We did that and commented on the fact that the babies did not look alike; they were one girl and two boys. In the course of the encounter we learned a little about the incidence of fraternal triplets.

Later that same day we noticed a man using a prosthetic arm with a hook to hold and measure two-by-four beams at the local hardware store. Another child and his parents noticed, too; and when that little boy saw the hook he said to his dad: "Look, there's a guy with a hook instead of a hand. Neat!" But the rest of the story was quite a different scenario. The father pulled his son close to him, and loudly "whispered": "Don't stare! You're gonna embarrass that man!" The lessons to be learned are many,

but the one most significant to me is that, comparing the two incidents, I
noticed that children readily learn that in our society, even though it is
appropriate to be curious about the world around you, there exists a
hierarchy of differences—some of which (such as physical differences) we
not only do not talk about, we do not even look at.

This brings me back to Anthony and his stand-in, the puppet Mark. It
seems that the fifth-graders experienced, along with me, the power that
puppetry has had through the ages and continues to have today. Even
though these fifth-graders had internalized society's message of drawing
away from persons with disabilities, nobody had ever told them not to talk
to puppets! Puppets historically have not only encouraged children's natural curiosity, they have rewarded it by talking, moving, and behaving in an
open and engaging manner. Puppets have created safe ground for audiences, allowing them to suspend reality long enough to believe that these
foam, cloth, or papier mâché concoctions are real. As a consequence,
children drop their defenses and learn something new.

When Anthony returned to his class, the children talked to him immediately. "Hey, we had this guy in here last week," said one, referring to
Mark's visit. "He had the same thing you got and told us about why he talks
like that. Is that why you talk like that?"

Mark, the puppet, had provided these children with a nonthreatening
way to practice new behaviors to use when they encountered Anthony. It
gave both Anthony and the other children a forum from which to initiate a
conversation. In short, it worked. So the puppet family grew.

When people come to visit our offices, they notice that the puppets
today are taller and heavier than the original Mark and his friends. I believe
that the size and stature of the puppets grew in direct proportion to my
confidence in the program. That is, over the year I have learned that when
children are given the opportunity to experience differences in a comfortable and controlled atmosphere, they can relax and learn. Jean Piaget
calls this "the teachable moment," that near-magical point in time when
an educational tool has sparked interest and creativity and enabled children to comfortably explore and adopt new, more productive behaviors.

In a typical appearance, The Kids on the Block perform several different
scripts. Each script focuses on a different disability or difference. In addition, the nondisabled puppet expresses some of the typical fears or misconceptions that many people have about disabled people—fears that are
directly addressed by the disabled character. When "Melody James," for
example, tells Mark that she bets his wheelchair prevents him from "doing
some of the things that other kids do," Mark responds, "I can do about a
hundred million things." He tells her that he can swim, explains how he
learned to ride horseback (at "Camp Courageous," he says, with tongue in

cheek), and tells her that he uses his wheelchair to push a soccer ball down the field.

When the skit is over, the puppets invite the children in the audience to ask questions—as important a part of the performance as the script itself. This question time allows children to ask about what is on their minds. They continue to ask as sensitive and interesting questions today as did Anthony's classmates nearly 10 years ago.

The relationships that are portrayed between the disabled and non-disabled puppets are also an important part of the message. By modeling a relationship, we try to open the door for nondisabled children to explore normal, open friendships with their disabled peers.

My family has grown to 17 Kids, each with a difference to portray and a special story to tell. You have heard about Mark. Now, I'd like you to meet "Lynne Casey," the newest Kid on the Block.

> Hi, I'm Lynne Casey, and you can tell by looking at me that I got burned real bad in a fire. See, the furnace in our house exploded and when the firefighters came they got my Mom out first because she was in the living room. By the time they got to me, upstairs, I was already burned pretty badly. I was in the hospital a real long time and had lots of operations, called plastic surgery, to help the scars heal properly. One time my best friend, Melody James, got real upset because I was planning on singing my favorite song in our school's talent show. The song is "I Feel Pretty," and it's the one Maria sings in *West Side Story*. Anyway, Melody was upset because she thought that since some of the kids at school think I'm not pretty anymore, that I just shouldn't sing the song. I understood how Melody felt. My Grandma had a real hard time looking at me when all the bandages came off, but my Mom and Dad helped her understand that lots of times when people are talking about what's pretty, what they're really talking about is what's the same. I look different now but I think of myself as a pretty person and always will!

Lynne is an important addition to the Kids on the Block because she helps them confront differences in one of its most dramatic forms. Since she is facially disfigured, Lynne talks not only about the trauma of severe burns, but also about the way we perceive each other when differences are starkly apparent. Through her and the other Kids, children have the opportunity to learn first hand that people with differences can be friendly, warm, and interesting; that differences can be as enabling as they can be disabling; and that it is a function of learned perception whether enablement or disablement is emphasized.

As we approach our tenth birthday, it is important for me and for those who use the puppet program to consider if the puppets "work." That is, do they do the job they say they can do? Have attitudes changed for the better as a result of their introduction into the lives of children who are not disabled?

The Kids on the Block have been the subject of at least five research studies conducted in the United States and Canada. The results have been not only positive but statistically significant as well. In May 1985 the Kids on the Block puppets were used to determine the level of disability awareness and attitudes of nonhandicapped children toward severely disabled children. Powell (1985) concluded that "the treatment [the puppet progam] used did improve student attitudes toward the severely handicapped."

In 1985, at the College of William and Mary, Williamsburg, Virginia, researcher Dr. Sarah Hawkins Grider found that the use of the Kids on the Block, combined with the use of role-playing and disability simulations created a significantly measurable change in the development of positive attitudes for fifth- and sixth-grade students.

At the department of pediatrics at the Chedoke-McMaster Hospital in Hamilton, Ontario, Rosenbaum, Armstrong, and King (1985) used a variety of programs to examine attitude change among elementary school children. The Kids on the Block puppets were used; in addition, nondisabled children were paired with disabled classmates in a "buddy" program. Although researchers felt that this unique combination would result in marked development of positive attitudes, a different scenario appeared. Children who saw The Kids on the Block but were not buddies were significantly more likely to show a positive attitude change than were children who received both interventions. Clearly, there are implications for work to be done on the part of both the special- and regular education communities in bringing together "the world as it could be, " as portrayed by the puppets, and "the world as it is," as perceived by disabled and nondisabled children alike.

Finally, in addition to empirical evidence, my professional intuition tells me the Kids work for one very important reason. They portray disabled children as real children. I am reminded of several instances in which disabled persons were the subject of television programs and films. E. Keith Byrd and Timothy R. Elliott examine this issue comprehensively in Chapter 7 of this Volume. But allow me to reiterate by citing three recent portrayals.

Not long ago, Bette Davis, in a highly regarded made-for-TV film, starred as a flyer who taught a paraplegic girl how to fly a plane. Prior to her solo flight this girl had had no friends, no interests, and little enthusiasm for life. After Ms. Davis's intervention, the phone never stopped ringing and she was literally belle of the ball.

For the younger viewers, I am reminded of an episode of "Fat Albert," in which a character who represented a child with Down's syndrome was taunted and teased by the neighborhood gang until he won first place in a track meet held by Special Olympics. Then the teasing stopped. Or a donkey named "Nestor," who was run out of his corral because his ears were so long he tripped over them, and looked funny to boot. Nestor was one miserable donkey until he had the chance to carry Mary on his back on her journey to Bethlehem. During the arduous trip through the desert it was Nestor's long ears that wrapped around Mary and protected her from a sandstorm. When Nestor returned home, he was welcomed as a hero. No donkey teased him or would even think of it because now he was special in a positive way.

What this means to me and The Kids on the Block is that for too long disabled persons have been portrayed in the media as helpless, dependent "cripples," people who generated pity and pathos from those around them. With the advent of P.L. 94-142 and other significant reforms, disabled people have moved from pitiable positions to the roles of "superhero," as seen in the three examples above. Yet this new development is often as separating, as disabling, as the pitiable portrayal. Kids learn from Fat Albert, Nestor, and countless other shows, books, and movies that disabled people must be better at something than regular people, special at something that most of us cannot do, before they, the nondisabled majority, will deign to have them as friends.

My point is that there are far too many occasions on which disabled persons are told that they are either "less than" or "better than." The Kids on the Block address the more than plausible alternative—that persons with disabilities have a right to be accepted on their own terms, as regular people who need neither our pity nor our applause as a basis for establishing contact and friendship.

CHAPTER 17

Self-Help Groups: Empowerment Attitudes and Behaviors of Disabled or Chronically Ill Persons

Mark A. Chesler and Barbara K. Chesney

Since the primary focus of this volume is attitudes toward persons with disabilities, it is important to emphasize the distinctive nature of our work, as well as both its divergence from and relevance to the topic at hand. First, we have not focused primarily on persons with disabilities, at least not as that label is commonly utilized. Our research and action projects are primarily concerned with families of chronically and seriously ill children, particularly children with cancer. However, since over 10% of this nation's children are affected by chronic illness or disabling conditions (Haggerty, 1983), such a focus is relevant to this book. Second, our work with self-help groups of families of children with cancer has not focused primarily on their attitudinal predispositions; rather it has concentrated upon the organizational structures, processes, programs, and mobilization efforts of these groups. However, since such group-level features flow from and have an impact upon individuals' attitudes, this focus also seems important and relevant here. We know that chronic illness is not the same as disability, although they may have much in common; that groups for parents and families are not the same as groups for patients, although they may share similar origins and dynamics; and that ill or disabled children are not the same as ill or disabled adults, although they may become one or the other. The combination of our orientation with that of others in this volume should multiply our perspectives and knowledge.

In this chapter we address three major issues: (1) What is empowerment? (2) Why is empowerment an important issue in discussions of chronic illness or disability? (3) In what ways are self-help groups actually or potentially empowering of members?

WHAT IS EMPOWERMENT?

Empowerment means different things to different people in different personal circumstances and in different social and cultural settings. For instance, it means something different to most men than to most women; it has different meanings in the United States and in the Union of Soviet Socialist Republics; it means different things to people with a lot of power than to people with very little power. To begin, we need both the skeleton of an abstract definition, one that may fit many different situations, and some particulars that fit our own explorations.

From the standpoint of psychology, Rappaport (1983–84) suggests that empowerment means to have (or gain) some positive sense of control over oneself and one's life opportunities. From a more sociological perspective, it probably also involves the feeling that one is part of a larger collectivity, a group in which one encounters "people like myself." Meaningful participation in such a collectivity involves formal or informal roles in a family, a friendship group, a race or gender group, a work group, an organization, or a total community. Finally, empowerment probably involves the feeling and evidence that one's collectivity is stable and potent, that it has access to necessary and valued resources, both those of a material (money, food, shelter) and a symbolic (reputation, respect, the vote) character.

In the context of chronically ill or disabled people, empowerment has some special and concrete meanings. First is the ability and resources to provide effective care for oneself, including the maintenance (or development) of a coherent identity (as an ill or disabled person or as the family member of such a person), emotional stability, and a positive self-concept (Kieffer, 1983–84). Second is the ability and resources to provide effective care for one's disabled or ill child or family member, including having (or getting) adequate information, expressing parental (or spousal) loving attitudes and behavior, and participating in the provision of medical and psychosocial care. All these intrapersonal characteristics are vital to the ability to care for oneself or others and to deal effectively with the interpersonal or institutional environment. Third is the ability and resources to care for significant others in the family, friendship network, and formal or informal collectivities of other ill or disabled people. Clearly, more than the self must be empowered for one to be whole; whatever community we live in, it is a social community. Fourth is the ability and resources to take action on behalf of self and community, to improve the medical and environmental resource system that provides care for ill or disabled people and thus affects their lives so importantly. This may involve efforts at public education, fund raising, community organization, political protest, planned social change, and so forth (Asch, 1986; Checkoway, 1985).

These defining features of empowerment speak to individual characteristics as well as to collective characteristics of groups of individuals. They identify attitudinal components of human beings (cognitive/informational, affective/emotional, evaluational) as well as behavioral components (action-taking, action-receiving). In sum, empowerment probably requires a positive sense of self, a coherent and accurate analysis of one's personal and collective situation (including limitations and opportunities), and a good understanding of oneself as part of a broader collectivity or class of affected people. Obviously, people cannot be empowered alone; it requires connection, identification, and action with other people.

WHY IS EMPOWERMENT AN ISSUE?

Despite our personal commitments, or national rhetoric, the possibility of empowerment is threatened or jeopardized for many people in these United States and, indeed, throughout the world. People without food and shelter, without wealth, without freedom, without self- or other-respect, without an available and caring collectivity, without the ability to influence the major decisions affecting their lives, are effectively disempowered. The possibility of empowerment is especially jeopardized for chronically ill and disabled people, because the personal and social conditions that define them as ill or disabled are potentially disempowering. Therefore, it is important to discuss the stresses of illness/disability and the ways these stresses may be disempowering.

Illness itself may be disempowering. The real constraints an illness or disability places on persons may limit some physical functions and impose constraints on their range of accessible roles and abilities. As Checkoway and Norsman (n.d.) note, illness or disability may result in impairments that limit travel, communication, or access to physical facilities and social functions. The diagnosis of a serious or life-threatening illness, especially for a child, is often shocking to the entire family. It creates fear and anxiety and often drains physical and emotional energy. It may also seriously compromise personal and familial finances. When an illness or disability is chronic, the strains of care (medication, transportation to a hospital, reorganization of household chores, etc.) continue over an extended period of time.

The actions of significant others may be disempowering. Friends and family who do not know how to act in the presence of an ill or disabled person often increase the stress of illness/disability and threaten the possibility of empowerment (Chesler & Barbarin, 1984). Although illness and disability are physical conditions, they are also social constructs, and often these subjective interpretations affect the attitudes and behaviors of others more than do the physical markers of illness. People who withdraw from former friends or acquaintances because they are frightened, awkward, or disgusted at an illness or disability threaten their friends' emotional integrity and self-esteem. People who cannot respond to requests for help, or who offer "nonhelpful help," compound the difficulties of normal social relations. Moreover, it is typical for ill or disabled persons (and their family members) to be stigmatized by others and labeled as non-normal, as somehow outside the range of normal human experience (Goffman, 1963).

The medical and human service system that provides services to people with chronic illness or disability often operates in ways that create added stress and heighten feelings of disempowerment. For example, the typical model of medical practice presses for compliant patient roles, treats patients and their family members as dependent and passive, and retards peoples' abilities to act independently and assertively (Antonovsky, 1980; Featherstone, 1980). Treatment in a complex medical organization, typical for patients with chronic disabling conditions, adds the impersonal trappings of bureaucracy to the medical treatment model itself, further depersonalizing and dehumanizing patients (Taylor, 1979). Even when the care is life-saving in nature, as in the case of childhood cancer and other serious illnesses, these aspects of the medical care system are distressing. Although these issues are related to the attitudes of caregivers (developed as part of their preprofessional socialization and training), they also reflect the structure of medical and human service institutions, and the roles mandated and adopted in these settings.

Finally, *the actions of community institutions* may contribute to the disempowerment of chronically ill and disabled persons, especially as these institutions fail to guarantee the legal and humane rights and privileges all citizens should expect. To the extent that ill people are deprived of adequate medical and psychosocial care, to the extent that chronically ill or disabled children and adults are denied fair and equal access to educational services, to insurance programs, to employment, or to public and private functions and facilities, they are disempowered.

In the particular case of seriously ill children, there is another disempowering element: *the challenge to the parental role*. Parents are the

TABLE 17-1 Stress and Employment in Self-Help Groups for Families of Children with Cancer

Categories of stress or disempowering threats	Self-help group activities	Empowering aspects of self-help groups
Intellectual		
Confusion	Lectures by staff	Share of experiental expertise
Ignorance of medical terms	Group discussions among parents	Access to professional expertise
Ignorance of where things are in the hospital	Handbooks and newsletters	Development of assertive links to the medical staff
Unclarity about how to explain the illness to others	Library of articles, films, and videotapes	Promote understanding of illness/treatment
Instrumental/Practical		
Disorder and chaos at home	Funds for wigs, prostheses, parking	Develop new skills in coping with illness
Financial pressures	Facilities for transportation, lodging	Learn "tricks" to solve problems
Lack of time and transport to hospital	Efforts to improve medical care	Learn about organizations
Need to monitor treatments	Raise funds for research, added staff, and needed services	Find new material resources
Reallocation of family time and tasks	Develop and run an organization (SHG)	
Dealings with other community agencies	Discuss coping strategies (e.g., nutrition, childrearing, family cohesion, etc.)	
Interpersonal		
Needs of other family members	Discuss problems with and feelings about the staff	Compare oneself with others
Friends' reactions and needs/ pressures	Meet new people	Learn how others deal with family, friends, and staff
Relations with the medical staff	Talk with others "like oneself"	Care for others . . . give *and* receive help
Behaving in public as the parent of an ill child . . . stigma	Family recreational activities	Feel "together" with others . . . not alone

(*continued*)

TABLE 17-1 (*Continued*)

Categories of stress or disempowering threats	Self-help group activities	Empowering aspects of self-help groups
Emotional		
Shock	Peer counseling	Share emotional experiences
Lack of sleep, nutrition	Be listened to and affirmed (and do listening and affirming)	Test new identity
Feelings of fear, defeat, anger, sadness, powerlessness	Discussion of intimate feelings	Promote disclosure
Feelings of hope, joy, victory.	Referral to professional counselling	Rely on self
Physical or psychosomatic reactions		Develop sense of competence
Existential		
Confusion about "why this happened to me" and "my child"	Talk about religious beliefs	Test new beliefs
Uncertainty about the future	Discussion of the common struggle	Test new social identity, plans
Changes in future goals, career	Create a long-term group . . . community	Help others
Uncertainty about God, fate and a "just world"		Feel part of a larger group

primary caretakers of the young, and when medical treatment of chronically ill children is accomplished on an outpatient basis, parents are frontline medical caregivers as well. Sometimes parents feel supplanted by medical professionals or do not feel they have the personal ability and social resources to care for their ill child; then they are lessened in their self-concept and performance of this important social role and this vital aspect of one's identity.

Table 17-1 (column 1) conceptualizes these threats to the well-being and empowerment of chronically ill or disabled persons from the vantage point of our work with families of children with cancer (Chesler & Barbarin, 1986). Partly as a guide to the remaining portions of this chapter, column 2 indicates some of the specific programs and activities of self-help groups that respond to these disempowering aspects of chronic disease and disability, and column 3 indicates some of the dynamic processes in self-help groups that may help empower ill and disabled people.

WHAT IS A SELF-HELP GROUP?

In the face of these stresses, or threats to one's well-being, ill and disabled people (and their family members) cope in a variety of ways. One of the most common coping strategies is the search for some kind of social support. Social support may be sought, and may be forthcoming, from a wide variety of sources: family members, friends, distant relatives, neighbors, medical staff members, clergy, and so forth. People in different life circumstances, or with different illnesses or disabling conditions, find some of these sources of support more helpful or available than others.

One interesting source of social support is a self-help group. A self-help group is a more or less formally organized group of people who share a similar life situation or who are coping with a similar set of stresses or conditions. A key characteristic of self-help groups, as distinguished from counseling or support groups in general, is that participants come together on a voluntary basis, to "help oneself and themselves." They may call upon professional resources or agencies for assistance, but often leadership is provided and maintained by group members themselves.

The literature on self-help groups suggests that there is a great variety of organizational structures and processes in these groups and that they create a varied set of programs and activities. Our own research with a sample of 50 self-help groups formed by and for families of children with cancer bears out this finding (Yoak & Chesler, 1985). Some groups are small (less than 10 members) and some are large (over 100 active members); some have formal bylaws, charters, and officers, others are like bowling clubs or coffee klatches; some have regular and announced programs, perhaps with outside visitors, others are informal discussion groups.

Their programs and activities also vary, as indicated in column 2 of Table 17-1. Some groups concentrate on dealing with the intellectual stresses of illness and disability, providing informational and educational programs that utilize professional and parental perspectives on the medical problem and its treatment. Others focus primarily upon providing instrumental assistance to parents and families, including small financial allocations, housing near the treatment center, and other practical services, facilities, and coping aids or hints. In some groups the primary concern is to generate an alternative social network and to provide an arena within which parents can socialize with one another. Many groups try to respond to the emotional stresses of illness or disability via discussions in which parents share their worries and hopes, their reactions and concerns, taking advantage of the trust that is built up among people who are "in the same boat." And some programs and activities respond to the existential threats of illness and disability, focusing on the search for answers to "why this happened to me" and what the meaning is of a cruel and unreasonable God or fate.

HOW ARE SELF-HELP GROUPS (POTENTIALLY) EMPOWERING?

What these groups share in common, despite their variety, is a membership of people experiencing a similar stressful situation and the commitment to meet with one another in an attempt to reduce the stresses or disempowering threats that often accompany their situation. As Suler notes, "The therapeutic potential of the self-help ideology is its ability to encourage people to overcome powerlessness, to feel and use their own strength to resolve problems" (1984, p. 30). The dynamic processes in self-help groups that help their members realize these empowerment objectives are not always articulated self-consciously, but they include:

1. Promoting disclosure and networking. This process permits and encourages the test of a new part of one's personal identity and the development of a heightened consciousness as an ill or disabled person (or parent). "Going public" is a crucial part of adapting to a new life situation, and mutual support groups encourage such self-assertion and self-acknowledgment. Levy (1976) emphasizes the importance of this function, and Bloch and Seitz (1985) also discuss families' needs for "a place to identify, explore, and deal with their concerns" (p. 8). Such processes help to counteract the culture of silence that sustains mutual ignorance and a sense of isolation from other people. It also helps develop a climate of trust based upon shared pain and shared experience. In such a climate, social comparisons can help people find role models and combat aloneness and alienation, as well as the sense that one's fate is unique. When effective, mutual disclosure also helps create a new social network, composed of people similarly ill or disabled, that has resources and options greater than those available in any single member.

2. Sharing emotional experiences. The sharing of intense and intimate feelings aids the expression and catharsis of emotions, as well as emotional problem solving. In discussing the deep sharing that occurs among bereaved parents, Sunderland notes that "illusions about the grieving process are gently examined, the opportunity to learn how others have survived this horror have occurred, and the helping and healing process of affirmation has involved everyone" (1982, p. 8). A self-help group is a place where people can share feelings (hopes as well as fears) that they may have kept secret from others, perhaps out of concern to protect themselves or to

spare their loved ones. As these secrets are shared, many people discover that they are neither incompetent nor "going crazy," and that their distressed emotional reactions may be quite normal.

3. Gaining access to information. In a group focusing on a particular illness or disability, people can concentrate on obtaining professional expertise that informs them of technical and psychosocial aspects of their condition. In addition, "veterans" share their "experiential expertise" (Borkman, 1976), unique information that only "people like us" know. Some of this information relates to an understanding of the way in which the medical system works, promoting more coherent analysis and personal action-taking. Such expertise aids problem solving and heightens a sense of intellectual competence with regard to the illness or disability and with regard to the medical and social environment within which one acts.

4. Gaining new coping skills and practical resources. As practical problems and solutions to problems are shared, many people discover new skills as well as new ways of dealing with deficits and needs. The emphasis on strength and self-reliance, and on viewing others' coping tactics, helps many people convert problems and limitations into resources and opportunities and encourages personal and institutional assertiveness. Levy (1976), Videcka-Sherman (1982), and Bloch and Seitz (1985) all emphasize the importance of such expanded skills and resources in helping people deal with practical problems, as well as gain and display their strength in general. As Sunderland notes, "Thanks to these strengths self love is restored bit by bit; families are reconstructed bit by bit; the world of work can be mastered a little at a time; and the pattern of life can be rewoven with new threads which will be woven next to the old" (1982, p. 8). Some of the skills developed in a self-help group also involve learning how to run an organization, develop new liaisons with the medical and psychosocial treatment systems, counsel others, exercise leadership, and so forth (Yoak, Chesney, & Schwartz, 1985).

5. Contributing to the welfare of others. The dynamic by which people who themselves are ill or disabled grow as they give aid and comfort to others occurs through the "helper-therapy" principle (Riessman, 1965). By helping others one announces the existence of spare resources and the ability to overcome loneliness and desolation. Giving of oneself to others is a significant route to receiving many benefits.

6. Mobilizing and acting for change. Efforts to improve or make changes in the social and medical environment occur as people conceptualize their experiences as common, rather than as individual and unique. They thus establish the basis for collective action. Withorn notes that, "As self-help groups grow in their criticism of the health and social welfare system . . . [they] organize new found understanding and anger into group pressure for change" (1980, pp. 8-9). It may be essential that this realiza-

tion and organization happen in a group context, for, as Hatfield argues, "By organizing themselves, people gain strength to stand up to powers against which they feel alone" (1981, p. 412). Many self-help groups generate the resources that permit them to help make changes in the delivery of care, in the educational and rehabilitative programs available for chronically ill and disabled people, and in the enactment of laws and public policies (Dickson, 1981).

Tables 17-2 and 17-3 illustrate the operation of some of these processes in self-help groups. The data represent the reports of empowerment-relevant attitudes and behaviors present in or gained from self-help groups of families of children with cancer. In visits with 50 self-help groups organized by and for families of children with cancer (the number of groups is indicated by the symbol *NN* in the tables), we asked active participants to indicate what groups did and what benefits they derived from group participation (the numbers of individuals is indicated by the symbol *N* in the tables). Analyses of these data are not complete and are available at present only in descriptive form. They are presented here as illustrations of the kinds of activities and benefits of self-help groups that embody the aforementioned processes and that they may contribute to participant empowerment.

In Table 17-2 self-help group members report activities that are potentially empowering and benefits they derive from their participation in a group. In both cases the activities and benefits occur at the attitudinal level. Disclosure and networking is the most common source of empowering attitudes in these groups: 97% of participants report much or some benefit from "being able to talk with other parents" and 94% report much or some benefit from "meeting others with similar problems." Sixty-four percent report that people "plan to get together socially" in their group a lot or some. Sharing emotional experiences also is a common activity (71% and 70% report these activities occur a lot or some of the time) and a common source of member benefit (81%–87% report much or some benefit on these items). Gaining access to information occurs commonly, and 66%–88% of members report much or some benefits from these activities. Finally, learning new coping skills and solving practical problems is reported as occurring a lot or some of the time by 79% and 87% of participants and as a source of much or some benefit by between 67% and 85% of participants. One of the items in this set, "coping with the death of my child," illustrates some of the problems in examining only the overall results in these tables: 44% of all participants report much benefit from this aspect of group activity; however, when these reports are differentiated by the life status of the child, only 17% of the parents of a living child report much benefit from such discussions, but 65% of the parents of deceased children report much benefit. Obviously, on this and other items, parents'

TABLE 17-2 Empowerment Attitudes

What do groups do that is empowering for members? $(N = 228, NN = 43)^*$				Self-help group process
	A lot	Some	Never or a little	
Plan to get together socially	22%	42%	36%	Disclosure and networking
Talk about very personal feelings	28	43	29	Sharing emotional experiences
Learn how to deal with emotional issues	29	41	30	
Talk about death	10	31	59	
Cry	19	38	43	
Discuss recent advances in treatment	23	46	31	Gaining access to information
Learn more about the disease	25	41	34	
Discuss the quality of medical care	30	40	30	
Discuss the quality of social work care	14	30	56	
Talk about the stresses on the family	50	37	13	Gaining coping skills/ resources
Talk about reactions of other family members	35	44	21	

*Table Ns and NNs differ from the total sample when individuals or total failed to provide any information.

particular life circumstances affect their choice of group activities and the level of benefit they derive from participation. Further analyses of these data will differentiate the overall results by several aspects of the social and demographic backgrounds of informants.

Table 17-3 presents members' reports of group activities and benefits that occur at the behavioral level. Activities and benefits related to processes of social disclosure and networking are once again most common. Activities where parents "sit and talk with one another" are reported as occurring a lot or some of the time by 95% of informants. Although many groups appear to plan activities that might be of practical coping assis-

TABLE 17-2 (Continued)

What benefits do members derive from group participation?
($N = 146$, $NN = 37$)

	Much	Some	None or a little
Being able to talk with other parents	68%	29%	3%
Meeting others with similar problems	68	26	6
Understand how well off I am	38	35	27
Feeling part of a large group	30	42	28
Expressing my feelings	44	43	13
Being more optimistic or hopeful	40	41	10
Getting in touch with my feelings	33	54	13
Getting information about cancer	48	40	12
Understanding the treatments	40	39	21
Learning who's who in the hospital	28	38	34
Coping with problems in my family	24	49	27
Coping with the death of someone else's child	51	29	20
Coping with the death of my child	44	23	33
Deciding how to discipline my child	12	43	45
Coping with my child's problems	35	50	15
Learning my "rights" as a parent	37	33	30
Developing self-confidence	30	42	28

tance, it does not appear that many parents derive substantial benefit from these processes: only 23% report financial assistance as of much or some benefit, and 15% report such benefit from assistance with lodging. Aid (learning or direct assistance) in "dealing with my child's school" is more often reported as a substantial benefit (55%). Further analysis should clarify whether most parents simply had little need for financial and lodging assistance, or whether groups did not deliver such benefits, regardless of the amount of group discussion and planning of these issues. Contributing to the welfare of others is reported as common (55%–59% reported it occurred a lot or some in their group), and 94% derived much

TABLE 17-3 Empowerment Behaviors

What do groups do that is empowering for members?
(*N* = 228, *NN* = 43)   Self-help group process

	A lot	Some	Never or a little	
Eat and drink together	29%	36%	35%	Disclosure and
Have a party for families	20	40	40	networking
Sit and talk with one another	74	21	5	
Visit other parents at home	8	22	70	
Pray with others	7	17	76	
Plan a newsletter	25	27	48	Gaining coping skills/
Plan to raise money	27	23	50	resources
Support a parent whose child was dying	28	31	41	Contributing to others
Counsel or support parents at the hospital	23	32	45	
Plan to change things in the hospital	12	27	61	Acting for change
Talk with drs/nrs about personal feelings toward them	7	21	72	

or some benefit from "being helpful to other parents." Substantially less common were activities focused on making changes in the hospital and in gaining benefits from such processes. Only 39% of participants report that their group often planned to make changes in the hospital, and only 44% and 46% of parents indicate that they derived much or some benefit from "being an active part of the medical care system" or from "changing things in the hospital."

It is interesting to compare some of the differences between reports of empowerment attitudes and behaviors (either in group activities or personal benefits). For instance, 70% of participants report that in their group they "discuss the quality of medical care"; but only 39% report a group "plan to change things in the hospital," and only 28% reported that

TABLE 17-3 (Continued)

What benefits do members derive from group participation?
($N = 146$, $NN = 37$)

	Much	Some	None or a little
Getting help from other parents	52%	38%	10%
Having a more active social life	14	36	50
Getting financial assistance	7	16	77
Finding a place to stay while my child was in the hospital	4	11	85
Dealing with my child's school	19	36	45
Being helpful to other parents	58	36	6
Being an active part of the medical care system	23	21	56
Changing things in the hospital	15	31	54
Getting help from the medical staff	21	25	54

in their group they "talk with doctors and nurses about their personal feelings towards them." This gap between attitudes ("discussing") and behavior ("doing") is another priority for future analysis of these data. However, we already know this discrepancy is common in the organizing efforts of disempowered people, especially where such action might make one vulnerable to even subtle retaliation by powerful persons (i.e., doctors and nurses upon whom one is dependent).

Some of the activities and benefits reported in Tables 17-2 and 17-3 focus on changes in the self and in the way in which people choose to live out their personal lives. Others refer to the ways in which people relate to others in their immediate or distal social world. Some important activities and benefits refer to efforts to change the outlooks of others in the social environment, and not solely to adapt to the pressures of that environment. Finally, some reports indicate the extent to which members of self-help groups attempt to change the structure and operations of organizations that deliver medical, psychosocial, or other services to them and their families. As noted earlier, empowerment can occur at all levels of human attitude and action.

Not only individuals are empowered; organized groups also act in ways that empower themselves and their members. Of the 50 self-help groups we visited and studied, about one-third (17) indicated that they did more than create patterns of individual benefits; they engaged in collective action to alter the system of health care delivery that impacted on them and their children. Direct evidence of public and political empowerment effects included:

- Feedback sessions with medical staffs that led to collaborative problem solving on issues of health care
- Public meetings and protests that eventually led hospitals to reinstitute a specialty clinic, to fire incompetent or insensitive staff members, to hire more staff for specialty purposes
- Public fund-raising programs that led to the construction of group homes or of Ronald McDonald–type Houses, the sponsorship of medical research on the illness and treatment, the hiring of additional medical and psychosocial staff members
- Public educational efforts aimed at educators, insurance executives, funeral directors, medical and nursing students, clinic or hospital staffs, the public at large
- Organizing activities that led to formal group representation in staff hiring processes and advocacy programs for patients and their families

Not reported by these groups, but discussed in the literature on self-help groups formed by/for disabled people, are lobbying activities resulting in the passage of legislation that improves this population's life chances and opportunities.

CONCLUSIONS

Empowerment, by means of self-help groups or through other mechanisms, is a central concern for all who value personal competence and well-being and the politics of democracy. It affects all who desire to be whole in the midst of a crisis, even a serious and chronic medical crisis. There is great skill and talent in the American public, although much of it is untrusted and undiscovered by institutional leaders (including human service professionals). Some of that talent is in the minds and hearts and hands of the ill and disabled. Indeed, sometimes those skills only surface, or are forced to the surface, by the life-changing crises of illness and disability. Those skills can be discovered, nurtured, refined, and mobilized through the operation of self-help groups. Supportive attitudes, and complementary actions by professionals, would contribute greatly to the empowerment of chronically ill and disabled people.

No one is fully empowered by the actions of others, however. Therefore, self-empowering attitudes and complementary actions by chronically ill and disabled people themselves constitute the essence of empowerment of self and others. No one is empowered alone, moreover. The central contribution of self-help groups is to provide an arena and an opportunity for people to empower themselves and the broader collectivities of which they are a part.

CHAPTER 18

Attitudes That Affect Employment Opportunities for Persons with Disabilities

Henry McCarthy

Even today, when leisure-time interests exert increasing influence in our lives, employment is, for most adults, the primary source of not only income, but also identity and interactions, if not satisfactions. Unfortunately, for most adults with disabilities employment represents only a yet-to-be-fulfilled hope, a close but inaccessible goal, a daily reminder that they are not among the majority. Survey statistics estimate the employment rate in the disabled population to be 34.5% (27.4% full-time and 7.1% part-time) among men and 19.4% (11.9% full-time and 7.5% part-time) among women (Bowe, 1983). Comparative rates for the general population are 79.7% (70.4% full-time and 9.3% part-time) and 58.6% (41.0% full-time and 17.6% part-time), respectively. Thus persons with disabilities are gainfully employed at a rate one-quarter to two-fifths that of the general working-age population. This inequity in employment is compounded by the fact that many persons with disabilities work in the secondary labor market (Dunn, 1981); thus they experience underemployment in seasonal or low-level jobs, with less pay, security, and promotional opportunities than their skill and motivation warrant.

Although recent, this information is hardly new. Since 1920, a massive public system of vocational rehabilitation (VR) throughout the states has attempted to remedy this problem by providing assessment, training, support, and placement services to get disabled persons permanently and (preferably) competitively employed. Much of the personal frustration, for both VR professionals and their clients, that the poor employment statistics summarize is mirrored in our inadequate understanding of the problem and what we can do to tackle it effectively. Considerable speculation, debate, and research have been carried out for the last two decades for purposes of identifying, clarifying, and altering factors that contribute to the employment inequity that confronts persons with disabilities. This chapter delineates the prominent streams of analysis and interpretation of the problem and outlines a career-development framework of multiple, interacting spheres of causal influence and potential intervention.

PRINCIPAL EXPLANATIONS FOR THE POOR EMPLOYMENT RATES OF PERSONS WITH DISABILITY

Several of the pioneers in the social psychology of disability were students of Kurt Lewin and thus had a strong Gestalt orientation (e.g., Barker & Wright, 1954). From the beginnings of rehabilitation theory and research, there was an appreciation of how characteristics of both the individual and the environment interact to shape the definition and outcome of life events in general and goal-directed behavior in particular. At the same time, the emerging practice of rehabilitation was being shaped by physical medicine and vocational education, disciplines that are emphatically more geared to clinical assessment and treatment of individual differences and deficits than to person–environment interaction. These disciplines' change-the-client orientation took hold and became the implicit assumption of rehabilitation programming and philosophy (Berkowitz, 1984; Stubbins, 1982). Since the mid 1960s, however, the various civil rights and consciousness-raising movements have revived consideration of the role of the environment in human affairs, particularly as a perpetrator of social disadvantage. Reflections of this trend are evident in the philosophy of the Independent Living movement (Crewe & Zola, 1983; Frieden, 1980, 1984), in the shift from positivist to social constructionist theories in medical sociology (Szasz, 1961), and in the critical writings of rehabilitation scholars like Finkelstein (1980), Hahn (1984), and Stubbins (1984a). Table 18-1 lists the major causes that have been advanced to explain the poor outcomes that persons with disabilities have experienced in the labor market. The author has subsumed the common explanations under three principal paradigms that differ in the definition of the source of the problem and the consequent change strategies to be pursued.

TABLE 18-1 Explanations for Employment Inequities Experienced by Persons with Disabilities

Clinical Services Model
  Functional limitations
  Poor motivation to work
  Social-skill deficits
  Occupational-skill deficits
  Job-search–skill deficits
Social Systems Model
  Architectural and worksite inaccessibility
  Lack of accessible and affordable transportation
  Disability income and benefits disincentives
  Tight labor-market conditions and policies
  Prejudice of employers and co-workers
Career Development Model
  Short-sighted perspective (finding a job instead of developing a career)
  Neglected or sheltered work socialization
  Unilateral and isolated approach to vocational programming
  Narrow concept and application of accommodation for employment
  Insufficient self-responsibility for own career activities and outcomes

Clinical Services Model

Explanations based on this *client-focused* model attribute the problem of unemployment to some failing(s) within the individual who has the disability. Thus the person is seen as the source of the problem and the appropriate target for intervention efforts. The VR system is dedicated to the evaluation and remediation of these personal handicaps to employment. Functional limitations carry major weight in professionals' and laypersons' perceptions of the vocational consequences of disability, despite repeated research and informal evidence showing a very complicated and by no means direct relationship between severity of disability and either occupational (Levitan & Taggart, 1977) or psychological (Schontz, 1971) status. Poor work motivation has long been presumed as a personality maladjustment or lifestyle choice based on secondary gains preferred by persons with disabilities. In fact, it has generated more complaints from counselors and programming for clients (Roessler & Bolton, 1978) than any other clinical issue. The social-skill deficits discussed with reference to rehabilitation clients have included resistance to or chronic dependence on supervision, as well as withdrawn, hostile, or otherwise unacceptable behavior in conversation and interaction with co-workers. Occupational-skill deficits among persons with disabilities have typically been attributed to the inferior quality of many vocational training programs that continue to operate with obsolescent equipment and an outmoded conception of job requirements and opportunities. Finally, job-search skills, such as information collection, realistic self-assessment, confident self-presentation, and appropriate assertiveness are often reported lacking in rehabilitation clients.

Although this model focuses on the client, only one of its five principal explanations (inadequate work motivation) tends to imply the person with the disability is responsible. Functional limitations are usually seen as an unavoidable consequence of the disabling condition itself; and the three types of skill deficits (social, occupational, job-search) are as likely blamed on the family or involved professionals as on the individual. Accordingly, it is worth recognizing that even though the clinical model defines the problem as existing within the person, it often extends responsibility for it to the social environment. Likewise, it is notable that the explanation that rehabilitation clients are unmotivated to seek and retain employment is also only one of the widely held clinical causes that has a significant attitudinal base to it. The conclusion that adherents to this clinical ideology draw is a recommendation to increase services and professional specialization to wage a better attack on eliminating the personal deficits of the clients.

Social Systems Model

Given their sensitivity to the influence of the many facets of society, it is not surprising that the proponents of this *ecological* (Stubbins & Albee, 1984) or *political* (Vash, 1981) model have identified a broader scope of contextual barriers than the personal handicaps that comprise the clinical model. The most concrete of these barriers is the inaccessibility of the environment in general and worksites in particular. Even getting *to* barrier-ridden buildings is difficult or impossible, it is pointed out, because public transportation is largely inaccessible and private transportation options usually unaffordable. Labor-market constraints exist when there is a lack of jobs due to depressions in local economies or a lack of compensating federal commitment to a full-employment policy such as Holland and Sweden have (Conte, 1982). Furthermore, our system maintains some explicit regulations that can create significant financial disincentives by inadvertently discouraging qualified clients with severe physical handicaps from accepting employment because they would have to relinquish their welfare income or subsidized medical coverage and attendant care.

Although often unexpressed, discriminatory attitudes of people in employment settings have not gone unacknowledged as a major perceived cause of the vocational problems of persons with disabilities. Whether conceived as ignorance, inexperience, or interaction strain, the prejudice of employers and co-workers has been the subject of more research and remediation efforts (Phillips & Smith, 1982; Schroedel & Jacobsen, 1978;

Schweitzer & Deely, 1981) than possibly the four other principal systemic barriers combined. Expression of this emphatic attribution to employers' negative attitudes ranges from the pointed to the implied, from scholarly writing (Hahn, 1984; U. S. Commission on Civil Rights, 1983) to bumper stickers declaring that attitudinal barriers are the biggest handicap that persons with disabilities face. Even the adherents of the clinical model operate in ways that reflect, in part, an underlying assumption that employers and co-workers are particularly unaccepting of this minority. For example, prolonged tenures in sheltered workshops and in other capacity-building rehabilitation programs are often the consequence of rehabilitation personnel's underestimation of client competence. However, they may likewise be misguided by exaggeration of community employers' discriminatory practices, believed to be counteracted by making persons with disabilities overcompensate just so they can compete (Rickard, Triandis, & Patterson, 1963). Explanations and implications of this strong belief in the existence of negative employer attitudes are discussed in the next section. Before detailing this specific explanation, it should be noted that the strategy consistent with all of the causes identified by the socioenvironmental model is one of advocacy for social change that will reduce or eliminate the systemic barriers.

DISABILITY PREJUDICE AS A PROXIMAL AND APPEALING CAUSE OF EMPLOYMENT INEQUITY

Negative attitudes toward persons with handicaps in the workplace have become somewhat blown out of proportion among employment barriers, due to their immediate plausibility and intervention appeal. That is, the most immediate reason why a person who is in the complex and subjectively evaluated situation of applying for a job gets rejected would appear to be something involved in the judgment of the evaluator. And the most salient stimulus that an unknown applicant presents to an employer/evaluator is the negatively valued disability. The plausibility seems indisputable. Furthermore, in a topological analysis, the evaluator stands as a gatekeeper controlling entry to employment; therefore, being the first encounter as we search backwards from the rejection event for explanations, he emerges as the proximal cause. In addition, most people, regardless of how important they believe the other system barriers to be, would be more personally motivated and professionally prepared to attempt to change the attitude of the evaluator than to work for architectural barrier removal, lobby for regulatory revisions in benefits programs, and the like. Not that attitude change is an easy task; but it has a definite appeal that has long captivated the rehabilitation community.

Some rehabilitationists may also have a self-protective motive for publicizing employer prejudice. Given the pressure on them to improve their success rate at job placement (reported in Combs and Omvig, 1986, as only 25% for 1981), it helps to have a clear and accepted external complication to blame when accountability knocks on their door. Finally, pointing the finger at employers has been easy because of the mutual suspicion and isolation in which the majority of the two groups (rehabilitationists and employers) have until recently operated. Contrastingly, among rehabilitation professionals who have worked collaboratively with the business community the typical opinion does not attribute negative attitudes toward clients to employers.

My point is not that negative attitudes toward persons with disabilities in the workplace are negligible, but that there are numerous other issues and agendas that also need to be addressed to improve the employment opportunity structure. We should not be trapped by the proximal and appealing cause.

Data from persons who themselves have handicaps are an important source of perspective on these issues and provide direction for determining needed interventions. In a Louis Harris (1986) survey, for example, the percentage of respondents whose employers had made some sort of accommodation to enable them to do their jobs was 10% greater than the percentage who said that they had encountered job discrimination because of their disabilities (35% vs. 25%). Even the perception of barriers by those from this survey who were not working full-time was telling. The most frequently acknowledged reasons for their unemployment were the handicapping consequences of the disability (78%) and the treatment it requires (51%). Forty-seven percent did believe that employers would not recognize that they are capable of doing a job because of their disability; however, almost as many (40%) felt that the lack of available jobs was an important reason why they were not working; 38% felt that their inadequate education and lack of marketable skills hindered them; and 28% considered the lack of accessible and affordable transportation a problem. Among the respondents who reported still facing barriers in their lives, only 1% suggested that changing employer attitudes was the most important thing that could be done to help them, and only another 1% offered this secondarily as a remedy.

Another survey (McCarthy, 1986) of persons with disabilities asked them why they thought they had not been hired for jobs for which they had applied. The most frequent reasons identified by the respondents, who were in their twenties, were extent of their (limited) work experience (43%), competition from other candidates (23%), and prejudice of employers (14%).

In summary, we have to consider seriously how each of several factors can create for persons with disabilities problems comparable to or greater than those stemming from employer prejudice. The next sections will be devoted to delineating attitudinal dimensions of some distal as well as proximal events, as well as some insidious as well as obvious interferences that persons with disabilities may encounter on the long journey to and through the world of work.

ATTITUDES, DISABILITY, AND EMPLOYABILITY: A CAREER DEVELOPMENT ANALYSIS

In order to capture a broader picture of factors that can influence the occupational achievement of persons with handicaps, it is useful to consider not the event of getting a job (or even *the* job of one's dreams), but the long-range, evolving process of career development (Akridge, 1985; Navin & Myers, 1983; Vandergoot, Jacobsen, & Worrall, 1977). The proposed career development perspective consists of three distinct but potentially overlapping phases. The first is the stage of *work socialization*, during which children and young adults are shaped by education and experience, mostly indirect and informal, to value challenge and effort, to accept responsibility and independence, to demonstrate both initiative and teamwork. In short, it is not only the means by which society inculcates the work ethic, but also the process by which individuals develop concepts of their interests, strengths, and weaknesses, as well as notions of what will be expected of them as adult workers. A large portion of this socialization is communicated by subtle messages and feedback that are no less effective and enduring for not being explicit, perhaps because the primary agents of socialization are such significant and controlling people in children's lives as their family members, teachers, and peers.

The second phase of career development involves intensive *vocational habilitation or rehabilitation*. This is accomplished through a variety of services typically referred to as career education and exploration, vocational evaluation, training (e.g., personal adjustment, work adjustment, occupational skill, work hardening), and job placement. These services can be obtained free or for a fee through a complex array of governmental and private agencies, which include schools and training institutes, the state employment service, private employment agencies, and VR agencies and facilities. These organizations are intended to function ultimately as brokers between job seekers and job providers (Granovetter, 1979).

The third phase of career development concerns *entry, integration, and advancement in employment*. Particularly in our age of high mobility and midlife career change, many persons experience this stage in cycles until a meaningful retirement is achieved. Another important aspect of this model is that it gives explicit recognition to multiple benchmarks by which career success and satisfaction are measured, including becoming socially integrated and being promoted on the job. In contrast, many theories of vocational development bring us up only to the point of deciding one's occupational choice. Therefore, they do not consider the critical roles employers play as both gatekeepers to jobs and investors in human resources, nor do they examine postemployment problems of employees, such as involuntary termination, quitting, and career stagnation.

Even this brief outline of a career development paradigm demonstrates how it offers some advantages in being either more analytic or more comprehensive than the clinical services or social systems models, particularly for investigating potential attitudinal influences. As a case in point, note that because the various participants (e.g., socialization agents) who contribute at each stage of the process can be specified, the focus of analysis and intervention for some causal factors (e.g., degree of work motivation) is not restricted to the person (i.e., the client) assumed responsible, but is opened to broader examination. Furthermore, the model encourages an understanding of normative and deviant experiences and how they relate to the formation of assets and deficits crucial to each phase of career development. Perhaps most importantly, by encompassing the whole lifespan, it provides a framework for addressing the occupational needs of the total population of persons with disabilities, ranging from the life fulfillment of those who have never managed to qualify for a vocational (re)habilitation program to the re-employment of injured workers with a long-time record of career advancement. Let us examine the utility of the model for generating and reconceptualizing causal explanations for the inordinate unemployment of persons with disabilities by considering the implications of some contrasting attitudes that can be adopted at each phase of career development.

NEGLECTED VERSUS NORMAL WORK SOCIALIZATION

Our potential for employment is seeded and nurtured from early childhood experiences that seem merely to be the pragmatic requirements of immediate situations, but which cumulatively teach us to follow instructions, accept feedback, cooperate with peers, and stick to a task. Such early work socialization begins the development of two ingredients essential for eventual employment: *generic work skills and self-concept as a capable person.* As previously noted, these are in large measure shaped by the environments, expectations, and experiences to which we are exposed by family, teachers, and friends. Unfortunately, many youth with disabilities have been controlled by agents of socialization whose well-meaning but defeating psychological influence stunted the development of their work skills and self-concepts.

A classic attitudinal barrier that has persisted with regard to the education of persons with disabilities is manifested by imposition of the "handicapped role" (Gliedman & Roth, 1980). This involves tolerating, and sometimes encouraging, passive attendance and excessive absence in school until time has ticked away and the school system, no longer legally responsible, can "graduate" them to some one else's custodial care. Teachers have also been inclined to maintain lowered performance expectations for students with disabilities (Career Planning and Placement Center, 1981). Youth tend to assimilate such expectations of their superiors, which leads to their setting lower aspirations for themselves (Bartel & Guskin, 1971). Hence it is imperative that disabled youth be challenged to perform to their maximum and be allowed to experience independence, adventure, risk, and even failure, rather than continually being protected from them. Parents can likewise be guilty of attempting to maximize security and self-confidence in their children with disabilities by sheltering them from the stress of developmental demands and honest feedback, thereby depriving them of critical opportunities for strengthening their self-concept and coping capacity through personal growth and skill development.

Neither special education nor rehabilitation has attended sufficiently to ensuring that the work socialization process was carried out in an adequate and timely way for their consumers. If special educators envisioned any employment prospects for their students, they tended to relegate the vocational domain to rehabilitationists, whom they counted on to assume counseling and placement responsibilities after the students graduated; but they rarely informed students or referred them to the VR agency in order to initiate the client relationship. Because youth are not eligible for rehabilitation services, these professionals did not concern themselves with the issue of work socialization until adult clients were assessed as needing to be given it remedially in a program like personal- or work-adjustment training.

The results of these postures has been a lack of attention to anticipating and compensating for experiences that militate against the normative socialization and career education of young people with disabilities. Of the several examples presented by Chubon (1985), three will be noted. The authoritarian character of most treatment environments can foster immaturity in children with disabilities who must frequent them; such social immaturity can easily be mistaken for limited mental ability. The atypical role situations and models, which they observe because of being removed from the usual home, school, and play activities and settings (due to treatment regimens, inaccessibility, etc.), limit the amount and scope of their exposure to the world of work. This might easily result in a distorted view of the nature and diversity of work. Even those lucky enough to get decent exposure to the world of work are not likely to have the benefit of a specifically useful role model in the form of a worker with an obvious disability. A reasonable conclusion that would be drawn (and get reinforced by the stereotyped views held by others) would be that the various occupations observed are outside the realm of possibility for them. Furthermore, educators and counselors who do not embrace lifelong learning for their students and clients are unlikely themselves to keep abreast of developments in their field and, consequently, serve as less adequate resources and role models for the vocational preparation of their students.

On the positive side, the philosophy and movement of normalization (Nirje, 1969; Wolfensberger & Tullman, 1982) is making progress in sensitizing professionals and parents to providing persons with disabilities exposure to appropriate educational and social environments and expectations. Recently, the career education and transition-to-work movements have greatly improved the levels of awareness, programming, and service coordination for providing normalized work socialization for youth with handicaps (Brolin, 1983; McCarthy, 1983; Palmer, 1984; Will, 1985). The field of education in general has also undergone some important improvements in its philosophy and practice. Many of these changes have directly benefited the entire range of student groups, including those with special needs. For example, the incorporation into the classroom of behavioral technologies such as computer-assisted and computer-managed instruction has facilitated educational mainstreaming by enhancing teachers' capability of individualizing the curriculum without straining their personal capacity to attend to all students simultaneously. The burgeoning of community colleges has offered the first feasible option for post-secondary and adult education to many individuals at the lower end not only of the socioeconomic but also of the intellectual scale. The spirit of these advances continues in accommodative efforts such as prescriptive teaching on the basis of students' preferred learning style and whole-mind instruction or imaginal education principles that encourage learning through many modalities, including nontraditional, experiential ways usable by people within a wide range of ability and motivation.

UNILATERAL AND ISOLATED VERSUS COLLABORATIVE AND INTEGRATED VOCATIONAL PROGRAMMING

The fatal flaw in the structure of the VR and counterpart service systems, and in the mindsets of its employees and patrons, has been their unilateral nature. This is manifested in many ways. For example, the ultimate recipient of VR's output (rehabilitated job seekers) is the local employment-providing community, members of which have had no role in designing, implementing, or monitoring its services. Thus there is a built-in imbalance in the broker relationship that distances VR personnel from the information and trust they should be exchanging with employers. This imbalance is increased through the typical recruitment and training of VR staff, which is heavily concentrated on clinician characteristics and skills for treating the rehabilitant client, to the neglect of business etiquette and negotiation skills for dealing with the corporate client (Galloway, 1982; McCarthy, 1984). Indeed, many VR counselors would find it a distortion to consider as their clients the local employment community, or even firms where they have placed rehabilitants. Others who have an interest in serving the business community as clientele claim the system sabotages, or at least does not support, their efforts in job placement by its policies and practices (Smits & Emener, 1980). The imbalanced relationship with VR's obvious clientele is reflected in the passive recipient role that many persons with disabilities still play in their rehabilitation, despite early and cogent recommendations for co-management by clients (Wright, 1960).

Fortunately, changes for the better are occurring in all these relationships. But we still have a long way to go to establish organizational and attitudinal commitment to collaboration throughout the VR process. For the past decade or so several successful initiatives have been made to include local employers not merely as advisors to, but as active partners in, the ongoing administration, delivery, and evaluation of rehabilitation services, particularly through Projects with Industry and other cooperative programs (Magee, Fleming, & Geletka, 1982; McCarthy, 1985; Pati & Morrison, 1982; Puleo, 1979). Such partnerships significantly benefit all three groups involved. For a minor investment of time, business representatives can display their corporate social responsibility while having informative first-hand contact with, and shaping influence on the training of, prospective employees. Rehabilitation organizations can gain gratis access to such resources for program improvement as technical expertise, labor-market information, colleague/employer contacts, and corporate foundation funding (McCarthy, 1986). Rehabilitants may reap the general benefits of a program that is better designed and equipped, as well as the personal advantages that accrue from pre-employment association with, and even mentoring from, members of the corporate community.

Consumer contributions to the rehabilitation enterprise have likewise expanded. Peer counseling and other self-help modalities are increasingly being accepted and sponsored as integral options for persons with disabilities, not just as alternatives to participation in the formal system. These are in addition to the Individualized Written Rehabilitation Plan, Client Assistance Projects, and other legislatively mandated mechanisms for ensuring that clients are directly involved in decisions that determine their rehabilitation.

Clearly, a collaborative approach to the design and delivery of rehabilitation services is much more than a sweet gesture. By generating appreciation and talent for networking, it maximizes the outcomes of three crucial objectives of any organizational mission, vocational rehabilitation included (McCarthy, 1982). Specifically, *information* is more immediately accessed, evaluated, and utilized, whether it is about the capabilities of a job applicant referred by rehabilitation or future occupational trends projected by corporate representatives. Secondly, *human and material resources* are greatly expanded without additional financial expenditure. Simply by redefining and cultivating both employer and rehabilitant clients as providers as well as consumers of its services, VR could harness a considerable amount and variety of personpower, not to mention some corporate donations of equipment and supplies. Finally, and most importantly for our discussion of attitudinal issues, the social networks that form through sharing responsibilities and rewards of a common endeavor stimulate a sense of *mutual strength and support* that can eliminate the competitiveness or alienation that such different groups otherwise often feel toward one another. Examples highlighting the impact of each of the three groups are worth specifying. Rehabilitation professionals' collegial contact with corporate employers, through which the worth of their services is recognized and reciprocated, should decrease staff burnout and turnover by increasing available resources and opportunities for being stimulated and appreciated. As participants in a collaborative service program such as a job-hunt club (Azrin & Besalel, 1980), rehabilitants' effort and experience are recognized and rewarded, thereby reducing feelings of impotence or isolation. Similarly, employers' network participation should diminish their feelings of being singled out and pressured by government authorities and advocacy groups to shoulder and solve the complex labor-force–participation problems of persons with disabilities.

"HIRING THE HANDICAPPED" VERSUS HUMAN RESOURCES ACCOMMODATION AND DEVELOPMENT

Once the bold slogan for getting persons with disabilities into the economic mainstream, "hiring the handicapped" is now recognized as having strategic and semantic disadvantages. From a career development perspective, it is not sufficient to establish hiring (or getting oneself or one's client hired) as the goal. When coupled with pity or paranoia (about governmental intrusion for lack of compliance with nondiscrimination legislation), such a short-sighted orientation could lead to creating and

accepting less-than-desirable, if not downright dysfunctional, matches between job vacancies and applicants (Daniels, 1985; Young, Rosati, &
Vandergoot, 1986). Instead, initiating employment should be conceived
of as merely one significant step in a process that continues to evolve,
while several equally important issues, such as satisfactory job performance, career advancement, job satisfaction, skill enhancement, and
wellness in the workplace, are pursued.

Part of the agenda of every civil rights group is working to effect positive
attitude change by promoting more affirmative terms for its constituency
and activities. Much has been written, for example, about sexist terminology in our everyday language and the impact this can have on limiting our
images and expectations of women. The disabled community has likewise
combined its search for equality with a scrutiny of the terms by which it is
referred. Among the preferred terms, *the handicapped* is not included. It
homogenizes a group that is truly heterogeneous and should be recognized
and treated accordingly. Particularly in the context of employment, the
term highlights problems and deficiencies rather than assets. Nor is this
just a matter of terminological niceties, for one could easily imagine the
consequences of a strict "hire the handicapped" mentality. If hiring is
done from a motive based on charity or tokenism, the employee is hardly
going to be given the experience, challenge, and consideration—regardless of her or his potential—that it takes to get promoted. Furthermore, if
job performance problems (actual or anticipated) are perceived as an
inevitable function of disability, they will be unnecessarily tolerated, instead of investigated and ameliorated. Usually the simplest and cheapest
solution to the problem is to accommodate the disability.

Accommodation has become synonymous with the practical solutions
to specific problems posed by disability or other special circumstances; but
fundamentally, *accommodation is an attitude* that allows for the full
expression of human talent. It does so either by removing whatever barriers (attitudinal, physical, procedural) interfere with accomplishing a goal
or by providing whatever assistance or support is needed to bring someone
to the level where goals can be approached by standard or alternative
means. Accordingly, accommodation should be thought of as a right by
which to obtain equal opportunity to participate, not as a special privilege.
By analogy, accommodation could be said to encompass the concept of a
negative right (e.g., guarantee against interference with individual decision making) and a positive right (e.g., guarantee of provision of resources
needed by an individual), as discussed by Scull (1981).

This broader conception of what accommodation means is at the crux of
the labor policies of many European, and particularly Scandinavian, countries (Habeck, Galvin, Frey, Chadderdon, & Tate, 1985), as well as the
developing movement for "supported work" in the United States (Ellien &

Vandergoot, 1985; Mank, Rhodes, & Bellamy, 1985). Although almost thirty federal laws prohibit discrimination on the basis of handicap, many of them explicitly or implicitly providing for accommodation (U.S. Commission on Civil Rights, 1983), this principle is incompatible with the spirit of rugged individualism that has pervaded American culture and has been absorbed by its social institutions, including rehabilitation (Stubbins, 1982). Thus the typical attitude toward accommodation connotes something special being done for a few who do not fit in, rather than a benefit that we all enjoy, both directly and indirectly. Adherents of this attitude fail to acknowledge the ample evidence demonstrating the general usefulness and cost-effectiveness of many accommodations. For example, barrier-free buildings qualify for lower insurance rates (Asher & Asher, 1976); they also ease access for workers transporting heavy loads, pregnant women, and many others in addition to persons with permanent mobility limitations.

Findings from a nationwide study of corporate accommodation practices for employees with handicaps clearly indicated that the firms most likely to consider and successfully implement accommodations were those with a philosophy emphasizing the importance of the individual and with a notably low turnover (Berkeley Planning Associates, 1982). Such qualities reflect not merely a policy for personnel management, but a commitment to human resource development. Typically, this approach is also characterized by extra efforts to ensure the safety, wellness, career enhancement, and self-fulfillment of employees. These goals are reflected in corporate support of carpooling, childcare, health promotion, recreation, volunteerism, continuing education, flex-time and job-sharing options, and assistance and rehabilitation programming for troubled employees and injured workers. By embracing a philosophy of accommodation and pursuing a human resources development strategy (Campbell, 1985), employers will end up screening in, integrating, and promoting many more useful employees with disabilities than by waiting to react to "hire the handicapped" appeals. And that is how it should be.

PASSIVITY VERSUS SELF-RESPONSIBILITY IN PURSUING ONE'S CAREER DEVELOPMENT

The previous discussions of socializers, brokers, and employers have indicated how their lack of awareness of, or attention to, the career development process, and particularly their participation in it, leads to lost opportunities for enhancing, if not detrimental effects on, the eventual employment of persons with disabilities. Only when each group recognizes and fulfills the responsibilities of its role will the employment preparation and integration of this minority be achieved. One of these groups is persons with disabilities. Indeed, they have the ultimate responsibility for securing the extent and quality of experience and assistance needed to accomplish their career goals. Unfortunately, many of the same factors that detract specifically from their vocational success can also have a deleterious effect on their general abilities to determine and satisfy their needs. For example, the lack of self-concept as a skillful person and potential worker discussed in relation to overprotective socialization practices could be merely one manifestation of a larger sense of inferiority and learned helplessness. There is extensive literature describing the second-class treatment allotted to persons who have disabilities or other stigmas in our society (e.g., Eisenberg, Griggins, & Duval, 1982) and the ways in which the consequences of this mistreatment are exacerbated by becoming internalized by its very victims.

Neither the deprived situation nor the succumbing reaction, however, is inevitable or, these days, more likely to occur than not. The rippling effects of consciousness-raising efforts and advocacy campaigns have taught many persons with disabilities to take initiative in shaping their lives, to familiarize and assert themselves with the established service systems and the laws protecting their rights. Their energies need to be applied to fulfilling their own responsibilities as well as making the system accountable. Those who seek change through growth accept the burdens of engaging in self-development activities, such as acquiring knowledge and skills, cultivating support systems, and seizing opportunities for enrichment. Recognition is rightly given to the Independent Living movement for effecting an enormous elevation in the levels of consciousness and commitment of persons with disabilities to directing their own destinies. Among its various agendas, however, career development issues have typically been a lower priority than psychosocial peer counseling, transportation, housing, health care benefits, and assistive devices. While all of these concerns contribute to employment prospects, it would be desirable for Independent Living centers to intensify their efforts toward directly maximizing the career development of their patrons.

CONCLUSIONS

The thesis of this chapter is that, in order to understand how attitudes affect the employability of persons with disability, it is necessary to consider more broadly than has traditionally been done both the processes and the participants involved in the employment enterprise. Specifically, it is argued that research and practice have focused exclusively on client deficits or employers' negative attitudes as the cause of underemployment among persons with handicaps. This results in a disproportionate emphasis on or downright restriction of intervention effort to a single stage and group, rather than the lifelong career development process, which many individuals, groups, and systems influence. We need to acknowledge the impact of, and encourage collaboration among, the constellation of people who shape the work socialization, career education, vocational (re)habilitation, and equal access to employment, integration, and advancement of persons with disabilities in our society.

CHAPTER 19

The Effects of Contact on Attitudes Toward Disabled Persons: Some Empirical Generalizations

Harold E. Yuker

The many studies dealing with the relationship between contact and attitudes toward disabled persons have yielded discrepant results. Some yielded positive correlations, a few yielded negative correlations, and many have shown no relationship.

Positive attitudes can result from mainstreaming disabled children, teaching disabled children, caring for or rehabilitating disabled persons, interacting socially with disabled persons, working with disabled persons, and so forth; but so can negative attitudes. Findings such as these indicate that the effect of contact on attitudes is complex. Contact under "favorable" conditions leads to positive attitudes, while contact under other conditions either does not affect attitudes or leads to negative attitudes (Amir, 1969).

Yuker and Block (1986) reported that although 70% of 33 correlation coefficients between contact measures and the Attitude Toward Disabled Persons Scales were positive, the values ranged from +.43 to −.35, with a median value of +.09. A more inclusive tabulation prepared for this chapter utilized the results of 318 comparisons obtained in 274 research studies of the effect of contact. These data revealed that 51% reported positive effects of contact; 10%, negative; and 39%, nonsignificant differences related to contact. Chi-square analysis of these data yielded a value of 84.3, which is significant beyond the .001 level, indicating that more studies had positive effects and fewer had negative effects than would be expected by chance. These data support Homans's (1950) hypothesis that liking and positive attitudes tend to be related to the amount of contact; but they also indicate that the relationship is not a simple one.

The purpose of the present chapter is to integrate the results of studies of the effects of contact on attitudes toward persons with disabilities in order to determine which variables tend to be associated with a positive change in attitudes. We will look for convergence in the research literature, without considering the quality of the research. Although some studies have been methodologically unsophisticated, they will be cited when their results either converge with data from other studies or support theory. If only methodologically adequate studies were cited, this would be a very short paper.

The data have been organized using a communication paradigm. Contact is examined in terms of the information that is provided. It is hypothesized that contact with persons who are disabled will result in positive attitudes when the contact yields persuasive positive information about disabled persons. The components of contact are organized in a variation of the paradigm discussed by McGuire (1969), who said that the variables that influence the effects of a message are the source, the message content, the conditions, and the receiver. We shall discuss the characteristics of the disabled person (source and message), the characteristics of the nondisabled person (receiver), and the characteristics of the interaction between the two (conditions and message). Although this organization confounds message with both the source and the interaction, it appears to be the most meaningful way of organizing the material.

CHARACTERISTICS OF THE DISABLED PERSON

Since the characteristics of the disabled person represent a confounding of the source and the message, they are of double importance. On the one hand, the disabled person should have the characteristics of any effective source: attractiveness and credibility. In addition, the disabled person's characteristics and interactive behavior should convey a positive message about persons who are disabled. The effects of many variables have been studied.

Attractiveness

Information sources that are perceived as attractive are more effective than those that are not so perceived. Attractive sources tend to be perceived as having qualities such as competence, social skills and likeability, communication skills, a positive self-image, and athletic skills. In addition, disabled persons perceived, as competent tend to have mild rather than severe disabilities.

Competence is very important. Competent persons tend to be perceived as both attractive and credible. School children who exhibit academic competence tend to be liked by both teachers and peers (Austin & Draper, 1984; Gottlieb, 1974; MacMillan & Morrison, 1980; Pliner & Hannah, 1985; Siperstein, Bopp, & Bak, 1978). Perceived imcompetence, on the other hand, contributes to the rejection of both mentally retarded and learning-disabled children. Nevertheless, children with these disabilities may be accepted in play situations, where different abilities are valued (Gottlieb, 1969; Siperstein, Bopp, & Bak, 1978). Most employers are willing to hire disabled persons with superior abilities (Oberle, 1975).

Social skills make a person more attactive and likeable. They have been shown to be important in both successful mainstreaming (Gresham, 1982; Strain & Shores, 1977) and employment (Collman & Newlyn, 1957). While data indicate that teaching social skills to children can result in increased acceptance, follow-up studies sometimes indicate remission to baseline behavior (Strain, Kerry, & Ragland, 1979).

On the other hand, *misbehavior* (negative, antisocial, and inappropriate behavior), which may be related to inadequate social skills, is a negative influence. It is often cited as a major factor in the rejection of mentally retarded children by both peers and teachers (Baldwin, 1958; Johnson, 1950; MacMillan & Morrison, 1980), though it appears to be less important in other disabilities (MacMillan & Morrison, 1980). But teachers tend to reject all students who are aggressive or defiant (Kedar-Voivodas, 1983).

Communication skills influence the way a person is reacted to by others. Persons who have difficulty communicating may evoke feelings of discomfort among some of their listeners. Lack of these skills results in problems for persons with disabilities that make oral communication difficult, for example, deaf persons, some persons with cerebral palsy, persons with speech problems, and some mentally retarded persons. In school, children with speech problems are rejected more in play and friendship situations than in academic situations. Although extended acquaintance usually leads to decreasing awareness of a disability, familiarity with persons who have speech problems apparently does not change negative beliefs (Ford, 1977). One study reported that after preschoolers were trained to communicate with deaf children they showed increased avoidance of these children (Vandell, Anderson, Ehrhardt, & Wilson, 1982). Data indicate that oral communication skills are very important for deaf children who are mainstreamed (Reich, Hambleton, & Houldin, 1977).

Athletic skills are often valued by children. When children describe the disabled children they "know best," their descriptions emphasize athletic ability and appearance (Clark, 1964). Learning-disabled children who are good athletes are liked better than other LD children (Siperstein, Bopp, & Bak, 1978).

Age also plays a role. Most young children are considered cute, even disabled children. This probably accounts for their frequent use on telethons. Teachers of kindergarten children have more positive attitudes than junior high school teachers (Larrivee & Cook, 1979), but this could be due to characteristics of the teacher rather than the characteristics of the child.

Education is important. Data indicate contact in college is likely to lead to positive attitudes (Genskow & Maglione, 1965; Gosse & Sheppard, 1979; Weinberg, 1978). In grammar or high school, contact often has no effect (Gosse & Sheppard, 1979; Weinberg, 1978), but sometimes leads to positive attitudes (Gosse & Sheppard, 1979), other times to negative attitudes (Centers & Centers, 1963; Gottlieb, 1974; Johnson, 1950). In precollege educational settings other variables may be relatively more important.

Personality also comes into play. Attitudes of persons in helping occupations are influenced by client characteristics such as manageability, likability, and treatability (Wills, 1978). Teachers prefer students who are high achievers (Brophy & Good, 1970) and those who are passive and conforming (Kedar-Voivodas, 1983). The importance of positive personality characteristics is also indicated by a study reporting that mentally retarded individuals who get along well with others tend to experience employment success (Collman & Newlyn, 1956).

Credibility

The credibility of a source of information is primarily a function of that person's perceived expertise. Since many people, probably incorrectly, perceive disabled persons as experts on disability, they are usually considered credible sources. The expressed attitudes of persons with disabilities, and their behaviors that reflect those attitudes, convey important messages to the persons they interact with (Wright, 1960; Wright, 1983; Yuker, Block, & Younng, 1966/1970). Disabled persons who answer questions about their disability, even though such questions may be annoying (Evans, 1976), give important information about their disability as well as about themselves and can have positive effects on the attitudes and behaviors of both children and adults. This is exemplified by the effect of performances of The Kids on the Block (Aiello, Chapter 16 in this volume).

Disability Characteristics

The characteristics of a person's disability can convey positive or negative information. Data indicate that school interaction with mentally retarded peers can result in increased negative attitudes (see Goodman, Gottlieb, & Harrison, 1972; Gottlieb & Budoff, 1973; Gottlieb & Davis, 1973), while interaction with children with other disabilities usually does not have this effect. Many teachers perceive emotionally disturbed children as presenting many problems, while physically disabled children tend to be perceived as presenting few problems (Yaffe, 1979). Similarly, teachers are more accepting of learning-disabled than of mentally retarded children (Moore & Fine, 1978).

Persons with nonvisible disabilities tend to be more acceptable than those with visible disabilities (Yuker, 1982). Physically attractive disabled persons are rejected less often than those who are not attractive (Kleck & DeJong, 1983; Kleck, Richardson, & Ronald, 1974). Normal-appearing mentally retarded persons tend to evoke fewer negative attitudes (Richardson, Koller, & Katz, 1985). Similarly, research indicates that contact with healthy older persons improves attitudes, while contact with older persons who are sick does not have this effect (Bennett, 1976). Dress and grooming are important. When children describe children they "know best," their descriptions emphasize appearance and athletic ability (Clark, 1964).

People who demonstrate a positive self-image and self-acceptance often are perceived positively by others. Persons who demonstrate self-acceptance by acknowledging their disabilities and being willing to discuss them are usually positively evaluated (Blood & Blood, 1982). The positive evaluation results even when the disabled person is nervous (Hastorf, Wildfogel, & Cassman, 1979). Coping behavior often results in positive evaluations by others, but apparently not when the disability is not acknowledged (Bazakas, 1978). Nonstereotyped behavior tends to result in greater acceptance than stereotyped behavior (Donaldson, 1980).

Gender may influence reactions. Two studies reported female educable mentally retarded children are rated more favorably by their peers than are male EMR children (Clark, 1964; Gottlieb, 1971), while learning-disabled boys are rated more favorably than learning-disabled girls (Scranton & Ryckman, 1979).

A review of the literature on disability hierarchies by Yuker (1982) demonstrated that messages conveyed by disabilities are influenced by the situation. Some disabilities are reacted to differently in social situations, employment situations, and "service" situations, such as rehabilitation or teaching. Persons who are blind rate high in social situations, in the middle on service, very low on employment. Mentally ill persons are in the middle for service, low for employment, very low socially. Other disabilities are evaluated similarly regardless of circumstances: persons with missing limbs are near the top of each hierarchy; persons with hearing problems are near the middle; persons who have neuromuscular problems or are mentally retarded are near the bottom of the list.

The hierarchy data also indicate that persons with mild disabilities tend to be reacted to more positively than those with severe disabilities (Guralnick, 1980; Hirshoren & Burton, 1979; Jones, Gottfried, & Owens, 1966). Other data show that persons with minor disabilities had only 18% unemployment, compared to 31% among those with severe disabilities (Wilson & Richards, 1975). Disability severity is influenced by perception and tends to decrease as one gets to know a disabled person, for example, when a nondisabled person has a close relationship to a mentally ill person, perception of that person as dangerous does not result in increased rejection (Chin-Shong, 1968).

CHARACTERISTICS OF THE NONDISABLED PERSON

In the contact paradigm the nondisabled person is the one who receives the message. A given message will be perceived differently by people with different characteristics, positively by one person and negatively by another. Important receiver characteristics include the types and strength of prior beliefs, the influence of training and experience, and demographic and personality variables.

Prior Beliefs and Attitudes

The beliefs and attitudes that a nondisabled person brings to an interaction influence the way the person perceives the messages conveyed by the interaction. Negative beliefs can hinder positive interaction and positive attitude change.

1. Persons who believe that disability is a very important characteristic of disabled persons have a high level of awareness of the disability and tend to ignore other characteristics of the person. They are "mindful" of the disability, whereas mindlessness about the disability and mindfulness about the competencies of the person tend to be related to positive attitudes (Langer & Chanowitz, Chapter 6 in this volume).

2. Persons who focus on the disability usually believe that disabled people are different, incompetent, inferior, and/or have negative characteristics. Teachers with negative attitudes toward disabled children tend to believe: (1) disabled children require special attention, extra time, and special knowledge (Frith & Edwards, 1981; Hudson, Graham, & Warner,

1979; Kingsley, 1967), (2) mentally retarded children get little benefit from schooling (Alexander & Strain, 1978; Moore & Fine, 1978), (3) disabled children create disturbances in class (Hudson and associates, 1979; Shotel, Iano, & McGettigan, 1972), (4) some disabled children restrict the progress of, or somehow "harm," nondisabled children (Alexander & Strain, 1978; Graham, Hudson, Burdg, & Carpenter, 1980; Vacc & Kirst, 1977). These beliefs can lead to self-fulfilling prophecies (Rosenthal & Jacobson, 1968). Many persons who work in mental institutions perceive "inmates" in negative terms (Rabkin, 1972; Wills, 1978) and have custodial rather than humanitarian attitudes (Cohen & Struening, 1962, Gilbert & Levinson, 1956).

3. Persons who consider themselves unable to cope with disabled persons tend to have negative attitudes. Some family members are concerned about their ability to provide adequate care and supervision and worry about the future of the disabled individual (Kreisman & Joy, 1974). Many teachers perceive themselves as lacking the skills needed to teach "special" children (Alexander & Strain, 1978; Harasymiw & Horne, 1976; Horne, 1983; Martin, 1976; Stephens & Braun, 1980; Vacc & Kirst, 1977). Teachers who believe that children with handicaps achieve more in special than in regular classes usually have negative attitudes (Barngrover, 1971; Gickling & Theobold, 1975; Hudson and associates, 1979; Kingsley, 1967; Vacc & Kirst, 1977). This belief is prevalent among resource-room and special-education teachers (Graham and associates, 1980; Vacc & Kirst, 1977).

In contrast to the above, other beliefs predispose the believer toward positive perceptions of persons with disabilities and positive attitude change as a consequence of contact. These include the beliefs that disabled people have many abilities, that they are similar to nondisabled people, and that special skills or training are not necessary for "dealing with" disabled persons. Data indicate teacher confidence is more important than special-education courses; teachers who believe they are able to teach disabled children usually can do so (Stephens & Braun, 1980; Warger & Trippe, 1982; Williams & Algozzine, 1977).

Occupational Training and Experience

Prior beliefs based on occupational socialization and personal experience are often strong and resistant to change. They can be positive or negative, depending on the content of the experience. Training that emphasizes the central role of the disability and the competence of the professional in contrast to the incompetence of the person with the disability tends to predispose one toward negative attitudes. Training that emphasizes the "personhood" and competence of the disabled person as well as dialog and teamwork leads to positive attitudes.

Occupational socialization produces attitudinal differences: psychologists and social workers tend to have more favorable attitudes than physicians and nurses (Rabkin, 1972). Courses in special education tend to promote positive attitudes (Brooks & Bransford, 1971; Geskie, 1985; Jaffe, 1972; Stephens & Braun, 1980), although some studies show no effects (Hjermstad, 1974). Regular class teachers who have contact with disabled children tend to develop positive attitudes (Harasymiw & Horne, 1976; Kennon & Sandoval, 1978).

Some studies show special-education teachers have more positive attitudes than other teachers (Efron & Efron, 1967; Hendlin, 1981; Moore & Fine, 1978). This may be attributable to the fact that they have more factual information (Jordan & Proctor, 1969; Proctor, 1967). Other studies show no differences between special-education teachers and other teachers (Kennon & Sandoval, 1978; Rouse, 1978; Semmel, 1959). A few studies have shown that regular teachers with mainstreamed disabled children in their classrooms have more positive attitudes than special-education teachers (Allen, 1978; Graham and associates, 1980; Hendlin, 1981). Regular teachers with contact with disabled children have more positive attitudes than those who do not have contact (Kennon & Sandoval, 1978). There is some indication that educational administrators tend to have positive attitudes (Guerin & Szatlocky, 1974).

Studies of the effect of medical education show that although many experiences result in no attitude change, some result in positive changes. A psychiatric clerkship that included a self-exploratory group experience resulted in more positive attitudes toward mentally ill persons, but this effect had disappeared by the time of a six-month follow-up (Elizur & Rosenheim, 1982). Psychiatric training resulted in positive changes on several scales of the OMI (Gelfand & Ullmann, 1961). A nursing program involving theory and supervised clinical experiences with mentally retarded persons resulted in an increase in positive attitudes (Gibson & Reed, 1974).

On-the-job experience can result in either positive or negative attitudinal predispositions. Some studies indicate a negative relationship between attitudes and years of experience (Dillon, 1979; Harasymiw & Horne, 1975; Mandell & Strain, 1978), possibly related to burnout, although others fail to report this (Combs & Harper, 1967; Greene, 1977; Levine, 1976; Semmel, 1979). A few studies report a positive relationship between experience and attitudes (e.g., Geskie, 1985). On the other hand, experience with persons with a specific type of disability often results in increased willingness to serve that group (Condell & Tonn, 1965).

Demographic and Personality Characteristics

A person's attitudes tend to be similar to those of others with similar demographic and educational backgrounds (McGuire, 1969; Rabkin, 1972). Friendship is strongly influenced by *similarity* in favorite activities, likes, dislikes, values, and so forth (Lott & Lott, 1965). Persons who have disabled friends have more positive attitudes than those who do not (Bell, 1962; Chin-Shong, 1968; Conine, 1969). The number of years of *education* is related to acceptance of persons who are different and is positively correlated with acceptance of persons who are disabled (Gosse & Sheppard, 1979; Yuker et al., 1966/1970).

The relationship between *age* and attitudes is both complex and confounded. After a detailed literature review Ryan (1981) concluded that the data are best explained by a "double inverted U model" covering the period from early childhood to adulthood. Among adults the effects of age are confounded by both education and type and extent of contact (Yuker et al., 1966/1970). Many studies show that in the United States either women have more positive attitudes than men or there is no relationship between *gender* and attitudes (Fonosch, 1979; Yuker et al., 1966/1970). This may be changing as a result of the trend toward gender equality (Yuker, Dill, & Hurley, 1987).

Relative Status

The way that nondisabled persons perceive their status relative to the status of disabled persons can be a strong influence on the outcome of interaction (Amir, 1969). If disabled persons are perceived as having a status equal to or superior to the status of the person with whom they are interacting, positive attitudes tend to result. Inferior status is apt to engender negative attitudes. This may be related to either characteristics and the occupational socialization of the nondisabled person or to characteristics of the disabled person, such as perceived competence and attractiveness.

INTERACTION VARIABLES

Important interaction variables include characteristics of the interaction itself (cooperation, reward value, personal closeness) and characteristics of the setting, including the norms that operate within a given setting. The type of contact that occurs will influence the perception of the disabled person, that is, both the source and the message. Only some types of interaction tend to result in positive perceptions and positive attitude change. The effects of each variable is influenced both by other interaction variables and by the disabled and nondisabled personal attributes discussed earlier.

Cooperation

Both theory and data indicate cooperative interaction tends to produce positive intergroup attitudes: competitive interaction may produce negative attitudes (Amir, 1969; Deutsch, 1949). Studies of cooperative behavior have yielded positive changes in attitude toward persons with several different types of disabilities: emotionally disturbed children (Fahl, 1970; Rynders et al., 1980); learning-disabled children (Armstrong, Johnson, & Balow 1981); and mentally retarded children (Ballard et al., 1977; Chennault, 1967; Johnson et al., 1979). However, data pertaining to the persistence of these changes is lacking, and one can question whether engaging in cooperative activities for a short period of time will produce long-term improvement in attitudes.

Reciprocity, which is related to cooperation, seems to be a basic aspect of positive social interaction (Gouldner, 1960). Data indicate positive behaviors tend to elicit positive behaviors from one's peers (Strain & Shores, 1977, Strain et al., 1976, 1977). One study indicated that although negative behavior was usually responded to in kind by peers, positive behavior tended to be followed by either no response or neutral behavior (Moore & Simpson, 1984).

Rewarding Interaction

Interaction that has positive consequences for the nondisabled person, such as success or goal achievement, tends to result in positive attitudes. Success in a team enterprise results in positive attitudes (Gibbons et al., 1980). Regular teachers' perception of their degree of success in dealing with special students is an important influence on teacher attitudes (Larrivee & Cook, 1979).

Personal Interaction

Interaction on a personal, intimate level tends to have positive effects (Amir, 1969). This involves getting to know the person as an individual, rather than as a label or a stereotype. When this happens the disability often seems to disappear; it is no longer perceived by the nondisabled person. Physical appearance is important in initial contacts; once people get to know one another it becomes relatively unimportant.

Family interaction presumably involves intimate personal interaction. Family members of disabled persons might be predicted to have positive attitudes. But since the interaction is influenced by the characteristics and behavior of both the disabled and nondisabled family members, this is not necessarily the case. One of four studies of the attitudes of siblings of disabled persons revealed positive attitudes (Begab, 1969), one revealed neutral attitudes (Adams, 1965), and two revealed negative attitudes (Knittel, 1963; Steinzor, 1967). In studies of family members compared to other persons, none reported more positive attitudes of family members, four reported no significant differences (Bowman, 1979; Chin-Shong, 1968; Hjermstad, 1974; Roeher, 1959), and two reported that family members' attitudes were more negative (Chin-Shong, 1968; Roeher, 1959). When a disabled person gets married, the marriage usually works out; but if a person becomes disabled after marriage it can have a negative effect on the marriage (Thompson, 1981).

Friendship also involves intimate personal interaction. Several studies indicate that persons who say they have disabled friends have positive attitudes (Bell, 1962; Chin-Shong, 1968; Conine, 1969; Jaques et al., 1970). Friends should not be grouped with family members. One study that separates the two reports more positive attitudes for friends than for family members (Conine, 1969), as would be expected from the above discussion.

Helping Relationships

Helping relationships are complex. They range from simple, single occurrences to long-term relationships. Helpers can be strangers, acquaintances, family members, friends, or persons whose occupation involves helping, rehabilitating, and so forth. The characteristics of both the helper and the person being helped are very important, as is their relative status (Fisher, Nadler, & Whitcher-Alagna, 1982; Wright, 1983). Ladieu, Hanfmann, and Dembo (1947) have an excellent discussion of the ways that help can be interpreted by a disabled recipient. Wright (1983) has discussed several recommendations for help givers that can facilitate the formation of positive attitudes. Equal status is important; persons with a disability are most willing to accept help when they believe they need it and when it does not create a status differential that places them in an inferior status position (Dembo, Leviton, & Wright, 1956/1975).

A special type of helping relationship is provided by volunteers who work in hospitals. Approximately 50% of the studies of the attitudes of volunteers who work in mental hospitals show positive effects on attitudes. Positive results include positive attitudes toward patients (Chinsky & Rappaport, 1970; Holzberg & Gewirtz, 1963; Keith-Spiegel & Spiegel, 1970; Kish & Hood, 1974) and negative attitudes toward mental hospitals (Chinsky &

Rappaport, 1970). Most of the rest show no effects, while at least one study shows that volunteers tend to develop negative attitudes. The negative results were reported by Vernallis and St. Pierre (1964), who reported that volunteer attitudes tended to be similar to those of aides, the group with whom they had the most contact. Aides generally have the most negative attitudes of any occupational group in a hospital.

Teaching

Teaching is another complex type of interaction. The effect of contact on teachers' attitudes depends very much on the characteristics of the teacher and the characteristics of the disabled students. These topics are discussed in Chapters 12 and 13 in this volume, by Hannah and Fichten, respectively. Peer tutoring, a special kind of teaching, is discussed in Chapter 15, by Horne.

Settings and Norms

These can either emphasize or deemphasize disabilities. They can either promote equal status and positive attitudes or unequal status and negative attitudes. Segregation, whether in classrooms, schools, school buses, or similar situations, tends to emphasize the differences between persons with and without disabilities and thus has negative effects.

Sometimes there is not a carryover of attitudes from one setting to another. Data indicate that friendships at school are often not reflected in out-of-school activities (Ladd, Munsen, & Miller, 1984). Norwegian elementary school children expressed more positive attitudes toward educable mentally retarded children in the play situation than in academic work (Gottlieb, 1969), whereas children with speech problems were rejected more in play and friendship than in academic situations (Woods & Carrow, 1959).

While intergroup contact in a residential setting may encourage acquaintanceship, provide information, and remove barriers to communication (Allport, 1954), the specific pattern of living arrangements can either foster or inhibit acquaintance (Deutsch & Collins, 1951; Festinger, Schachter, & Back, 1950). A study of a housing project for elderly persons and young physically disabled persons reported that the attitudes of elderly persons toward physically disabled persons became more positive; the attitudes of the physically disabled persons toward the elderly did not change (Johns, 1967). While data indicate that most persons who live in neighborhoods containing residential facilities for mentally retarded individuals develop more positive attitudes over time, the quality of interaction between mentally retarded persons and their neighbors is more important than the quantity (Sigelman, Spanhel, & Lorenzen, 1979).

The importance of the setting is indicated in studies of the effect of *institutional tours.* In most of these cases there is limited interaction, the contact consisting mostly of observation. Data indicate that tours of institutions for retarded or mentally ill persons either result in an increase in negative attitudes (Cleland & Chambers, 1959; Hall, 1970) or no change in attitudes (Cleland & Cochran, 1961; Lillis & Wagner, 1977). While some studies have demonstrated positive effects, the results are confounded by having the tours as part of a course with lectures and discussions of disability (Levinson & Distefano, 1979). As Rabkin has stated: "Tours of institutions, like tours of zoos, may arouse feelings of pity or revulsion, but almost never stimulate a sense of respect and empathy regarding the inmates; it is only when roles are transformed and patients are given 'normal' role assignments that they seem like you or me" (1972, p. 23).

SUMMARY

The attitudinal consequences of contact with disabled persons are mediated by the characteristics of the disabled person, the nondisabled person, and the interaction. The data indicate that for contact to result in positive attitudes, the disabled person should be (1) competent in the areas that are valued by the other parties to the interaction, (2) socially skillful and able to communicate successfully, and (3) accepting of his/her disability and willing to discuss it. Demographic and disability characteristics appear most important in initial contacts; under conditions of extended contact, which is an important factor in attitude change, they tend to be relatively unimportant.

For positive attitudes, the nondisabled person should be free of negative beliefs that could hamper positive attitudes; that is, the beliefs that (1) disability is the most important characteristic of disabled persons, (2) disabled people are different, incompetent, inferior, and/or have negative characteristics, and (3) they—the nondisabled persons—are unable to cope with disabled persons and their problems. In addition, the nondisabled person should have (4) demographic and personality characteristics similar to those of the disabled individuals with whom they interact, (5) status that is equal to the status of the disabled person, and (6) educational and occupational socialization that did not emphasize the negative beliefs or status differences mentioned above.

Finally, for positive attitudes the interaction should (1) involve cooperation and reciprocity, (2) be rewarding to both disabled and nondisabled participants, (3) result in the participants' getting to know one another as individuals, and (4) persist over time. When possible, the interaction should be structured to achieve these effects.

References

Abroms, K. I., & Kodera, T. L. (1979). Acceptance hierarchy of handicaps: Validation of Kirk's statement "Special education often begins where medicine stops." *Journal of Learning Disabilities, 12*, 15-20.

Adams, F. K. (1965). Comparison of attitudes of adolescents toward normal and toward retarded brothers. *Dissertation Abstracts, 27*, 662-663A.

Adler, C., Shanan, J., & Adler, E. (1968). *Cultural background, family structure and attitudes toward rehabilitation of hemiplegic patients after CVA.* Paper presented at a Seminar on Research in Rehabilitation, Israel Rehabilitation Council, Jerusalem.

Affleck, G. G. (1975). Role-taking ability and the interpersonal competencies of retarded children. *American Journal of Mental Deficiency, 80*, 312-316.

Aiello, B. (1979). *Kids on the Block teaching kit.* Washington, DC: Kids on the Block, Inc.

Airasian, P. W., & Bart, W. M. (1973). Ordering theory: A new and useful measurement model. *Educational Technology, 13*, 56-60.

Ajzen, I., & Fishbein, M. (1977). Attitude-behavior relations: A theoretical analysis and review of empirical research. *Psychological Bulletin, 84*, 888-918

Akridge, R. (1985). Rehabilitation, career development and self-awareness. *Journal of Rehabilitation, 51*, 24-30.

Alexander, C., & Strain, P. S. (1978). A review of educators' attitudes toward handicapped children and the concept of mainstreaming. *Psychology in the Schools, 15*, 390-396.

Algozzine, B. (1977). The emotionally disturbed child: Disturbed or disturbing? *Journal of Abnormal Child Psychology, 5*, 205-211.

Algozzine, B. (1980). The disturbing child: A matter of opinion. *Behavioral Disorders, 5*, 112-115.

Allen, V. L. (1976). *Children as teachers: Theory and research on tutoring.* New York: Academic Press.

Allon, R., & Graham, J. R. (1970). Intercorrelations of factor scores from the Opinions About Mental Illness Scale. *Psychological Reports, 26*, 805-806.

Allport, F. H. (1955). *Theories of perception and the concept of structure.* New York: Wiley.

Allport, G. W. (1935). Attitudes. In C. Murchinson (Ed.), *A handbook of social psychology* (pp. 798-844). Worcester, MA: Clark University Press.

Allport, G. W. (1954). *The nature of prejudice.* Reading, MA: Addison-Wesley.

Aloia, G. F., Beaver, R. J., & Pettus, W. F. (1978). Increasing initial interactions among integrated EMR students and their nonretarded peers in a game-playing situation. *American Journal of Mental Deficiency, 82*, 573-579.

Aloia, G. F., Knutson, R., Minner, S. H., & Von Seggen, M. (1980). Physical education teachers' initial perceptions of handicapped children. *Mental Retardation, 18*, 85-87.

Alper, S., & Retish, P. (1972). A comparative study of the effects of student teaching on the attitudes of students in special education, elementary education, and secondary education. *Training School Bulletin, 69*, 70-77.

Alpert, J. L. (1974). Teacher behavior across ability groups: A consideration of the mediation of Pygmalion effects. *Journal of Educational Psychology, 66*, 348-353.

American Foundation for the Blind. *What do you do when you meet a blind person?* [Film]. New York: Author.

American Psychiatric Association. (1980). *Diagnostic and statistical manual of mental disorders* (3rd. ed.). Washington, DC: Author.

Amir, Y. (1969). Contact hypothesis in ethnic relations. *Psychological Bulletin, 71*, 319-342.

Anthony, W. A. (1972). Societal rehabilitation: Changing societies' attitudes toward the physically and mentally disabled. *Rehabilitation Psychology, 19*, 117-126.

Anthony, W. A., & Carkhuff, R. R. (1970). The effects of rehabilitation counselor training upon trainee functioning. *Rehabilitation Counseling Bulletin, 13*, 333-342.

Antonak, R. F. (1979). An ordering-theoretic analysis of attitudes toward disabled persons. *Rehabilitation Psychology, 26*, 136-144.

Antonak, R. F. (1980). A hierarchy of attitudes toward exceptionality. *Journal of Special Education, 14*, 231-241.

Antonak, R. F. (1981a). *Developmental and psychometric analysis of the Scale of Attitudes Toward Disabled Persons.* Unpublished manuscript, University of New Hampshire, Durham.

Antonak, R. F. (1981b). Prediction of attitudes toward disabled persons: A multivariate analysis. *Journal of General Psychology, 104*, 119-123.

Antonak, R. F. (1982). Development and psychometric analysis of the Scale of Attitudes Toward Disabled Persons. *Journal of Applied Rehabilitation Counseling, 13*, 22-29.

Antonak, R. F. (1985a). *Construct validation and psychometric analysis of the Scale of Attitudes Toward Disabled Persons.* Unpublished manuscript, University of New Hampshire, Durham.

Antonak, R. F. (1985b). Construct validation of the Scale of Attitudes Toward Disabled Persons. *Journal of Applied Rehabilitation Counseling, 16*, 7-10, 48.

Antonak, R. F. (1985c). Societal factors in disablement. *Rehabilitation Counseling Bulletin, 28*, 188-201.

Antonovsky, A. (1980). *Health, stress, and coping.* San Francisco: Jossey-Bass.

Antonovsky, H., Meari, M., & Blanc, J. (1978). Changing family life in an Arab village. In J. Antonovsky & J. C. Chiland (Eds.), *The child in his family: Children and their parents in a changing world* (pp. 217-240). New York: Wiley.

Armstrong, B., Johnson, D. W., & Balow, B. (1981). Effects of cooperative vs. individualistic learning experiences on interpersonal attraction between learning-disabled and normal-progress elementary school students. *Contemporary Educational Psychology, 6*, 102–109.

Armstrong, S. H. (1975). The common structure of treatment staff attitudes toward adolescent dialysis patients. *Psychotherapy and Psychosomatics, 26*, 329–332.

Aronson, E., & Osherow, N. (1980). Cooperation, social behavior, and academic performance: Experiments in the desegregated classroom. In L. Bickman (Ed.), *Applied social psychology annual* (163-196). Beverly Hills, CA: Sage.

Asch, A. (1984). The experience of disability: A challenge for psychology. *American Psychologist, 39*, 529–536.

Asch, A. (1986). Will populism empower the disabled? *Social Policy, 16*, 12-18.

Asch, S. E. (1952). Forming impressions of personality. *Journal of Abnormal and Social Psychology, 41*, 258–290.

Asher, J., & Asher, J. (1976, October). How to accommodate workers in wheelchairs. *Job Safety and Health*, pp. 3-35.

Ashmore, R. D., & Del Boca, F. K. (1981). Conceptual approaches to stereotypes and stereotyping. In D. L. Hamilton (Ed.), *Cognitive processes in stereotyping and intergroup behavior* (pp. 1-35). Hillsdale, NJ: Lawrence Erlbaum.

Austin, A. M. B., & Draper, D. C. (1984). The relationship among peer acceptance, social impact, and academic achievement in middle childhood. *American Educational Research Journal, 21*, 597-604.

Ausubel, D. (1955). Relationships between shame and guilt in the socializing process. *Psychological Review, 62*, 378-390.

Avorn, J., & Langer, E. (1980). Self-induced dependence in the elderly: Negative effects of being helped. *Journal of the American Geriatrics Society, 30*, 397-401.

Azrin, N., & Besalel, V. (1980). *Job club counselor's manual.* Baltimore: University Park Press.

Babbitt, C. E., Burbach, H. J., & Iutcovich, M. (1979). Physically handicapped college students: An exploratory study of stigma. *Journal of College Student Personnel, 20*, 403-407.

Badt, M. I. (1957). Attitudes of university students toward exceptional children and special education. *Exceptional Children, 28*, 286-290.

Baker, F., & Schulberg, D. C. (1967). The development of a community mental health ideology scale. *Community Mental Health Journal, 3*, 216-225.

Baker, L. D. (1974). Authoritarianism, attitudes toward blindness, and managers: Implications for the employment of blind persons. *New Outlook for the Blind, 68*, 308-314.

Baker, L. D., & Reitz, H. J. (1978). Altruism toward the blind: Effects of sex of helper and dependency of victim. *The Journal of Social Psychology, 104*, 19-28.

Baldwin, W. K. (1958). The social position of the educable mentally retarded child in the regular grades in the public schools. *Exceptional Children, 106-108*, 112.

Ballard, M., Corman, L., Gottlieb, J., & Kaufman, M. J. (1977). Improving the social status of mainstreamed retarded children. *Journal of Educational Psychology, 69*, 605-611.

Barber, K. (1985). *The influence of handicapping condition and achievement level on teachers' attitude toward children.* Unpublished master's thesis, University of Detroit, Detroit, MI.

Barker, D. G. (1948). The social psychology of physical disabilities. *Journal of Social Issues, 4*, 28-38.

Barker, R. G. (1964). Concepts of disabilities. *Personnel and Guidance Journal,* 43, 371-374.

Barker, R. G., & Wright, B. (1954). Disablement: The somatopsychological problem. In E. Wittkower & R. Cleghorn (Eds.), *Recent developments in psychosomatic medicine* (pp. 419-435). Philadelphia: Lippincott.

Barker, R. G., Wright, B. A., Meyerson, L., & Gonick, M. R. (1953). *Adjustment to physical handicap and illness: A survey of the social psychology of physique and disability* (rev. ed.). New York: Social Science Research Council.

Barngrover, E. (1971). A study of educators' preferences in special education programs. *Exceptional Children,* 37, 754-755.

Barrell, R. P., DeWolfe, A. S., & Cummings, J. W. (1965). A measure of staff attitudes toward care of physically ill patients. *Journal of Consulting Psychology,* 29, 218-222.

Barrell, R. P., DeWolfe, A. S., & Cummings, J. W. (1967). Personnel attitudes and patients' emotional response to hospitalization for physical illness. *Journal of Psychology,* 65, 253-260.

Barsch, R. H. (1964). The handicapped ranking scale among parents of handicapped children. *American Journal of Public Health,* 54, 1560-1567.

Bart, W. M., & Krus, D. (1973). An ordering theoretic method to determine hierarchies among items. *Educational and Psychological Measurements,* 33, 291-300.

Bartel, N. R., & Guskin, S. L. (1971). A handicap is a social phenomenon. In W. M. Cruickshank (Ed.), *Psychology of exceptional children and youth* (3rd ed.) (pp. 75-113). Englewood Cliffs, NJ: Prentice-Hall.

Barton, L. E., Snart, F. D., & Hillyard, A. L. (1958). Attitudes of teachers and peers toward multiply handicapped students during the first year of public school integration. *B. C. Journal of Special Education,* 9, 111-120.

Bateman, B. (1962). Sighted children's perceptions of blind children's abilities. *Exceptional Children,* 29, 42-46.

Bauer, C. J., Campbell, N. J., & Troxel, V. (1985). Altering attitudes toward the mentally handicapped through print and nonprint media. *School Library Media Quarterly,* 13, 110-114.

Begab, M. J. (1970). Impact of education on social work students' knowledge and attitudes about mental retardation. *American Journal of Mental Deficiency,* 74, 801-808.

Begab, M. J. (1969). The effect of differences in curricula and experiences on social work student attitudes and knowledge about mental retardation. *Dissertation Abstracts International,* 29, 4111-4112.

Belgrave, F. Z. (1984). The effectiveness of strategies for increasing social interaction with a physically disabled person. *Journal of Applied Social Psychology,* 14, 147-161.

Belgrave, F. Z. (1985). Reactions to a black stimulus person under disabling and nondisabling conditions. *Journal of Rehabilitation,* 51(2), 53-57.

Belgrave, F. Z., & Mills, J. (1981). Effect upon desire for social interaction with a physically disabled person of mentioning the disability in different contexts. *Journal of Applied Social Psychology,* 11, 44-57.

Bell, A. H. (1962). Attitudes of selected rehabilitation workers and other hospital employees toward the physically disabled. *Psychological Reports,* 10, 183-186.

Bellah, R. N., et al. (1985). *Habits of the heart: Individualism and commitment in American life.* Berkeley, CA: University of California Press.

Bem, D. J. (1970). *Beliefs, attitudes and human affairs.* Belmont, CA: Wadsworth.

Bender, L. F. (1981). 1980 Presidential Address to the American Academy for Cerebral Palsy and Developmental Medicine. *Developmental Medicine and Child Neurology, 23,* 103-108.

Bennett, R. (1976). Attitudes of the young toward the old: A review of research. *Personnel and Guidance Journal, 55,* 136-139.

Berger, P. L., & Luckman, T. (1966). *The social construction of reality.* New York: Doubleday.

Berkeley Planning Associates. (1982). *Study of accommodations provided by federal contractors.* Washington, DC: U.S. Department of Labor, Employment Standards Administration.

Berkowitz, E. (1984). Professionals as providers: Some thoughts on disability and ideology. *Rehabilitation Psychology, 29,* 211-216.

Berkowitz, L. (1975). *A survey of social psychology.* Hinsdale, IL: Dryden.

Berman, D. S., & Fry, P. B. (1978). Pariah or paragon: Student teachers' evaluations of enrolling mentally ill students. *Psychology in the Schools, 15,* 529-532.

Bernotavicz, F. (1979). *Changing attitudes towards the disabled through visual presentations: What the research says.* Portland: University of Southern Maine, Human Services Development Institute, Center for Research and Advanced Study.

Berrigan, C. R. (1979). Effects of an inservice education workshop on the attitudes of regular classroom teachers toward disabled students (Doctoral dissertation). *Dissertation Abstracts International, 40,* 5009A.

Berryman, J. D., Neal, W. R., & Robinson, J. (1980). The validation of a scale to measure attitudes toward the classroom integration of disabled students. *Journal of Educational Research, 73,* 199-203.

Bierman, K. L., & Furman, W. (1981). Effects of role and assignment rationale on attitudes formed during peer tutoring. *Journal of Educational Psychology, 73,* 33-40.

Billings, H. K. (1963). An exploratory study of the attitudes of non-crippled children in three selected elementary schools. *Journal of Experimental Education, 31,* 381-387.

Blaney, P. (1975). Implications of the medical model and its alternatives. *American Journal of Psychiatry, 132,* 911-914.

Blank, H. R. (1957). Psychoanalysis and blindness. *Psychoanalytic Quarterly, 26,* 1-24.

Blatt, B. (1960). Some persistently recurring assumptions concerning the mentally subnormal. *Training School Bulletin, 57,* 48-59.

Bledstein, B. J. (1976). *The culture of professionalism.* New York: W. W. Norton.

Bloch, J., & Seitz, M. (1985). *Empowering parents of disabled children.* Syosset, NY: Variety Pre-schooler's Workshop.

Block, J. (1961). *The Q-sort method in personality assessment and psychiatric research.* Springfield, IL: Thomas.

Blood, G. W., Blood, I. M., & Danhauer, J. L. (1978). Listeners' impressions of normal-hearing and hearing-impaired children. *Journal of Communication Disorders, 11,* 513-518.

Blood, I. M., & Blood, G. W. (1982). Classroom teachers' impressions of hearing impaired and deaf children. *Perceptual and Motor Skills, 54,* 877-878.

Bogardus, E. S. (1925). Measuring social distances. *Journal of Applied Sociology, 9,* 216-226.

Bogardus, E. S. (1932). A social distance scale. *Sociology and Social Research*, *17*, 265-271.

Bogatz, G. A., & Ball, S. (1971). *The second year of Sesame Street: A continuing evaluation*. Princeton, NJ: Educational Testing Service.

Borg, W. R., Langer, P., & Wilson, J. (1975). Teacher classroom management skills and pupil behavior. *Journal of Experimental Education*, *44*, 52-58.

Borkman, R. (1976). Experiential knowledge: A new concept for the analysis of self-help groups. *Social Service Review*, *50*, 445-456.

Boucher, C. R., & Dino, S. L. (1979). Learning disabled and emotionally disturbed: Will the labels affect teacher planning? *Psychology in the Schools*, *16*, 395-402.

Bowe, F. (1978). *Handicapped America: Barriers to disabled people*. New York: Harper & Row.

Bowe, F. (1983). *Demography and disability: A chartbook for rehabilitation*. Fayetteville, AR: Arkansas Rehabilitation Research and Training Center, University of Arkansas.

Bowen, W. T., Twemlow, S. W., & Boquet, R. E. (1978). Assessing community attitudes toward mental illness. *Hospital and Community Psychiatry*, *29*, 251-254.

Bowman, J. (1979). A study of the attitudinal responses of nondisabled subjects toward amputation, blindness, and facial disfigurement. *Dissertation Abstracts International*, *401*, 4458-4459B.

Bradfield, R. H., Brown, J., Kaplan, P., Rickert, E., & Stannard, R. (1973). The special child in the regular classroom. *Exceptional Children*, *39*, 384-390.

Brigham, J. C. (1971). Ethnic stereotypes. *Psychological Bulletin*, *76*, 15-38.

Brightman, A. J. (Ed.). (1984). *Ordinary moments: The disabled experience*. Baltimore: University Park Press.

Britton, S. (1983). Who should be mainstreamed? A multidimensional scale of eleven disabilities. In P. Dunn-Rankin (Ed.), *Scaling methods* (pp. 186-201). Hillsdale, NJ: Lawrence Erlbaum.

Brolin, D. (Ed.). (1983). *Life-centered career education: A competency based approach* (2nd ed.). Reston, VA: Council for Exceptional Children.

Brooks, B. L., & Bransford, L. A. (1971). Modification of teachers' attitudes toward exceptional children. *Exceptional Children*, *38*, 259-260.

Brophy, J. E., & Good, T. L. (1970). Teachers' communication of differential expectations for children's classroom performance: Some behavioral data. *Journal of Educational Psychology*, *61*, 365-374.

Brown, J. A., & MacDougall, M. A. (1973). Teacher consultation for improved feelings of self-adequacy in children. *Psychology in the Schools*, *10*, 320-326.

Brown, R. (1958). How shall a thing be called? *Psychological Review*, *65*, 14-21.

Brownell, G. A. (1978). The effect of teachers' expressed attitude on interactions, sociometric ratings, and academic achievement of mentally retarded children in the integrated classroom (Doctoral dissertation). *Dissertation Abstracts International*, *38*, 6003A.

Brulle, A. R., Barton, L. E., Barton, C. L., & Wharton, D. L. (1983). A comparison of teacher time spent with physically handicapped and able-bodied students. *Exceptional Children*, *49*, 543-545.

Bruner, J. S. (1964). On perceptual readiness. In R. J. C. Harper, C. C. Anderson, C. M. Christensen, & S. M. Hunka (Eds.), *The cognitive process* (pp. 254-276). Englewood Cliffs, NJ: Prentice-Hall.

Bruner, J. S., Goodnow, J., & Austin, G. (1956). *A study of thinking*. New York: Wiley.

Bryan, T., Donahue, M., & Pearl, R. (1981). Learning disabled children's peer interactions during a small-group problem-solving task. *Learning Disability Quarterly, 4*, 13-22.

Bryan, T., & McGrady, H. J. (1972). Use of a teacher rating scale. *Journal of Learning Disabilities, 5*, 199-206.

Burstein, N. D. (1986). The effects of classroom organization on mainstreamed preschool children. *Exceptional Children, 52*, 425-434.

Burton, L. (1975). *The family life of sick children: A study of families coping with chronic childhood disease*. London: Routledge & Kegan Paul.

Buttery, T. J. (1978). Affective response to exceptional children by students preparing to be teachers. *Perceptual & Motor Skills, 46*, 288-290.

Byrd, E. K. (1979a). Magazine articles and disability. *American Rehabilitation, 4*, 18-20.

Byrd, E. K. (1979b). Television programming: A rating of programs depicting disability. *Alabama Personnel and Guidance Journal*, 19-21.

Byrd, E. K. (1979c). Television's portrayal of disability. *Disabled USA, 3*, 5.

Byrd, E. K., Byrd, P. D., & Allen, C. (1977). Television programming and disability. *Journal of Applied Rehabilitation Counseling, 8*, 28-32.

Byrd, E. K., & Elliott, T. R. (1985). Feature films and disability: A descriptive study. *Rehabilitation Psychology, 30*, 47-51.

Byrd, E. K., McDaniel, R. S., & Rhoden, R. B. (1979). *Television programming and disability: A replication study*. Manuscript submitted for publication.

Byrd, E. K., McDaniel, R. S., & Rhoden, R. B. (1980). Television programming and disability: A ten year span. *International Journal of Rehabilitation Research, 3*, 321-326.

Byrd, E. K., & Pipes, R. B. (1981). Feature films and disability. *Journal of Rehabilitation, 47*, 51-53.

Byrd, E. K., Williamson, W., & Byrd, P. D. (1986). Literary characters who are disabled. *Rehabilitation Counseling Bulletin, 30*, 57-61.

Byrne, D. (1969). Attitudes and attraction. In L. Berkowitz (Ed.), *Advances in experimental social psychology* (Vol.4) (pp. 314-330). New York: Academic Press.

Cameron, P., Titus, D. G., Kostin, J., & Kostin, M. (1973). The life satisfaction of non-normal persons. *Journal of Consulting and Clinical Psychology, 41*, 207-214.

Campbell, J. (1985). Approaching affirmative action as human resource development. In H. McCarthy (Ed.), *Complete guide to employing persons with disabilities* (pp. 14-30). Albertson, NY: Human Resources Center.

Canter, F. M. (1963). The relationship between authoritarian attitudes, attitudes toward mental patients, and effectiveness of clinical work with mental patients. *Journal of Clinical Psychology, 19*, 124-127.

Canter, F. M., & Shoemaker, R. (1960). The relationship between authoritarian attitudes and attitudes toward mental patients. *Nursing Research, 9*, 39-41.

Career Planning and Placement Center. (1981). *Careers in science: A guide for the counselors, teachers and parents of students with disabilities*. Irvine: University of California.

Carroll, C. F., & Repucci, N. D. (1978). Meanings that professionals attach to labels of children. *Journal of Consulting and Clinical Psychology, 46*, 372-374.

Carroll, J. D. (1980). Multidimensional scaling. *Annual Review of Psychology, 17*, 321-324.

Cartledge, G., Frew, T., & Zaharias, J. (1985). Social skill needs of mainstreamed students: Peer and teacher perceptions. *Learning Disability Quarterly, 8*, 132-140.

Cartledge, G., & Milburn, J. F. (1978). The case for teaching social skills in the classroom. *Review of Educational Research, 1*, 133-156.

Carver, C. S., Gibbons, F. X., Stephan, W. G., Glass, D. C., & Katz, I. (1979). Ambivalence and evaluative response amplification. *Bulletin of the Psychonomic Society, 13*, 50-52.

Carver, C. S., Glass, D. C., & Katz, I. (1978). Favorable evaluations of blacks and the handicapped: Positive prejudice, unconscious denial, or social desirability. *Journal of Applied Social Psychology, 8*, 97-106.

Carver, C. S., Glass, D. C., Snyder, M. L., & Katz, I. (1977). Favorable evaluation of stigmatized others. *Personality and Social Psychology Bulletin, 3*, 232-235.

Casey, K. (1978). The semantic differential technique in the examination of teacher attitudes to handicapped children. *The Exceptional Child, 25*, 41-52.

Cassie, P. (1984). *So who's perfect?* Scottdale, PA: Herald Press.

Cauthen, N. R., Robinson, I. E., & Krauss, H. H. (1971). Stereotypes: A review of the literature 1926-1968. *Journal of Social Psychology, 84*, 103-125.

Centers, L., & Centers, R. (1963). Peer group attitudes toward the amputee child. *Journal of Social Psychology, 61*, 127-132.

Chanowitz, B., & Langer, E. (1981a). Knowing more (or less) than you can show: Understanding control through the mindfulness/mindlessness distinction. In M. E. P. Seligman & J. Garber (Eds.), *Human helplessness* (pp. 167-181). New York: Academic Press.

Chanowitz, B., & Langer, E. (1981b). Premature cognitive commitment. *Journal of Personality and Social Psychology, 41*, 1051-1063.

Checkoway, B. (1985, Fall). Models for empowering citizens in human services. *Patterns for Participation*, Wisconsin Association for Developmental Disabilities Newsletter, pp. 5-6.

Checkoway, B., & Norsman, A. (n.d.). *Activating citizens with disabilities.* Unpublished manuscript.

Chelune, G. J. (1983, August). Neuropsychological assessment: Beyond deficit testing. Paper presented at the 91st annual convention of the America Psychological Association, Anaheim, CA.

Chennault, M. (1967). Improving the social acceptance of unpopular educable mentally retarded pupils in special classes. *American Journal of Mental Deficiency, 72*, 455-458.

Chesler, M. (1965). Ethnocentrism and attitudes toward the physically disabled. *Journal of Personality and Social Psychology, 2*, 877-882.

Chesler, M., & Barbarin, O. (1984). Difficulties of providing help in a crisis: Relationships between parents of children with cancer and their friends. *Journal of Social Issues, 40*, 113-134.

Chesler, M., & Barbarin, O. (1986). *Childhood cancer and the family.* New York: Brunner/Mazel.

Chigier, E., & Chigier, M. (1968). Attitudes to disability of children in the multicultural society in Israel. *Journal of Health and Social Behavior, 9*, 310-317.

Chin-Shong, E. (1968). *Rejection of the mentally ill: A comparison with the findings on ethnic prejudice.* Unpublished doctoral dissertation, Columbia University, New York.

Chinsky, J. M., & Rappaport, J. (1970). Attitude change in college students and chronic patients: A dual perspective. *Journal of Consulting and Clinical Psychology, 35,* 388–394.

Chubon, R. (1985). Career-related needs of school children with severe physical disabilities. *Journal of Counseling and Development, 64,* 47–51.

Clark, A. W., & Binks, N. M. (1966). Relation of age and education to attitudes toward mental illness. *Psychological Reports, 19,* 649–650.

Clark, E. T. (1964). Children's perceptions of a special class for educable mentally retarded children. *Exceptional Children, 30,* 289–295.

Cleland, C. C., & Chambers, W. R. (1959). Experimental modification of attitudes as a function of an institutional tour. *American Journal of Mental Deficiency, 64,* 124–130.

Cleland, C. C., & Cochran, L. L. (1961). The effect of institutional tours on attitudes of high school seniors. *American Journal of Mental Deficiency, 65,* 473–481.

Cleland, C. C., Manaster, G., King, M., & Iscoe, I. (1975). The mentally ill and mentally retarded via adjectival descriptions. *Mental Retardation, 13,* 28–30.

Cliff, N. (1973). Scaling. *Annual Review of Psychology, 24,* 473–506.

Cliff, N., & Young, F. W. (1968). On the relation between unidimensional judgements and multidimensional scaling. *Organizational Behavior and Human Performance, 3,* 269–285.

Cloerkes, G. (1979). Determinants of attitudes and behavior toward physically disabled persons: Results of a secondary analysis. *International Journal of Rehabilitation Research, 2,* 382–383.

Cloerkes, G. (1981). Are prejudices against disabled persons determined by personality characteristics? *International Journal of Rehabilitation Research, 4,* 35–46.

Clore, G. L., & Jeffery, K. M. (1972). Emotional role playing, attitude change, and attraction toward a disabled person. *Journal of Personality and Social Psychology, 23,* 105–111.

Clore, G. L., & McMillan, J. K. (1972). Emotional role playing, attitude change, and attraction toward a disabled person. *Journal of Personality and Social Psychology, 23,* 105–111.

Cohen, J. S. (1963). Employer attitudes toward hiring mentally retarded individuals. *American Journal of Mental Deficiency, 67,* 705–713.

Cohen, J. S. (1986). Theoretical considerations of peer tutoring. *Psychology in the Schools, 32,* 175–186.

Cohen, J. S., & Struening, E. L. (1959). Factors underlying opinions about mental illness in the personnel of a large mental hospital. *American Psychologist, 14,* 339.

Cohen, J. S., & Struening, E. L. (1960). Attitudes toward the mentally ill of psychiatric hospital personnel as a function of occupation, education, age, and sex. *American Psychologist, 15,* 417.

Cohen, J. S., & Struening, E. L. (1962). Opinions about mental illness in the personnel of two large mental hospitals. *Journal of Abnormal and Social Psychology, 64,* 349–360.

Cohen, J. S., & Struening, E. L. (1965). Opinions about mental illness: Hospital differences in attitudes for eight occupational groups. *Psychological Reports, 17,* 25–26.

Cohen, P. A., Kulik, J. A., & Kulik, C. C. (1982). Educational outcomes of tutoring: A meta-analysis of findings. *American Educational Research Journal, 19*, 237–248.

Coleman, M. C., & Gilliam, J. E. (1983). Disturbing behaviors in the classroom: A survey of teacher attitudes. *Journal of Special Education, 2*, 121–129.

Collmann, R. D., & Newlyn, D. (1956). Employment success of mentally dull and intellectually normal ex-pupils in England. *American Journal of Mental Deficiency, 61*, 484–490.

Combs, I., & Omvig, C. (1986). Accommodation of disabled people into employment: Perceptions of employers. *Journal of Rehabilitation, 52*, 42–45.

Combs, R. H., & Harper, J. L. (1967). Effects of labels on attitudes of educators toward handicapped children. *Exceptional Children, 33*, 399–403.

Comer, R. J., & Piliavin, J. A. (1972). The effects of physical deviance upon face to face interaction: The other side. *Journal of Personality and Social Psychology, 23*, 33–39.

Comer, R. J., & Piliavin, J. A. (1975). As others see us: Attitudes of physically handicapped and normals toward own and other groups. *Rehabilitation Literature, 36*, 206–225.

Condell, J. F., & Tonn, M. H. (1965). A comparison of MTAI scores. *Mental Retardation Journal, 3*, 23–24.

Conine, T. A. (1968). Teachers' attitudes toward disabled persons. *Dissertation Abstracts International, 29*, 4102A.

Conte, L. (1982). Manpower policy and the disabled person: An international perspective. *Rehabilitation Literature, 43*, 130–135.

Cook, S. W. (1969). Motives in a conceptual analysis of attitude-related behavior. In W. J. Arnold & D. Levine (Eds.), *Nebraska symposium on motivation* (pp. 179–231). Lincoln: University of Nebraska Press.

Cook, S. W., & Pelfrey, M. (1985). Reactions to being helped in cooperating interracial groups: A context effect. *Journal of Personality and Social Psychology, 49*, 1231–1245.

Cooke, T. P., & Apolloni, T. (1976). Developing positive social-emotional behaviors: A study of training and generalization effects. *Journal of Applied Behavior Analysis, 9*, 65–78.

Coombs, C. H. (1964). *A theory of data.* New York: Wiley.

Cooper, L., Johnson, D. W., Johnson, R., & Wilderson, F. (1980). The effects of cooperative, competitive, and individualistic experiences on interpersonal attraction among heterogeneous peers. *The Journal of Social Psychology, 111*, 243–252.

Corbet, B. (1980). *Options: Spinal cord injury and the future.* Newton Falls, MA: National Spinal Cord Injury Foundation.

Cornes, P. (1984). *The future of work for people with disabilities: A view from Great Britain.* New York: World Rehabilitation Fund.

Cosden, M., Pearl, R., & Bryan, T. H. (1985). The effects of cooperative and individual goal structures on learning disabled and nondisabled students. *Exceptional Children, 52*, 103–114.

Costin, F., & Kerr, W. D. (1962). The effect of an abnormal psychology course on students' attitudes toward mental illness. *Journal of Educational Psychology, 53*, 214–218.

Couch, A., & Kenniston, K. (1960). Yeasayers and naysayers: Agreeing response set as a personality variable. Journal of Abnormal and Social Psychology, 60, 151–174.

Cowen, E. I., Underberg, R. P., & Verillo, R. T. (1958). The development and testing of an attitudes to blindness scale. *Journal of Social Psychology, 48,* 297-304.

Coxon, A. P. M., & Jones, C. L. (1978). *The images of occupational prestige: A study in social cognition.* New York: St. Martin's Press.

Crandell, J. M. (1969). The genesis and modification of attitudes toward the child who is different. *Training School Bulletin, 66,* 72-79.

Crewe, N. M., & Zola, I. K. (Eds.). (1983). *Independent living for physically disabled people.* San Francisco: Jossey-Bass.

Crockenburg, S. B., Bryant, B. K., & Wilce, L. S. (1976). The effects of cooperatively and competitively structured learning environments on inter-and intrapersonal behavior. *Child Development, 47,* 386-396.

Croxen, M. (1983). *Disability and employment: Choosing a way of life.* Milton Keynes, England: The Open University.

Csapo, M. (1972). Peer models reverse the "one bad apple spoils the barrel theory." *Teaching Exceptional Children, 5,* 20-24.

Cumming, E., & Cumming, J. (1957). *Closed ranks.* Cambridge, MA: Commonwealth Fund, Harvard University Press.

Custer, J. D., & Osguthorpe, R. T. (1983). Improving social acceptance by training handicapped students to tutor their nonhandicapped peers. *Exceptional Children, 50,* 173-174.

Daniels, S. (1985). Attitudinal influences on affirmative action implementation. In H. McCarthy (Ed.), *Complete guide to employing persons with disabilities* (pp. 31-47). Albertson, NY: Human Resources Center.

Davis, D. L. (1967). Teacher behavior toward boys and girls during first grade reading instruction. *American Educational Research Journal, 4,* 261-270.

Davis, F. (1961). Deviance disavowal: The management of strained interaction by the visibly handicapped. *Social Problems, 9,* 121-132.

Davison, M. L. (1983). *Multidimensional scaling.* New York: Wiley.

Dawes, R. M. (1984). Approaches to attitude measurement. In R. L. Jones (Ed.), *Attitude and attitude change in special education: Theory and practice* (pp. 70-92). Reston, VA: Council for Exceptional Children.

DeFleur, M. L., & Westie, F. R. (1963). Attitude as a scientific concept. *Social Forces, 42,* 17-31.

Delquadri, J., Greenwood, C. R., Whorton, D., Carta, J. J., & Hall, R. V. (1986). Classwide peer tutoring. *Exceptional Children, 52,* 535-542.

Dembo, T. (1964). Sensitivity of one person to another. *Rehabilitation Literature, 25,* 231-235.

Dembo, T. (1970). The utilization of psychological knowledge in rehabilitation. *Welfare Review, 8,* 1-7.

Dembo, T., Leviton, G. L., & Wright, B. A. (1956/1975). Adjustment to misfortune: A problem of social-psychological rehabilitation. *Artificial Limbs, 3,* 4-62. (Reprinted in *Rehabilitation Psychology,* 1975, *2,* 1-100.)

Deutsch, M. (1949). A theory of cooperation and competition. *Human Relations, 2,* 129-152.

Deutsch, M. (1962). Cooperation and trust: Some theoretical notes. In M. Jones (Ed.), *Nebraska symposium on motivation* (Vol. 10) (pp. 275-320). Lincoln: University of Nebraska Press.

Deutsch, M., & Collins, M. E. (1951). *Interracial housing: A psychological evaluation of a social experiment.* Minneapolis: University of Minnesota Press.

Dickson, J. (1981). *Organizing the disabled.* San Francisco: Organizer Training Center.

Dielman, T. E., Stiefel, G., & Cattell, R. B. (1973). A check on the factor structure of the Opinions of Mental Illness Scale. *Journal of Clinical Psychology, 29,* 92-95.

Dienstbier, R. A. (1970). Positive and negative prejudice: Interactions of prejudice with race and social desirability. *Journal of Personality, 38,* 198-215.

Dillon, S. L. (1979). Attitudes of in-service elementary school teachers in the San Diego public schools regarding persons with epilepsy (Doctoral dissertation). *Dissertation Abstracts International, 39,* 11A.

Distefano, M. K., & Marr, M. W. (1970). Stability of attitudes in psychiatric attendants following training. *Mental Hygiene, 54,* 433-435.

Distefano, M. K., & Pryer, M. W. (1975). Effects of brief training on mental health knowledge and attitudes of nurses and nurses aides in a general hospital. *Nursing Research, 24,* 40-42.

Dixon, D. R. (1967). Courses in psychology and student's attitudes toward mental illness. *Psychological Reports, 29,* 50.

Doernberg, N. L. (1978). Some negative effects for young handicapped children. *Rehabilitation Literature, 39,* 107-110.

Donaldson, J. (1980). Changing attitudes toward handicapped peers: A review and analysis of research. *Exceptional Children, 46,* 504-514.

Donaldson, J. (1981). The visibility and image of handicapped people on television. *Exceptional Children, 47,* 413-416.

Donaldson, J., & Martinson, M. C. (1977). Modifying attitudes toward physically disabled persons. *Exceptional Children, 43,* 337-341.

Donder, D., & Nietupski, J. (1981). Nonhandicapped adolescents teaching playground skills to their mentally retarded peers: Toward a less restrictive middle school environment. *Education and Training of the Mentally Retarded, 16,* 270-276.

Drabman, R., Spitalnik, R., & Spitalnik, K. (1974). Sociometric and disruptive behavior as a function of four types of token reinforcement programs. *Journal of Applied Behavior Analysis, 7,* 93-101.

Drake, G. A. (1977, April). *A comparative study of pre- and post-semester attitudes toward handicapped students in introductory special education classes.* Paper presented at the annual convention of the Council for Exceptional Children, Atlanta, GA. (ERIC Document Reproduction Service No. ED 139-221).

Drass, S. D., & Jones, R. L. (1971). Learning disabled children as behavior modifiers. *Journal of Learning Disabilities, 4,* 16-23.

Dreyfus, H. L., & Rabinow, P. (1982). *Michel Foucault: Beyond structuralism and hermeneutics.* Chicago: University of Chicago Press.

Dunn, D. (1981). Current placement trends. *Annual Review of Rehabilitation, 2,* 113-146.

Durfee, R. (1971). Personality characteristics and attitudes toward the disabled by students in the health profession. *Rehabilitation Counseling Bulletin, 15,* 35-44.

Eareckson, J. (1976). *Joni.* Grand Rapids, MI: Zondervan.

Easton, D. (1971). *The political system: An enquiry into the state of political science.* Chicago: University of Chicago Press.

Eberly, C., Eberly, B., & Wright, K. (1981). Mental health professionals' attitudes toward physically handicapped groups in attributionally ambiguous and non-ambiguous situations. *Counseling Psychology, 28,* 276-278.

Edelson, R. I., & Paul, G. L. (1976). Some problems in the use of "attitude" and "atmosphere" scores as indicators of staff effectiveness in institutional treatment. *Journal of Nervous and Mental Disease, 162,* 248-256.

Edelson, R. I., & Paul, G. L. (1977). Staff "attitude" and "atmosphere" scores as a function of ward size and patient chronicity. *Journal of Consulting and Clinical Psychology, 45,* 874-884.

Edgerton, R. B. (1967). *The cloak of competence: Stigma in the lives of the mentally retarded.* Berkeley: University of California Press.

Edsall, T. B. (1984). *The new politics of inequality.* New York: W. W. Norton.

Edwards, A. L. (1957). *The social desirability variable in personality assessment and research.* New York: Dryden Press.

Edwards, A. L., & Kilpatrick, F. P. (1948). A technique for the construction of attitude scales. *Journal of Applied Psychology, 32,* 374-384.

Efron, R. E., & Efron, H. Y. (1967). Measurement of attitudes toward the retarded and an application with educators. *American Journal of Mental Deficiency, 72,* 100-107.

Ehrlich, H. J., & Rinehart, J. W. (1965). A brief report on the methodology of stereotype research. *Social Forces, 43,* 564-575.

Eisenberg, M., Griggins, C., & Duval, R. (Eds.). (1982). *Disabled people as second-class citizens.* New York: Springer.

Eisenman, R., & Foulks, E. F. (1970). Usefulness of Mussen's TAT scoring system. *Psychological Reports, 22,* 129-185.

Elizur, A., & Rosenheim, E. (1982). Empathy and attitudes among medical students: The effects of group experience. *Journal of Medical Education, 57,* 675-683.

Ellien, V., & Vandergoot, D. (1985). *A supported work approach: Employer-based rehabilitation facilities services.* Washington, DC: National Association of Rehabilitation Facilities.

Elliott, T. R., & Byrd, E. K. (1982). Media and disability. *Rehabilitation Literature, 43,* 348-355.

Elliott, T., & Byrd, E. K. (1983). Attitude change toward disability through television portrayal. *Journal of Applied Rehabilitation Counseling, 14,* 35-37.

Elliott, T. R., & Byrd, E. K. (1984a). Attitude change toward disability through television: Portrayal with male college students. *International Journal of Rehabilitation Research, 7,* 330-332.

Elliott, T. R., & Byrd, E. K. (1984b). Video depictions of blindness and attitudes toward disability. *Journal of Rehabilitation, 50,* 49-52.

Elliott, T. R., Byrd, E. K., & Byrd, P. D. (1983). An examination of disability as depicted on prime television programming. *Journal of Rehabilitation, 49,* 39-42.

Ellsworth, R. B. (1965). A behavioral study of staff attitudes toward mental illness. *Journal of Abnormal and Social Psychology, 70,* 194-200.

Ellsworth, R., Bryant, A., & Butler, G. (1960). Psychiatric aide inservice training: An experimental approach. *Nursing Research, 9,* 12-16.

Elstein, A. S., & Van Pelt, J. D. (1966). Dimensions in the perception of psychiatric patients by hospital staff. *Journal of Consulting Psychology, 30,* 213-218.

Elstein, A. S., & Van Pelt, J. D. (1968). Structure of staff perceptions of psychiatric patients. *Journal of Consulting and Clinical Psychology, 32,* 550-559.

Emerton, G. R., & Rothman, G. (1978). Attitudes towards deafness: Hearing students at a hearing and deaf college. *American Annals of the Deaf, 123,* 588-593.

Endres, J. E. (1979). Fear of death and attitudinal dispositions toward physical disability. *Dissertation Abstracts International, 39,* 7161A. (University Microfilms No. 79-11825).

Engel, K. L., & Paul, G. L. (1981). Staff performance: Do attitudinal "effectiveness profiles" really assess it? *Journal of Nervous and Mental Disease, 169,* 529–540.

English, R. W. (1971). Correlates of stigma toward physically disabled persons. *Rehabilitation Research and Practice Review, 2,* 1–17.

English, R. W. (1977). The application of personality theory to explain psychological reactions to physical disability. In J. Stubbins (Ed.), *Social and psychological aspects of disability* (pp. 227–238). Baltimore: University Park Press.

Enright, R. D., & Lapsley, D. K. (1980). Social role-taking: A review of the constructs, measures, and measurement properties. *Review of Educational Research, 50,* 647–674.

Epstein, J. (1960). *The faith of Judaism.* London: Sonsino.

Epstein, L. (1978). The effects of intraclass peer tutoring on the vocabulary development of learning disabled children. *Journal of Learning Disabilities, 11,* 63–66.

Erdelyi, M. H. (1974). A new look at the new look: Perceptual defense and vigilance. *Psychological Review, 81,* 1–25.

Evans, J. H. (1976). Changing attitudes toward disabled persons: An experimental study. *Rehabilitation Counseling Bulletin, 19,* 572–579.

Everton, C., Brophy, J., & Good, T. (1973). *Communication of teacher expectations: Second Grade* (Report No. 92). Austin: University of Texas, Center for Teacher Education.

Fahl, M. (1970). Emotionally disturbed children: Effects of cooperative and competitive activity on peer interaction. *American Journal of Occupational Therapy, 24,* 31–33.

Farina, A., Allen, J. G., & Saul, B. B. (1968). The role of the stigmatized person in affecting social relationships. *Journal of Personality, 36,* 169–182.

Farina, A., & Ring, K. (1965). The influence of perceived mental illness on interpersonal relations. *Journal of Abnormal Psychology, 70,* 47–51.

Farina, A., Thaw, J., Felner, R. D., & Hust, B. E. (1976). Some interpersonal consequences of being mentally ill or mentally retarded. *American Journal of Mental Deficiency, 80,* 414–422.

Featherstone, H. (1980). *A difference in the family.* New York: Basic Books.

Federal Register. (1974). *39,* 42470-42507.

Feigl, H. (1953). The scientific outlook: Naturalism and humanism. In H. Feigl & M. Brodbeck (Eds.), *Readings in the philosophy of science* (pp. 8–18). New York: Appleton-Century-Crofts.

Feldman, E. (1976). *Attitudes of Jewish and Arab village leaders toward rehabilitation of the disabled.* Unpublished master's thesis, Hebrew University, Jerusalem.

Fenrick, N. J., & Petersen, T. K. (1984). Developing positive changes in attitudes towards moderate/severely handicapped students through a peer tutoring program. *Education and Training of the Mentally Retarded, 19,* 83–89.

Festinger, L., Schachter, S., & Back, K. (1950). *Social pressures in informal groups: A study of human factors in housing.* New York: Harper & Row.

Fichten, C. S. (1986). Self, other and situation-referent automatic thoughts: Interaction between people who have a physical disability and those who do not. *Cognitive Therapy and Research, 10,* 571–587.

Fichten, C. S., & Amsel, R. (in press). Thoughts concerning interaction between college students who have a physical disability and their nondisabled peers. *Rehabilitation Counseling Bulletin.*

Fichten, C. S., & Amsel, R. (1986b). Trait attributions about physically disabled college students: Circumplex analyses and methodological issues. *Journal of Applied Social Psychology, 16,* 410–427.

Fichten, C. S., Amsel, R., Bourdon, C. V., & Creti, L. (in press). Interaction between college students with a physical disability and their professors. *Journal of Applied Rehabilitation Counseling.*

Fichten, C. S., Amsel, R., Robillard, K., & Judd, D. (1987). *College students with a physical disability: Myths and realities concerning self-esteem, social anxiety and stereotypes.* Manuscript submitted for publication.

Fichten, C. S., & Bourdon, C. V. (1986). Social skill deficit or response inhibition: Interaction between wheelchair user and able-bodied college students. *Journal of College Student Personnel, 27,* 326–333.

Fichten, C. S., Bourdon, C. V., Amsel, R., & Fox, L. (in press). Validation of the College Interaction Self-Efficacy Questionnaire: Students with and without disabilities. *Journal of College Student Personnel.*

Fichten, C. S., Bourdon, C. V., Creti, L., & Martos, J. G. (1987). Facilitation of teaching and learning: What professors, students with a physical disability and institutions of higher education can do. In H. I. Day and R. I. Brown (Eds.), *Natcon: Special Edition—Vocational Counselling in Rehabilitation* (Vol 14, pp 45–69). Ottawa, Canada: Employment and Immigration Canada.

Fichten, C. S., Compton, V., & Amsel, R. (1985). Imagined empathy and attributions concerning activity preferences of physically disabled college students. *Rehabilitation Psychology, 30,* 235–239.

Fine, J. A. (1979). Castration anxiety and self-concept of physically normal children as related to perceptual awareness of attitudes toward physical deviance (Doctoral dissertation). *Dissertation Abstracts International, 39,* 4819A.

Finkelstein, V. (1980). *Attitudes and disabled people* (Monograph No. 5). New York: World Rehabilitation Fund.

Finn, T. E. (1980). Teacher inservice education to ease the mainstreaming process and enhance student development (Doctoral dissertation). *Dissertation Abstracts International, 40,* 4524A.

Fish, D. E. (1981). Counselor effectiveness: Relationship to death anxiety and attitudes toward disabled persons (Doctoral dissertation). *Dissertation Abstracts International, 42,* 1488A.

Fishbein, M. (Ed.). (1967). *Readings in attitude theory and measurement.* New York: Wiley.

Fishbein, M., & Ajzen, I. (1972). Attitudes and opinions. *Annual Review of Psychology, 23,* 487–544.

Fishbein, M., & Ajzen, I. (1974). Attitudes toward objects as predictors of single and multiple behavioral criteria. *Psychological Review, 81,* 59–74.

Fisher, J. D., Nadler, A., Whitcher-Alagna, S. (1982). Recipient reactions to aid. *Psychological Bulletin, 91,* 27–54.

Fisher, R. (1955). Statistical method and scientific induction. *Journal of the Royal Statistical Society, 17,* 69–78.

Fishman, J. A. (1956). An examination of the process and function of social stereotyping. *Journal of Social Psychology, 43,* 27–64.

Fletcher, B. L. (1984). *The growth value of troubling experiences as seen by insiders and outsiders.* Unpublished doctoral dissertation, University of Kansas, Lawrence.

Florian, V. (1977). A comparison of attitudes toward the physically disabled between Jewish and Arab high school students. *Megamot, 2,* 184-192.

Florian, V., & Katz, S. (1983). The impact of cultural, ethnic, and national variables on attitudes toward the disabled in Israel: A review. *Intercultural Journal of Intercultural Relations, 7,* 167-179.

Florian, V., & Shurka, E. (1981). Jewish and Arab parents' coping patterns with their disabled child in Israel. *International Journal of Rehabilitation Research, 4,* 201-204.

Follansbee, A. (1981). *Object representation and castration anxiety: Personality determinants of attitudes toward physically disabled persons.* Unpublished doctoral dissertation, New York University, New York.

Fonosch, G. G. (1979). *Attitudes of selected university faculty members toward disabled students.* Unpublished doctoral dissertation, University of Nebraska, Lincoln.

Fonosch, G. G., & Schwab, L. O. (1981). Attitudes of selected university faculty members toward disabled students. *Journal of College Student Personnel, 22,* 229-235.

Ford, A. B., Liske, R. E., & Ort, R. S. (1962). Reactions of physicians and medical students to chronic illness. *Journal of Chronic Diseases, 15,* 785-794.

Ford, P. S. (1977). An investigation of attitudes toward, and beliefs about, people with speech disorders. *Dissertation Abstracts International, 38,* 2625B.

Foster, G. G., Ysseldyke, J. E., & Reese, J. H. (1975). "I wouldn't have seen it if I hadn't believed it." *Exceptional Children, 41,* 469-473.

Foster, S., McClanahan, L. D., & Overley, T. (1974). Mental hospital staff attitudes as a function of experience, discipline, and hospital atmosphere. *Journal of Abnormal Psychology, 83,* 569-577.

Foster, S. L., & Ritchey, W. L. (1979). Issues in the assessment of social competence in children. *Journal of Applied Behavior Analysis, 12,* 625-638.

Foucault, M. (1965). *Madness and civilization.* New York: Vintage Books.

Foucault, M. (1972). *The archeology of knowledge.* New York: Harper Colophon.

Foucault, M. (1973). *The birth of the clinic.* New York: Vintage Books.

Foucault, M. (1978). *The history of sexuality.* New York: Vintage Books.

Foucault, M. (1979). *Discipline and punish.* New York: Vintage Books.

Freed, E. X. (1964). Opinions of psychiatric hospital personnel and college students toward alcoholism, mental illness, and physical disability: An exploratory study. *Psychological Reports, 15,* 615-618.

Freedman, J. (1978). *Happy people.* New York: Harcourt, Brace.

Freeman, H. E., & Kassenbaum, G. G. (1960). Relationships of education and knowledge to opinions about mental illness. *Mental Hygiene, 44,* 43-47.

Frericks, A. H., & Adelman, S. I. (1974). *Labelling of students by prospective teachers.* (ERIC Document Reproduction Service No. ED 088 827).

Freud, S. (1957). On narcissism: An introduction. In J. Strachey (Ed. and Trans.), *The standard edition of the complete psychological works of Sigmund Freud* (Vol. 14, pp. 73-102). London: Hogarth Press. (Original work published 1914)

Freud, S. (1961). The ego and the id. In J. Strachey (Ed. and Trans.), *The standard edition of the complete psychological works of Sigmund Freud* (Vol. 19, pp. 3-66). London: Hogarth Press. (Original work published 1923).

Frieden, L. (1980). Independent living models. *Rehabilitation Literature, 41,* 169-173.

Frieden, L. (1984). From independent living to interdependent living: The future for people with disabilities. *American Rehabilitation, 10,* 23-26.

Friedson, E. (1965). Disability as social deviance. In M. B. Sussman (Ed.), *Sociology and rehabilitation* (pp. 71-99). Washington, DC: American Sociological Association.

Frith, G. H., & Edward, R. (1981). Misconceptions of regular classroom teachers about physically handicapped students. *Exceptional Children, 48,* 182-184.

Furnham, A., & Gibbs, M. (1984). School childrens' attitudes toward the handicapped. *Journal of Adolescence, 7,* 99-117.

Furnham, A., & Pendred, J. (1983). Attitudes towards the mentally and physically disabled. *British Journal of Medical Psychology, 56,* 179-187.

Gable, R. A., Strain, P. S., & Henrickson, J. M. (1979). Strategies for improving the status and social behavior of learning disabled children. *Learning Disability Quarterly, 2,* 33-39.

Galloway, C. (1982). *Employers as partners: A guide to negotiating jobs for people with disabilities.* Rohnert Park, CA: Sonoma State University, Institute on Human Resources.

Garvar, A. (1986). *Principals', special educators', and regular teachers' perceptions of disabilities and attitudes toward mainstreaming: A multidimensional scaling approach.* Doctoral dissertation in progress, Hofstra University.

Gartner, A., Kohler, M., & Reissman, F. (1971). *Children teach children.* New York: Harper.

Gelfand, S., and Ullmann, L. P. (1961). Attitude change associated with psychiatric affiliation. *Nursing Research, 10,* 200-204.

Gellman, W. (1959). Roots of prejudice against the handicapped. *Journal of Rehabilitation, 40,* 115-123.

Genskow, J. K., & Maglione, F. D. (1965). Familiarity, dogmatism and reported student attitudes toward the disabled. *Journal of Social Psychology, 67,* 329-341.

Gergen, K. L., & Jones, E. E. (1963). Mental illness, predictability and affective consequences as stimulus factors in person perception. *Journal of Abnormal and Social Psychology, 67,* 95-104.

Geskie, M. A. (1985). Relationship between empathy, attitudes toward disabled persons and level of nursing education (Doctoral dissertation, Hofstra University, Hempstead, NY) *Dissertation Abstracts International, 47,* 850B.

Giaconia, R. M., & Hedges, L. V. (1982). Identifying features of effective open education. *Review of Educational Research, 52,* 579-602.

Gibbons, F. X., Stephan, W. G., Stephenson, B., & Petty, C. R. (1980). Reactions to stigmatized others: Response amplification vs. sympathy. *Journal of Experimental Social Psychology, 16,* 19-22.

Gibson, B. S., & Reed, J. C. (1974). Training nurses in MR. *Mental Retardation, 12,* 591-605.

Gickling, E. E., & Theobold, J. T. (1975). Mainstreaming: Affect or effect? *Journal of Special Education, 9,* 317-328.

Gilbert, D. C., & Levinson, D. J. (1956). Ideology, personality and institutional policy in the mental hospital. *Journal of Applied Social Psychology, 53,* 263-271.

Gilbert, D. C., & Levinson, D. J. (1957). "Custodialism" and "humanism" in mental hospital structure and staff ideology. In M. Greenblatt, D. J. Levinson, & R. H. Williams (Eds.), *The patient and the mental hospital* (pp. 20-35). Glencoe, IL: Free Press.

Giles, F. L., & Byrd, E. K. (in 1986). Disability and human services in popular literature in relation to recent presidential administrations. *Journal of Applied Rehabilitation Counseling, 17*(4), 54-56.

Gladstone, L. R. (1977). A study of the relationship between ego style preference and experimental pain tolerance and attitudes toward physical disability (Doctoral dissertation). *Dissertation Abstracts International, 37*, 4679B.

Glass, R. M., & Meckler, R. S. (1972). Preparing elementary teachers to instruct mildly handicapped children in regular classrooms: A summer workshop. *Exceptional Children, 39*, 152-156.

Gliedman, J., & Roth, W. (1980). *The unexpected minority: Handicapped children in America.* New York: Harcourt, Brace.

Goffman, E. (1960). *Asylums: Essays on the social situation of mental patients and other inmates.* Garden City, NY: Doubleday.

Goffman, E. (1963). *Stigma: Notes on management of spoiled identity.* Englewood Cliffs, NJ: Prentice-Hall.

Golden, C. J. (Ed.) (1984). Current topics in rehabilitation psychology. Orlando, FL: Grune & Stratton.

Goldin, G. J. (1966). Some rehabilitation counselor attitudes toward their professional role. *Rehabilitation Literature, 27*, 360-364.

Goldstein, K., & Blackman, S. (1975). Generalizations regarding deviant groups. *Psychological Reports, 37*, 279-283.

Golin, A. K. (1970). Stimulus variables in the measurement of attitudes toward disability. *Rehabilitation Counseling Bulletin, 14*, 20-26.

Good, T., & Brophy, J. (1972). Behavioral expression of teacher attitudes. *Journal of Educational Psychology, 63*, 617-624.

Goodman, H., Gottlieb, J., & Harrison, R. H. (1972). Social acceptance of EMRs integrated into a nongraded elementary school. *American Journal of Mental Deficiency, 76*, 412-417.

Goodspeed, M. T., & Celotta, B. K. (1982). Professors' and teachers' views of competencies necessary for mainstreaming. *Psychology in the Schools, 19*, 402-407.

Gordon, C. (Ed.). (1980). *Power/knowledge: Michel Foucault.* New York: Pantheon Books.

Gorn, G. J., Goldberg, M. E., & Kanungo, R. N. (1976). The role of educational television in changing the intergroup attitudes of children. *Child Development, 47*, 277-280.

Gosse, V. F., & Sheppard, G. (1979). Attitudes toward physically disabled persons: Do education and personal contact make a difference? *Canadian Counselor, 13*, 131-135.

Gottlieb, J. (1969). Attitudes toward retarded children: Effects of evaluator's psychological adjustment and age. *Scandinavian Journal of Educational Research, 13*, 170-182.

Gottlieb, J. (1971). Attitude of Norwegian children toward the retarded in relation to sex and situational context. *American Journal of Mental Deficiency, 75*, 635-639.

Gottlieb, J. (1974). Attitudes toward retarded children: Effects of labeling and academic performance. *American Journal of Mental Deficiency, 79*, 268-273.

Gottlieb, J. (1975). Public, peer, and professional attitudes toward mentally retarded persons. In M. J. Begab & S. A. Richardson (Eds.), *The mentally retarded in society: A social science perspective* (pp. 99–125). Baltimore: University Park Press.

Gottlieb, J. (1980). Improving attitudes toward retarded children by using group discussions. *Exceptional Children, 47,* 106–111.

Gottlieb, J., & Budoff, M. (1973). Social acceptability of retarded children in nongraded schools differing in architecture. *American Journal of Mental Deficiency, 78,* 215–219.

Gottlieb, J., Cohen, L., & Goldstein, L. (1974). Social contact and personal adjustment as variables relating to EMR children. *Training School Bulletin, 71,* 9-16.

Gottlieb, J., Corman, L., & Curci, R. (1984). Attitudes toward mentally retarded children. In R. L. Jones (Ed.) *Attitudes and attitude change in special education: Theory and practice, 143–156.* Reston, VA: Council for Exceptional Children.

Gottlieb, J., & Corman, L. (1975). Public attitudes toward mentally retarded children. *American Journal of Mental Deficiency, 80,* 72–80.

Gottlieb, J., & Davis, J. (1973). Social acceptance of EMRs during overt behavioral interactions. *American Journal of Mental Deficiency, 78,* 141–143.

Gottlieb, J., Semmel, M. I., & Veldman, D. J. (1978). Correlates of social status among mainstreamed mentally retarded children. *Journal of Educational Psychology, 70,* 396–405.

Gottlieb, J., & Siperstein, G. N. (1976). Attitudes toward mentally retarded persons: Effects of attitude referent specificity. *American Journal of Mental Deficiency, 80,* 376–381.

Gottwald, H. (1970). *Public awareness about mental retardation.* Reston, VA: Council for Exceptional Children.

Gough, H. G. (1960). Adjective Check List as a personality assessment research scale. *Psychological Reports, 6,* 107–122.

Gould, C. (1984). *Personality determinants of distressed identification: An attitude component of the Disability Factor Scales.* Unpublished doctoral dissertation, New York University, New York.

Gouldner, A. W. (1960). The norm of reciprocity: A preliminary statement. *American Sociological Review, 25,* 161-179.

Gowman, A. G. (1957). *The war blind in American social structure.* New York: American Foundation for the Blind.

Graham, J. R. (1968). Effects of introductory and abnormal psychology courses on students' attitudes toward mental illness. *Psychological Reports, 22,* 448.

Graham, S., Hudson, F., Burdg, N. B., & Carpenter, D. (1980). Education personnel's perceptions of mainstreaming and resource room effectiveness. *Psychology in the Schools, 17,* 128–134.

Grand, S. A., Bernier, J. E., & Strohmer, D. C. (1982). Attitudes toward disabled persons as a function of social context and specific disability. *Rehabilitation Psychology, 27,* 165–174.

Grand, S. A., & Strohmer, D. C. (1983). Minority perception of the disabled. *Rehabilitation Counseling Bulletin, 27,* 117–119.

Granovetter, M. (1979). Placement as brokerage: Information problems in the labor market for rehabilitated workers. In D. Vandergoot & J. Worrall (Eds.), *Placement in rehabilitation: A career development perspective* (pp. 85–101). Baltimore: University Park Press.

Green, K., Rock, D. L., & Weisenstein, G. R. (1983). Validity and reliability of a scale assessing attitudes toward mainstreaming. *Exceptional Children, 50*, 182-183.

Green, S. C., Kappes, B. M., & Parish, T. S. (1979). Attitudes of educators to handicapped and nonhandicapped children. *Psychological Reports, 44*, 829-830.

Greenbaum, J. J., & Wang, D. D. (1965). A semantic-differential study of the concepts of mental retardation. *Journal of General Psychology, 73*, 257-272.

Greene, M. A., & Retish, P. M. (1973). A comparative study of attitudes among students in special education and regular education. *Training School Bulletin, 70*, 10-14.

Greene, W. R. (1977). Teacher attitudes in Nevada toward inclusion of mentally retarded children in the public schools (Doctoral dissertation). *Dissertation Abstracts International, 37*, 6401A.

Greenwald, A. G. (1975). Consequences of prejudice against the null hypothesis. *Psychological Bulletin, 82*, 1-20.

Gresham, F. M. (1981). Social skills training with handicapped children: A review. *Review of Educational Research, 51*, 139-176.

Gresham, F. M. (1982). Misguided mainstreaming: The case for social skills training with handicapped children. *Exceptional Children, 48*, 422-433.

Guerin, G. R. (1979). Regular teacher concerns with mainstreamed learning handicapped children. *Psychology in the Schools, 16*, 543-545.

Guerin, G. R., & Szatlacky, K. (1974). Integration programs for the mildly retarded. *Exceptional Children, 41*, 173-179.

Guralnick, M. J. (1980). Social interactions among preschool children. *Exceptional Children, 46*, 248-253.

Guskin, S. (1963a). Dimensions of judged similarity among deviant types. *American Journal of Mental Deficiency, 68*, 218-224.

Guskin, S. L. (1963b). Measuring the strength of the stereotype of the mental defective. *American Journal of Mental Deficiency, 67*, 569-575.

Guskin, S. (1963c). Social psychologies of mental deficiency. In N. R. Ellis (Ed.), *Handbook of mental deficiency: Psychological theory and research* (pp. 89-10). New York: McGraw-Hill.

Guttman, L. (1944). A basis for scaling qualitative data. *American Sociological Review, 9*, 139-150.

Habeck, R., Galvin, D., Frey, W., Chadderdon, L., & Tate, D. (1985). *Economics and equity in employment of people with disabilities: International policies and practices*. East Lansing: Michigan State University Center for International Rehabilitation.

Haber, R. N. (Ed.). (1969). *Information-processing approaches to visual perception*. New York: Holt, Rinehart & Winston.

Haber, R. N. (1974). Information processing. In E. C. Carterette & M. P. Friedman (Eds.), *Handbook of perception: Historical and philosophical roots of perception* (Vol. 1) (pp. 149-162). New York: Academic Press.

Hafer, M., & Narcus, M. (1979). Information and attitudes toward disability. *Rehabilitation Counseling Bulletin, 23*, 95-102.

Haggerty, R. (1983). Epidemiology of childhood disease. In D. Mechanic (Ed.), *Handbook of health care and health professions* (pp. 321-338). New York: Free Press.

Hahn, H. (1983). Paternalism and public policy. *Society, 20* (2), 36-46.

Hahn, H. (1984). *Equality and disability: European perceptions of employment policy.* New York: World Rehabilitation Fund.

Hahn, H. (Ed.). (1985a). Disability and rehabilitation [Special issue]. *American Behavioral Scientist, 28* (3).

Hahn, H. (1985b). *Physical differences: A personal quest for understanding.* Unpublished manuscript, University of Southern California, Department of Political Science, Los Angeles.

Hall, E. L., & Mueller, B. S. (1968). Effects of training on the mental illness ideology of nursing assistance. *Nursing Research, 17,* 172–174.

Hall, E. P. (1970). An experimental study of the modification of attitudes toward the mentally retarded (Doctoral dissertation). *Dissertation Abstracts International, 30,* 4828A.

Hallinan, M. T. (1976). Friendship patterns in open and traditional classrooms. *Sociology of Education, 49,* 254–265.

Hallinan, M. T. (1979). Structural effects on childrens' [sic] friendships and cliques. *Social Psychology Quarterly, 42,* 43–54.

Hamady, S. (1960). *Temperament and character of the Arabs.* New York: Twayne Publishers.

Hamera, E. K., & Shontz, F. C. (1978). Perceived positive and negative effects of life-threatening illness. *Journal of Psychosomatic Research, 22,* 419–424.

Hamilton, D., & Gifford, R. (1976). Illusory correlation in interpersonal perceptions: A cognitive basis of stereotype judgments. *Journal of Experimental Social Psychology, 12,* 392–404.

Hamilton, D. L. (Ed.). (1981). *Cognitive processes in stereotyping and intergroup behavior.* Hillsdale, NJ: Lawrence Erlbaum.

Hamza, N. (1964). *The psychology of the handicapped.* Cairo: Egypt Press.

Handlers, A., & Austin, K. (1980). Improving attitudes of high school students toward handicapped peers. *Exceptional Children, 47,* 228–229.

Hannah, M. E., & Doherty, C. (1982, October). *Child age and sex: Do they make a difference in attitude?* Paper presented at the annual convention of the National Association of School Psychologists, Toronto.

Hannah, M. E., & Pliner, S. (1983). Teacher attitudes toward handicapped children: A review and synthesis. *School Psychology Review, 12,* 12–55.

Harasymiw, S. J., & Horne, M. D. (1975). Integration of handicapped children: Its effect on teacher attitudes. *Education, 96,* 153–158.

Harasymiw, S. J., & Horne, M. D. (1976). Teacher attitudes toward handicapped children and regular classroom integration. *Journal of Special Education, 10,* 393–400.

Harasymiw, S. J., Horne, M. D., & Lewis, S. C. (1976). A longitudinal study of disability group acceptance. *Rehabilitation Literature, 37,* 98–102.

Harasymiw, S. J., Horne, M. D., & Lewis, S. C. (1978). Age, sex, and education as factors in acceptance of disability groups. *Rehabilitation Psychology, 25,* 201–208.

Harper, D. C., & Wacker, D. P. (1985). Children's attitudes toward disabled peers and the effects of mainstreaming. *Academic Psychology Bulletin, 7,* 87–98.

Harris, L. and Associates. (1986). *The ICD survey of disabled Americans: Bringing disabled Americans into the mainstream.* New York: Author.

Hastorf, A. H., Wildfogel, I., & Cassman, T. (1979). Acknowledgement of handicap as a tactic in social interaction. *Journal of Personality and Social Psychology, 37,* 1790–1797.

Hatfield, A. (1981). Self-help groups for families of the mentally ill. *Social Work, 26,* 409–413.

Hazzard, A. (1983). Children's experience with, knowledge of, and attitude toward disabled persons. *Journal of Special Education, 17,* 131–139.

Hazzard, A. P., & Baker, B. L. (1982). Enhancing children's attitudes toward disabled peers using a multi-media intervention. *Journal of Applied Developmental Psychology, 3,* 247–262.

Heider, F. (1958). *The psychology of interpersonal relations.* New York: Wiley.

Hendlin, R. J. (1981). The attitude of educators toward handicapped children. *Dissertation Abstracts International, 42,* 1400A.

Henrich, E. (Ed.). (1961). *Experiments in survival.* New York Association for the Aid of Crippled Children.

Hicks, J. M., & Spaner, F. E. (1962). Attitude change and mental hospital experience. *Journal of Abnormal and Social Psychology, 65,* 112–120.

Higgins, P. C. (1985). *The rehabilitation detectives: Doing human service work.* Beverly Hills, CA: Sage.

Hirshoren, A., & Burton, T. (1979). Willingness of regular teachers to participate in mainstreaming handicapped children. *Journal of Research and Development in Education, 12,* 93–100.

Hjermstad, E. J. (1974). An exploratory study of undergraduate students in special education in relation to attitudes toward the handicapped. *Dissertation Abstracts International, 35,* 2807A.

Hogan, R. (1969). Development of an Empathy Scale. *Journal of Consulting and Clincal Psychology, 39,* 307–316.

Hollinger, C. S., & Jones, R. L. (1970). Community attitudes toward slow learners and mental retardates: What's in a name. *Mental Retardation, 8,* 19–23.

Holzberg, J. D., & Gewirtz, H. (1963). A method of altering attitudes toward mental illness. *Psychiatry Quarterly, 37,* 56–61.

Homans, G. C. (1950). *The human group.* New York: Harcourt.

Horne, M. D. (1978). Cultural effect on attitudes toward labels. *Psychological Reports, 43,* 1051–1058.

Horne, M. D. (1980). *How attitudes are measured: A review of investigations of professional, peer, and parent attitudes toward the handicapped* (Report No. TM-78). Princeton, NJ: ERIC Clearinghouse on Tests, Measurements, and Evaluation. (ERIC Document Service Reproduction No. ED 198 154).

Horne, M. D. (1983). Elementary classroom teacher attitudes toward mainstreaming. *The Exceptional Child, 30,* 93–98.

Horne, M. D. (1985). *Attitudes toward handicapped students: Professional, peer and parent reactions.* Hillsdale, NJ: Lawrence Erlbaum.

Horowitz, L. S., & Rees, N. S. (1962). Attitudes and information about deafness. *The Volta Review, 64,* 180–189.

Horwitz, R. A. (1979). Psychological effects of the "open classroom." *Review of Educational Research, 49,* 71–86.

Hudson, F., Graham, S., & Warner, M. (1979). Mainstreaming: An examination of the needs of regular classroom teachers. *Learning Disability Quarterly, 2,* 58–62.

Hughes, J. N., & Hall, D. M. (1985). Performance of disturbed and nondisturbed boys on a role play test of social competence. *Behavioral Disorders, 11,* 24–29.

Hughes, S. L., Kaufman, J. M., & Wallace, G. (1973). What do labels really mean to classroom teachers? *Academic Therapy, 3,* 285–289.

Hunt, P. (Ed.). (1966). *The experience of disability*. London: Geoffrey Chapman.

Huston-Stein, A., Friedrick-Cofer, L., & Susman, E. J. (1977). The relation of classroom structure to social behavior, imaginative play, and self-regulation of economically disadvantaged children. *Child Development, 48*, 908-916.

Hutton, J. B., & Roberts, T. G. (1982). Relationships of sociometric status and characteristics of emotional disturbance. *Behavioral Disorders, 1*, 19-24.

Jaffe, J. (1966). Attitudes of adolescents toward the mentally retarded. *American Journal of Mental Deficiency, 70*, 907-912.

Jaffe, J. (1972). The effects of work conferences on attitudes towards the mentally retarded. *Rehabilitation Counseling Bulletin, 15*, 220-227.

Jaffe, Y., Moaz, B., & Avram, L. (1979). Mental hospital experience, classroom instruction, and change in conceptions and attitudes toward mental illness. *British Journal of Medical Psychology, 52*, 253-258.

Jamieson, J. D. (1984). Attitudes of educators toward the handicapped. In R. L. Jones (Ed.), *Attitudes and attitude change in special education: Theory and practice* (pp. 206-222). Reston, Va: Council for Exceptional Children.

Janicki, M. P. (1970). Attitudes of health professionals toward twelve disabilities. *Perceptual and Motor Skills, 30*, 77-78.

Jankey, L. (1978). Illusion and reality: Coming together during coming home. *Disabled USA, 1*, 4-6.

Jaques, M. E., Linkowski, D. C., & Seika, F. L. (1970). Cultural attitudes toward disability: Denmark, Greece and the United States. *International Journal of Social Psychiatry, 16*, 54-62.

Johannsen, W. J., Redel, Sister M. S., & Engel, R. G. (1964). Personality and attitudinal changes during psychiatric nursing affiliation. *Nursing Research, 13*, 342-345.

Johns, C. T. (1976). The effect of housing on attitudes toward the elderly and physically disabled (Doctoral dissertation). *Dissertation Abstracts International, 38*, 961-962.

Johnson, A. B., & Cartwright, C. A. (1979). The roles of information and experience in improving teachers' knowledge and attitudes about mainstreaming. *Journal of Special Education, 13*, 453-462.

Johnson, D. W. (1980). Group processes: Influences of student–student interaction on school outcomes. In J. H. McMillan (Ed.), *The social psychology of school learning* (pp. 324-342). New York: Academic Press.

Johnson, D. W., & Johnson, R. T. (1975). *Learning together and alone: Cooperation, competition, and individualization*. Englewood Cliffs, NJ: Prentice-Hall.

Johnson, D. W., & Johnson, R. T. (1979). Conflict in the classroom: Controversy and learning. *Review of Educational Research, 49*, 51-70.

Johnson, D. W., Johnson, R. T., & Maruyama, G. (1983). Interdependence and attraction among heterogeneous and homogeneous individuals. *Review of Educational Research, 53*, 45-54.

Johnson, D. W., Maruyama, G., Johnson, R. T., Nelson, D., & Skon, L. (1981). Effects of cooperative, competitive, and individualistic goal structures on achievement: A meta-analysis. *Psychological Bulletin, 89*, 47-62.

Johnson, G. O. (1950). A study of the social position of mentally handicapped children in the regular grades. *American Journal of Mental Deficiency, 55*, 60-88.

Johnson, G. O., & Kirk, S. A. (1950). Are mentally handicapped children segregated in the regular grades? *Exceptional Children, 17*, 65-68, 87-88.

Johnson, R., & Heal, L. W. (1976). Private employment agency responses to the physically handicapped applicant in a wheelchair. *Journal of Applied Rehabilitation Counseling, 7*, 12–21.

Johnson, R., Rynders, J. R., Johnson, D. W., Schmidt, B., & Haider, S. (1979). Interaction between handicapped and non-handicapped teenagers as a function of situational goal structuring: Implications for mainstreaming. *American Educational Research Journal, 16*, 161–167.

Jones, E. E., & Berglass, S. (1978). Control of attributions about the self through self-handicapping strategies: The appeal of alcohol and the role of underachievement. *Personality and Social Psychology Bulletin, 4*, 200–206.

Jones, E. E., Farina, A., Hastorf, A. H., Markus, H., Miller, D. T., & Scott, R. A. (1984). *Social stigma: The psychology of marked relationships.* New York: W. H. Freeman.

Jones, E. E., & Pittman, T. S. (1980). Toward a general theory of strategic self-presentation. In J. Schuls (Ed.), *Psychological perspectives on the self* (pp. 278–293). Hillsdale, NJ: Lawrence Erlbaum.

Jones, E. E., & Sigall, H. (1971). The bogus pipeline: A new paradigm for measuring affect and attitude. *Psychological Bulletin, 76*, 349–364.

Jones, R. L. (1974). The hierarchical structure of attitudes toward the exceptional. *Exceptional Children, 40*, 430–435.

Jones, R. L., & Gottfried, N. W. (1962). Preferences and configurations of interest in special class teaching. *Exceptional Children, 28*, 371–377.

Jones, R. L., & Gottfried, N. W. (1966). The prestige of special education teaching. *Exceptional Children, 32*, 465–468.

Jones, R. L., Gottfried, N. W., & Owens, A. (1966). The social distance of the exceptional: A study at the high school level. *Exceptional Children, 32*, 551–556.

Jones, R. L., Gottlieb, J., Guskin, S., & Yoshida, R. K. (1978). Evaluating mainstreaming programs: Models, caveats, considerations and guidelines. *Exceptional Children, 44*, 588–601.

Jones, R. L., & Guskin, S. L. (1984). Attitudes and attitude change in special education. In R. L. Jones (Ed.), *Attitude and attitude change in special education: Theory and practice* (pp. 1–20). Reston, VA: Council for Exceptional Children.

Jones, R. L., & Sisk, D. A. (1967). Early perceptions of orthopedic disability. *Exceptional Children, 34*, 42–43.

Jones, T. W., Sowell, V. M., Jones, J. K., & Butler, L. G. (1981). Changing children's perceptions of handicapped people. *Exceptional Children, 47*, 365–368.

Jordan, J. E. (1971). Attitude-behavior research on physical-mental-social disability and racial-ethnic differences. *Psychological Aspects of Disability, 18*, 5–26.

Jordan, J. E., & Friesen, E. W. (1968). Attitudes of rehabilitation personnel toward physically disabled persons in Columbia, Peru, and the United States. *Journal of Social Psychology, 74*, 151–161.

Jordan, J. E., & Proctor, D. I. (1969). Relationship between knowledge of exceptional children, amount of experience with them, and teacher attitude toward their classroom integration. *Journal of Special Education, 3*, 433–439.

Kane, B. J., & Alley, G. R. (1980). A peer-tutored, instructional management program in computational mathematics for incarcerated, learning disabled juvenile delinquents. *Journal of Learning Disabilities, 13*, 148–151.

Kang, Y. W., & Masoodi, B. A. (1977). Attitudes toward blind people among theological and education students. *Visual Impairment and Blindness, 71,* 394-400.

Kanouse, D. E. (1971). Language, labeling and attribution. In E. E. Jones et al. (Eds.), *Attribution: Perceiving the causes of behavior* (pp. 86-101). Morristown, NJ: General Learning Press.

Kanouse, D. E., & Hanson, L. R., Jr. (1971). Negativity in evaluations. In E. E. Jones et al. (Eds.), *Attribution: Perceiving the causes of behavior* (pp. 42-61). Morristown, NJ: General Learning Press.

Kaplan, K. J. (1972). On the ambivalence-indifference problem in attitude theory and measurement. *Psychological Bulletin, 77,* 361-372.

Katz, D. (1960). The functional approach to the study of attitudes. *Public Opinion Quarterly, 24,* 163-204.

Katz, I. (1981). *Stigma: A social psychological analysis.* Hillsdale, NJ: Lawrence Erlbaum.

Katz, I., Glass, D. C., & Cohen, S. (1973). Ambivalence, guilt, and the scapegoating of minority group victims. *Journal of Experimental Social Psychology, 9,* 423-436.

Katz, I., Glass, D. C., Lucido, D. J., & Farber, J. (1977). Ambivalence, guilt, and the denigration of a physically handicapped victim. *Journal of Personality, 45,* 419-429.

Katz, I., Glass, D. C., Lucido, D. J., & Farber, J. (1979). Harm-doing and victim's racial or orthopedic stigma as determinants of helping behavior. *Journal of Personality, 47,* 340-364.

Katz, S., Kravetz, S., & Karlinsky, M. (1986). The impact of disability framework and responsibility for the disability on attitudes of a sample of high school students in the U.S.A.: A replication of an Israeli study. *Rehabilitation Counseling Bulletin, 30,* 102-109.

Katz, S., & Shurka, E. (1982). The influence of contextual variables on evaluation of the physically disabled by the nondisabled. *Rehabilitation Literature, 38,* 369-373.

Kedar-Voivodas, G. (1983). The impact on elementary children's school roles and sex roles on teacher attitudes: An interactional analysis. *Review of Educational Research, 53,* 415-437.

Kehle, T., Bramble, W., & Mason, E. (1974). Teachers' expectations: Ratings of student performance as biased by student characteristics. *The Journal of Experimental Education, 43,* 54-60.

Keith-Spiegel, P., & Spiegel, D. E. (1970). Effects of mental hospital experiences on attitudes of teen age students toward mental illness. *Journal of Clinical Psychology, 26,* 387-388.

Kellam, S. G., Durell, J., & Shader, R. J. (1966). Nursing staff attitudes and the clinical course of psychotic patients. *Archives of General Psychiatry, 14,* 190-202.

Kelley, H. (1967). Attribution theory in social psychology. In D. Levine (Ed.), *Nebraska symposium on motivation* (pp. 192-238). Lincoln: University of Nebraska Press.

Kelly, B. A. (1984). Attitudes toward disabled persons of selected collegiate coordinators for disabled students. *Journal of College Student Personnel, 25,* 255-259.

Kelly, N. K., & Menolascino, F. J. (1975). Physicians' awareness and attitudes toward the retarded. *Mental Retardation, 13*(6), 10-13.

Kennon, A. F., & Sandoval, J. (1978). Teacher attitudes toward the educable mentally retarded. *Education and Training of the Mentally Retarded, 13,* 139-145.

Keogh, B. K., Tchir, C., & Winderguth-Behn, A. (1974). Teachers' perceptions of educationally high risk children. *Journal of Learning Disabilities, 7,* 367-374.

Kernberg, O. (1966). Structural derivatives of object relationships. *International Journal of Psychoanalysis, 47,* 236-253.

Kieffer, C. (1983-84). Citizen empowerment: A developmental perspective. *Prevention in Human Services, 3,* 9-36.

Kingsley, R. F. (1967). Prevailing attitudes toward exceptional children. *Education, 87,* 426-430.

Kirchner, C., & Simon, Z. (1984a). Blind and visually handicapped college students—Part I: Estimated numbers. *Journal of Visual Impairment and Blindness, 78,* 78-81.

Kirchner, C., & Simon, Z. (1984b). Blind and visually handicapped college students—Part II: Settings and Services. *Journal of Visual Impairment and Blindness, 78,* 164-168.

Kirschenbaum, D. S., & Mushkat, M. A. (1980). Volunteer paraprofessional mental health workers' participation in an inner city early intervention program: A dose of reality. *Journal of Community Psychology, 8,* 251-255.

Kiser, B. (1974). *New light of hope.* New Canaan, CN: Keats Publishing.

Kish, G. B., & Hood, R. W. (1974). Voluntary activity promotes more realistic conceptions of the mentally ill by college students. *Journal of Community Psychology, 2,* 30-32.

Kitano, M. K., Stiehl, J., & Cole, J. T. (1978). Role taking: Implications for special education. *Journal of Special Education, 12,* 59-74.

Kleck, R. E. (1968). Physical stigma and non-verbal cues emitted in face-to-face interactions. *Human Relations, 21,* 19-28.

Kleck, R. E. (1969). Physical stigma and task oriented interactions. *Human Relations, 22,* 53-60.

Kleck, R. E., & DeJong, W. (1983). Physical disability, physical attractiveness, and social outcomes in children's small groups. *Rehabilitation Psychology, 2,* 79-92.

Kleck, R. E., Ono, H., & Hastorf, A. H. (1966). The effect of physical deviance upon face-to-face interaction. *Human Relations, 19,* 425-436.

Kleck, R. E., Richardson, S. A., & Ronald, L. (1974). Physical appearance clues and interpersonal attraction in children. *Child Development, 45,* 305-310.

Knittel, M. G. (1963). *A comparison of attitudes toward the disabled between subjects who had a physically disabled sibling and subjects who did not have a physically disabled sibling.* Unpublished Doctoral Dissertation, University of South Dakota.

Knoff, H. (1985). Attitudes toward mainstreaming: A status report and comparison of regular and special educators in New York and Massachusetts. *Psychology in the Schools, 22,* 410-418.

Kramer, J. R. (1985). *Family interfaces: Transgenerational patterns.* New York: Brunner/Mazel.

Kreisman, D. E., & Joy, V. D. (1974). Family response to the mental illness of a relative: A review of the literature. *Schizophrenia Bulletin, 10,* 34-57.

Krohn, A., & Mayman, M. (1974). Object representations in dreams and projective tests. *Bulletin of the Menninger Clinic, 28,* 455-466.

Krus, D. J. (1975). *Order analysis of binary data matrices.* Los Angeles: Theta Press.

Krus, D. J. (1977). Order analysis: An inferential model of dimensional analysis and scaling. *Educational and Psychological Measurement, 37,* 587-602.

Krus, D. J., & Bart, W. M. (1974). An ordering-theoretic method of multidimensional scaling of items. *Educational and Psychological Measurement, 34,* 525-535.

Krus, D. J., Bart, W. M., & Airasian, P. W. (1975). *Ordering theory and methods.* Los Angeles: Theta Press.

Kruskal, J. B., & Wish, M. (1978). *Multidimensional scaling.* Beverly Hills, CA: Sage.

Kuhn, T. S. (1971). The relations between history and the history of science. In P. Rabinow & W. M. Sullivan (Eds.), *Interpretative social science: A reader* (pp. 136-160). Berkeley, CA: University of California Press.

Kvaraceus, W. C. (1956). Acceptance-rejection and exceptionality. *Exceptional Children, 22,* 328-331.

Ladd, G. W., Munson, H. L., & Miller, J. K. (1984). Social integration of deaf adolescents in secondary level mainstreamed programs. *Exceptional Children, 50,* 420-428.

Ladieu, G., Hanfmann, E., & Dembo, T. (1947). Studies in adjustment to visible injuries: Evaluation of help by the injured. *Journal of Abnormal & Social Psychology, 42,* 169-192.

La Greca, A. M., & Mesibov, G. B. (1979). Social skills intervention with learning disabled children: Selecting skills and implementing training. *Journal of Clinical Child Psychology, 8,* 234-241.

Lancioni, G. E. (1982). Normal children as tutors to teach social responses to withdrawn mentally retarded schoolmates: Training, maintenance and generalization. *Journal of Applied Behavior Analysis, 15,* 17-40.

Lange, M. (1986). *A comparison of attitudes of male and female secondary teachers toward mainstreaming acting out versus shy/withdrawn children.* Unpublished master's thesis, University of Detroit, Detroit, MI.

Langer, E. (1979a). The illusion of incompetence. In L. Perlmuter & R. Monty (Eds.), *Choice and perceived control* (pp. 261-267). Hillsdale, NJ: Lawrence Erlbaum.

Langer, E. (1979b). Rethinking the role of thought in social interaction. In J. Harvey, W. Ickes, & R. Kidd (Eds.), *New directions in attribution research* (pp. 210-219). Hillsdale, NJ: Lawrence Erlbaum.

Langer, E. (1980). Old age: An artifact? In S. Kiesler & J. McGaugh (Eds.), *Biology, behavior, and aging* (pp. 138-145). New York: Academic Press.

Langer, E., & Abelson, R. (1974). A patient by any other name. . . . Clinician group differences in labelling bias. *Journal of Consulting and Clinical Psychology, 42,* 4-9.

Langer, E. J., Bashner, R. S., & Chanowitz, B. (1985). Decreasing prejudice by increasing discrimination. *Journal of Personality and Social Psychology, 49,* 113-120.

Langer, E., Blank, A., & Chanowitz, B. (1978). The mindlessness of ostensibly thoughtful action: The role of placebic information in interpersonal interaction. *Journal of Personality and Social Psychology, 36,* 635-642.

Langer, E. J., Fiske, S., Taylor, S. E., & Chanowitz, B. (1976). Stigma, staring, and discomfort: A novel-stimulus hypothesis. *Journal of Experimental and Social Psychology, 12,* 451-463.

Langer, E., & Imber, L. (1980). The role of mindlessness in the perception of deviance. *Journal of Personality and Social Psychology, 29,* 360–367.

Langer, E., & Newman, H. (1979). The role of mindlessness in a typical social psychology experiment. *Personality and Social Psychology Bulletin, 5,* 295–299.

Langer, E., Piper, A., & Friedus, J. (1986). *Dyslexia and mindfulness: Self-instigated prevention of mindlessness.* Prepublication manuscript, Harvard University.

Larrivee, B. (1981). Effects of inservice training intensity on teachers' attitudes toward mainstreaming. *Exceptional Children, 48,* 34–39.

Larrivee, B., & Cook, L. (1979). Mainstreaming: A study of the variables affecting teacher attitude. *Journal of Special Education, 13,* 315–324.

Larson, M. S. (1977). *The rise of professionalism: A sociological analysis.* Berkeley, CA: University of California Press.

Lawton, M. P. (1964). Studies on the psychiatric aide. *Mental Hospitals, 15,* 512–515.

Lawton, M. P. (1965). Personality and attitudinal correlates of psychiatric aide performance. *Journal of Social Psychology, 66,* 215–226.

Lazar, A. L., Gensley, J. T., & Orpet, R. E. (1971). Changing attitudes of young mentally gifted children toward handicapped persons. *Exceptional Children, 37,* 600–602.

Lazar, A. L., Houghton, D., & Orpet, R. (1975, April). *A study of attitude acceptance and social adjustment.* Paper presented at the annual convention of the California Educational Research Association, San Diego, CA. (ERIC Document Reproduction Service No. ED 116 407).

Lazarsfield, P. F., & Henry, N. W. (1968). *Latent structure analysis.* Boston: Houghton-Mifflin.

Lazerson, D. B. (1980). "I must be good if I can teach!"—Peer tutoring with aggressive and withdrawn children. *Journal of Learning Disabilities, 13,* 43–48.

Leek, D. F. (1966). *Formation of impressions of persons with a disability.* Unpublished master's thesis, University of Kansas, Lawrence.

Leinhardt, G., & Pallay, A. (1982). Restrictive educational settings: Exile or haven. *Review of Educational Research, 52,* 557–578.

Lemon, N. (1973). *Attitudes and their measurement.* New York: Wiley.

Leonard, B. D. (1978). Impaired view: Television portrayal of handicapped people (Doctoral dissertation). *Dissertation Abstracts International, 39,* 2603A–2604A.

Leung, E. K. (1980). Evaluation of a children's literature program designed to facilitate the social integration of handicapped children into regular elementary classrooms (Doctoral dissertation). *Dissertation Abstracts International, 40,* 4528-A

Levine, B. G. (1976). Attitudes of head start teachers and aides toward handicapped children (Doctoral dissertation). *Dissertation Abstracts International, 37,* 2112–2113A.

Levinson, M., & Distefano, M. K., Jr. (1979). Effects of brief training on mental health knowledge and attitudes of law enforcement officers. *Journal of Police Science and Administration, 7,* 241–244.

Levitan, S., & Taggart, R. (1977). *Jobs for the disabled.* Baltimore: Johns Hopkins University Press.

Levy, L. (1976). Self-help groups: Types and psychological processes. *Journal of Applied Behavioral Science, 12,* 310-322.

Lieberman, L. L. (1983). *The effects of stimulus elaboration on the perception of disabilities: A multidimensional scaling approach.* Unpublished doctoral dissertation, Hofstra University, Hempstead, NY.

Lieberman, L. P. (1970). Attitudes toward the mentally ill, knowledge of mental illness, and personal adjustment. *Psychological Reports, 26,* 47-52.

Likert, R. (1932). A technique for the measurement of attitudes. *Archives of Psychology,* No. 140.

Lillis, L., & Wagner, R. M. (1977). Nursing education: Its effect upon attitudes toward the mentally retarded. *Rehabilitation Literature, 38,* 358-363.

Lilly, M. S. (1971). Improving social acceptance of low sociometric status, low achieving students. *Exceptional Children, 37,* 341-348.

Lindsey, E., & Frith, G. H. (1983). Detrimental student behaviors as perceived by elementary teachers. *Education, 103,* 306-308.

Lingoes, J. C. (1963). Multiple scalogram analysis: A set theoretic model for analyzing dichotomous items. *Educational and Psychological Measurements, 23,* 501-524.

Linkowski, D. C. (1971). A scale to measure acceptance of disability. *Rehabilitation Counseling Bulletin, 14,* 236-244.

Linkowski, D. C., Jaques, M. C., & Gaier, E. L. (1969). Reactions to disabilities: A thematic analysis. *Journal of Social Psychology, 77,* 201-214.

Lippman, W. (1922). *Public opinion.* New York: Macmillan.

Litton, F. W., Banbury, M. M., & Harris, K. (1980). Materials for educating nonhandicapped students about their handicapped peers. *Teaching Exceptional Children, 13,* 39-43.

Livneh, H. (1982). On the origins of negative attitudes toward people with disabilities. *Rehabilitation Literature, 43,* 338-347.

Livneh, H. (1983). Application of smallest space analysis to the study of attitudes toward disabled persons. *Professional Psychology: Research and Practice, 14,* 406-413.

Livneh, H. (1985). Death attitudes and their relationship to perceptions of physically disabled persons. *Journal of Rehabilitation, 51,* 38-41, 80.

Lonnquist, D. E. (1979). Employment rates among severely physically disabled and nondisabled college graduates and dropouts. *Journal of Applied Rehabilitation Counseling, 10,* 24-27.

Lott, A., & Lott, B. (1965). Group cohesiveness as interpersonal attraction: A review of relationships with antecedent and consequent variables. *Psychological Bulletin, 64,* 259-309.

Lyth, M. (1973). Employers' attitudes to the employment of the disabled. *Occupational Psychology, 47,* 67-70.

MacDonald, A. P., Jr., & Hall, J. (1969). Perception of disability by the nondisabled. *Journal of Consulting and Clinical Psychology, 33,* 654-660.

Macklin, G. F., & Matson, J. L. (1985). A comparison of social behaviors among nonhandicapped and hearing impaired children. *Behavioral Disorders, 11,* 60-65.

MacMillan, D. L., & Morrison, G. M. (1984). Sociometric research in special education. In R. L. Jones (Ed.), *Attitude and attitude change in special education: Theory and practice* (pp. 70-92). Reston, VA: Council for Exceptional Children.

MacMillan, D. L., & Morrison, G. M. (1980). Correlates of social status among mildly handicapped learners in self-contained special classes. *Journal of Educational Psychology, 72*, 437–444.

MacPherson, C. B. (1962). *The political theory of possessive individualism: Hobbes to Locke*. New York: Oxford University Press.

Magee, J., Fleming, T., & Geletka, J. (1982). The new wave in rehabilitation: Projects with industry. *American Rehabilitation, 7*, 21–24.

Magill, F. N. (Ed.). (1963). *Cyclopedia of literary characters*. New York: Harper & Row.

Maher, C. A. (1984). Handicapped adolescents as cross-age tutors: Program description and evaluation. *Exceptional Children, 51*, 56–63.

Makarim, S. (1974). *The Druze faith*. Delmar, NY: Caravan Books.

Mandel, G., Palgi, P., Pinkis, H., & Greenberger, A. (1969). The attitudes of parents toward children with cerebral palsy from different ethnic origins in Israel. *Public Health, 12*, 67–73.

Mandell, C. J., & Strain, P. B. (1978). An analysis of factors related to the attitudes of regular classroom teachers toward mainstreaming mildly handicapped children. *Contemporary Educational Psychology, 3*, 154–162.

Mandoli, M., Mandoli, P., & McLaughlin, T. F. (1982). Effects of same-age peer tutoring on the spelling performance of a mainstreamed elementary LD student. *Learning Disability Quarterly, 5*, 185–189.

Manis, M., Houts, P. S., & Blake, J. B. (1962). Beliefs about mental illness as a function of psychiatric status and psychiatric hospital. *Journal of Abnormal and Social Psychology, 67*, 226–233.

Mank, D., Rhodes, L., & Bellamy, T. (1985). Four supported employment alternatives. In W. Kiernan & J. Stark (Eds.), *Pathways to employment for developmentally disabled adults*. Baltimore: Paul H. Brookes.

Margo, B. C. (1983). Modifying attitudes toward physically handicapped children. *Perceptual and Motor Skills, 56*, 1002.

Marinelli, R. P., & Kelz, J. W. (1973). Anxiety and attitudes toward visibly disabled persons. *Rehabilitation Counseling Bulletin, 16*, 198–205.

Marion, P. B., & Iovacchini, E. V. (1983). Services for handicapped students in higher education: An analysis of national trends. *Journal of College Student Personnel, 24*, 131–137.

Marlowe, M. (1979). The games analysis intervention: A procedure to increase the peer acceptance and social adjustment of a retarded child. *Education and Training of the Mentally Retarded, 14*, 262–268.

Marlowe, M. (1980). Games analysis treatment of social isolation in a gender disturbed boy. *Behavioral Disorders, 6*, 41–50.

Marsh, V., & Friedman, R. (1972). Changing public attitudes toward blindness. *Exceptional Children, 38*, 426–428.

Martin, E. W. (1974). Some thoughts on mainstreaming. *Exceptional Children, 41*, 150–153.

Martin, E. (1976). Integration of the mildly handicapped into regular schools. In M. C. Reynolds (Ed.), *Mainstreaming: Origins and implications* (pp. 56–63). Reston, VA: Council for Exceptional Children.

Martin, J., Veldman, D. J., & Anderson, L. M. (1980). Within class relationships between student achievement and teacher behaviors. *American Educational Research Journal, 17*, 479–490.

Martin, R. (1972). Student sex and behavior as determinants of the type and frequency of teacher student contacts. *Journal of School Psychology, 10,* 339-347.

Martino, L., & Johnson, D. W. (1979). Cooperative and individualistic experiences among disabled and normal children. *Journal of Social Psychology, 107,* 177-183.

Mason, L., & Muhlenkamp, A. (1976). Patients' self-reported effective states following loss and caregivers' expectations of patients' affective states. *Rehabilitation Psychology, 23,* 72-76.

Matson, J. L., Rotatori, A. F., & Helsel, W. J. (1983). Development of a rating scale to measure social skills in children: The Matson Evaluation of Social Skills with Youngsters (MESSY). *Behavioral Research and Therapy, 21,* 335-340.

McCarthy, H. (1982). Partnership as a method of enhancing attitudes and behaviors toward employment of disabled individuals. *Rehabilitation Counseling Bulletin, 26,* 119-132.

McCarthy, H. (1983). Understanding motives of youth in transition to work: A taxonomy for rehabilitation counselors and educators. *Journal of Applied Rehabilitation Counseling, 14,* 52-61.

McCarthy, H. (1984). Redefining the scope of responsibilities and resources for rehabilitation counselors. *International Journal for the Advancement of Counseling, 7,* 217-224.

McCarthy, H. (1985). Models of productive partnership between business and rehabilitation. In H. McCarthy (Ed.), *Complete guide to employing persons with disabilities* (pp. 131-169). Albertson, NY: Human Resources Center.

McCarthy, H. (1986). Corporate social responsibility and services to people with disabilities. *Journal of Rehabilitation Administration, 10,* 60-67.

McCarthy, H. (1986a). Making it in able-bodied America: Career development in young adults with physical disabilities. *Journal of Applied Rehabilitation Counseling, 17*(4), 30-38.

McCarthy, R. M., & Stodden, R. A. (1979). Mainstreaming secondary students: A peer tutoring model. *Teaching Exceptional Children, 11,* 162-163.

McCarthy, T. (1978). *1978. The critical theory of Jurgen Habermas.* Cambridge, MA: MIT Press.

McClelland, D. (1961). *The achieving society.* New York: Free Press.

McDaniel, J. W. (1976). *Physical disability and behavior.* Elmsford, NY: Pergamon Press.

McGuire, W. J. (1969). The nature of attitudes and attitude change. In G. Lindsey & E. Aronson (Eds.), *The handbook of social psychology* (2nd ed.) (Vol. 3) (pp. 136-314). Reading, MA: Addison-Wesley.

McHale, S. M., Olley, J. G., Marcus, L. M., & Simeonsson, R. J. (1981). Nonhandicapped peers as tutors for autistic children. *Exceptional Children, 48,* 263-265.

McHale, S. M., & Simeonsson, R. J. (1980). Effects of interaction on nonhandicapped children's attitudes towards autistic children. *American Journal of Mental Deficiency, 85,* 18-24.

McMurran, K. (1985). Small? Who's small? Not exuberant Michael Petrucciani, the little big man of jazz piano. *People Weekly, 23,* 113-115.

McQuay, S. L. (1978). Attitudes of community college faculty toward the deaf: A Guttman facet theory analysis (Doctoral dissertation). *Dissertation Abstracts International, 38,* 6650-6651A.

Mechanic, D. (1962). Some factors in identifying and defining mental illness. *Mental Hygiene, 46,* 66-74.

Mercer, J. R. (1966). Patterns of family crisis related to reacceptance of the retardate. *American Journal of Mental Deficiency, 71,* 19-32.

Mertens, D. M. (1976). Expectations of teachers-in-training: The influence of a student's sex and a behavioral vs. descriptive approach in a biased psychological report. *Journal of School Psychology, 14,* 222-229.

Meyer, L. M. (1973). Comparison of attitudes toward mental patients of junior and senior nursing students and their university peers. *Nursing Research, 22,* 242-245.

Middleton, E. J., Morsink, C., & Cohen, S. (1979). Program graduates' perception of need for training in mainstreaming. *Exceptional Children, 45,* 258-261.

Middleton, J. (1953). Prejudices and opinions of mental hospital employees regarding mental illness. *American Journal of Psychiatry, 110,* 133-138.

Miller, M., Armstrong, S., & Hagan, M. (1981). Effects of teaching on elementary students' attitudes toward handicaps. *Education and Training of the Mentally Retarded, 16,* 110-113.

Mills, J., Belgrave, F. Z., & Boyer, K. M. (1984). Reducing avoidance of social interaction with a physically disabled person by mentioning the disability following a request for aid. *Journal of Applied Social Psychology, 14,* 1-11.

Minnes, P. M., & Tsuk, K. (1986, June). *Attitudes toward the limb deficient: The effect of prosthesis type.* Paper presented at the annual convention of the Canadian Psychological Association, Toronto.

Mitchell, J., & Allen, H. (1975). Perception of a physically disabled counselor in a counselling session. *Journal of Counseling Psychology, 22,* 70-73.

Moed, G., Wright, B., Feshbach, S., & Sandry, M. (1963). A picture story test for use in physical disability. *Perceptual and Motor Skills, 17,* 483-497.

Moore, G., & Castle, M. R. (1978). Intercorrelations among factors in the Opinions About Mental Illness Scale in scores of nonpsychiatric nurses: A comparison with other studies. *Psychological Reports, 43,* 876-878.

Moore, L., & Fine, M. J. (1978). Regular and special class teachers' perceptions of normal and exceptional children and their attitudes toward mainstreaming. *Psychology in the Schools, 15,* 253-259.

Moore, S. R., & Simpson, R. L. (1984). Reciprocity in the teacher–pupil and peer verbal interactions of learning disabled, behavior-disordered and regular education students. *Learning Disabled Quarterly, 7,* 30-38.

Morgan, S. R. (1978). A descriptive analysis of maladjusted behavior in socially rejected children. *Behavioral Disorders, 4,* 23-30.

Morris, G. S. D. (1976). *How to change the games children play.* Minneapolis, MN: Burgess.

Morris, R. S., & McCauley, R. W. (1977). *Placement of handicapped children by Canadian mainstream administrators and teachers: A Rucker-Gable Survey.* Minneapolis, MN: University of Minnesota. (ERIC Document Reproduction Service No. ED 100 714).

Morrison, J. K. (1976). Demythologizing mental patients' attitudes toward mental illness: An empirical study. *Journal of Community Psychology, 4,* 181-185.

Morrison, J. K. (1977). Changing negative attribution to mental patients by means of demythologizing seminars. *Journal of Clinical Psychology, 33,* 49-51.

Morrison, J. K., & Becker, R. E. (1975). Seminar-induced change in a community psychiatric team's reported attitudes toward "mental illness." *Journal of Community Psychology, 3,* 281-284.

Morrison, J. K., Yablonovitz, H., Harris, M. R., & Nevid, J. S. (1976). The attitudes of nursing students and others about mental illness. *Journal of Psychiatric Nursing and Mental Health Services, 14,* 17-19.

Murphy, A. T., Dickstein, J., & Dripps, E. (1960). Acceptance, rejection, and the hearing handicapped. *Volta Review, 62,* 208-216.

Murray, R. (1969). Attitudes of professional nonpsychiatric nurses toward mental illness. *Journal of Psychiatric Nursing and Mental Health Care, 20,* 117-123.

Mussen, P. H., & Barker, R. G. (1944). Attitudes toward cripples. *Journal of Abnormal and Social Psychology, 39,* 351-355.

Nader, A. (1984). Teacher attitude toward the elementary exceptional child. *International Journal of Rehabilitation Research, 7,* 37-46.

Nathanson, R. B. (1979). Campus interactions, attitudes and behaviors. *Personnel and Guidance Journal,* 39-62.

Navin, S., & Myers, J. (1983). A model of career development for disabled adults. *Journal of Applied Rehabilitation Counseling, 14,* 38-43.

Neff, W. S. (Ed.). (1971). *Rehabilitation psychology.* Washington, DC: American Psychological Association.

Newman, J. (1976). Faculty attitudes toward handicapped students. *Rehabilitation Literature, 37,* 194-197.

Newman, R. K., & Simpson, R. L. (1983). Modifying the least restrictive environment to facilitate the integration of severely emotionally disturbed children and youth. *Behavioral Disorders, 8,* 103-112.

Nirje, B. (1969). The normalization principle. In R. Kugel & A. Shearer (Eds.), *Changing patterns in residential services for the mentally retarded.* Washington, DC: President's Committee on Mental Retardation.

Noonan, J. R., Barry, J. R., & Davis, H. C. (1970). Personality determinants in attitudes toward visible disability. *Journal of Personality, 39,* 1-15.

Norales, F. O. (1982). Belizean secondary teachers' judgments of discipline problems and students' attitudes toward education. *Education, 4,* 348-353.

Novak, D. W., & Lerner, M. J. (1968). Rejection as a consequence of perceived similarity. *Journal of Personality and Social Psychology, 9,* 147-152.

Nunnally, J. (1961). *Popular conceptions of mental health: Their development and change.* New York: Holt, Rinehart.

Nunnally, J. C. (1978). *Psychometric theory* (2nd ed.). New York: McGraw-Hill.

Oberle, J. B. (1975). The effect of personalization and quality of contact on changing expressed attitudes and hiring preferences toward disabled persons (Doctoral dissertation). *Dissertation Abstracts International, 37,* 2144A.

Odom, S. L., Jenkins, J. R., Speltz, M. L., & DeKlyen, M. (1982). Promoting social integration of young children at risk for learning disabilities. *Learning Disability Quarterly, 5,* 379-387.

Odom, S. L., & Spelz, M. L. (1983). Program variations in preschools for handicapped and nonhandicapped children: Mainstreamed vs. integrated special education. *Analysis & Intervention in Developmental Disabilities, 3,* 89-103.

Oliphant, J. (1982). *Teachers attitudes toward learning disabled students.* Unpublished master's thesis, University of Detroit, Detroit, MI.

Olsen, D. H. (1978). The effects of a cross-age tutoring program on the reading achievement of mildly retarded student tutees (Doctoral dissertation). *Dissertation Abstracts International, 39,* 1442A.

Olson, J., Algozzine, B., & Schmid, R. (1980). Mild, moderate, and severe EH: An empty distinction? *Behavioral Disorders, 5,* 96-101.

Orlansky, M. D. (1979). Active learning and student attitudes toward exceptional children. *Exceptional Children, 46,* 49-52.

Osgood, C. E., Suci, G. J., & Tannenbaum, P. H. (1957). *The measurement of meaning.* Urbana, IL: University of Illinois.

Osguthorpe, R. T., Eiserman, W. D., & Shisler, L. (1985). Increasing social acceptance: Mentally retarded students tutoring regular class peers. *Education and Training of the Mentally Retarded, 20,* 235-240.

Osmond, H. (1970). The medical model in psychiatry. *Hospital and Community Psychiatry, 21,* 275-281.

Owen, L., & Barnes, J. (1982). The relationships between cooperative, competitive, and individualistic learning preferences and students' perceptions of classroom learning atmosphere. *American Educational Research Journal, 19,* 182-200.

Palardy, R. (1969). What teachers believe—What children achieve. *Elementary School Journal, 40,* 370-374.

Palgi, P. (1962). Attitudes toward the disabled among immigrants from middle-eastern countries. *Public Health, 3,* 16-17.

Palmer, J. (Ed.). (1984). *Education, career development and the physically disabled.* Chicago: Stoelting.

Palmerton, K. E., & Frumkin, R. M. (1969). Type of contact as a factor in attitudes of college counselors toward the physically disabled. *Perceptual and Motor Skills, 28,* 489-490.

Pancer, S. M., Adams, D. A., Mollard, D., Solsberg, D., & Tammen, L. (1979). Perceived distinctiveness of the handicapped. *Journal of Social Psychology, 108,* 275-276.

Panda, K. C., & Bartel, N. R. (1972). Teacher perception of exceptional children. *Journal of Special Education, 6,* 261-266.

Paolitto, P. P. (1976). The effect of cross-age tutoring on adolescence. An inquiry into theoretical assumptions. *Review of Educational Research, 46,* 215-237.

Parish, T. S., Bryant, W. T., & Shirazi, A. (1976). The personal attribute inventory. *Perceptual and Motor Skills, 42,* 715-720.

Parish, T. S., Eads, G. M., Reece, H. H., & Piscitello, M. A. (1977). Assessment and attempted modification of future teachers' attitudes toward handicapped children. *Perceptual and Motor Skills, 44,* 540-542.

Parkes, C. M. (1975). Psychosocial transitions: Comparison between reactions to loss of limbs and loss of a spouse. *British Journal of Psychiatry, 127,* 204-210.

Parson, L. R., & Heward, W. L. (1979). Training peers to tutor: Evaluation of a tutor training package for primary learning disabled students. *Journal of Applied Behavior Analysis, 12,* 309-310.

Parsons, T. (1951). Illness and the role of the physician: A sociological perspective. *American Journal of Orthopsychiatry, 21,* 452-460.

Parsons, T. (1958). Definition of health and illness in light of American values and social structure. In E. C. Jaco (Ed.), *Patients, physicians and illnesses.* Glencoe, IL: Free Press.

Pascal, J. I. (1954). The changing attitude toward the blind and partially sighted. *American Journal of Optometry, 31,* 319-324.

Pastalan, L. A. (1974). The simulation of age-related sensory losses: A new approach to the study of environmental barriers. *New Outlook for the Blind, 68,* 356-362.

Patai, R. (1973). *The Arab mind.* New York: Charles Scribner.

Pati, G., & Morrison, G. (1982). Enabling the disabled. *Harvard Business Review, 60,* 152-168.

Paul, G. L., & Lentz, R. J. (1977). *Psychosocial treatment of chronic mental patients: Milieu versus social learning programs*. Cambridge, MA: Harvard University Press.

Paul, G. L., & McInnis, T. A. (1974). Attitudinal changes associated with two approaches to training mental health techniques in milieu and social learning programs. *Journal of Consulting and Clinical Psychology, 42*, 21-33.

Paul, G. L., McInnis, T. A., & Mariotto, M. J. (1973). Objective performance outcomes associated with two approaches to training mental health technicians in milieu and social learning programs. *Journal of Abnormal Psychology, 82*, 523-532.

Payne, R., & Murray, C. (1974). Principals' attitudes toward the integration of the handicapped. *Exceptional Children, 41*, 123-125.

Pederson, L. L., & Carlson, P. M. (1981). Rehabilitation service providers: Their attitudes towards people with physical disabilities, and their attitudes towards each other. *Rehabilitation Counseling Bulletin, 24*, 275-282.

Pedhazur, E. J. (1982). *Multiple regression in behavioral research* (2nd ed.). New York: Holt, Rinehart, & Winston.

Penn, J. R., & Dudley, D. H. (1980). The handicapped student: Problems and perceptions. *Journal of College Student Personnel, 21*, 354-357.

Peres, Y., & Katz, R. (1980). Stability and centrality: The nuclear family in modern Israel. *Megamot, 26*, 27-56.

Perry, D. C. (1981). The disabled student and college counseling. *Journal of College Student Personnel, 22*, 533-538.

Perry, R. J. (1974). The effect of long term experience on the attitudes of psychiatric aides. *Journal of Community Psychology, 2*, 166-173.

Philips, G. B. (1975). An exploration of employer attitudes concerning employment opportunities for deaf people. *Journal of Rehabilitation of the Deaf, 9*, 1-9.

Phillips, D. L. (1963). Rejection: A possible consequence of seeking help for mental disorders. *American Sociological Review, 29*, 679-687.

Phillips, R., & Smith, R. (1982). Improving communications between counselor and employers. *Journal of Rehabilitation, 48*, 54-56.

Plas, J., & Cook, V. J. (1982). Variables that predict desire for work with special education adolescents. *Psychology in the Schools, 19*, 388-394.

Pliner, S., & Hannah, M. E. (1985). The role of achievement in teachers' attitudes toward handicapped children. *Academic Psychology Bulletin, 7*, 327-335.

Plummer, J. M. (1976). Projective techniques. In B. Bolton (Ed.), *Handbook of measurement and evaluation in rehabilitation*. Baltimore: University Park Press.

Pomazal, R. J., & Clore, G. L. (1973). Helping on the highway: The effects of dependency and sex. *Journal of Applied Social Psychology, 3*, 150-164.

Postman, L. (1951). Toward a general theory of cognition. In J. H. Rohrer & M. Sherif (Eds.), *Social psychology at the crossroads*. New York: Harper & Brothers.

Powell, K. R. (1985). Disability awareness and attitudes of nonhandicapped children toward severely disabled (Doctoral dissertation). *Dissertation Abstracts International, 46*, 1151A.

Power, P. W. (1985). Family coping behaviors in chronic illness: A rehabilitation perspective. *Rehabilitation Literature, 46*, 78-83.

Proctor, D. I. (1967). An investigation of the relationships between knowledge of exceptional children, kind and amount of experience, and attitudes toward their classroom integration (Doctoral dissertation). *Dissertation Abstracts,* 28, 1721A.

Pryer, M. W., & Distefano, M. K. (1977). Relationship between opinions about mental illness and mental health knowledge among psychiatric aides. *Psychological Reports,* 40, 241-242.

Pryer, M. W., Distefano, M. K., & Marr, L. W. (1977). Attitude changes in psychiatric attendants following experience and training. *Mental Hygiene,* 53, 253-257.

Puleo, C. (1979). Linking vocational rehabilitation and the world of work: The business and industry advisory council. In D. Vandergoot & J. Worrall (Eds.), *Placement in rehabilitation: A career development perspective* (pp. 127-136). Baltimore: University Park Press.

Pulton, T. W. (1976). Attitudes toward the physically disabled: A review and a suggestion for producing positive attitude change. *Physiotherapy Canada,* 28, 83-88.

Quilitch, H. R., & Risley, T. R. (1973). The effects of play materials on social play. *Journal of Applied Behavior Analysis,* 6, 573-578.

Rabkin, J. G. (1972). Opinions about mental illness: A review of the literature. *Psychological Bulletin,* 77, 153-171.

Rabkin, J. G. (1975). The role of attitudes toward mental illness in evaluation of mental health programs. In M. Guttentag & E. L. Struening (Eds.), *Handbook of evaluation research* (Vol. 2) (pp. 326-351). Beverly Hills: Sage Publications.

Rapier, J., Adelson, R., Carey, R., & Croke, K. (1972). Changes in children's attitudes toward the physically handicapped. *Exceptional Children,* 39, 219-223.

Rappaport, J. (1983-84). Studies in empowerment. *Prevention in Human Services,* 3, 1-8.

Reich, C., Hambleton, D., & Houdin, B. K. (1977). The integration of hearing impaired children in regular classrooms. *American Annals of the Deaf,* 122, 534-543.

Reznikoff, M. (1963). Attitudes of psychiatric nurses and attitudes toward psychiatric treatment and hospitals. *Mental Hygiene,* 47, 360-364.

Rice, C. E., Berger, D. G., Klett, S. L., & Sewall, L. G. (1966). Staff opinions about patient care. *Archives of General Psychiatry,* 14, 428-436.

Rice, D. M. (1980). An investigation of attitudes of the able-bodied college student toward the physically handicapped college student in the competitive academic setting (Doctoral dissertation). *Dissertation Abstracts International,* 40, 4533A.

Richardson, H. B., & Guralnick, M. L. (1978). Pediatric residents and young handicapped children: Curriculum evaluation. *Journal of Medical Education,* 53, 487-492.

Richardson, S. A., Goodman, N., Dornbusch, S. M., & Hastorf, A. H. (1963). Variant reactions to physical disabilities. *American Sociological Review,* 28, 429-435.

Richardson, S. A., Goodman, N., Hasdorf, A., & Dornbusch, S. M. (1961). Cultural uniformity in reaction to physical disabilities. *American Sociological Review,* 26, 241-247.

Richardson, S. A., Koller, H., & Katz, M. (1985). Appearance and mental retardation: Some first steps in the development and application of a measure. *American Journal of Mental Deficiency,* 89, 475-484.

Richardson, S. A., & Ronald, L. (1977). The effect of a physically handicapped interviewer on children's expression of values toward handicap. *Rehabilitation Psychology, 24,* 211–218.

Rickard, T., Triandis, H., & Patterson, C. (1963). Indices of employer prejudice toward disabled applicants. *Journal of Applied Psychology, 47,* 52–55.

Riessman, F. (1965). The "helper-therapy" principle. *Social Work, 10,* 27–32.

Ringlaben, R. P., & Price, J. R. (1981). Regular classroom teachers' perceptions of mainstreaming effects. *Exceptional Children, 47,* 302–304.

Rist, R. (1970). Student social class and teacher expectations: The self ful-filling prophecy in ghetto education. *Harvard Educational Review, 40,* 411–451.

Robillard, K., & Fichten, C. S. (1983). Attributions about sexuality and romantic involvement of physically disabled students: An empirical study. *Sexuality and Disability, 6,* 197–212.

Roeher, G. A. (1959). *A study of certain public attitudes toward the orthopaedically disabled.* Unpublished doctoral dissertation. New York University.

Roessler, R., & Bolton, B. (1978). *Psychosocial adjustment to disability.* Baltimore: University Park Press.

Rofe, C., Almagor, M., & Joffe, Y. (1980). The relationship between ethnic origin, affiliation to a disabled group, and attitude toward them. *Megamot, 54,* 487–494.

Romney, A. K., Shepard, R. N., & Nerlove, S. B. (Eds.). (1972). *Multidimensional scaling: Theory and applications in the behavioral sciences* (Vol. 2). New York: Seminar Press.

Rosch, E. (1978). Principles of categorization. In R. Rosch & B. Lloyd (Eds.), *Cognition and categorization.* Hillsdale, NJ: Lawrence Erlbaum.

Rosenbaum, P. L., Armstrong, R. W., & King, S. M. (1985). Improving attitudes toward the disabled: A randomized controlled trial of direct contact versus Kids-on-the-Block. *Journal of Developmental & Behavioral Pediatrics, 7,* 302–307.

Rosenbaum, M., Elizur, A., & Wijsenbeek, H. (1976). Attitudes toward mental illness and role conceptions of psychiatric patients and staff. *Journal of Clinical Psychology, 32,* 167–173.

Rosenfield, D., Sheehan, D. S., Marcus, M., & Stephan, W. G. (1981). Classroom structure and prejudice in desegregated schools. *Journal of Educational Psychology, 73,* 17–26.

Rosenholtz, S. J., & Rosenholtz, S. H. (1981). Classroom organization and the perception of ability. *Sociology of Education, 54,* 132–140.

Rosenthal, R., & Jacobsen, L. (1968). Teachers' expectancies: Determiners of pupils' IQ gains. *Psychological Reports, 19,* 113–118.

Ross, L., Rodin, J., & Zimbardo, P. (1969). Toward an attribution theory: The reduction of fear through induced cognitive-emotional misattribution. *Journal of Personality and Social Psychology, 12,* 279–288.

Rounds, J. B., & Neubauer, N. A. (1986, April). *Individual differences in perceptions of disabilities: An application to rehabilitation counseling students.* Paper presented at the annual meeting of the American Educational Research Association, San Francisco.

Rouse, H. W. (1978). Teacher control ideology and their attitudes toward the handicapped (Doctoral dissertation). *Dissertation Abstracts International, 39,* 226A.

Rowlett, J. D. (1982). Attitudes of peers toward physically limited students in university resident halls (Doctoral dissertation). *Dissertation Abstracts International, 42,* 4740A.

Rubin, R. A., & Barlow, B. (1978). Prevalence of teacher identified behavior problems: A longitudinal study. *Exceptional Children, 45,* 102–111.

Rucker C. N., & Vincenzo, F. M. (1970). Maintaining social acceptance gains made by mentally retarded children. *Exceptional Children, 36,* 679–680.

Russell, T., & Ford, D. F. (1983). Effectiveness of peer tutors vs. resource teachers. *Psychology in the Schools, 20,* 436–441.

Ryan, K. M. (1981). Developmental differences in reactions to the physically disabled. *Human Development, 24,* 240–256.

Rynders, J. E., Johnson, R. T., Johnson, D. W., & Schmidt, B. (1980). Producing positive interaction among Down syndrome and nonhandicapped teenagers through cooperative goal structuring. *American Journal of Mental Deficiency, 85,* 268–273.

Sadlick, M., & Penta, F. B. (1975). Changing nurse attitudes toward quadraplegics through the use of television. *Rehabilitation Literature, 36,* 274–278.

Safilios-Rothschild, C. (1970). *The sociology and social psychology of disability and rehabilitation.* New York: Random House.

Salasek, J. L. (1985). *Changes in behavior and attitudes toward individuals with mental disorders as a function of inservice training.* Unpublished doctoral dissertation, Hofstra University, Hempstead, NY.

Salend, S. J., & Moe, L. (1983). Modifying handicapped students' attitudes toward their handicapped peers through children's literature. *Journal of Special Education, 19,* 22–28.

Samoocha, S. (1980). *Orientation and politicization of Arab minority in Israel.* Haifa, Israel: Institute of Middle-East Studies.

Sampson, E. E. (1977). Psychology and the American ideal. *Journal of Personality and Social Psychology, 35,* 767–782.

Sampson, E. E. (1981). Cognitive psychology as ideology. *American Psychologist, 35,* 730–743.

Sandberg, L. D. (1982). Attitudes of nonhandicapped elementary school students toward school-aged trainable mentally retarded students. *Education and Training of the Mentally Retarded, 17,* 30–34.

Sandler, A., & Robinson, R. (1981). Public attitudes and community acceptance of mentally retarded persons: A review. *Education and Training of the Mentally Retarded, 16,* 97–103.

Sanua, V. D. (1970). A cross cultural study of cerebral palsy. *Social Science & Medicine, 4,* 461–512.

Sapon-Shevin, M. (1982). Mentally retarded characters in children's literature. *Children's Literature in Education, 13,* 19–31.

Sarason, S. B. (1967). Towards a psychology of change and innovation. *American Psychologist, 22,* 227–233.

Sarnoff, I. (1960). Psychoanalytic theory and social attitudes. *Public Opinion Quarterly, 24,* 251–279.

Scheibe, K. E. (1965). College students spend eight weeks in mental hospital: A case report. *Psychotherapy: Theory, Research and Practice, 2,* 117–120.

Scheier, M. F., Carver, C. S., Schultz R., Glass, D. C., & Katz, I. (1978). Sympathy, self-consciousness, and reactions to the stigmatized. *Journal of Applied Social Psychology, 8,* 270–282.

Schensul, S., & Schensul, J. (1982). Self-help groups and advocacy. In G. Weber & L. Cohen (Eds.), *Beliefs and self-help.* New York: Human Sciences Press.

Schiffman, S. S., Reynolds, M. L., & Young, F. W. (1981). *Introduction to multidimensional scaling: Theory, methods, and applications.* New York: Academic Press.

Schloss, P. J., & Schloss, C. N. (1985). Contemporary issues in social skills research with mentally retarded persons. *Journal of Special Education, 19,* 269-282.

Schmelkin, L. P. (1981). Teachers' and nonteachers' attitudes toward mainstreaming. *Exceptional Children, 48,* 42-47.

Schmelkin, L. P. (1982). Perceptions of disabilities: A multidimensional scaling approach. *Journal of Special Education, 16,* 161-177.

Schmelkin, L. P. (1983). *Attitudes to disability: A research study.* Workshop presented at the third New College Collegium, Hofstra University, Hempstead, NY.

Schmelkin, L. P. (1984). Hierarchy of preferences toward disabled groups: A reanalysis. *Perceptual and Motor Skills, 59,* 151-157.

Schmelkin, L. P. (1985). A multidimensional scaling of disability labels. *Rehabilitation Psychology, 30,* 221-233.

Schmelkin, L. P., & Lieberman, L. L. (1984). Education students awareness of mainstreaming concerns: Implications for improving training programs. *Education, 104,* 258-263.

Schmuck, R. A. (1968). Helping teachers improve classroom group processes. *Journal of Applied Behavioral Science, 4,* 401-435.

Schneider, C. R., & Anderson, W. (1980). Attitudes toward the stigmatized: Some insights from recent research. *Rehabilitation Counseling Bulletin, 23,* 299-313.

Schneider, D. J., Hastorf, A. H., & Ellsworth, P. C. (1979). *Person perception* (2nd ed.). Reading, MA: Addison-Wesley.

Schoggen, P. (1978). Environmental forces' effects on physically disabled children. In R. G. Barker et al., *Habitats, environments, and human behavior.* San Francisco: Jossey-Bass.

Schroedel, J., & Jacobsen, R. (1978). *Employer attitudes towards hiring persons with disability: A labor market research model.* Albertson, NY: Human Resources Center.

Schroedel, J. G., & Schiff, W. (1972). Attitudes towards deafness among several deaf and hearing populations. *Rehabilitation Psychology, 19,* 59-70.

Schultz, R. L. (1982). Educating the special needs student in the regular classroom. *Exceptional Children, 48,* 366-368.

Schwartz, B. (1955). The measurement of castration anxiety and anxiety over loss of love. *Journal of Personality, 24,* 204-219.

Schwebel, A. I., & Cherlin, D. L. (1972). Physical and social distancing in teacher-pupil relationships. *Journal of Educational Psychology, 63,* 543-550.

Schweitzer, N., & Deely, J. (1981). The awareness factor: A management skills seminar. *Journal of Rehabilitation, 47,* 45-50.

Scranton, T. R., & Ryckman, D. B. (1979). Sociometric status of learning disabled children in an integrated program. *Journal of Learning Disabilities, 12,* 402-407.

Scruggs, T. E., Mastropieri, M. A., & Richter, L. (1985). Peer tutoring with behaviorally disordered students: Social and academic benefits. *Behavioral Disorders, 10,* 283-294.

Scruggs, T. E., & Osguthorpe, R. T. (1986). Tutoring interventions within special education settings: A comparison of cross-age and peer tutoring. *Psychology in the Schools, 23,* 187-193.

Scruggs, T. E., & Richter, L. (1985). Tutoring learning disabled students: A critical review: *Learning Disability Quarterly, 8,* 286–298.

Scull, A. (1981). Deinstitutionalization and the rights of the deviant. *Journal of Social Issues, 37,* 6–20.

Sellin, D., & Mulchahay, R. (1965). The effect of an institutional tour upon opinions about mental retardation. *American Journal of Mental Deficiency, 70,* 408–412.

Semmel, D. S. (1979). Variables influencing educators' attitudes toward individualized education programs for handicapped children (Doctoral dissertation). *Dissertation Abstracts International, 39,* 5451A.

Semmel, M. I. (1959). Teacher attitudes and information pertaining to mental deficiency. *American Journal of Mental Deficiency, 63,* 566–574.

Semmel, M. I., & Dickson, S. (1966). Connotative reactions of college students to disability labels. *Exceptional Children, 32,* 443–450.

Sharabi, M. (1975). *Introduction to the study of Arab society.* Jerusalem: Salach-Alden.

Sharan, S. (1980). Cooperative learning in small groups: Recent methods and effects on achievement, attitudes and ethnic relations. *Review of Educational Research, 50,* 241–271.

Shaver, P. R., & Scheibe, K. E. (1967). Transformation of social identity: A study of chronic mental patients and college volunteers in a summer camp setting. *Journal of Psychology, 66,* 19–37.

Shaw, M. E., & Wright, J. M. (1967). *Scales for the measurement of attitudes.* New York: McGraw-Hill.

Sheare, J. B. (1974). Social acceptance of EMR adolescents in integrated programs, *American Journal of Mental Deficiency. 78,* 678–682.

Shears, L. M., & Jensema, C. J. (1969). Social acceptability of anomalous persons. *Exceptional Children, 36,* 91–96.

Shepard, R. N., Romney, A. K., & Nerlove, S. B. (Eds.). (1972). *Multidimensional scaling: Theory and applications in the behavioral sciences* (Vol. 1). New York: Seminar Press.

Shontz, F. (1971). Physical disability and personality. In W. S. Neff (Ed.), *Rehabilitation psychology* (pp. 33-73). Washington, DC: American Psychological Association.

Shotel, J. R., Iano, R. P., & McGettigan, J. F. (1972). Teacher attitudes associated with the integration of handicapped children. *Exceptional Children, 38,* 677–683.

Shurka, E. (1983). Attitudes of Israeli Arabs toward the mentally ill. *International Journal of Social Psychiatry, 29,* 101–110.

Shurka, E., and Florian, V. (1983). A study of Israeli Jewish and Arab parental perception of their disabled children. *Journal of Comparative Family Studies, 14,* 367–376.

Shurka, E., & Katz, S. (1978). The influence of variables related to the disabled on Arab and Jewish youth and their evaluation of persons with a physical disability. *Society and Welfare, 1,* 384–391.

Shurka, E., & Katz, S. (1982). Evaluation of persons with a physical disability: The influence of variables related to the disabled on Arab and Jewish youth. *Journal of Cross-Cultural Psychology, 13,* 105–116.

Shurka, E., Siller, J., & Dvonch, P. I. (1983). Coping behavior and personal responsibility as factors in the perception of disabled persons by nondisabled. *Rehabilitation Psychology, 27,* 225–233.

Siegel, S. (1956). *Nonparametric statistics for the behavioral sciences.* New York: McGraw-Hill.

Siegler, M., & Osmond, H. (1974). *Models of madness, models of medicine.* New York: Harper & Row.

Sigelman, C. K., Spanhel, C. L., & Lorenzen, C. D. (1979). Community reactions to deinstitutionalization. *Journal of Rehabilitation, 45,* 52-54, 60.

Sigler, G. R., & Lazar, A. L. (1976, April). *Prediction of teacher attitudes toward handicapped individuals.* Paper presented at the annual convention of the Council for Exceptional Children, Chicago. (ERIC Document Reproduction Service No. ED 125 235).

Silberman, M. (1971). Teachers attitudes and actions toward their students. In M. Silberman (Ed.), *The experience of schooling* (pp. 331-347). New York: Holt, Rinehart & Winston.

Siller, J. (1959/1964). *Reactions to physical disability by the disabled and the nondisabled.* Paper presented at the annual convention of the American Psychological Association, and in a revised form in *Research Bulletin, American Foundation for the Blind, 7,* 27-36.

Siller, J. (1963). Reactions to physical disability. *Rehabilitation Counseling Bulletin, 7,* 12-16.

Siller, J. (1964). Personality determinants of reactions to the physically disabled. *American Foundation for the Blind Research Bulletin, 7,* 37-52.

Siller, J. (1969). *The general form of the Disability Factor Scales.* Unpublished manuscript, New York University, New York.

Siller, J. (1970). The generality of attitudes toward the disabled. *Proceedings of the 78th annual convention of the American Psychological Association, 5,* 697-698.

Siller, J. (1976a). Attitudes toward disability. In H. Rusalem & D. Malikin (Eds.), *Comtemporary vocational rehabilitation* (pp. 67-80). New York: New York University Press.

Siller, J. (1976b). Psychosocial aspects of physical disability. In J. Meislin (Ed.), *Rehabilitation medicine and psychiatry* (pp. 222-233). Spingfield, IL: Thomas.

Siller, J. (1984a). Attitudes toward the physically disabled. In R. L. Jones (Ed.), *Attitudes and attitude change in special education: Theory and practice* (pp. 184-205). Reston, VA: Council for Exceptional Children.

Siller, J. (1984b). The role of personality in attitudes toward those with physical disabilities. In C. J. Golden (Ed.), *Current topics in rehabilitation psychology* (pp. 201-227). Orlando, FL: Grune & Stratton.

Siller, J., Chipman, A., Ferguson, L. T., & Vann, D. H. (1967). Studies in reactions to disability. *Attitudes of the nondisabled toward the physically disabled.* New York: New York University School of Education.

Siller, J., Ferguson, L. T., Vann, D. H., & Holland, B. (1967). *Structure of attitudes toward the physically disabled: Disability factor scales—Amputation, blindness, cosmetic conditions.* New York: New York University School of Education.

Silverman, L. H. (1967). Psychoanalytic theory: "The reports of my death are greatly exaggerated." *American Psychologist, 31,* 621-637.

Simpson, A. W., & Erickson, M. T. (1983). Teachers' verbal and nonverbal communication patterns as a function of teacher race, student gender and student race. *American Educational Research Journal, 20,* 183-198.

Simpson, C. (1981). Classroom structure and the organization of ability. *Sociology of Education, 54,* 120–132.

Simpson, R. L., Parrish, N. E., & Cook, J. J. (1976). Modification of attitudes of regular class children towards the handicapped for the purpose of achieving integration. *Contemporary Educational Psychology, 1,* 46–51.

Singleton, K. W. (1978). Creating positive attitudes and expectancies of regular classroom teachers toward mainstreaming handicapped children: A comparison of two inservice methods (Doctoral dissertation). *Dissertation Abstracts International, 38,* 186–187A.

Siperstein, G. N., Bak, J. J., & Gottlieb, J. (1977). Effects of group discussions on children's attitudes toward handicapped peers. *Journal of Educational Research, 70,* 131–134.

Siperstein, G. N., Bopp, M., & Bak, J. (1978). Social status of learning disabled. *Journal of Learning Disabilities, 11,* 98–102.

Siperstein, G. N., & Gottlieb, J. (1977). Physical stigma and academic performance as factors affecting children's first impressions of handicapped peers. *American Journal of Mental Deficiency, 81,* 455–462.

Skrtic, T. M., Sigler, G. R., & Lazar, A. L. (1978, April). *Attitudes of male and female TMR teachers toward the handicapped.* Paper presented at the annual convention of the Council for Exceptional Children, Dallas, TX. (ERIC Document Reproduction Service No. ED 086 699).

Smart, R., Wilton, K., & Keeling, B. (1980). Teacher factors and special class placement. *Journal of Special Education, 14,* 217–229.

Smits, S., & Emener, W. (1980). Insufficient/ineffective counselor involvement in job placement activities: A system failure. *Journal of Rehabilitation Administration, 4,* 147–155.

Snyder, M., Kleck, R. E., Strenta, A., & Mentzer, S. (1979). Avoidance of the handicapped: An attributional ambiguity analysis. *Journal of Personality and Social Psychology, 37,* 2297–2306.

Solso, R. L. (Ed.). (1973). *Contemporary issues in cognitive psychology: The Loyola symposium.* Washington, DC: Winston.

Souelem, O. (1955). Mental patients' attitudes toward mental hospitals. *Journal of Clinical Psychology, 11,* 181–185.

Speece, D. L., & Mandell, C. J. (1980). Resource room support services for regular teachers. *Learning Disabilities Quarterly, 3,* 49–53.

Stainback, W., Stainback, S., Hatcher, C., Strathe, M., & Healy, H. (1984). Teaching nonhandicapped students about individual differences: A pilot study. *Behavioral Disorders, 9,* 196–206.

Stake, J. E., & Katz, J. F. (1982). Teacher gender differences. *American Educational Research Journal, 19,* 465–471.

Steinzor, L. V. (1967). Siblings of visually handicapped children. *New Outlook for the Blind, 61,* 48-52.

Stephens, T. M., & Braun, B. L. (1980). Measures of regular classroom teachers' attitudes toward handicapped children. *Exceptional Children, 46,* 292–294.

Stephenson, W. (1953). *The study of behavior: Q-technique and its methodology.* Chicago: University of Chicago Press.

Stilwell, D. N., Stilwell, W. E., & Perrit, L. C. (1983). Barriers in higher education for persons with handicaps: A follow-up. *Journal of College Student Personnel, 24,* 337–343.

Storey, K. S. (1980). The effects of the television series "Feeling Free" on children's attitudes toward handicapped people (Doctoral dissertation). *Dissertation Abstracts International, 40,* 6119A.

Stotsky, B. A., & Rhetts, J. E. (1966). Changing attitudes toward the mentally ill in nursing homes. *Nursing Research, 15,* 175-177.

Stovall, C., & Sedlacek, W. E. (1983). Attitudes of male and female university students toward students with different physical disabilities. *Journal of College Student Personnel, 24,* 325-330.

Stowitschek, C. E., Hecimovic, A., Stowitschek, J. J., & Shores, R. E. (1982). Behaviorally disordered adolescents as peer tutors. *Behavioral Disorders, 7,* 136-148.

Strain, P. S. (1975). Increasing social play of severely retarded preschoolers with socio-dramatic activities. *Mental Retardation, 13,* 7-9.

Strain, P. S., Kerr, M. M., & Ragland, E. U. (1979). Effects of peer-mediated social initiations and prompting reinforcement procedures on the social behavior of autistic children. *Journal of Autism and Developmental Disorders, 9,* 41-54.

Strain, P. S., & Odom, S. L. (1986). Peer social initiations: Effective intervention for social skills development of exceptional children. *Exceptional Children, 52,* 543-551.

Strain, P. S., & Shores, R. E. (1977). Social interaction development among behaviorally handicapped preschool children: Research and educational implications. *Psychology in the Schools, 14,* 493-502.

Strain, P. S., Shores, R. E., & Kerr, M. M. (1976). An experimental analysis of "spillover" effects on the social interaction of behaviorally handicapped preschool children. *Journal of Applied Behavior Analysis, 9,* 31-40.

Strain, P. S., Shores, R. E., & Timm, M. A. (1977). Effects of peer social initiations on the behavior of withdrawn preschool children. *Journal of Applied Behavior Analysis, 10,* 289-298.

Strain, P. S., & Wiegerink, R. (1976). The effects of sociodramatic activities on social interaction among behaviorally disordered preschool children. *Journal of Special Education, 10,* 71-75.

Strauch, J. D. (1970). Social contact as a variable in the expressed attitudes of normal adolescents toward EMR pupils. *Exceptional Children, 36,* 485-494.

Strohmer, D. C., & Phillips, S. D. (1985). Counselor preferences of disabled and disadvantaged college students for personal versus vocational concerns. *Rehabilitation Counseling, 28,* 171-175.

Strong, E. K. (1931). *Changes of interest with age.* Palo Alto, CA: Stanford University Press.

Stubbins, J. (1982). *The clinical attitude in rehabilitation: A cross-cultural view.* New York: World Rehabilitation Fund.

Stubbins, J. (1984a). Rehabilitation services as ideology. *Rehabilitation Psychology, 29,* 197-202.

Stubbins, J. (1984b). (Symposium Ed.). Social science perspectives on vocational rehabilitation. *Rehabilitation Literature, 45,* 338-380.

Stubbins, J. (1984c). Vocational rehabilitation as social science. *Rehabilitation Literature, 45,* 375-380.

Stubbins, J., & Albee, G. W. (1984). Ideologies of clinical and ecological models. *Rehabilitation Literature, 45,* 349-353.

Stude, E. W. (1973). Evaluation of short-term training for rehabilitation counselors: Effectiveness of an institute on epilepsy. *Rehabilitation Counseling Bulletin, 16,* 146-154.

Suler, J. (1984). The role of ideology in self-help groups. *Social Policy, 14*, 29–36.

Summers, G. F. (Ed.). (1970). *Attitude measurement*. Chicago: Rand-McNally.

Sunderland, S. (1982). *The strengths of compassionate friends: Enduring life following the death of a child*. Cincinnati, OH: University of Cincinnati.

Swing, S. R., & Peterson, P. L. (1982). The relationship of student ability and small group interaction to student achievement. *American Educational Research Journal, 19*, 259–274.

Szasz, T. (1961). *The myth of mental illness*. New York: Harper.

Tagalakis, V., Amsel, R., & Fichten, C. S. (in press). Job interview strategies for people with a visible disability. *Journal of Applied Social Psychology*.

Tagiuri, R. (1969). Person perception. In G. Lindzey & E. Aronson (Eds.), *The handbook of social psychology* (Vol. 3) (2nd ed.) (pp. 395–449). Reading, MA: Addison-Wesley.

Talmage, H., Pascarella, E. T., & Ford, S. (1984). The influence of cooperative learning strategies on teacher practices, student perceptions of the learning environment, and academic achievement. *American Educational Research Journal, 21*, 163–179.

Taylor, S. (1979). Hospital patient behavior: Reactance, helplessness, or control. *Journal of Social Issues, 35*, 156–184.

Taylor, S. E. (1981). A categorization approach to stereotyping. In D. L. Hamilton (Ed.), *Cognitive processes in stereotyping and intergroup behavior* (pp. 83–114). Hillsdale, NJ: Lawrence Erlbaum.

Taylor, S., Lichtman, R., & Wood, J. (1984). Attributions, beliefs about control, and adjustment to breast cancer. *Journal of Personality and Social Psychology, 46*, 489–502.

Thede, D. L., & Antonak, R. F. (1981). An ordering-theoretic analysis of women's attitudes. *Journal of Social Psychology, 114*, 251–258.

Thomas, S. A., Foreman, P. E., & Remenyi, A. G. (1985). The effects of previous contact with physical disability upon Australian children's attitudes toward people with physical disabilities. *International Journal of Rehabilitation Research, 8*, 69–70.

Thompson, T. L. (1981). The impact of a physical handicap on communicative characteristics of the marital dyad. *Western Journal of Special Communication, 45*, 227–240.

Threlkeld, R. M., & DeJong, W. (1982). Changing behavior toward the handicapped: An evaluation of the film "First Encounters." *Rehabilitation Counseling Bulletin, 25*, 282–285.

Threlkeld, R. M. & DeJong, W. (1983). Hiring the disabled: An attempt to influence behavioral intentions through a media presentation. *Rehabilitation Psychology, 28*, 105–114.

Thurer, S. (1980). Disability and monstrosity: A look at literary distortions of handicapping conditions. *Rehabilitation Literature, 41*, 12–15.

Thurstone, L. L. (1928). Attitudes can be measured. *American Journal of Sociology, 33*, 529–554.

Titley, R. W. (1969). Imaginations about the disabled. *Social Science and Medicine, 3*, 29–38.

Towfighy-Hooshyar, N., & Zingle, H. W. (1984). Regular-class students' attitudes toward integrated multiply handicapped peers. *American Journal of Mental Deficiency, 88*, 630–637.

Triandis, H. C. (1971). *Attitude and attitude change*. New York: Wiley.

Triandis, H. C., Adamopoulos, J., & Brinberg, D. (1984). Perspectives and issues in the study of attitudes. In R. L. Jones (Ed.), *Attitude and attitude change in special education: Theory and practice* (pp. 21–40). Reston, VA: Council for Exceptional Children.

Triandis, H. C., & Triandis, L. M. (1965). Race, social class, religion, and nationality as determinants of social distance. *Journal of Abnormal and Social Psychology, 61*, 110–118.

Tringo, J. L. (1970). The hierarchy of preference toward disability groups. *Journal of Special Education, 4*, 295–306.

Tseng, M. S. (1972). Attitudes toward the disabled: A cross-cultural study. *Journal of Social Psychology, 87*, 311–312.

Twomey, L. C., & Kiefer, F. (1972). Attitude change following education in interpersonal dynamics among attendants in a state hospital for the criminally insane. *Psychological Reports, 50*, 989–990.

U. S. Commission on Civil Rights (1983). *Accommodating the spectrum of individual abilities.* Washington, DC: Author.

Vacc, N. A., & Kirst, N. (1977). Emotionally disturbed children and regular classroom teachers. *Elementary School Journal, 77*, 309–317.

Vandell, D. L., Anderson, L. D., Ehrhardt, G., & Wilson, K. S. (1982). Integrating hearing and deaf preschoolers: An attempt to enhance hearing children's interactions with deaf peers. *Child Development, 53*, 1354–1363.

Vandergood, D., Jacobsen, R., & Worrall, J. (1977). *New directions for placement-related research and practice in the rehabilitation process.* Albertson, NY: Human Resources Center.

VanderKolk, C. J. (1976a). Physiological and self-reported reactions to the disabled and deviant. *Rehabilitation Psychology, 23*, 77–83.

VanderKolk, C. J. (1976b). Physiological measures as a means of assessing reactions to the disabled. *New Outlook for the Blind, 70*, 101–103.

Van Hasselt, V. B., Hersen, M., Whitehill, M. B., & Bellack, A. S. (1979). Social skill assessment and training for children: An evaluative review. *Behavioral Research and Therapy, 17*, 413–437.

Vash, C. (1981). *The psychology of disability.* New York: Springer.

Vernallis, S. F., & St. Pierre, R. G. (1964). Volunteer workers' opinions about mental illness. *Journal of Clinical Psychology, 20*, 140–143.

Videcka-Sherman, L. (1982). Effects of participation in a self-help group for bereaved parents: Compassionate Friends. *Prevention in Human Services, 1*, 69–78.

Vidoni, D. O., Fleming, N. J., & Mintz, S. (1983). Behavior problems of children as perceived by teachers, mental health professionals, and children. *Psychology in the Schools, 20*, 93–98.

Vinacke, W. E. (1957). Stereotypes as social concepts. *Journal of Social Psychology, 46*, 229–243.

Voeltz, L. M. (1980). Children's attitudes toward handicapped peers. *American Journal of Mental Deficiency, 84*, 455–464.

Voeltz, L. M. (1982). Effects of structured interactions with severely handicapped peers on children's attitudes. *American Journal of Mental Deficiency, 86*, 380–390.

Wahl, O. F., Zastowny, T. R., & Briggs, D. (1980). A factor analytic reexamination of two popular surveys of mental health attitudes. *Multivariate Experimental Clinical Research, 5*, 29–39.

Walsh, J. E. (1971). Instruction in psychiatric nursing, level of anxiety, and direction of attitude change toward the mentally ill. *Nursing Research, 20,* 522–529.

Warger, C. L., & Trippe, M. (1982). Preservice teacher attitudes toward mainstreamed students with emotional impairments. *Exceptional Children, 49,* 246–252.

Warr, P. B., & Knapper, C. (1968). *The perception of people and events.* London: Wiley.

Warren, S. A., Turner, D. R. (1966). Attitudes of professionals and students toward exceptional children. *Training School Bulletin, 62,* 136–144.

Webb, N. M. (1982). Group composition, group interaction, and achievement in cooperative small groups. *Journal of Educational Psychology, 74,* 475–484.

Weinberg, N. (1973). Manipulating attraction toward the disabled: An application of the similarity–attraction model. *Rehabilitation Psychology, 20,* 156–164.

Weinberg, N. (1976). Social stereotyping of the physically handicapped. *Rehabilitation Psychology, 23,* 115–124.

Weinberg, N. (1978). Modifying social stereotypes of the physically disabled. *Rehabilitation Counseling Bulletin, 22,* 114–124.

Weinberg, N. (1984). Physically disabled people assess the quality of their lives. *Rehabilitation Literature, 45,* 13–15.

Weinberg, N., & Sebian, C. (1980). The Bible and disability. *Rehabilitation Counseling Bulletin, 23,* 273–282.

Weinberg, N., & Williams, J. (1978). How the physically disabled perceive their disabilities. *Journal of Rehabilitation, 44,* 31–33.

Weinberg-Asher, N. (1976). The effect of physical disability on self-perception. *Rehabilitation Counseling Bulletin, 23,* 15–20.

Weiner, B., & Sierad, J. (1975). Misattribution for failure and enhancement of achievement strivings. *Journal of Personality and Social Psychology, 31,* 415–421.

Weinstein, R. S. (1976). Reading group membership in first grade: Teacher behaviors and pupil experience over time. *Journal of Educational Psychology, 68,* 103–116.

Weisman, S. L., & Chigier, E. (1965). *A survey of paralyzed adolescents in the central region of Israel.* Tel Aviv: Ilan.

Wertheimer, M. (1923). Untersuchungen zu Lehre von der Gestalt. II. *Psychologische Forschung, 4,* 301–350.

Wesolowski, M. D., & Deichmann, J. (1980). Physiological activity and attitudes toward disabled persons. *Rehabilitation Counseling Bulletin, 23,* 218–226.

Westervelt, V. D., Brantley, J., & Ware, W. (1983). Changing children's attitudes toward physically handicapped peers: Effects of a film and teacher-led discussion. *Journal of Pediatric Psychology, 8,* 327–343.

Westervelt, V. D., & McKinney, J. D. (1980). Effects of a film on nonhandicapped children's attitudes toward handicapped children. *Exceptional Children, 46,* 294–296.

White, C. S., Karchmer, M. A., Armstrong, D. F., & Bezozo, C. E. (1983). Current trends in high school graduation and college enrollment of hearing-impaired students attending residential schools for deaf persons. *American Annals of the Deaf, 128,* 125–131.

Whiteman, M., & Lukoff, I. F. (1962). Public attitudes toward blindness. *New Outlook for the Blind, 56,* 153–158.

Whiteman, M., & Lukoff, I. F. (1965). Attitudes toward blindness and other physical handicaps. *Journal of Social Psychology, 66,* 135–145.

Whorf, B. (1956). *Language, thought, and reality.* Cambridge, MA: M.I.T. Press.
Wicas, E. A., & Carluccio, L. W. (1971). Attitudes of counselors toward three handicapped client groups. *Rehabilitation Counseling Bulletin, 15,* 25-34.
Wicker, A. (1969). Attitudes versus action: The relationship of verbal and overt behavioral responses to attitude objects. *Journal of Social Issues, 25,* 41-78.
Will, M. (1985). Bridges from school to working life. OSERS programming for the transition of youth with disabilities. *Rehabilitation World, 9,* 4-7.
Willey, N. R., & McCandless, B. R. (1973). Social stereotypes for normal, educable mentally retarded, and orthopedically handicapped children. *Journal of Special Education, 7,* 282-288.
Williams, R. F. (1986). Perceptions of mentally retarded persons. *Education and Training of the Mentally Retarded, 21,* 13-20.
Williams, R. J., & Algozzine, B. (1977). Differential attitudes toward mainstreaming: An investigation. *Alberta Journal of Educational Research, 23,* 207-212.
Williamson, J. B., Karp, D. A., Dalphin, J. R., & Gray, P. S. (1982). *The research craft: An introduction to social research methods* (2nd ed.). Boston: Little, Brown.
Willis, J. B., Feldman, N. S., & Ruble, D. N. (1977). Children's generosity as influenced by deservedness of reward and type of recipient. *Journal of Educational Psychology, 69,* 33-35.
Wills, T. A. (1978). Perceptions of clients by professional helpers. *Psychological Bulletin, 85,* 968-1000.
Wilson, E. D. (1971). A comparison of the effects of deafness simulation and observation upon attitudes, anxiety, and behavior manifested toward the deaf. *Journal of Special Education, 5,* 343-349.
Wilson, E. D. (1975). *Sociobiology: The new synthesis.* Cambridge, MA: Harvard University Press.
Wilson, E. D., & Alcorn, D. (1969). Disability simulation and development of attitudes toward the exceptional. *Journal of Special Education, 3,* 303-307.
Wilson, T. R., & Richards, J. A. (1975). Jobs for veterans with disabilities. *HumRRO Manpower R & D Monograph, 41.*
Wilson, T. R., Richards, J. A., & Bercini, K. R. (1975). Disabled veterans of the Vietnam era: Employment problems and prospects. *HumRRO Technical Report, 75*(1).
Withorn, A. (1980, May/June). Helping ourselves: The limits and potential of self-help. *Radical America,* pp. 1-9.
Wolfensberger, W. (1972). *The principle of normalization in human services.* Toronto, Canada: National Institute on Mental Retardation.
Wolfensberger, W., & Tullman, S. (1982). A brief outline of the principle of normalization. *Rehabilitation Psychology, 27,* 131-145.
Woods, F. J., & Carrow, M. A. (1959). Choice-rejection status of speech-defective children. *Exceptional Children, 25,* 279-283.
Wright, B. A. (Ed.). (1959). *Psychology and rehabilitation.* Washington, DC: American Psychological Association.
Wright, B. A. (1960). *Physical disability: A psychological approach.* New York: Harper & Row.
Wright, B. A. (1972). Psychological snares in the investigative enterprise. In E. P. Trapp & P. Himmelstein (Eds.) *Readings on the exceptional child* (rev. ed.) (pp. 359-371). New York: Appleton-Century-Crofts.
Wright, B. A. (1975a). Sensitizing outsiders to the position of the insider. *Rehabilitation Psychology, 22,* 129-135.

Wright, B. A. (1975b). Social-psychological leads to enhance rehabilitation effectiveness. *Rehabilitation Counseling Bulletin, 18*, 214-223.

Wright, B. A. (1978). The coping framework and attitude change: A guide to constructive role-playing. *Rehabilitation Psychology, 4*, 177-183.

Wright, B. A. (1980a). Developing constructive views of life with a disability. *Rehabilitation Literature, 41*, 274-279.

Wright, B. A. (1980b). Person and situation: Adjusting the rehabilitation focus. *Archives of Physical Medicine and Rehabilitation, 61*, 59-64.

Wright, B. A. (1983). *Physical disability: A psychosocial approach* (2nd ed.). New York: Harper & Row.

Wright, B. A., & Fletcher, B. L. (1982). Uncovering hidden resources: A challenge in assessment. *Professional Psychology, 13*, 229-235.

Wright, B. A., & Howe, M. (1969). *The fortune phenomenon as manifested in stigmatized and non-stigmatized groups.* Unpublished manuscript, University of Kansas, Lawrence.

Wright, B. A., & Muth, M. (1965). *The fortune phenomenon with rehabilitation clients.* Unpublished manuscript, University of Kansas, Lawrence.

Wright, F. H., & Klein, R. A. (1966). Attitudes of hospital personnel and the community regarding mental illness. *Journal of Counseling Psychology, 13*, 106-107.

Yaffe, E. (1979). Experienced mainstreamers speak out. *Teacher, 96*, 61-63.

Yager, S., Johnson, R. T., Johnson, D. W., & Snider, B. (1985). The effect of cooperative and individualistic learning experiences on cross-handicap relationships. *Contemporary Educational Psychology, 10*, 127-138.

Yamamato, K. (1971). To be different. *Rehabilitation Counseling Bulletin, 14*, 180-189.

Yamamoto, K., & Dizney, H. F. (1967). Rejection of the mentally ill: A study of attitudes of student teachers. *Journal of Counseling Psychology, 16*, 264-268.

Yamamoto, K., & Wiersma, J. (1967). Rejection of self and of deviant others among student teachers. *The Journal of Special Education, 1*, 401-408.

Yoak, M., & Chesler, M. (1985). Alternative professional roles in health care delivery: Leadership patterns in self-help groups. *Journal of Applied Behavioral Science, 21*, 427-444.

Yoak, M., Chesney, B., & Schwartz, N. (1985). Active roles in self-help groups for parents of children with cancer. *Children's Health Care, 14*, 38-45.

Young, J., Rosati, R., & Vandergoot, D. (1986). Initiating a marketing strategy by assessing employer needs for rehabilitation services. *Journal of Rehabilitation, 52*, 37-41.

Ysseldyke, J. E., & Foster, G. G. (1978). Bias in teachers' observations of emotionally disturbed and learning disabled children. *Exceptional Children, 44*, 613-615.

Yuker, H. E. (1976). *Attitudes of the general public toward handicapped individuals.* Washington, DC: White House Conference of Handicapped Individuals.

Yuker, H. E. (1982). *The disability hierarchies.* Unpublished manuscript, Center for the Study of Attitudes towards Persons with Disabilities, Hofstra University, Hempstead, NY.

Yuker, H. E. (1983). The lack of a stable order of preference for disabilities: A response to Richardson and Ronald. *Rehabilitiation Psychology, 28*, 93-103.

Yuker, H. E. (1986). Disability and the law: Attitudes of police, lawyers, and mental health professionals. *Rehabilitation Psychology, 31*, 13-26.

Yuker, H. E., & Block, J. R. (1979). *Challenging barriers to change: Attitudes toward disabled persons.* Albertson, NY: Human Resources Center.

Yuker, H. E., & Block, J. R. (1986). *Research with the Attitude Toward Disabled Persons Scales: 1960-1985.* Hempstead, NY: Hofstra University Center for the Study of Attitudes toward Persons with Disabilities.

Yuker, H. E., Block, J. R., & Campbell, W. J. (1960). *A scale to measure attitudes toward disabled persons.* Albertson, NY: Human Resources Center.

Yuker, H. E., Block, J. R., & Younng, J. H. (1966, reprinted 1970). *The measurement of attitudes toward disabled persons.* Albertson, NY: Human Resources Center.

Yuker, H. E., Dill, C. A., & Hurley, M. (1987). *Gender differences in attitudes toward disabled persons: A meta-analysis.* Manuscript submitted for publication.

Zajonc, R. B. (1968). Attitudinal effects of mere exposure [Monograph]. *Journal of Personality and Social Psychology, 9,* 1-27.

Zola, I. K. (1982). *Missing pieces: A chronicle of living with a disability.* Philadelphia: Temple University Press.

Index